冨 樫 義 博

Go on without me. I'll catch up in about two minutes.

Yoshihiro Togashi

Yoshihiro Togashi's manga career began in 1986 at the age of 20, when he won the coveted Osamu Tezuka Award for new manga artists. He debuted in the Japanese **Weekly Shonen Jump** magazine in 1989 with the romantic comedy **Tende Shôwaru Cupid**. From 1990 to 1994 he wrote and drew the hit manga **YuYu Hakusho**, which was followed by the dark comedy science-fiction series **Level E** and finally this adventure series **Hunter x Hunter**. In 1999 he married the manga artist Naoko Takeuchi.

HUNTER X HUNTER Volume 2
SHONEN JUMP ADVANCED Manga Edition

STORY AND ART BY
YOSHIHIRO TOGASHI

English Adaptation/Gary Leach
Translation/Lillian Olsen
Touch-up Art & Lettering/Mark Griffin
Design/Amy Martin
Editor/Pancha Diaz

Printed in the U.S.A.

Published by VIZ Media, LLC
P.O. Box 77010
San Francisco, CA 94107

10 9 8 7 6
First printing, April 2005
Sixth printing, May 2016

www.viz.com

THE WORLD'S MOST
CUTTING-EDGE MANGA
SHONEN JUMP
ADVANCED
www.shonenjump.com

SHONEN JUMP ADVANCED MANGA

HUNTER × HUNTER

ハンター × ハンター

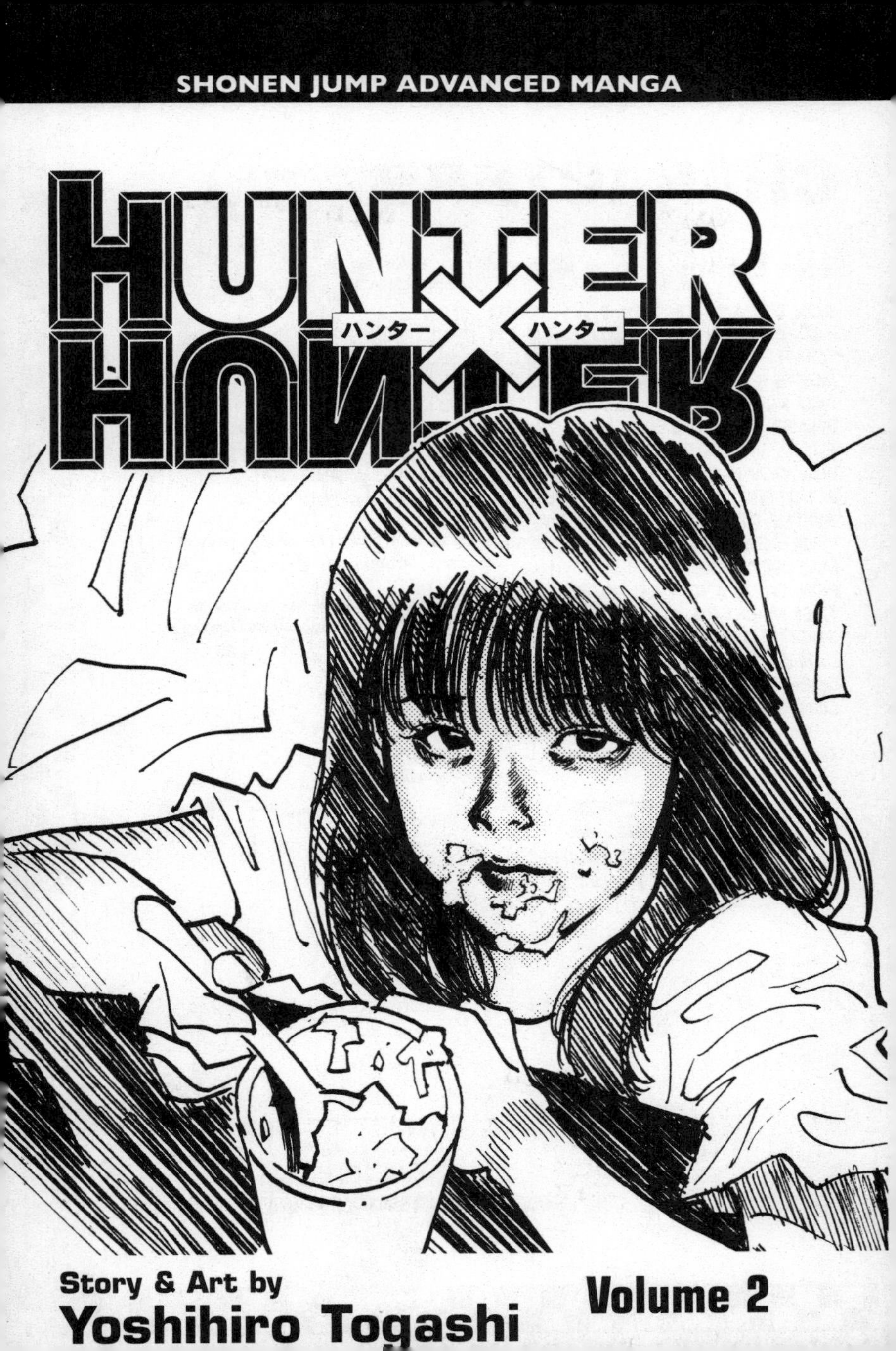

Story & Art by
Yoshihiro Togashi

Volume 2

CHARACTERS

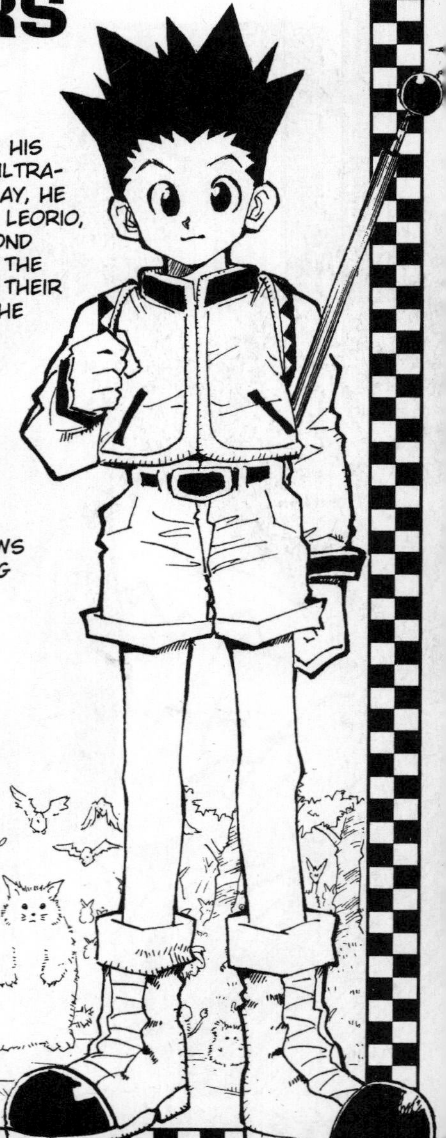

The Story Thus Far

GON DREAMS OF BEING A HUNTER LIKE HIS FATHER, AND SETS OUT TO TAKE THE ULTRA-TOUGH LICENSING EXAM. ALONG THE WAY, HE MEETS FELLOW APPLICANTS KURAPIKA, LEORIO, AND KILLUA. THE FOUR PASS THE SECOND PHASE OF THE EXAM AND MOVE ON TO THE THIRD, WHICH REQUIRES THEM TO FIND THEIR WAY DOWN THE TRICK TOWER WITHIN THE ALLOTTED TIME. GON'S GROUP, JOINED BY THE TREACHEROUS TONPA, MAKES PROGRESS THROUGH "THE PATH OF MAJORITY RULES," BUT WAITING FOR THEM ARE PRISONERS HIRED AS TASKMASTERS IN EXCHANGE FOR SHORTER SENTENCES. IF GON'S TEAM CAN GET THE "BEST OF FIVE" IN THE ONE-ON-ONE MATCHES, THEY MAY CONTINUE ON THEIR WAY. TONPA THROWS HIS MATCH, BUT GON WINS HIS, PUTTING THE SCORE AT 1-1...!!

Gon

OUR HERO ASPIRES TO BECOME A HUNTER, AND REUNITE WITH HIS FATHER!

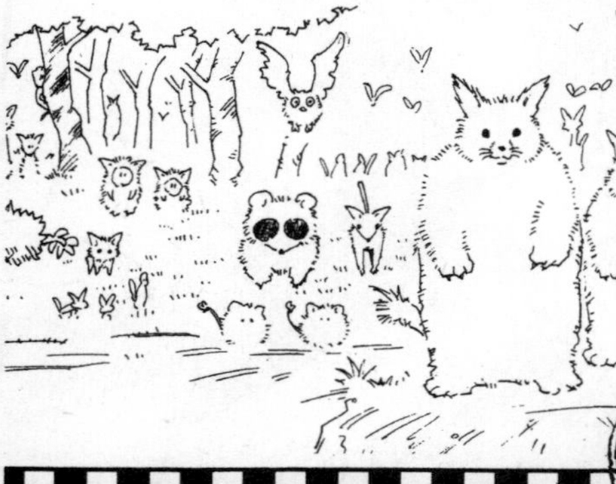

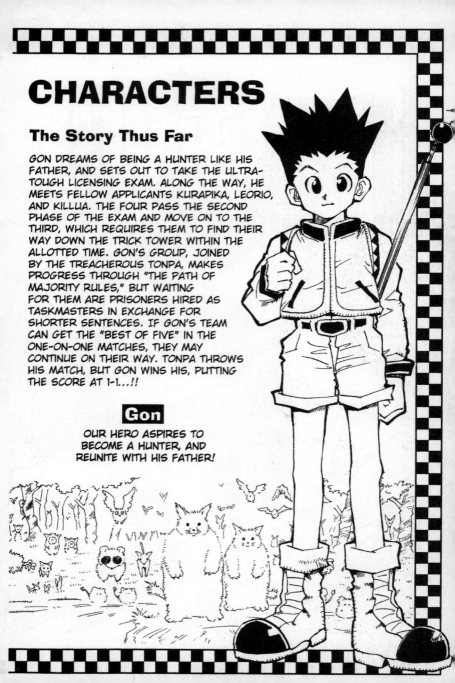

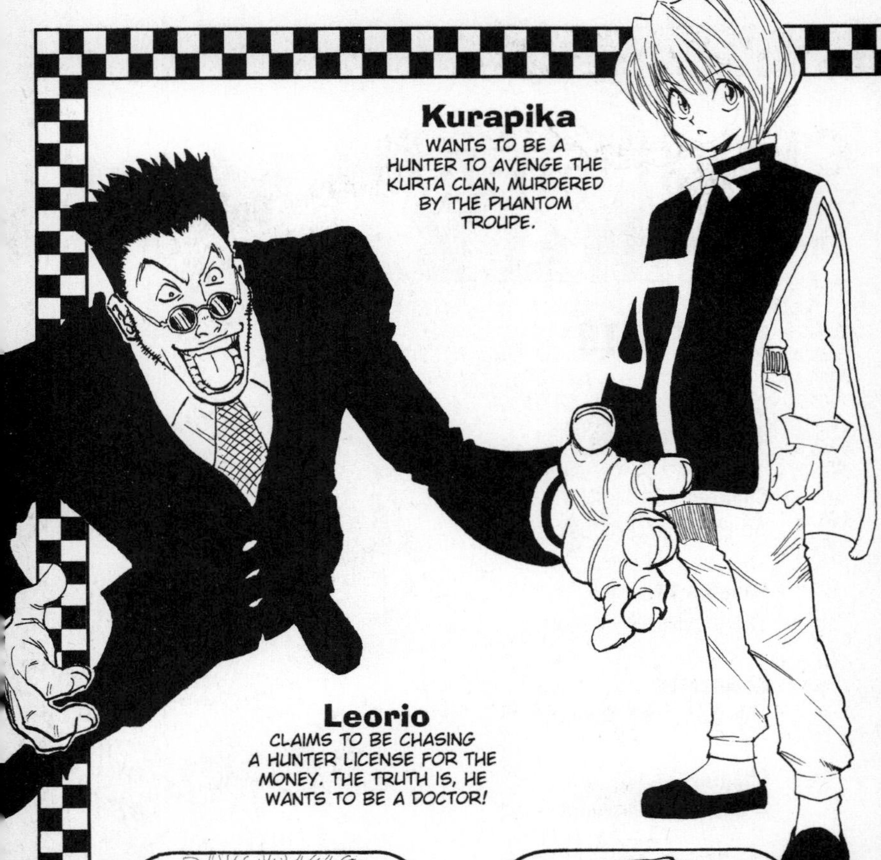

Kurapika

WANTS TO BE A HUNTER TO AVENGE THE KURTA CLAN, MURDERED BY THE PHANTOM TROUPE.

Leorio

CLAIMS TO BE CHASING A HUNTER LICENSE FOR THE MONEY. THE TRUTH IS, HE WANTS TO BE A DOCTOR!

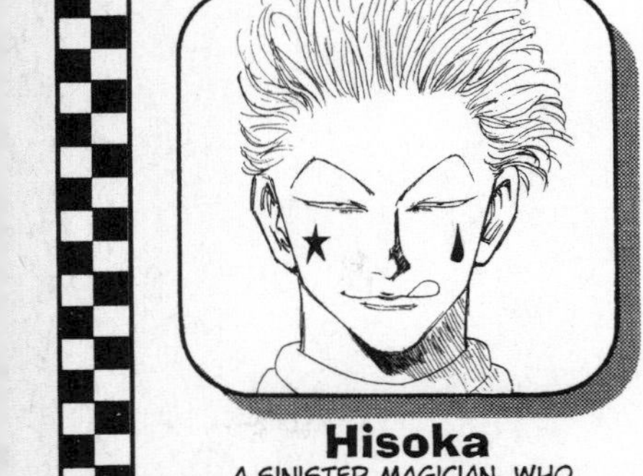

Hisoka

A SINISTER MAGICIAN, WHO DEALS DEATH FROM A DECK OF PLAYING CARDS! NO EXAMINEE IS SAFE FROM HIS BLOODLUST!

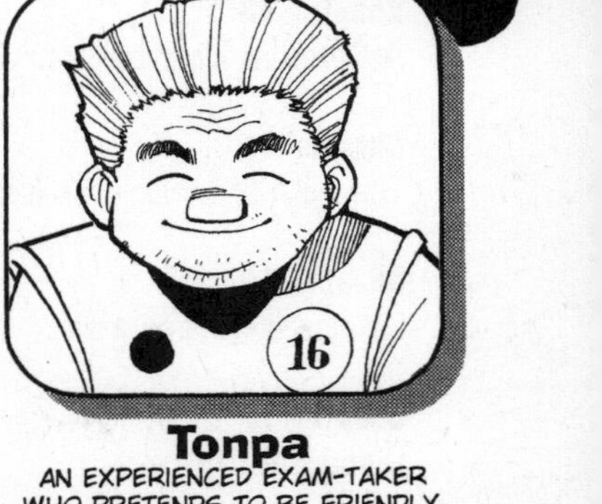
16

Tonpa

AN EXPERIENCED EXAM-TAKER WHO PRETENDS TO BE FRIENDLY, BUT ONLY TO INDULGE HIS HOBBY-CRUSHING NEWBIES.

Volume 2

CONTENTS

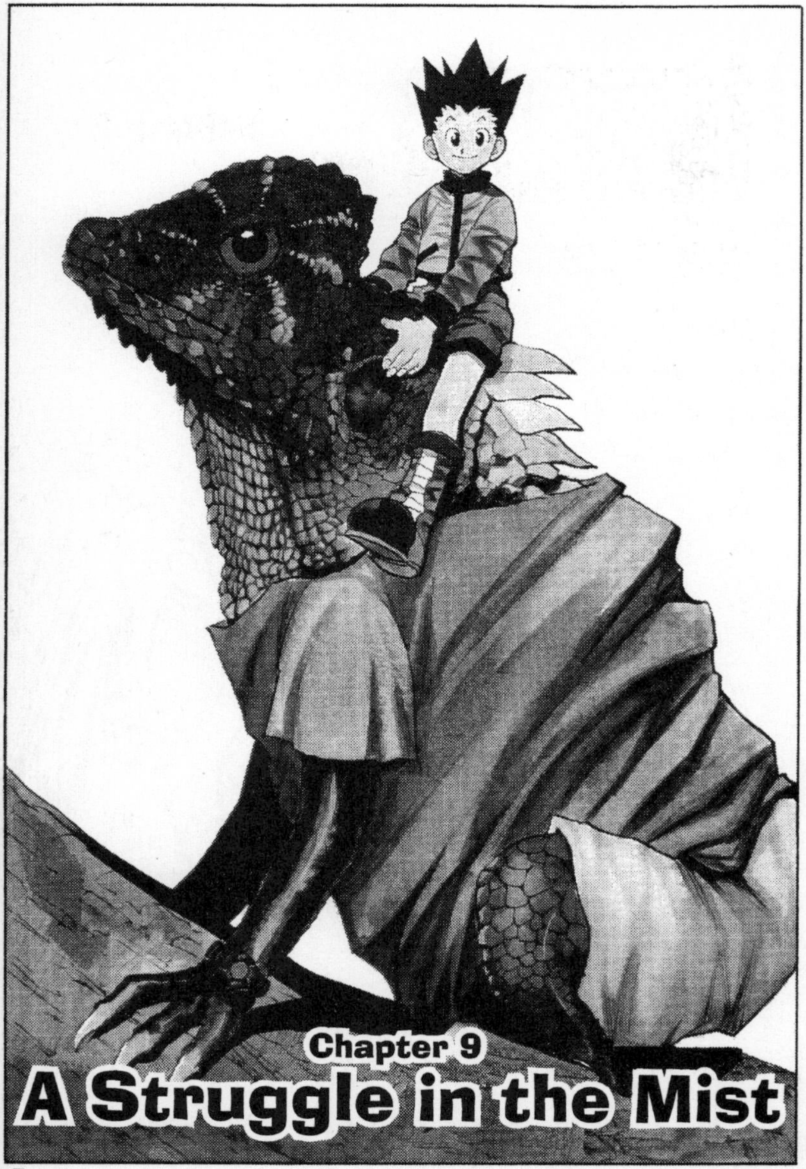
Chapter 9
A Struggle in the Mist

Satotz

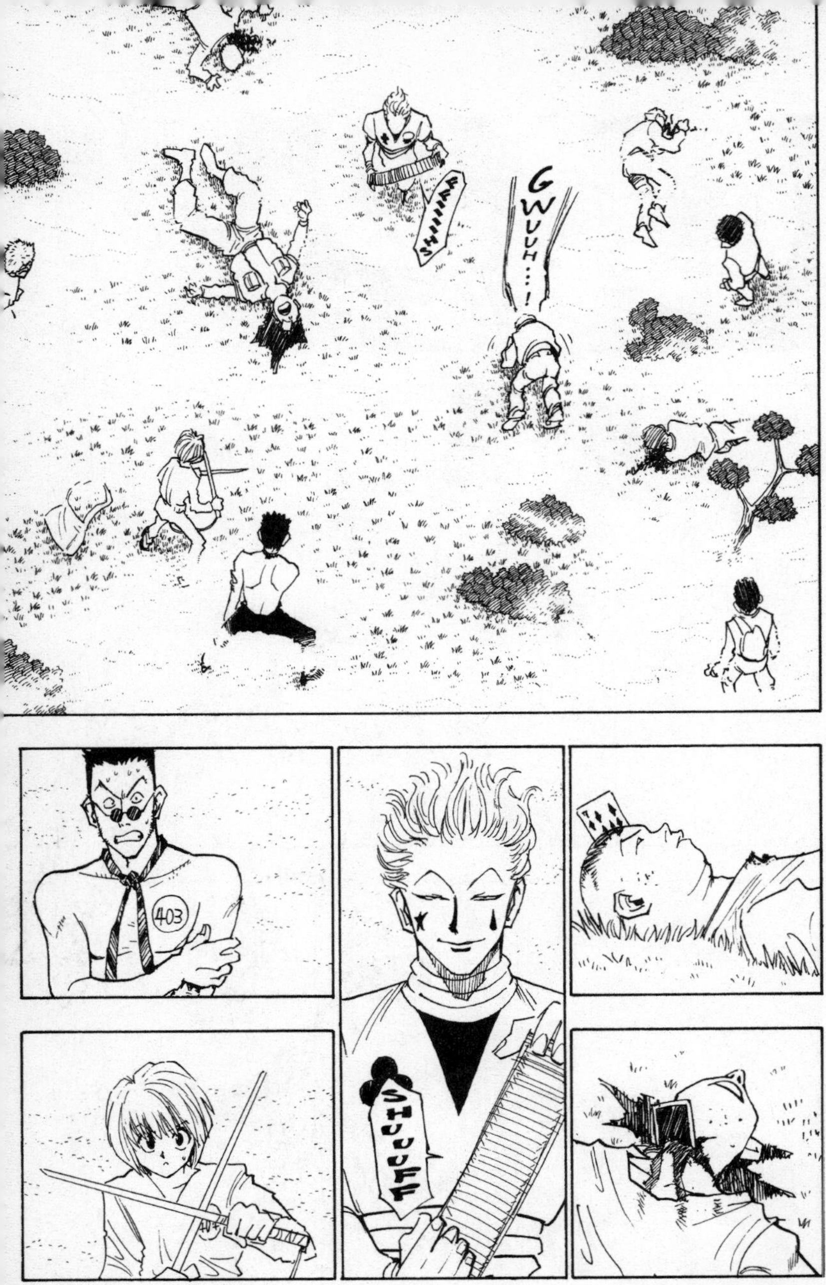
GWUUH...!
SHUUUFF

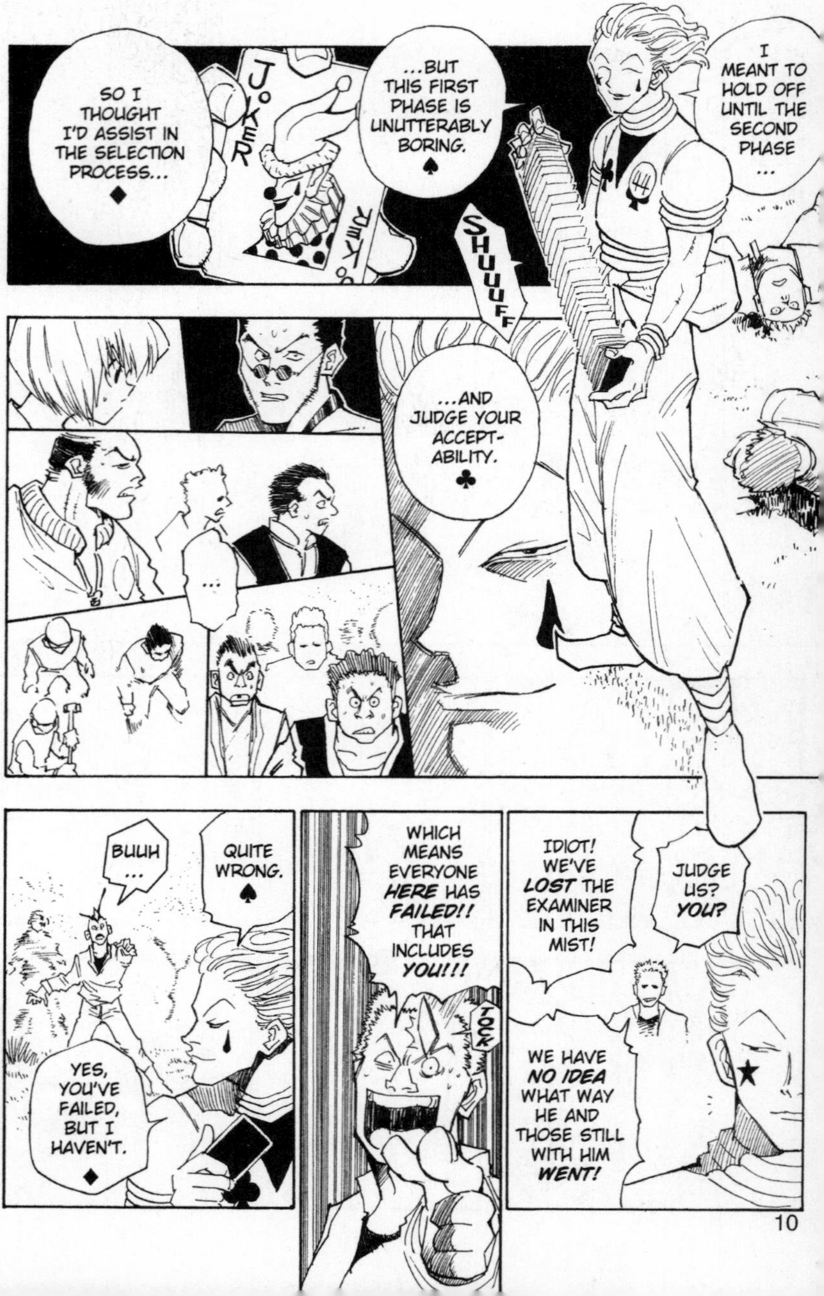
I MEANT TO HOLD OFF UNTIL THE SECOND PHASE ...
...BUT THIS FIRST PHASE IS UNUTTERABLY BORING. ♠
JOKER
SO I THOUGHT I'D ASSIST IN THE SELECTION PROCESS... ♦
SHUUUFF
...AND JUDGE YOUR ACCEPT-ABILITY. ♣
...
JUDGE US? ***YOU?***
IDIOT! WE'VE ***LOST*** THE EXAMINER IN THIS MIST!
WE HAVE ***NO IDEA*** WHAT WAY HE AND THOSE STILL WITH HIM ***WENT!***
WHICH MEANS EVERYONE ***HERE*** HAS ***FAILED!!*** THAT INCLUDES ***YOU!!!***
TOCK
QUITE WRONG. ♠
BUUH ...
YES, YOU'VE FAILED, BUT I HAVEN'T. ♦

READ THIS WAY

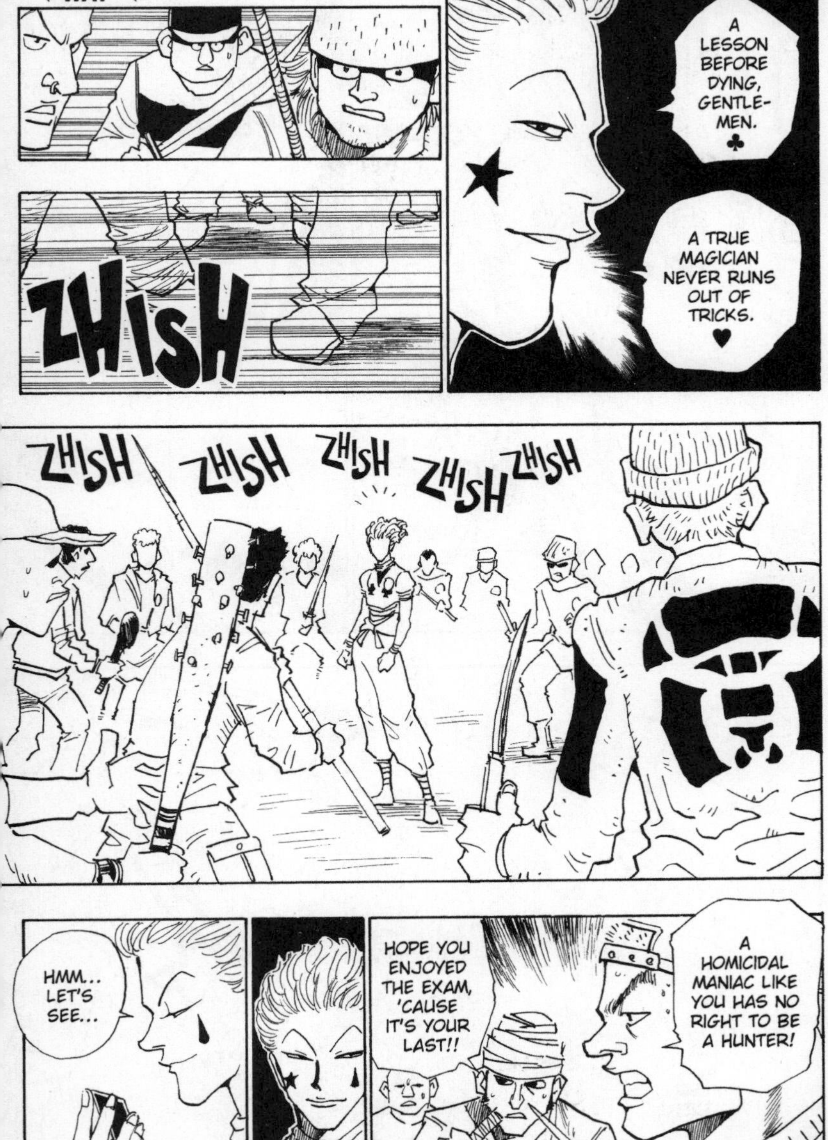
A LESSON BEFORE DYING, GENTLEMEN. ♣
A TRUE MAGICIAN NEVER RUNS OUT OF TRICKS. ♥
ZHISH
ZHISH
ZHISH
ZHISH
ZHISH
ZHISH
ZHISH
A HOMICIDAL MANIAC LIKE YOU HAS NO RIGHT TO BE A HUNTER!
HOPE YOU ENJOYED THE EXAM, 'CAUSE IT'S YOUR LAST!!
HMM... LET'S SEE...

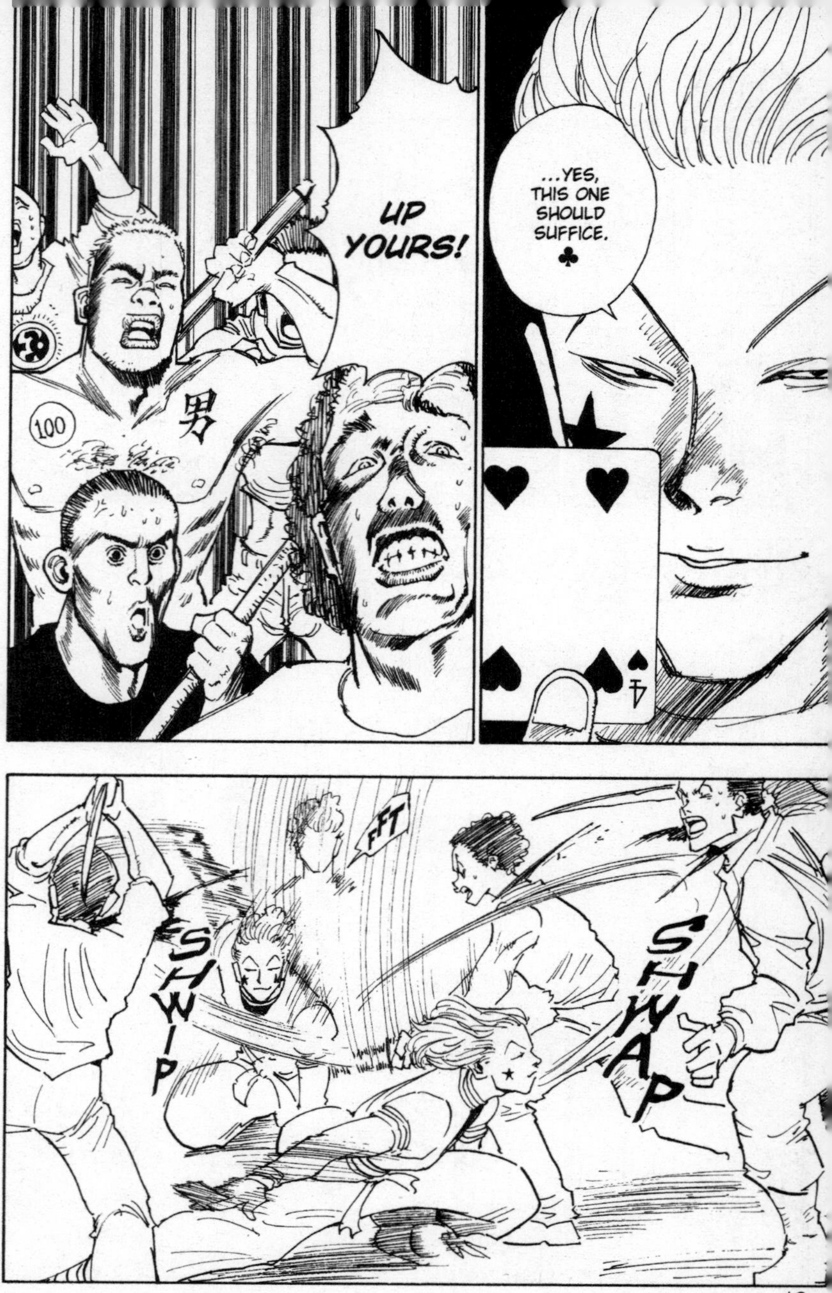
...YES, THIS ONE SHOULD SUFFICE. ♣
UP YOURS!
SHWAP
FFT
SHWIP

READ THIS WAY

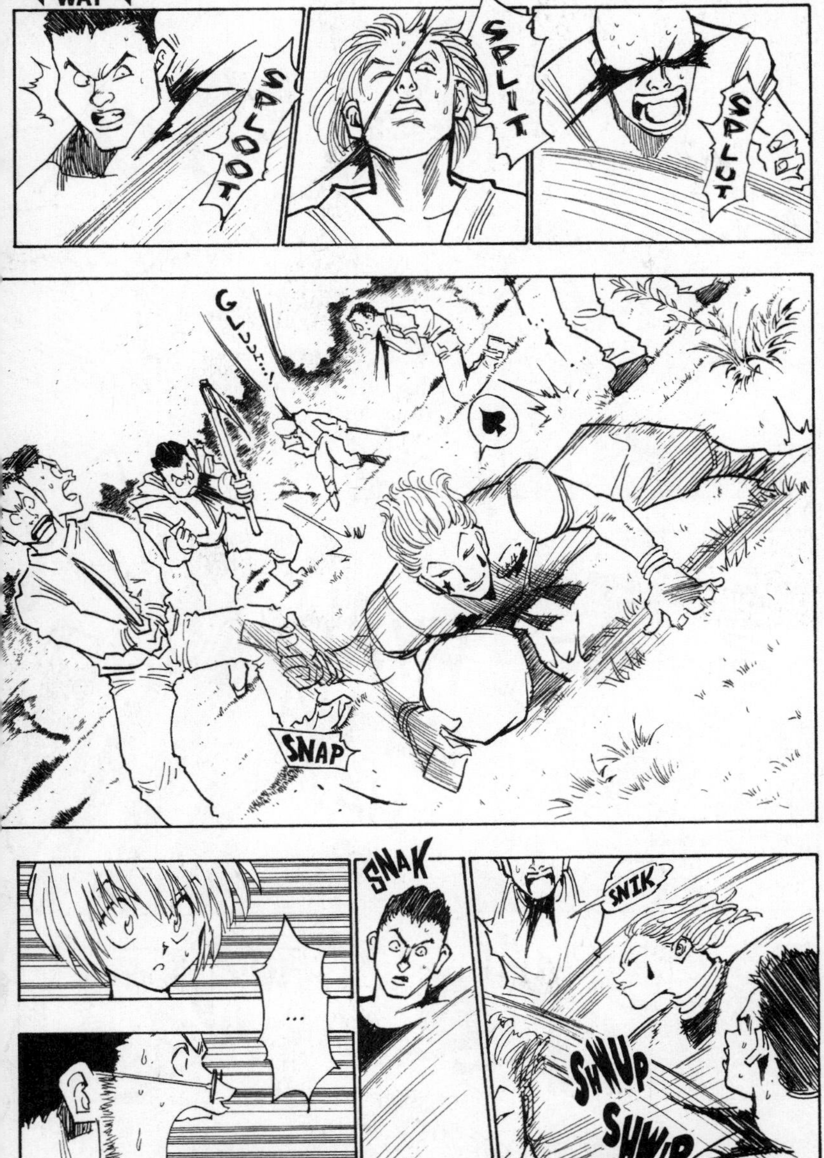

SPLUT
SPLIT
SPLOOT
GLUUH...!
♠
SNAP
SNIK
SHWUP
SHWIP
SNAK
...

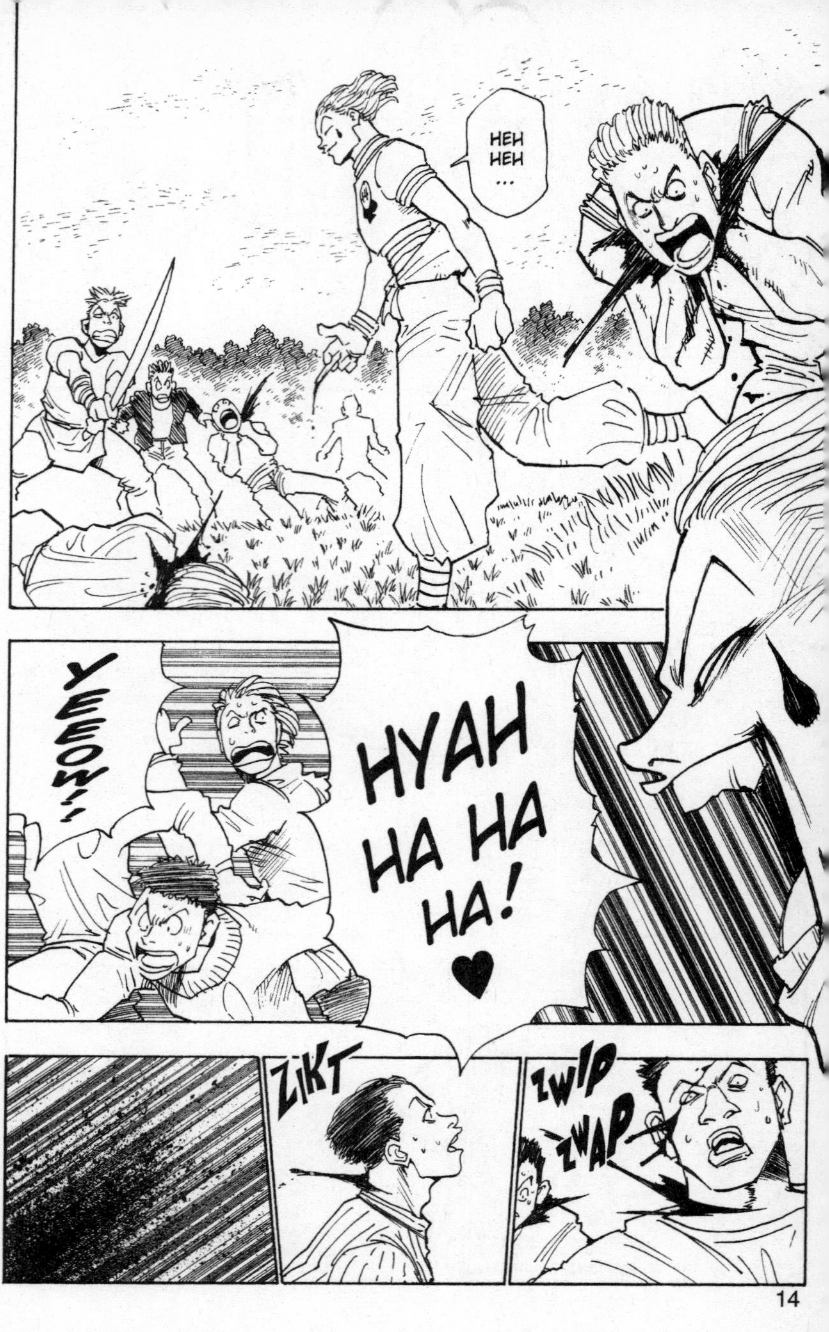
HEH HEH ...
HYAH HA HA HA! ♥
YEEEOW!!
ZWIP
ZWAP
ZIKT

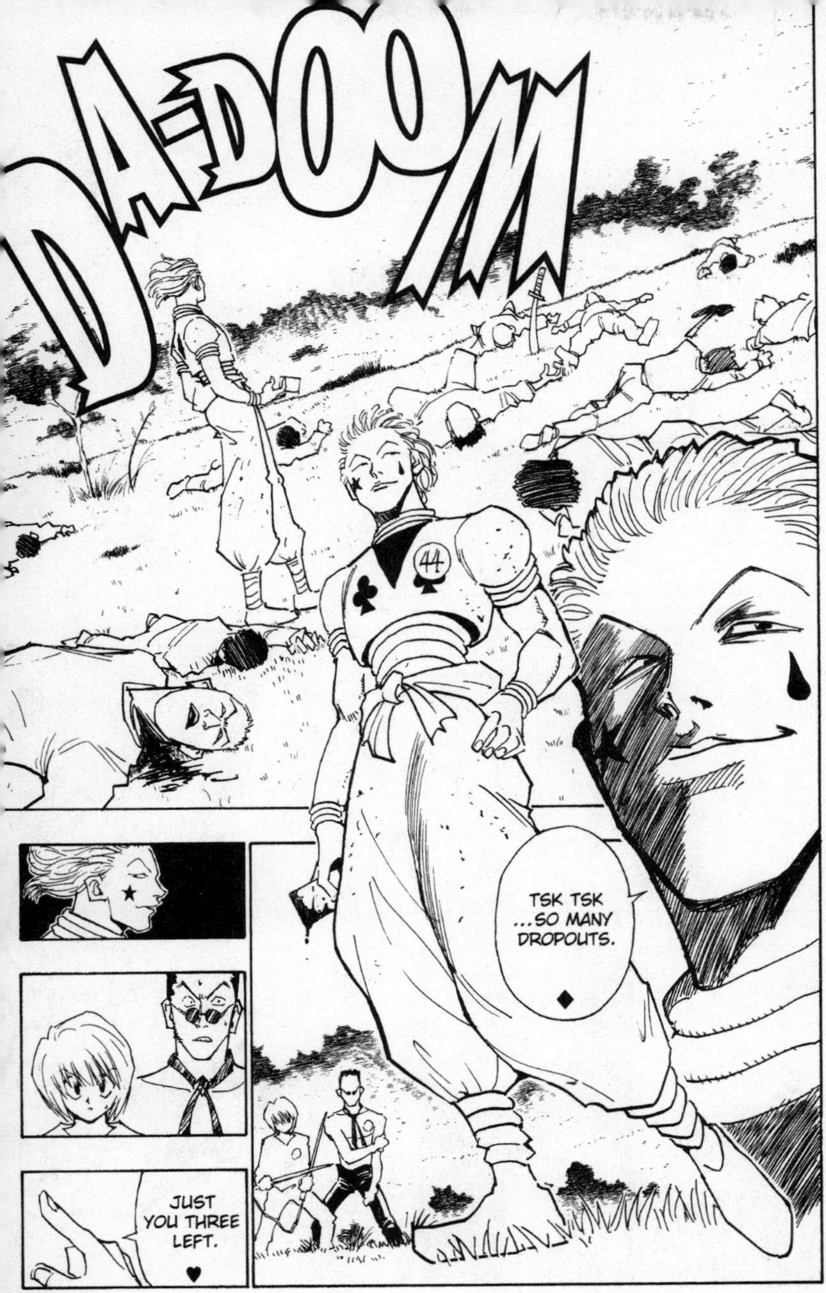
DA-DOOM
TSK TSK ...SO MANY DROPOUTS.
JUST YOU THREE LEFT.

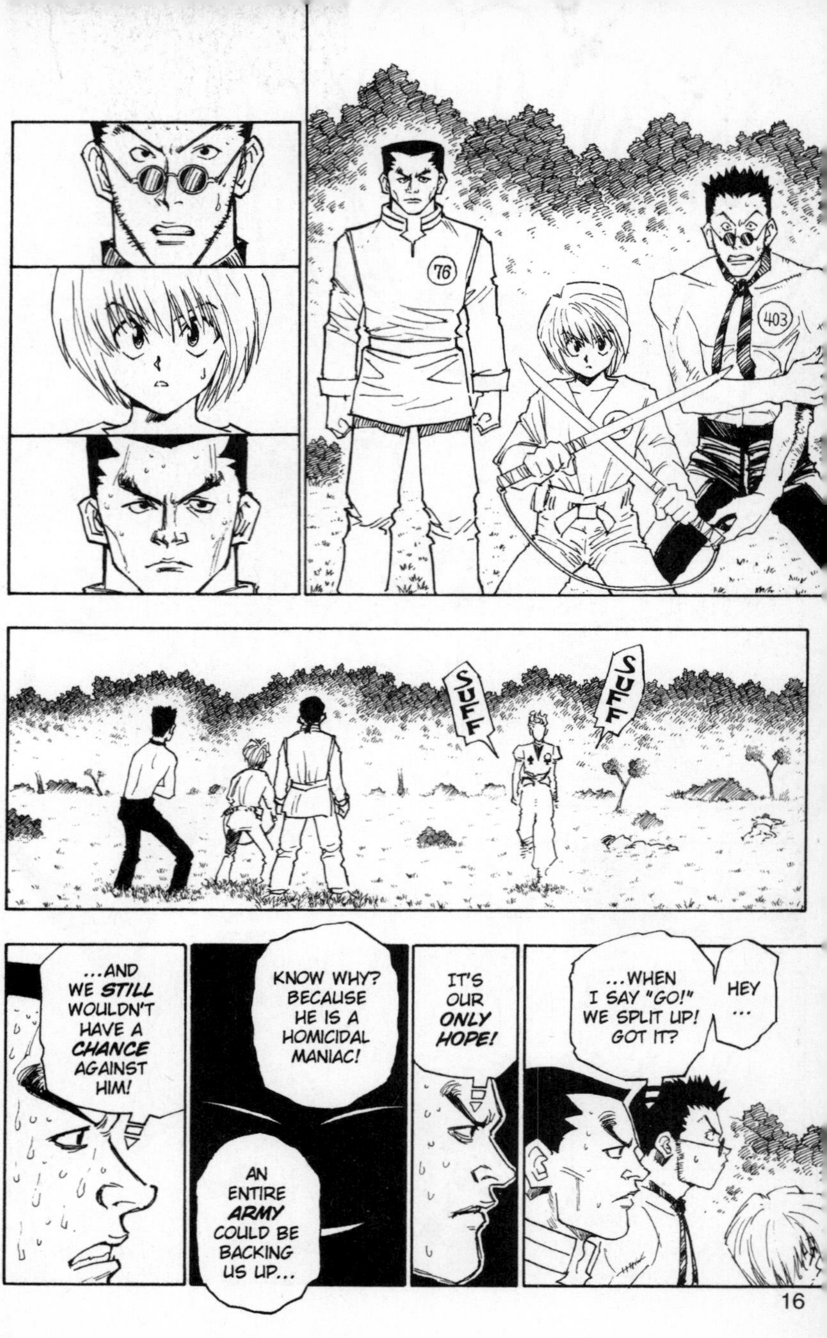
SUFF
SUFF
HEY ...
...WHEN I SAY "GO!" WE SPLIT UP! GOT IT?
IT'S OUR ONLY HOPE!
KNOW WHY? BECAUSE HE IS A HOMICIDAL MANIAC!
AN ENTIRE ARMY COULD BE BACKING US UP...
...AND WE STILL WOULDN'T HAVE A CHANCE AGAINST HIM!

READ THIS WAY

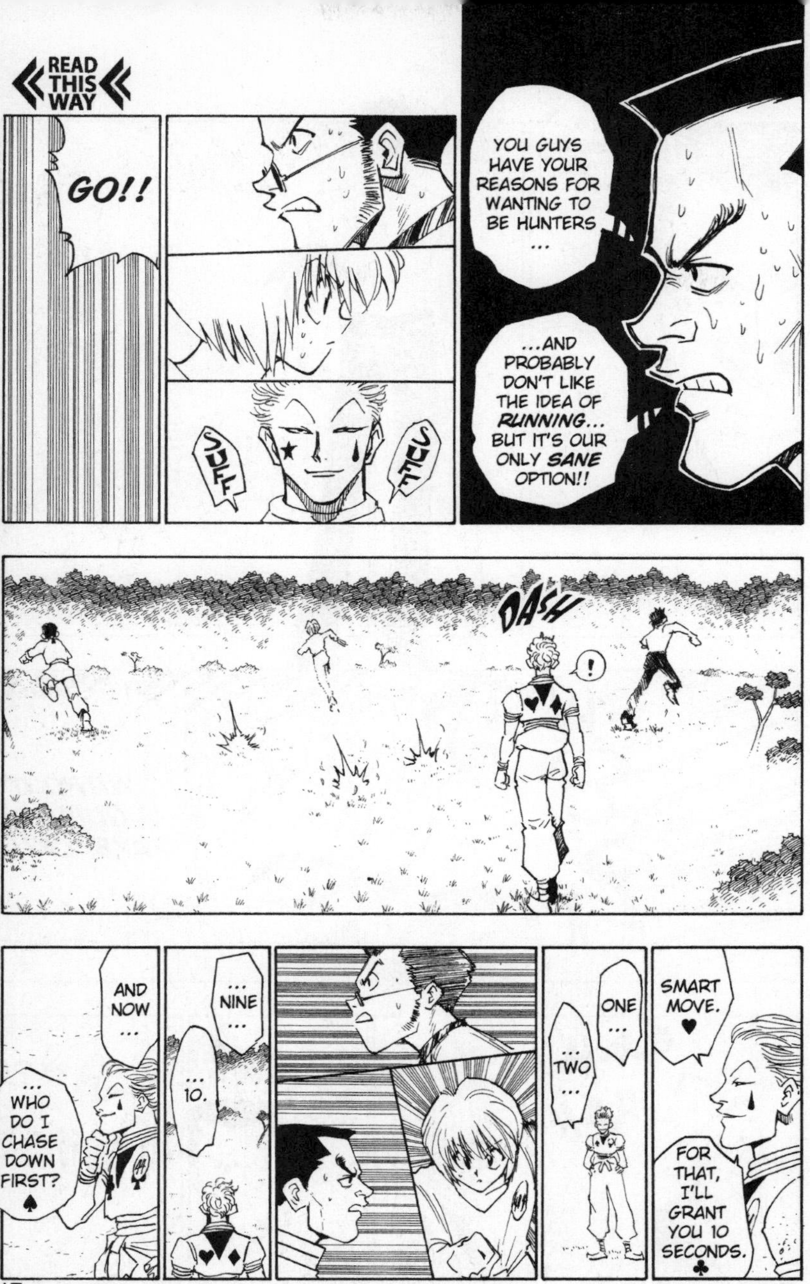

YOU GUYS HAVE YOUR REASONS FOR WANTING TO BE HUNTERS ...
...AND PROBABLY DON'T LIKE THE IDEA OF *RUNNING*... BUT IT'S OUR ONLY *SANE* OPTION!!
SUFF
SUFF
GO!!
DASH
!
SMART MOVE. ♥
FOR THAT, I'LL GRANT YOU 10 SECONDS. ♣
ONE ...
... TWO ...
... NINE ...
... 10.
AND NOW ...
... WHO DO I CHASE DOWN FIRST? ♠

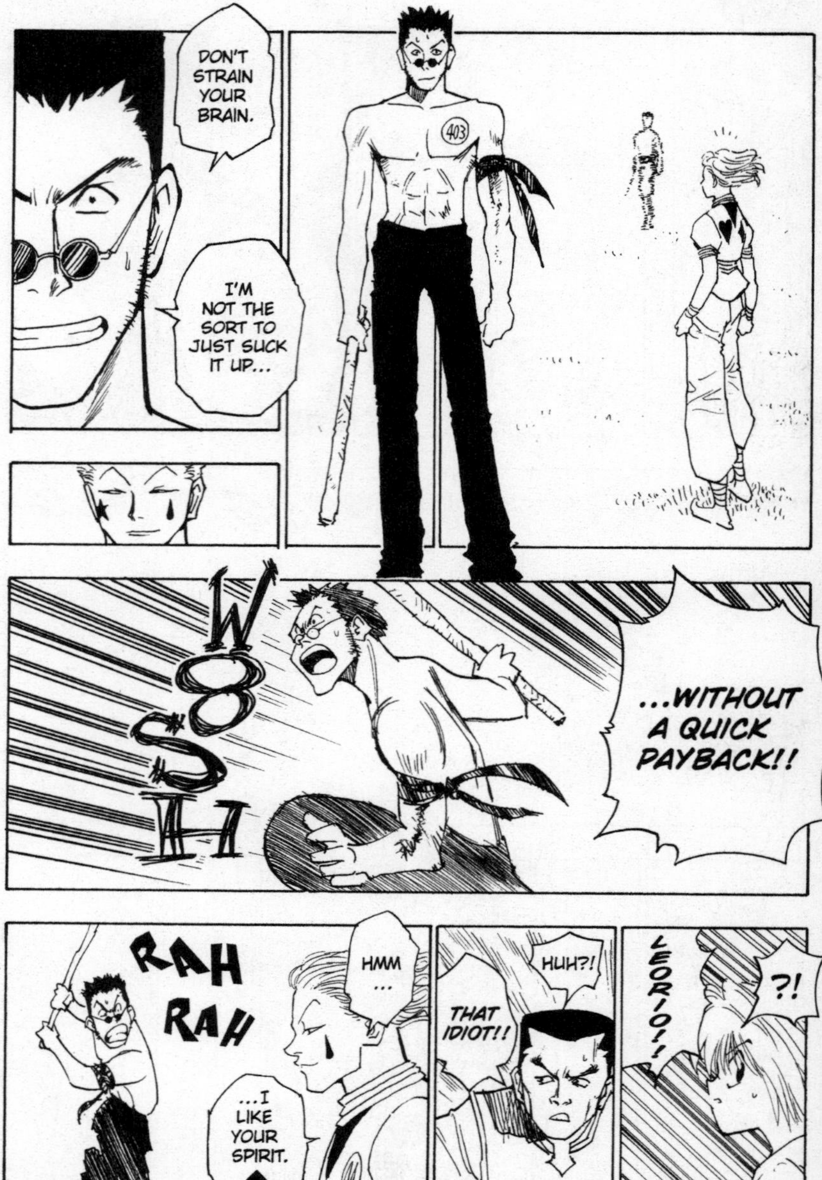
DON'T STRAIN YOUR BRAIN.
I'M NOT THE SORT TO JUST SUCK IT UP...
...WITHOUT A QUICK PAYBACK!!
?!
LEORIO!!
HUH?!
THAT IDIOT!!
HMM ...
...I LIKE YOUR SPIRIT. ◆
RAH RAH

READ THIS WAY

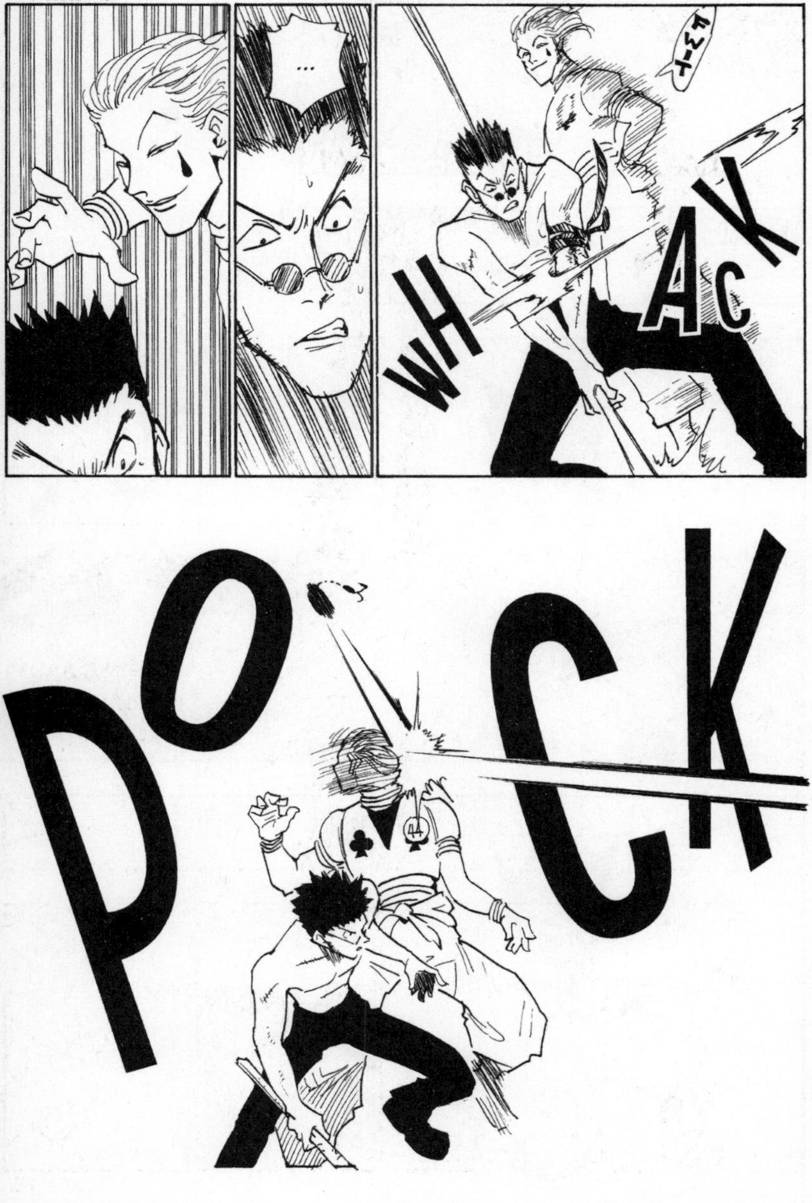
TWIT
WHACK
...
POCK

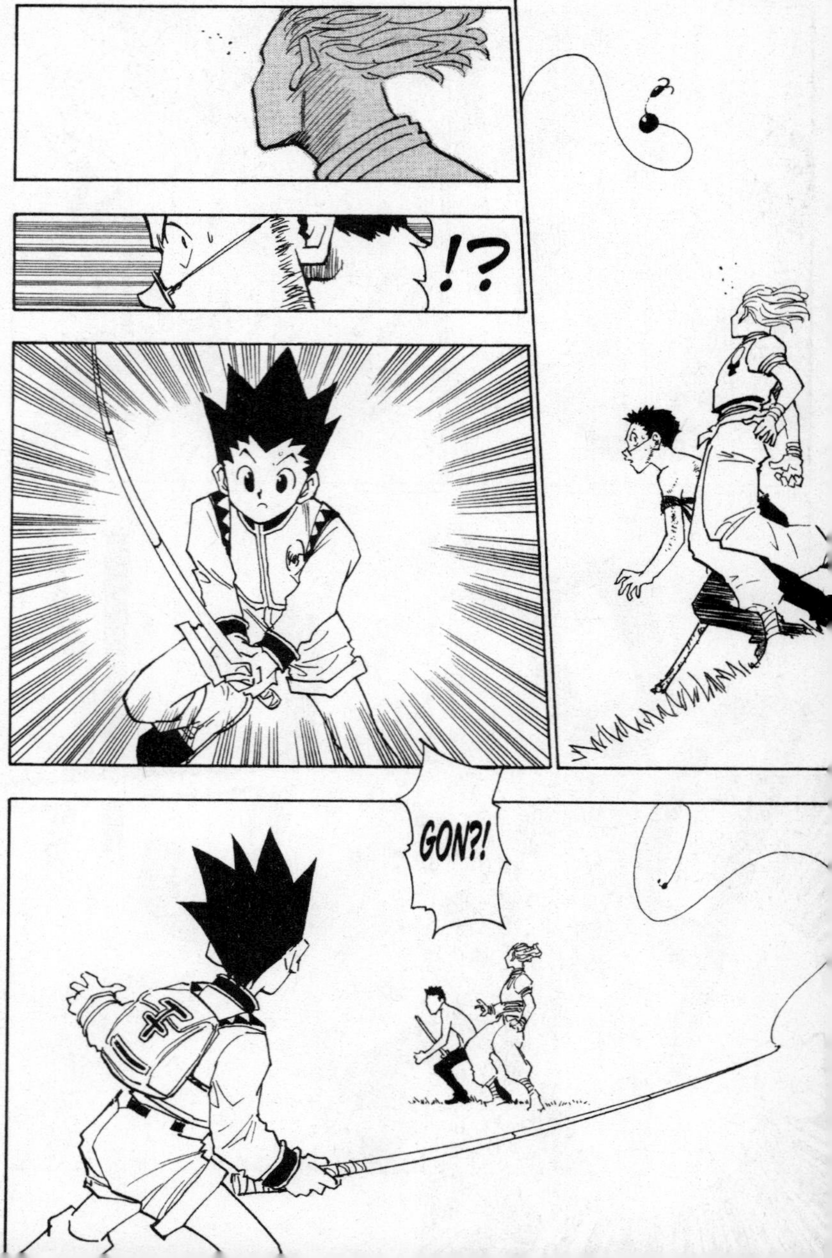
!?
GON?!

READ THIS WAY

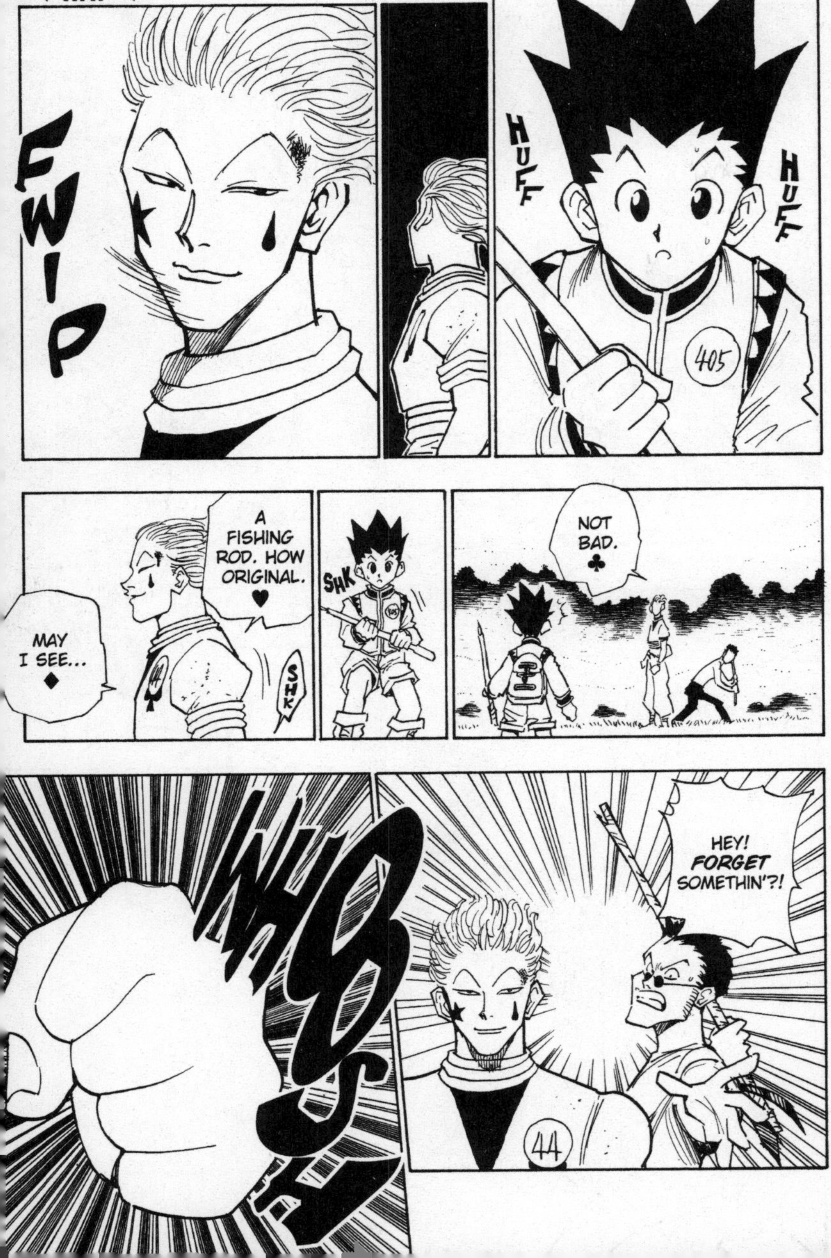
HUFF
HUFF
FWIP
NOT BAD. ♣
SHK
A FISHING ROD. HOW ORIGINAL. ♥
SHK
MAY I SEE... ♦
HEY! *FORGET* SOMETHIN'?!
WHOOSH

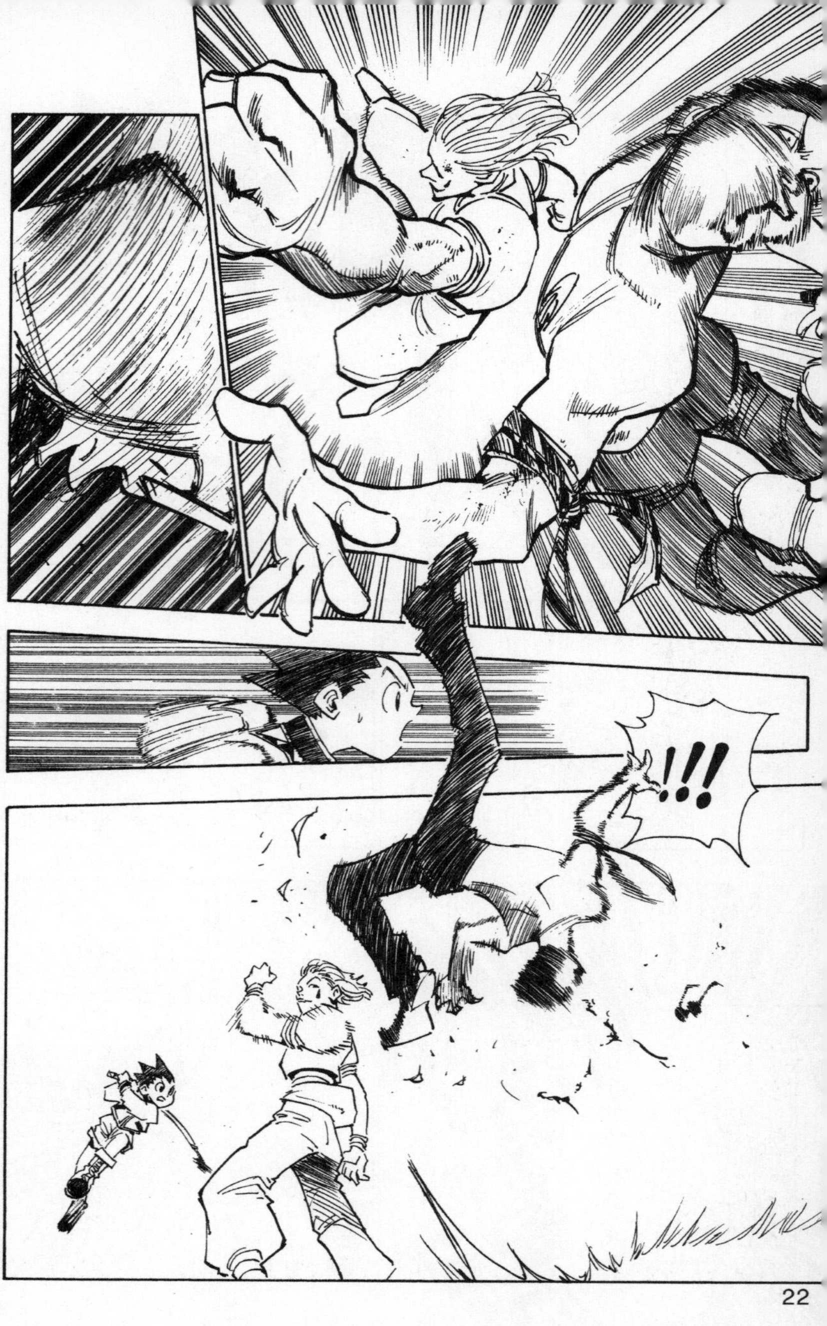
!!!

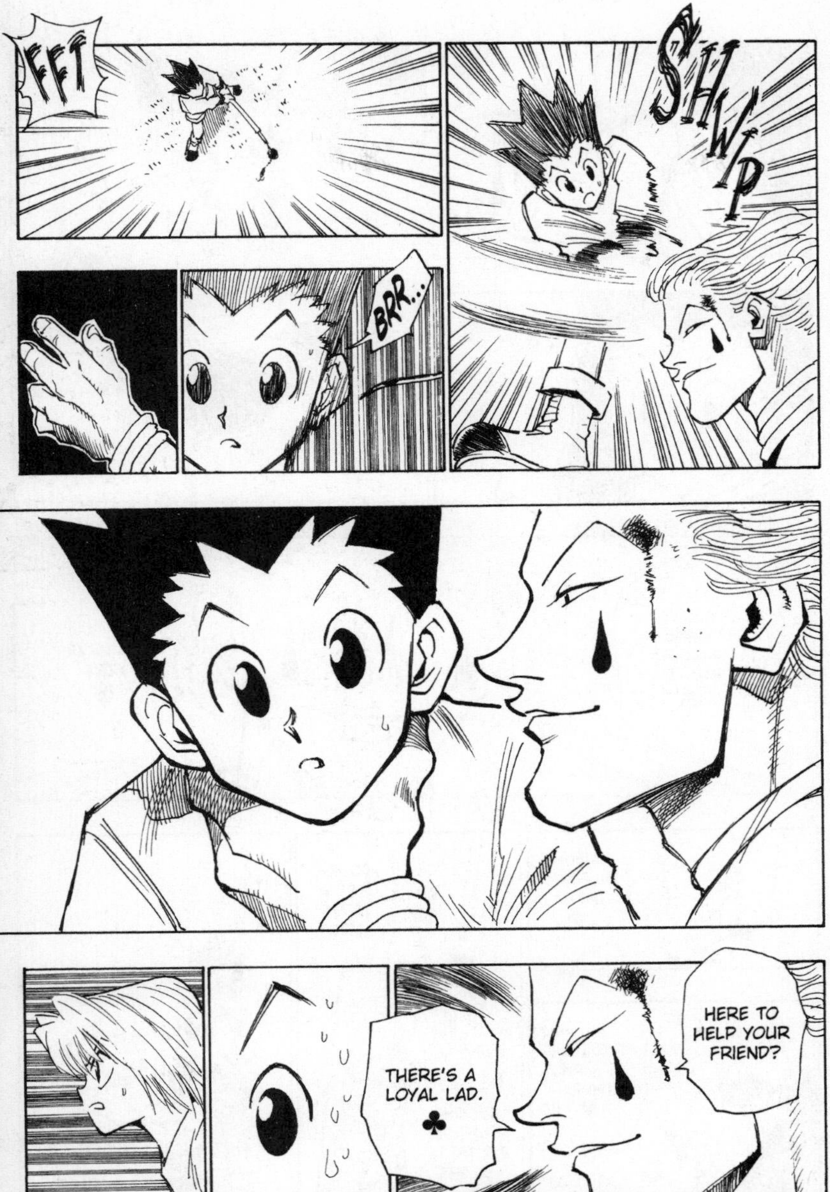
SHWIP
FFT
BRR...
HERE TO HELP YOUR FRIEND?
THERE'S A LOYAL LAD. ♣

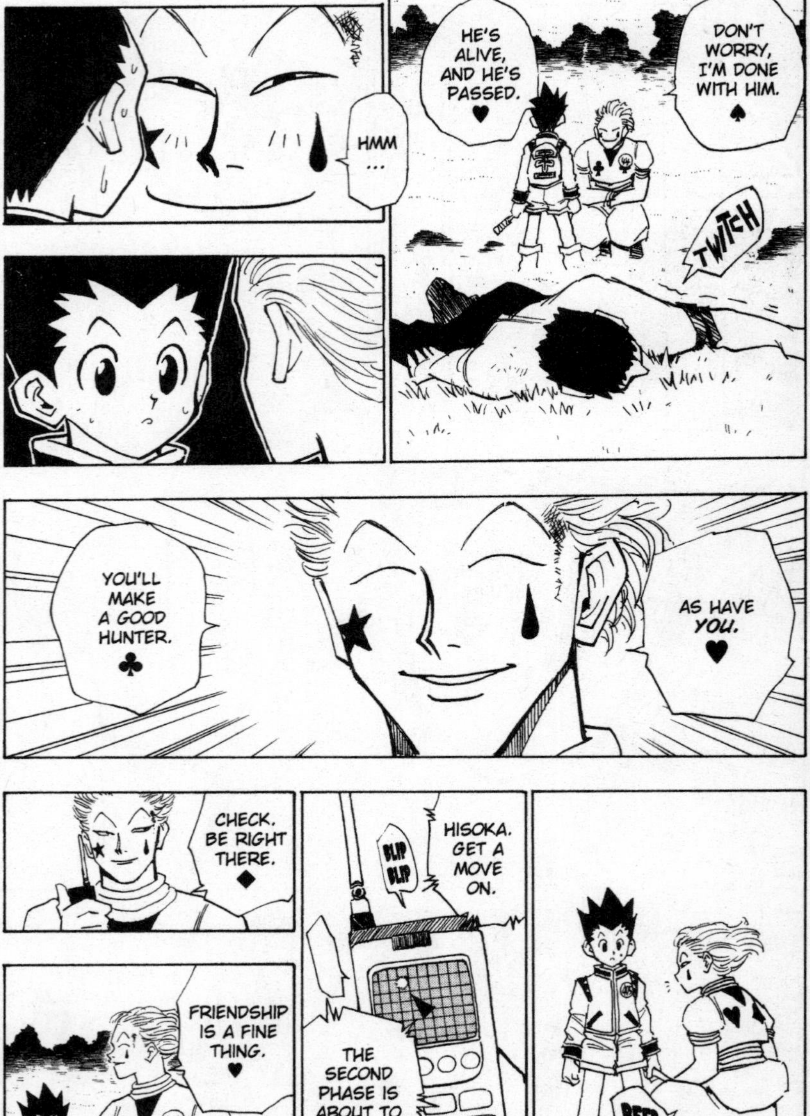
DON'T WORRY, I'M DONE WITH HIM. ♠
HE'S ALIVE, AND HE'S PASSED. ♥
TWITCH
HMM ...
AS HAVE YOU. ♥
YOU'LL MAKE A GOOD HUNTER. ♣
BEEP BEEP
HISOKA. GET A MOVE ON.
BLIP BLIP
THE SECOND PHASE IS ABOUT TO START.
CHECK. BE RIGHT THERE. ♦
FRIENDSHIP IS A FINE THING. ♥

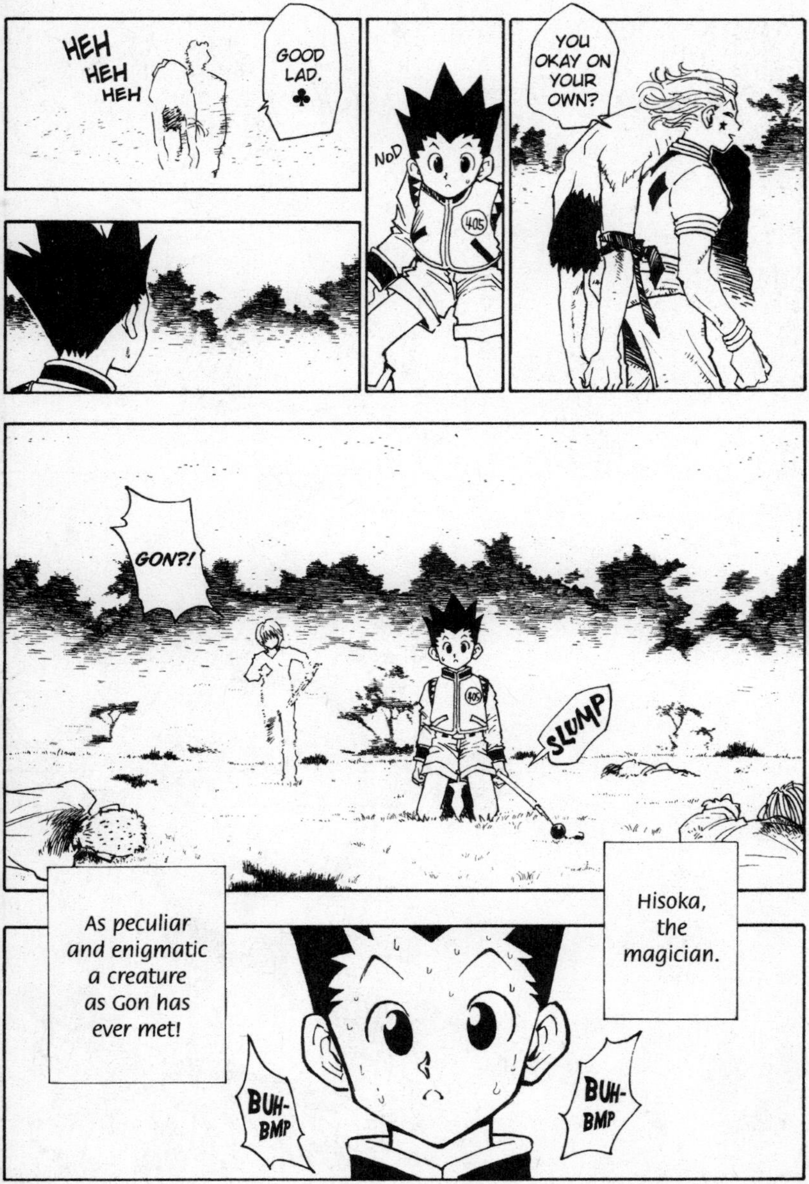
YOU OKAY ON YOUR OWN?
NOD
GOOD LAD. ♣
HEH HEH HEH
GON?!
SLUMP
Hisoka, the magician.
As peculiar and enigmatic a creature as Gon has ever met!
BUH-BMP
BUH-BMP

Menchi

Chapter 10
An Unexpected Task

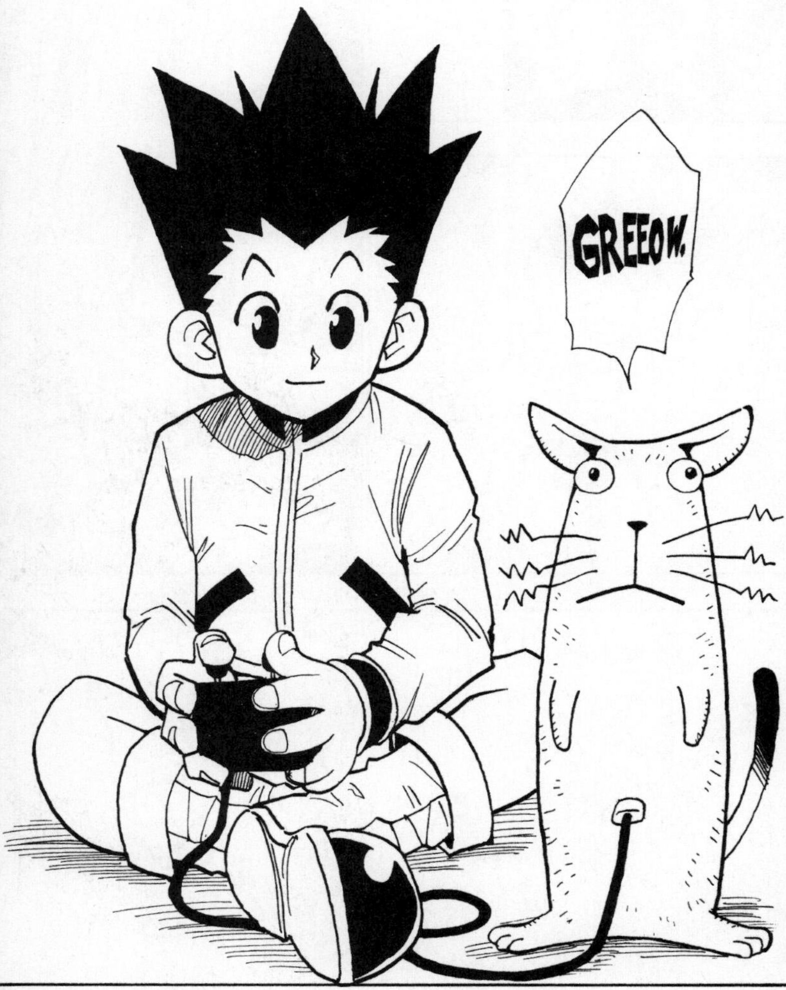
GREEOW.

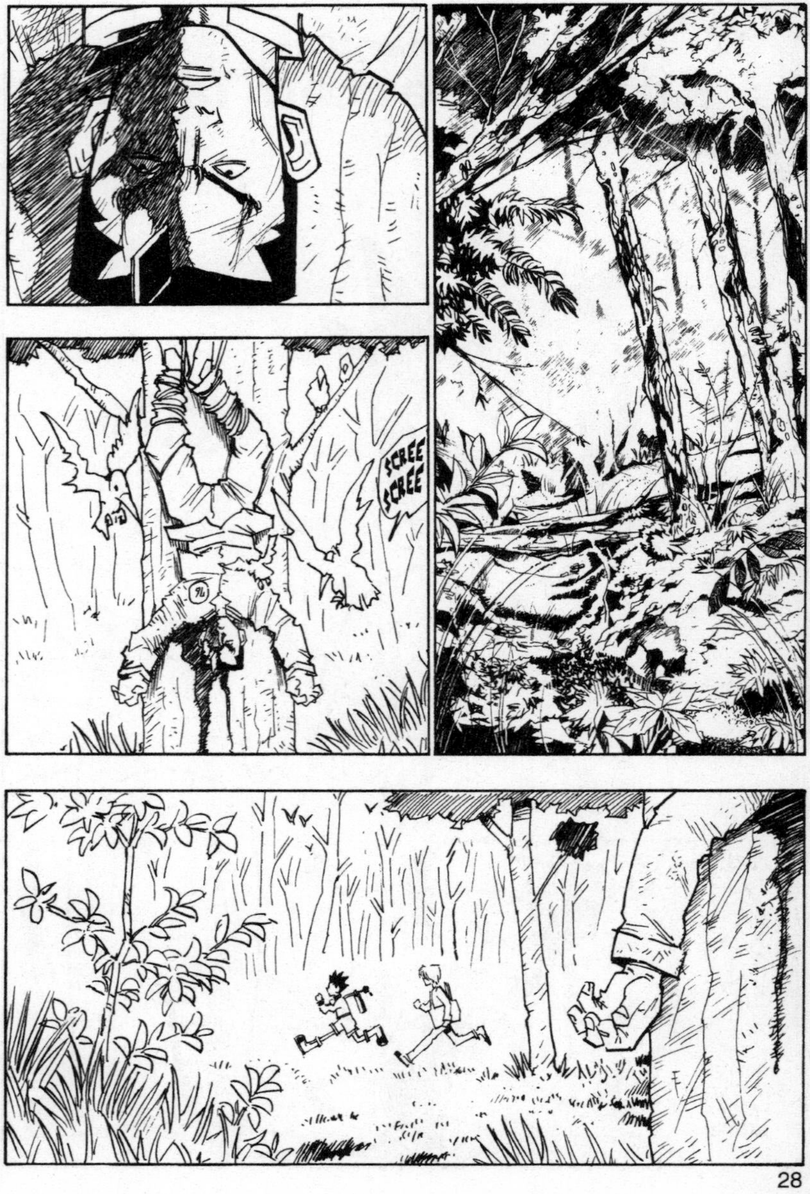
SCREE SCREE

READ THIS WAY

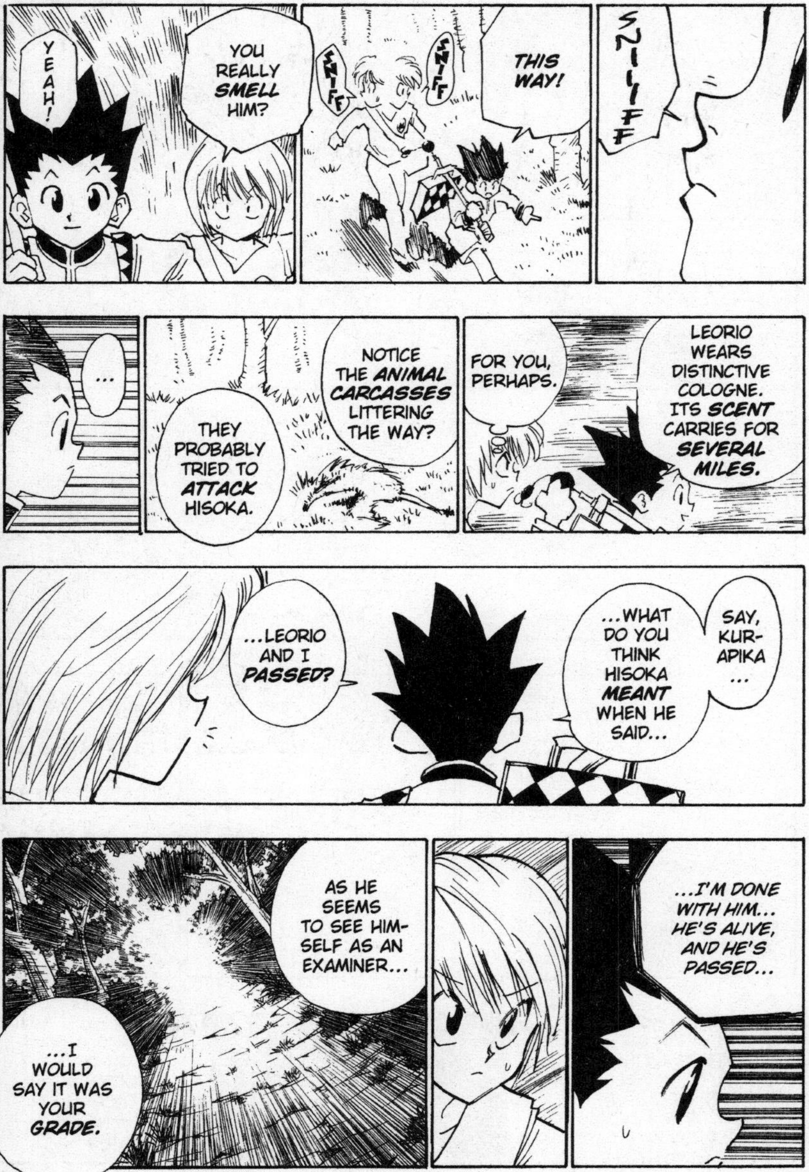
SNIIIFF
THIS WAY!
SNIFF
SNIFF
YOU REALLY SMELL HIM?
YEAH!
LEORIO WEARS DISTINCTIVE COLOGNE. ITS SCENT CARRIES FOR SEVERAL MILES.
FOR YOU, PERHAPS.
NOTICE THE ANIMAL CARCASSES LITTERING THE WAY?
THEY PROBABLY TRIED TO ATTACK HISOKA.
...
SAY, KUR-APIKA...
...WHAT DO YOU THINK HISOKA MEANT WHEN HE SAID...
...LEORIO AND I PASSED?
...I'M DONE WITH HIM... HE'S ALIVE, AND HE'S PASSED...
AS HE SEEMS TO SEE HIM-SELF AS AN EXAMINER...
...I WOULD SAY IT WAS YOUR GRADE.

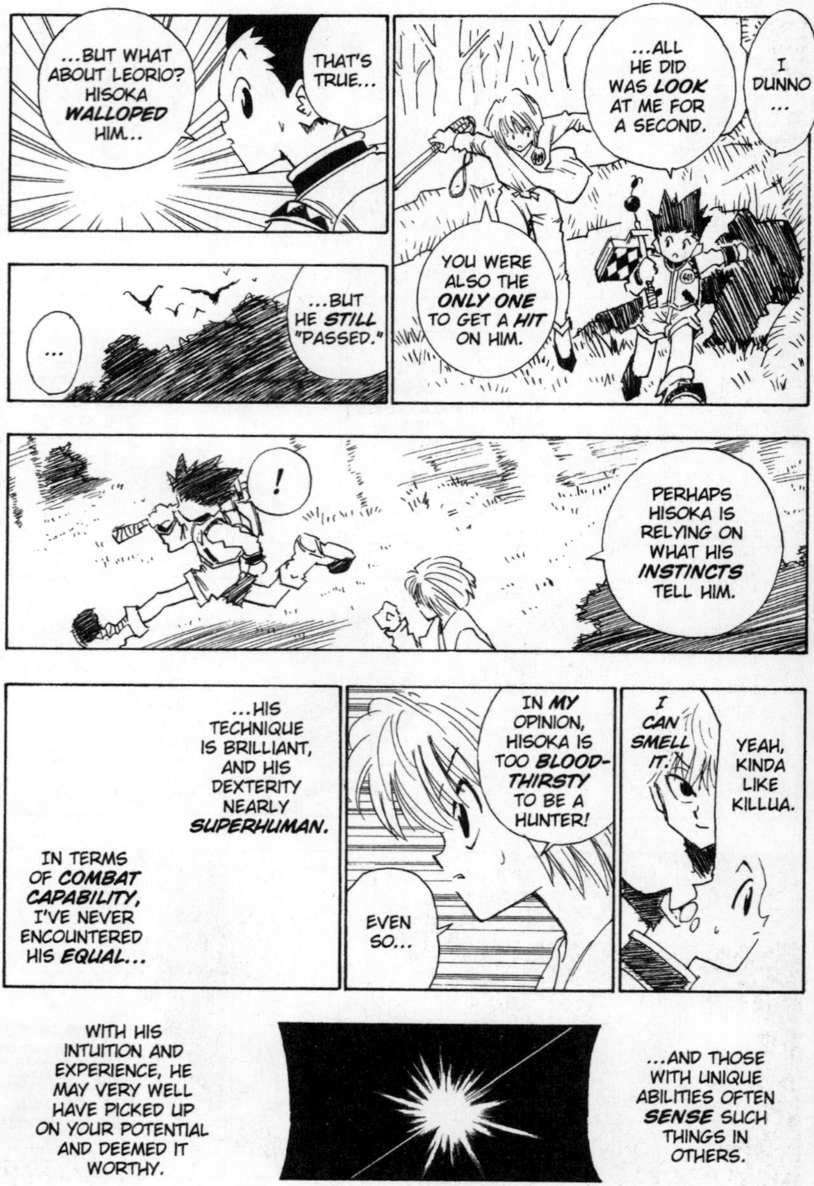
I DUNNO...
...ALL HE DID WAS LOOK AT ME FOR A SECOND.
YOU WERE ALSO THE ONLY ONE TO GET A HIT ON HIM.
THAT'S TRUE...
...BUT WHAT ABOUT LEORIO? HISOKA WALLOPED HIM...
...BUT HE STILL "PASSED."
...
PERHAPS HISOKA IS RELYING ON WHAT HIS INSTINCTS TELL HIM.
!
YEAH, KINDA LIKE KILLUA.
I CAN SMELL IT.
IN MY OPINION, HISOKA IS TOO BLOOD-THIRSTY TO BE A HUNTER!
EVEN SO...
...HIS TECHNIQUE IS BRILLIANT, AND HIS DEXTERITY NEARLY SUPERHUMAN.
IN TERMS OF COMBAT CAPABILITY, I'VE NEVER ENCOUNTERED HIS EQUAL...
...AND THOSE WITH UNIQUE ABILITIES OFTEN SENSE SUCH THINGS IN OTHERS.
WITH HIS INTUITION AND EXPERIENCE, HE MAY VERY WELL HAVE PICKED UP ON YOUR POTENTIAL AND DEEMED IT WORTHY.

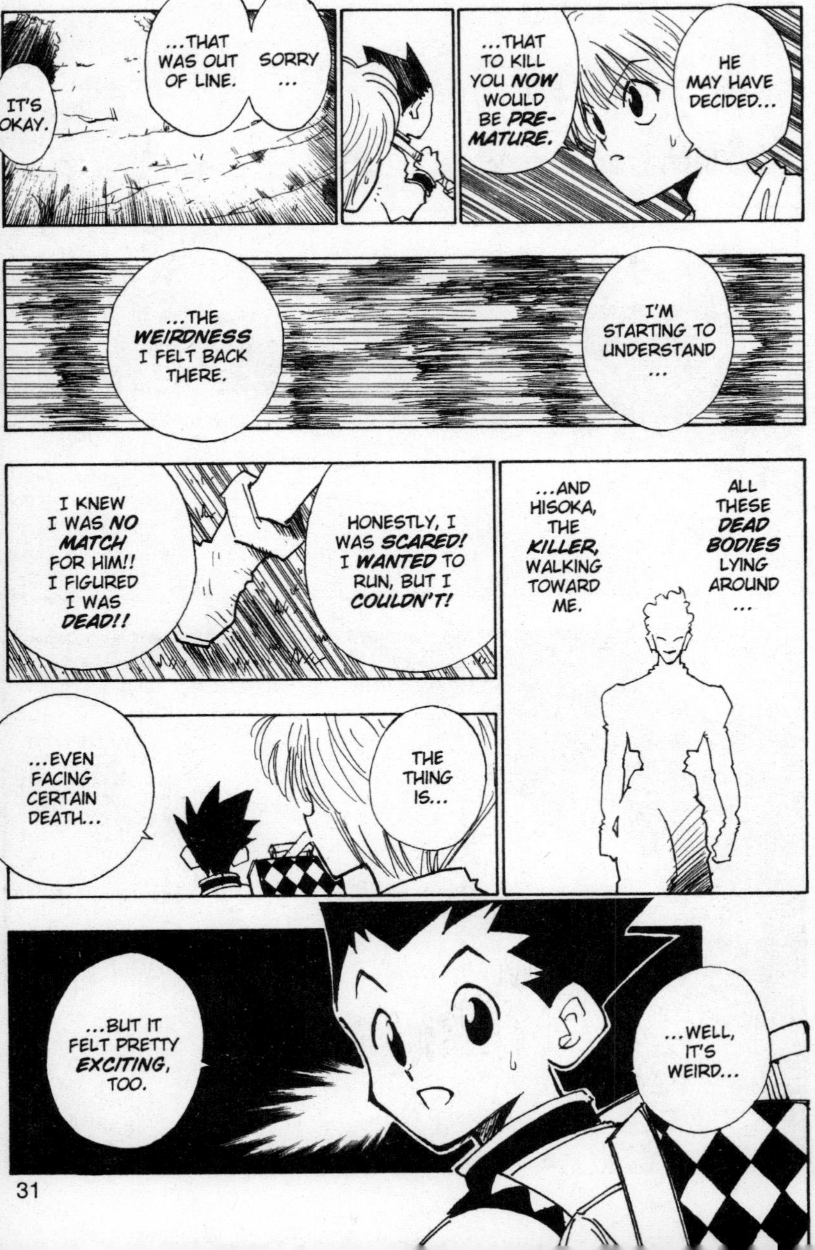
HE MAY HAVE DECIDED...
...THAT TO KILL YOU NOW WOULD BE PRE-MATURE.
SORRY...
...THAT WAS OUT OF LINE.
IT'S OKAY.
I'M STARTING TO UNDERSTAND...
...THE WEIRDNESS I FELT BACK THERE.
ALL THESE DEAD BODIES LYING AROUND...
...AND HISOKA, THE KILLER, WALKING TOWARD ME.
HONESTLY, I WAS SCARED! I WANTED TO RUN, BUT I COULDN'T!
I KNEW I WAS NO MATCH FOR HIM!! I FIGURED I WAS DEAD!!
THE THING IS...
...EVEN FACING CERTAIN DEATH...
...WELL, IT'S WEIRD...
...BUT IT FELT PRETTY EXCITING, TOO.

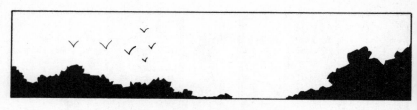

WE'VE COME THROUGH THE SWAMP. WELL DONE, ALL OF YOU.

THIS IS THE VISCA FOREST PRESERVE, WHERE WE WILL CONDUCT THE *SECOND PHASE.*

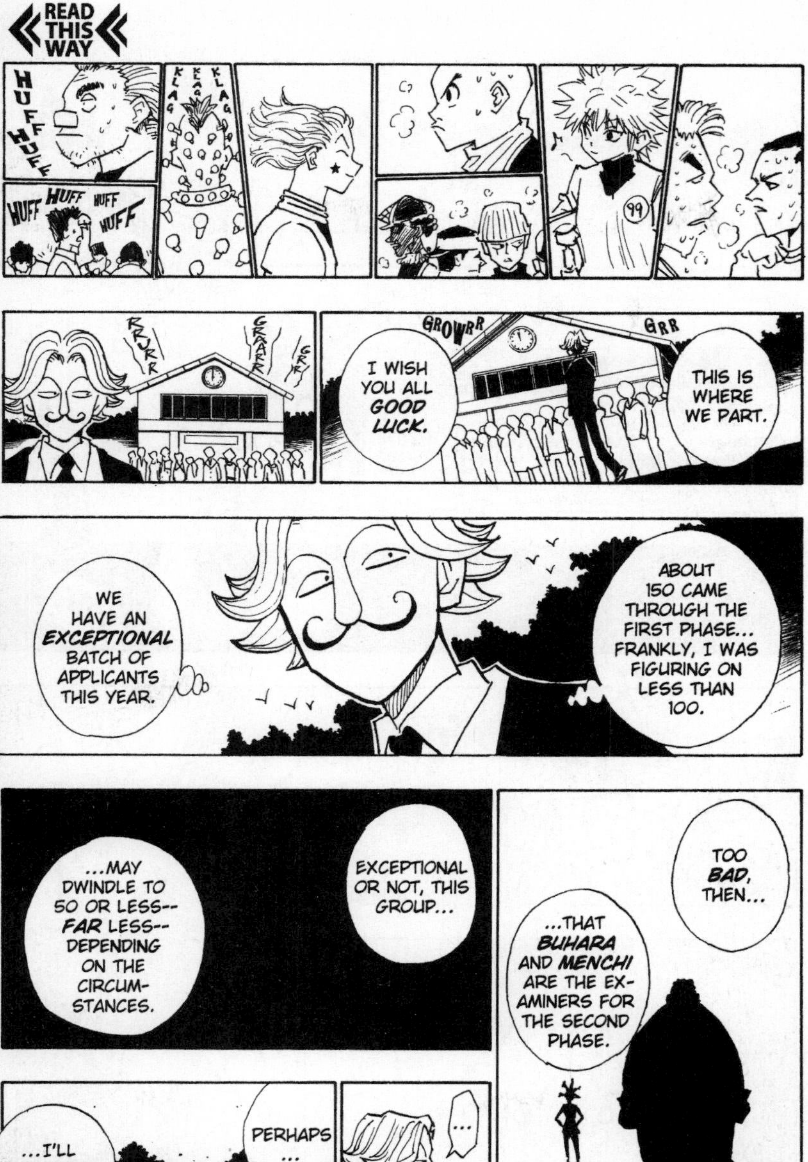
READ THIS WAY
KLAG KLAG KLAG
HUFF HUFF HUFF
HUFF HUFF HUFF HUFF
GROWRR
GRR
THIS IS WHERE WE PART.
I WISH YOU ALL GOOD LUCK.
RRURR
GRARR
GRR
ABOUT 150 CAME THROUGH THE FIRST PHASE... FRANKLY, I WAS FIGURING ON LESS THAN 100.
WE HAVE AN EXCEPTIONAL BATCH OF APPLICANTS THIS YEAR.
TOO BAD, THEN...
...THAT BUHARA AND MENCHI ARE THE EXAMINERS FOR THE SECOND PHASE.
EXCEPTIONAL OR NOT, THIS GROUP...
...MAY DWINDLE TO 50 OR LESS--FAR LESS--DEPENDING ON THE CIRCUMSTANCES.
...
PERHAPS ...
...I'LL STAY AND WATCH.

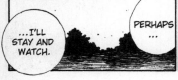

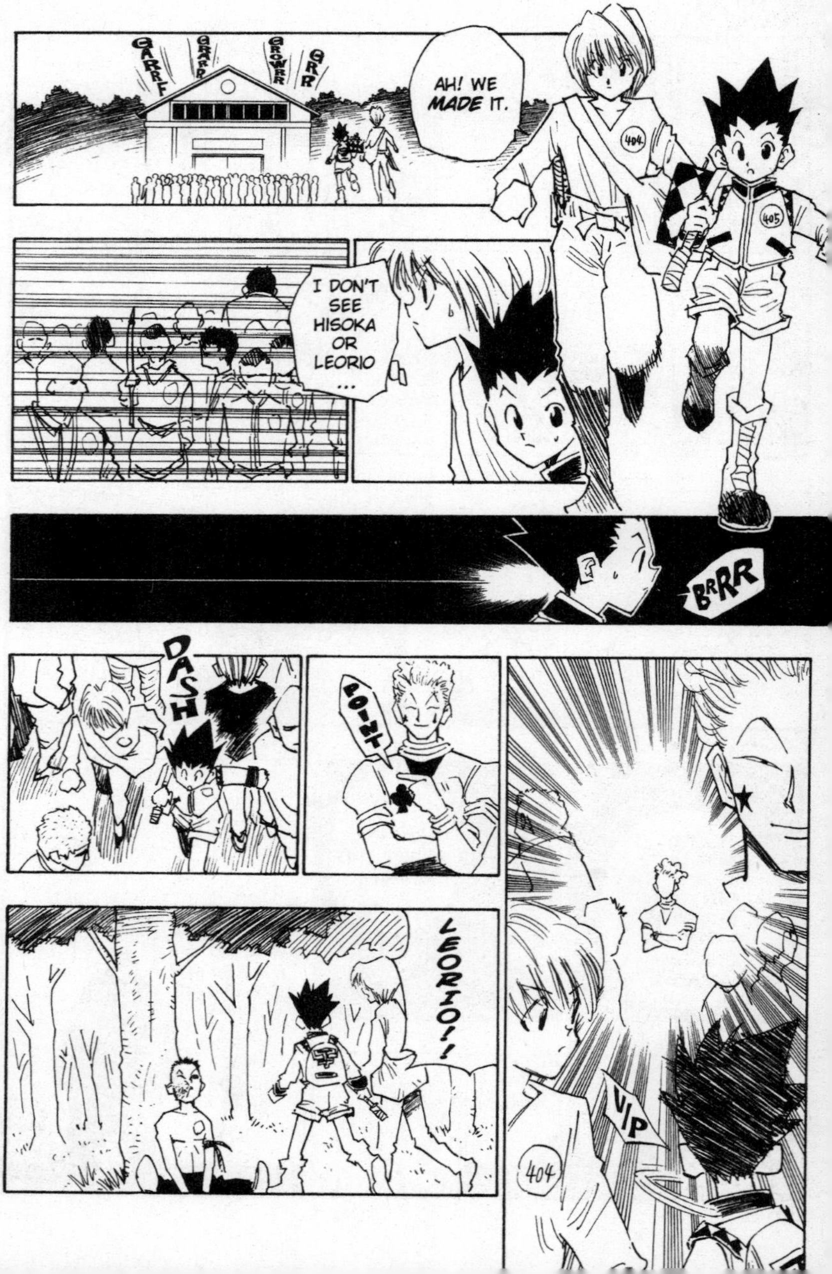
AH! WE *MADE* IT.
GRR
GROWRR
GRARR
GARRF
I DON'T SEE HISOKA OR LEORIO ...
BRRR
V/P
404
POINT
DASH
LEORIO!!

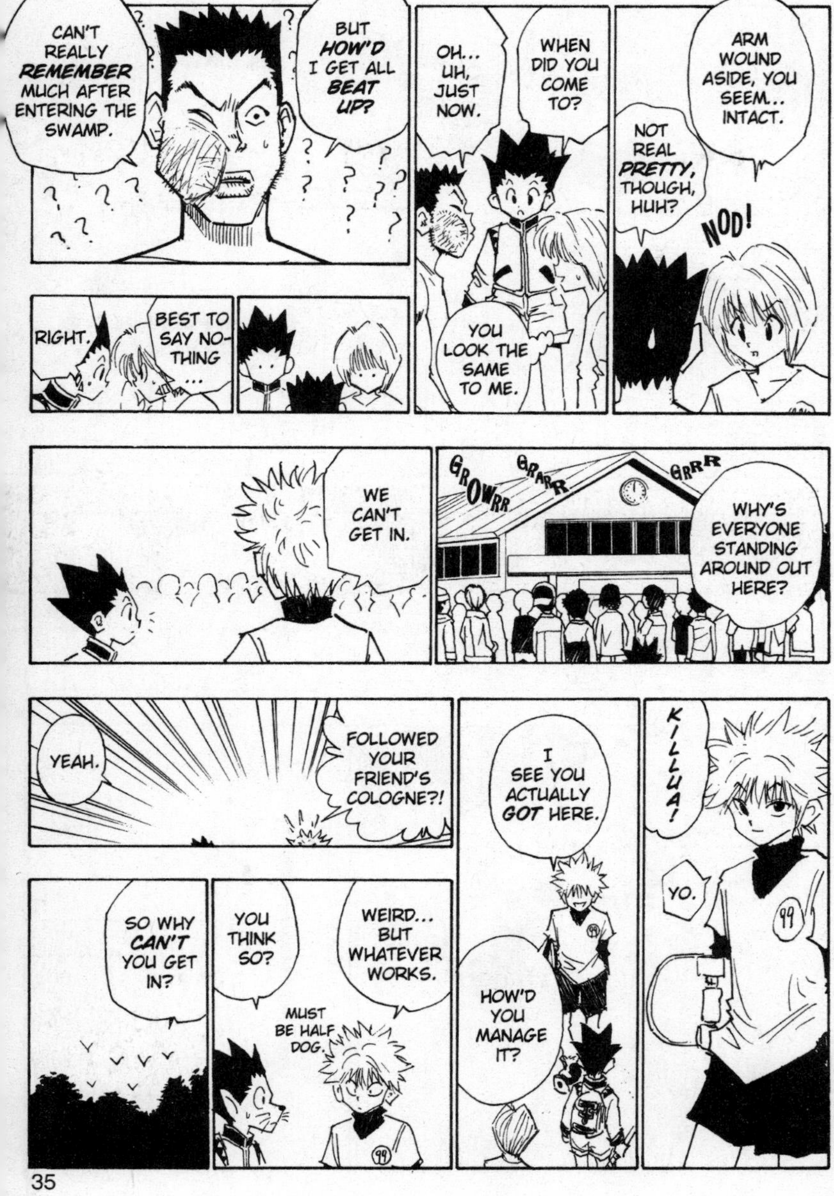

ARM WOUND ASIDE, YOU SEEM... INTACT.
NOT REAL PRETTY, THOUGH, HUH?
NOD!
WHEN DID YOU COME TO?
OH... UH, JUST NOW.
YOU LOOK THE SAME TO ME.
BUT HOW'D I GET ALL BEAT UP?
CAN'T REALLY REMEMBER MUCH AFTER ENTERING THE SWAMP.
BEST TO SAY NOTHING...
RIGHT.
GRRR
GRARRR
GROWRR
WHY'S EVERYONE STANDING AROUND OUT HERE?
WE CAN'T GET IN.
KILLUA!
YO.
I SEE YOU ACTUALLY GOT HERE.
HOW'D YOU MANAGE IT?
FOLLOWED YOUR FRIEND'S COLOGNE?!
YEAH.
WEIRD... BUT WHATEVER WORKS.
YOU THINK SO?
MUST BE HALF DOG.
SO WHY CAN'T YOU GET IN?

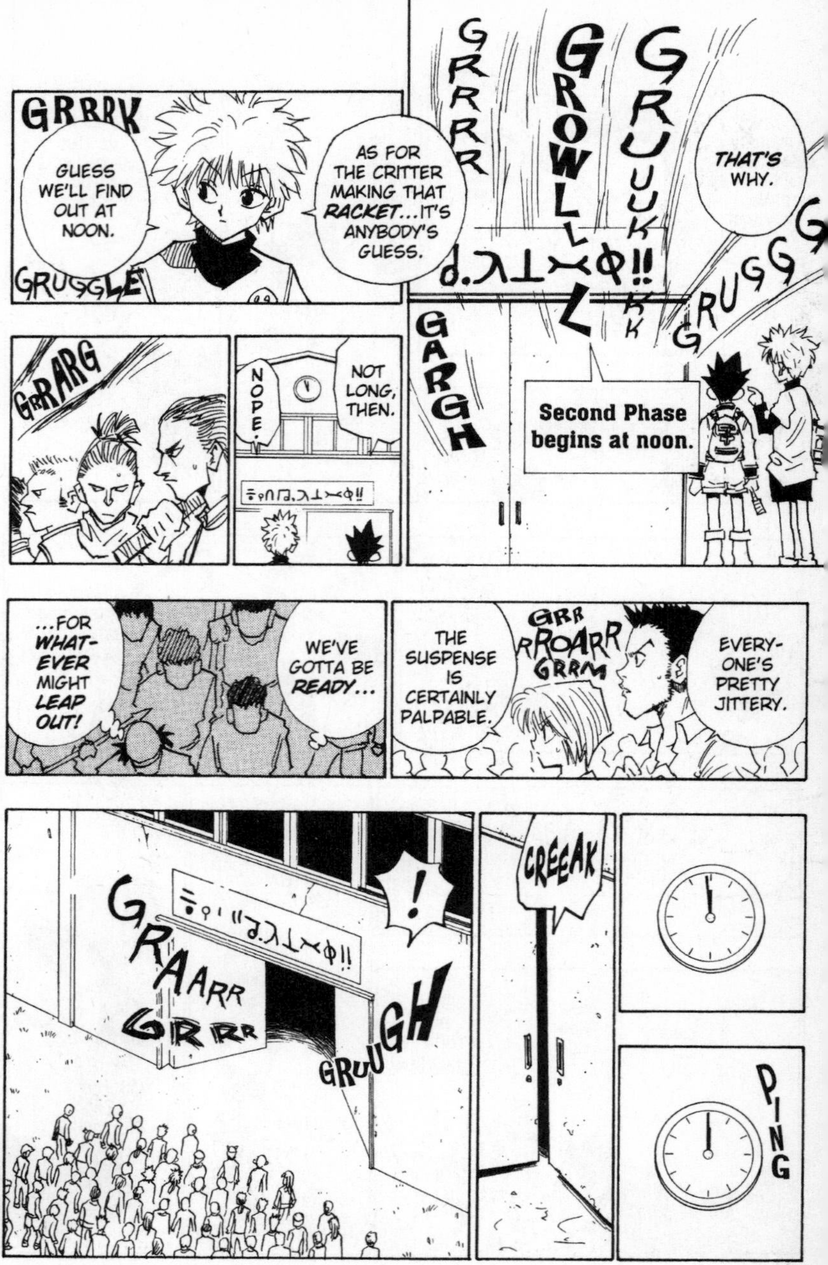
THAT'S WHY.
GRUUUKK!!KK
GROWLLL
GRRRR
GRUGGG
Second Phase begins at noon.
GARGH
AS FOR THE CRITTER MAKING THAT RACKET... IT'S ANYBODY'S GUESS.
GRRRK
GUESS WE'LL FIND OUT AT NOON.
GRUGGLE
NOT LONG, THEN.
NOPE.
GRRARG
EVERYONE'S PRETTY JITTERY.
GRR RROARR GRRM
THE SUSPENSE IS CERTAINLY PALPABLE.
WE'VE GOTTA BE READY...
...FOR WHATEVER MIGHT LEAP OUT!
PING
CREEAK
!
GRAARR GRRRR
GRUUGH

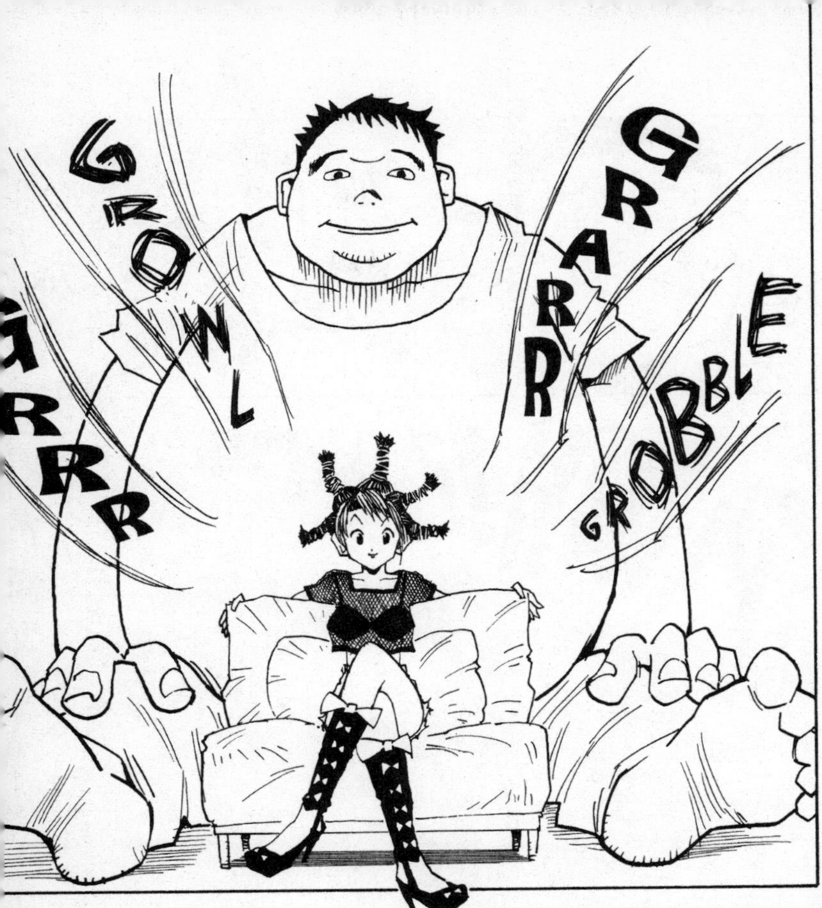
GRARR
GROBBLE
GROWL
GRRRR

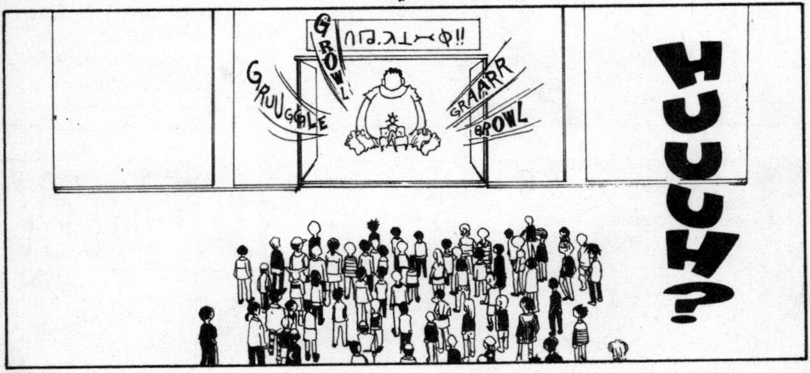
HUUUH?
GRAARR
GROWL
GROWL
GRUUGGLE

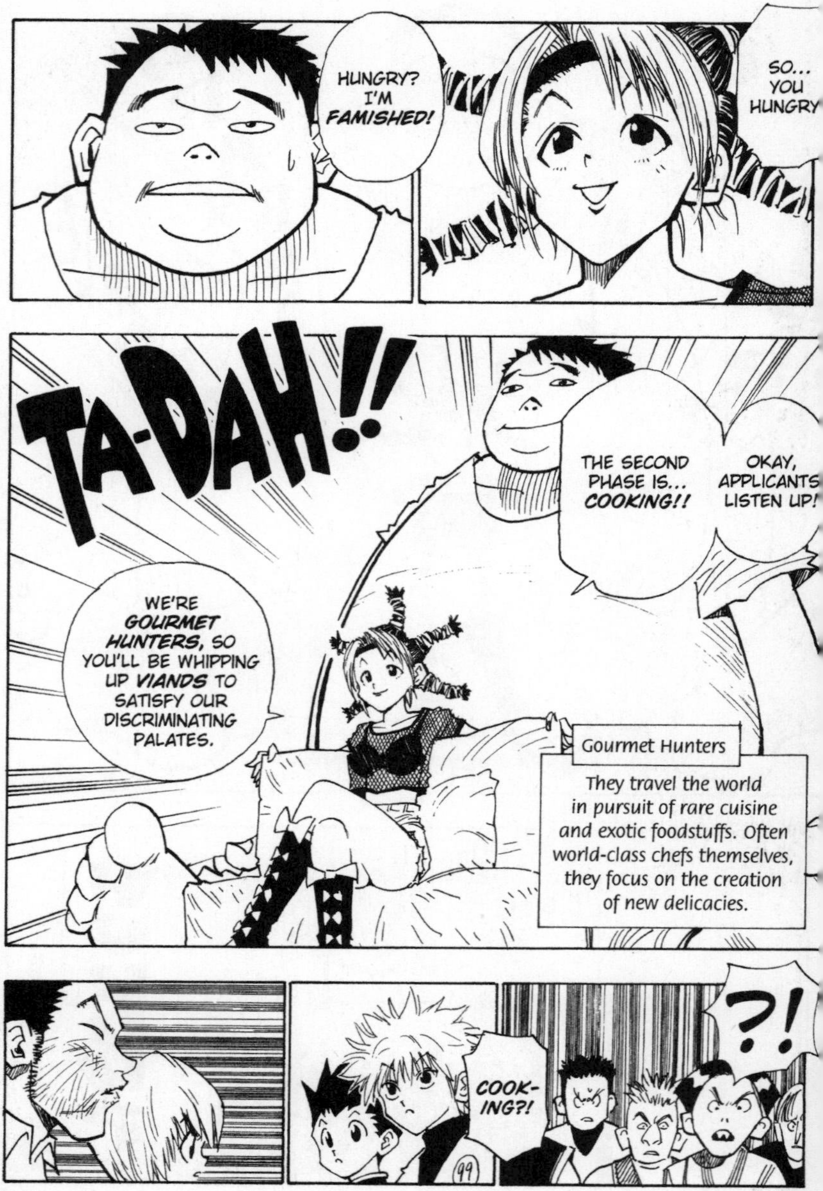
SO... YOU HUNGRY
HUNGRY? I'M FAMISHED!
OKAY, APPLICANTS LISTEN UP!
THE SECOND PHASE IS... COOKING!!
TA-DAH!!
WE'RE GOURMET HUNTERS, SO YOU'LL BE WHIPPING UP VIANDS TO SATISFY OUR DISCRIMINATING PALATES.
Gourmet Hunters
They travel the world in pursuit of rare cuisine and exotic foodstuffs. Often world-class chefs themselves, they focus on the creation of new delicacies.
?!
COOK-ING?!

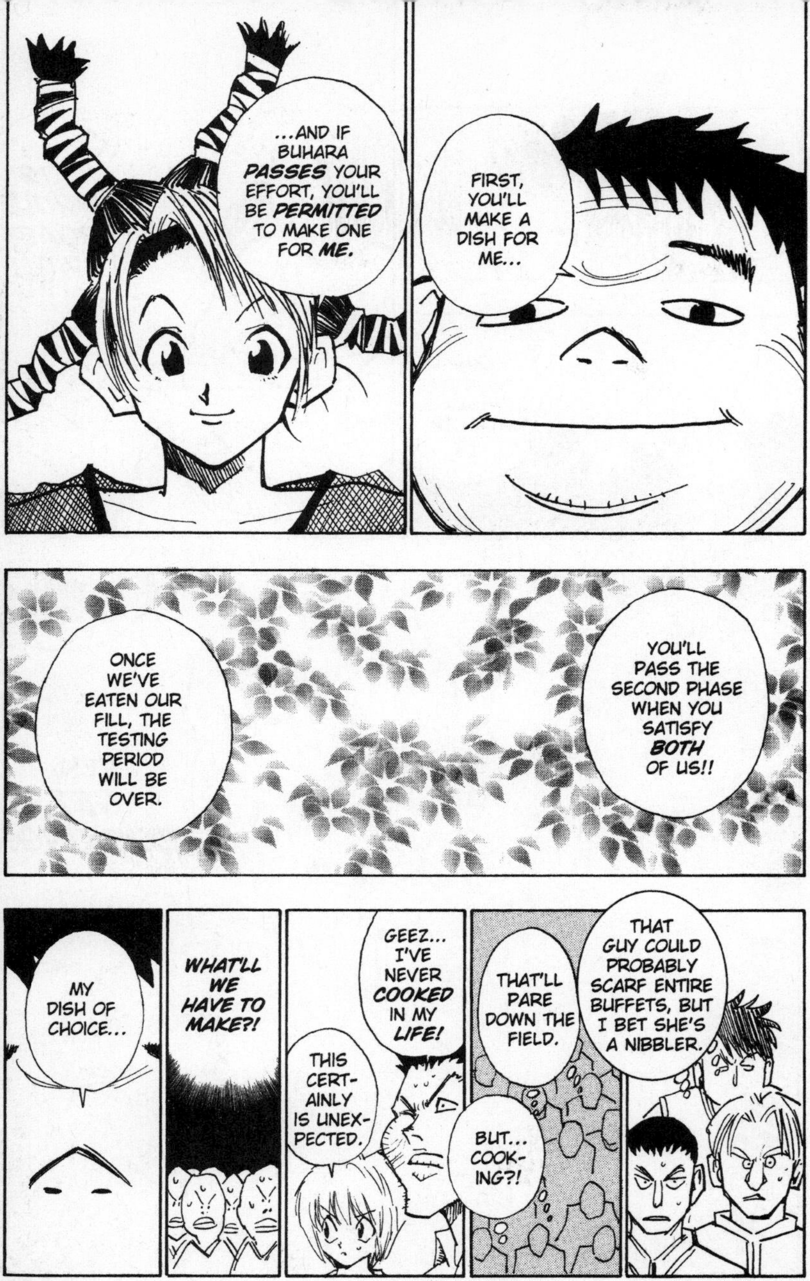
FIRST, YOU'LL MAKE A DISH FOR ME...
...AND IF BUHARA **PASSES** YOUR EFFORT, YOU'LL BE **PERMITTED** TO MAKE ONE FOR **ME.**
YOU'LL PASS THE SECOND PHASE WHEN YOU SATISFY **BOTH** OF US!!
ONCE WE'VE EATEN OUR FILL, THE TESTING PERIOD WILL BE OVER.
THAT GUY COULD PROBABLY SCARF ENTIRE BUFFETS, BUT I BET SHE'S A NIBBLER.
THAT'LL PARE DOWN THE FIELD.
BUT... COOKING?!
GEEZ... I'VE NEVER **COOKED** IN MY **LIFE!**
THIS CERTAINLY IS UNEXPECTED.
WHAT'LL WE HAVE TO MAKE?!
MY DISH OF CHOICE...

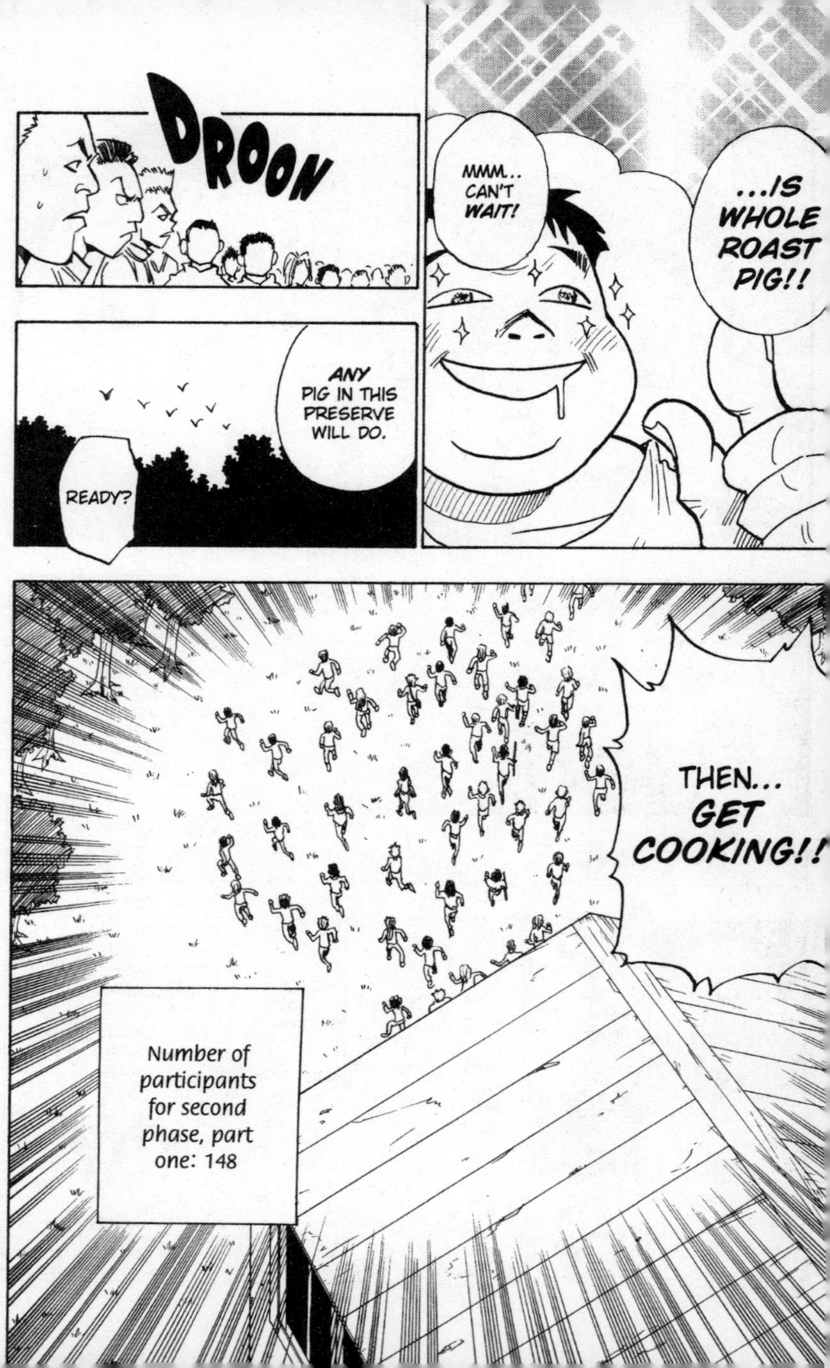
...IS WHOLE ROAST PIG!!
MMM... CAN'T WAIT!
DROON
ANY PIG IN THIS PRESERVE WILL DO.
READY?
THEN... GET COOKING!!
Number of participants for second phase, part one: 148

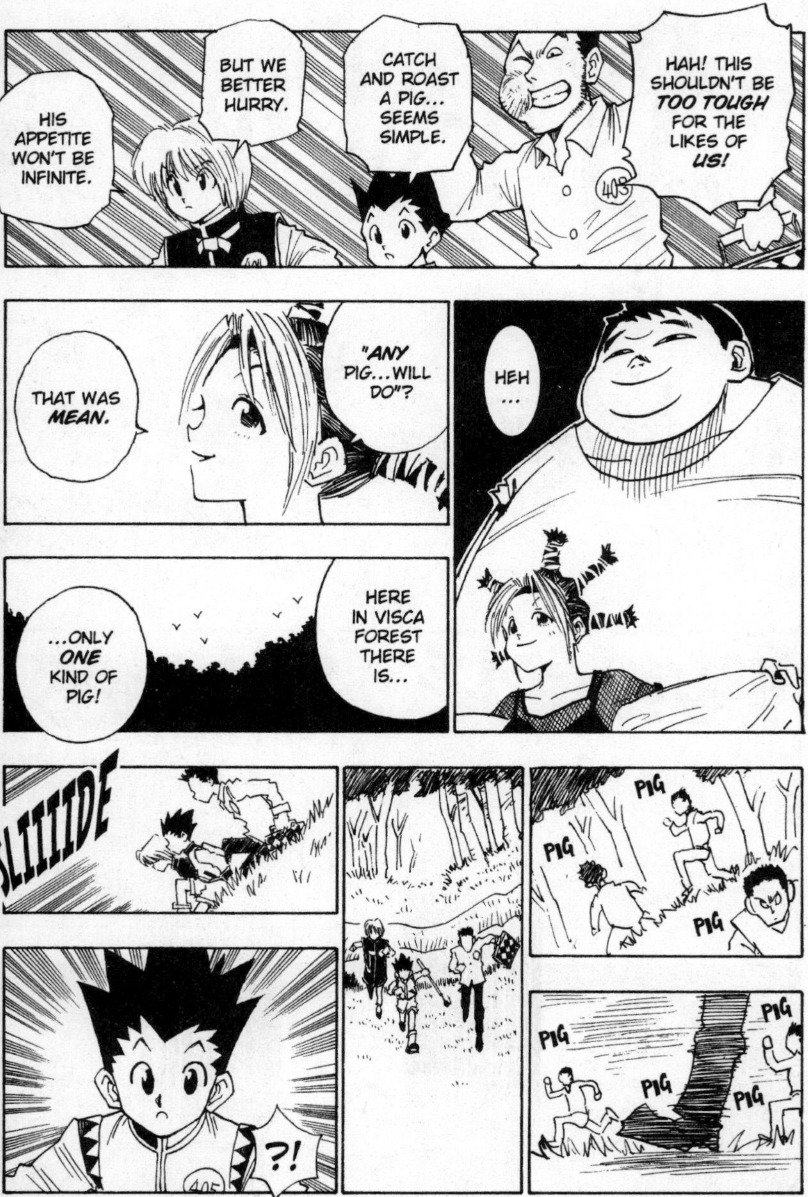
HAH! THIS SHOULDN'T BE *TOO TOUGH* FOR THE LIKES OF *US!*
CATCH AND ROAST A PIG... SEEMS SIMPLE.
BUT WE BETTER HURRY.
HIS APPETITE WON'T BE INFINITE.
HEH ...
"*ANY* PIG...WILL DO"?
THAT WAS *MEAN.*
HERE IN VISCA FOREST THERE IS...
...ONLY *ONE* KIND OF PIG!
PIG
PIG
PIG
PIG
PIG
PIG
PIG
SLIIIDE
?!

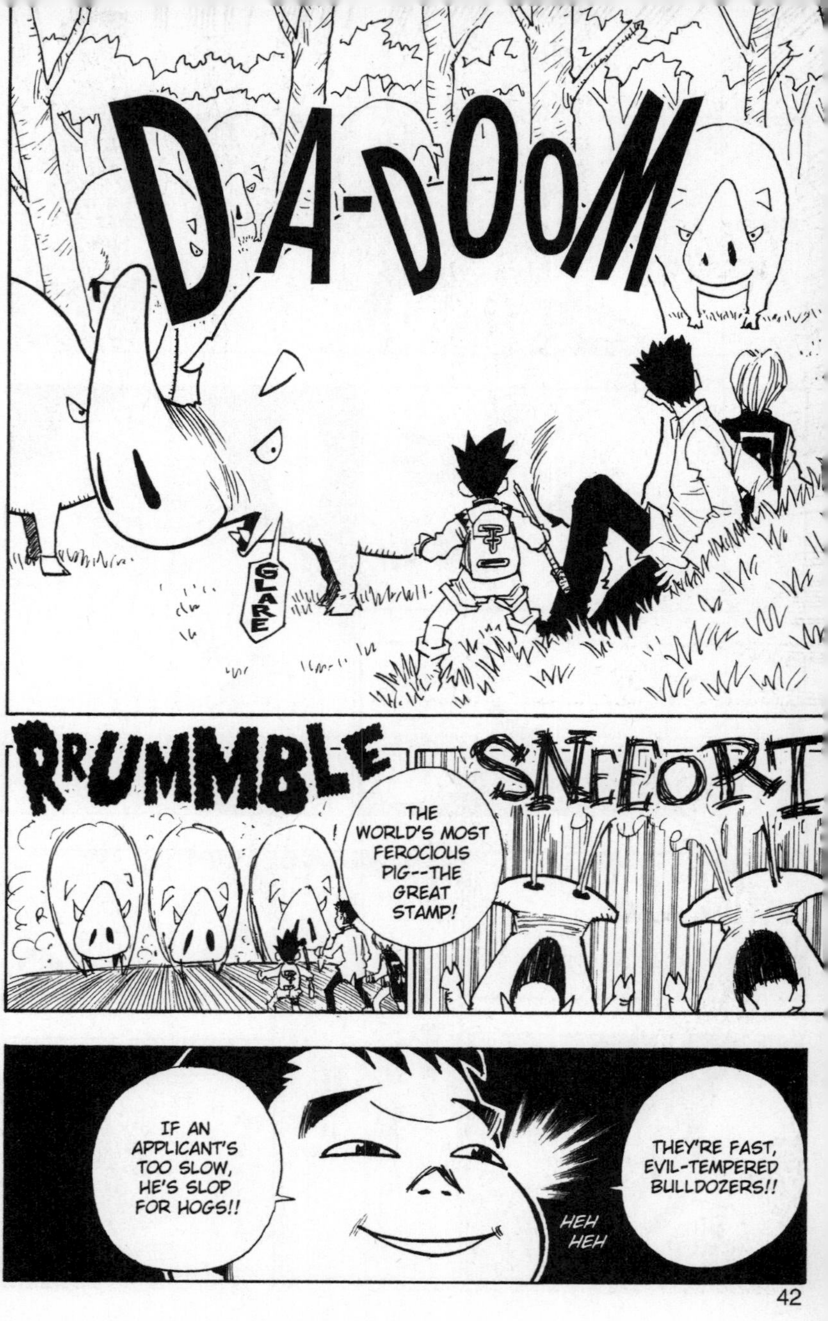
DA-DOOM
GLARE
SNEEORT
THE WORLD'S MOST FEROCIOUS PIG--THE GREAT STAMP!
RRUMMBLE
THEY'RE FAST, EVIL-TEMPERED BULLDOZERS!!
HEH HEH
IF AN APPLICANT'S TOO SLOW, HE'S SLOP FOR HOGS!!

YAAAH!!!

SLAM

...I FELT EARLIER!

...THE THRILL...

BRRR

THIS IS LIKE...

THAT WAS!..

...FACING HISOKA!

BUT IT'S STILL NOT LIKE...

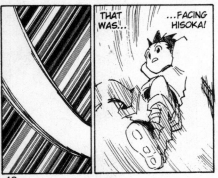

43

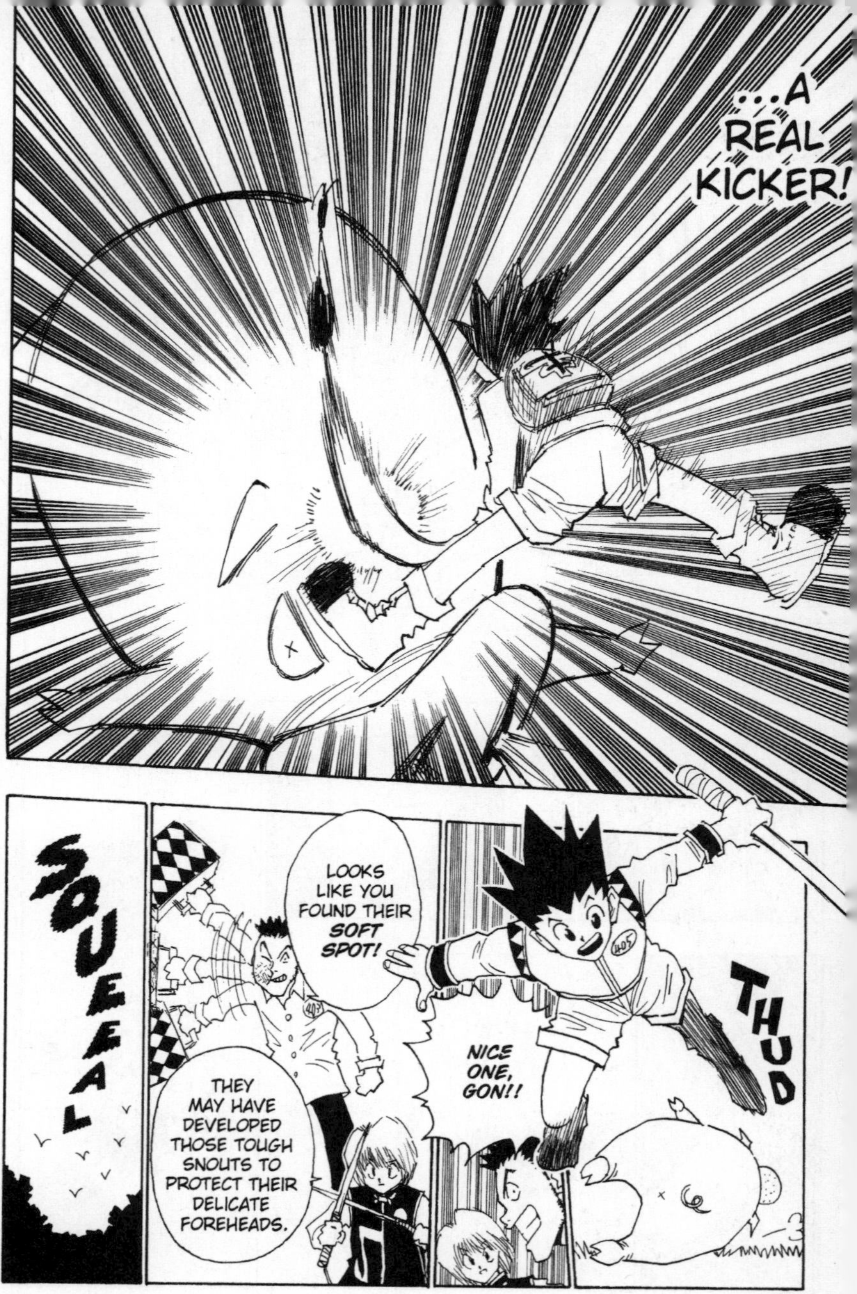
...A REAL KICKER!
THUD
LOOKS LIKE YOU FOUND THEIR *SOFT SPOT!*
NICE ONE, GON!!
THEY MAY HAVE DEVELOPED THOSE TOUGH SNOUTS TO PROTECT THEIR DELICATE FOREHEADS.
SQUEEEAL

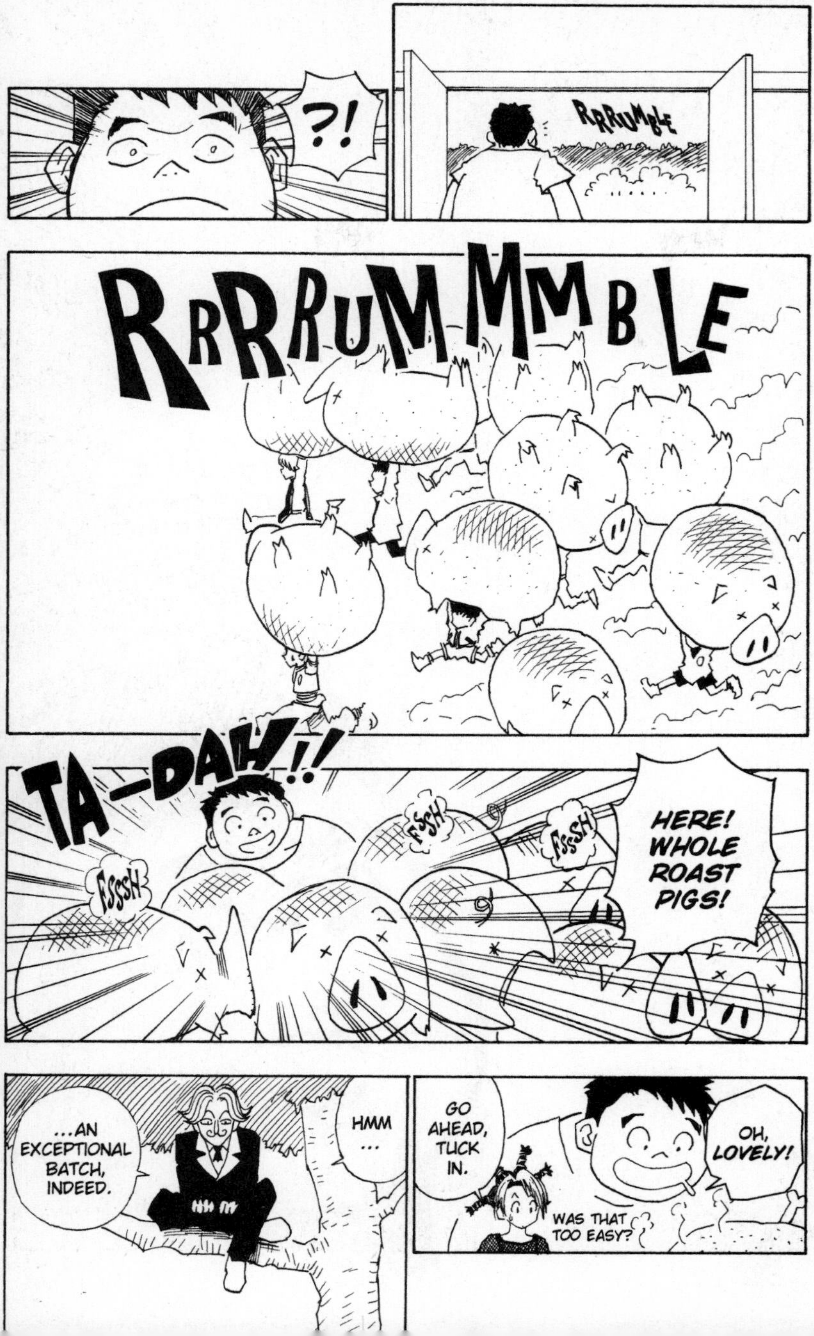
RRRUMBLE
?!
RRRUMMMBLE
HERE! WHOLE ROAST PIGS!
FSSSH
FSSSH
TA-DAH!!
FSSSH
OH, LOVELY!
GO AHEAD, TUCK IN.
WAS THAT TOO EASY?
HMM ...
...AN EXCEPTIONAL BATCH, INDEED.

Buhara

Chapter 11
The Inevitable Outcome

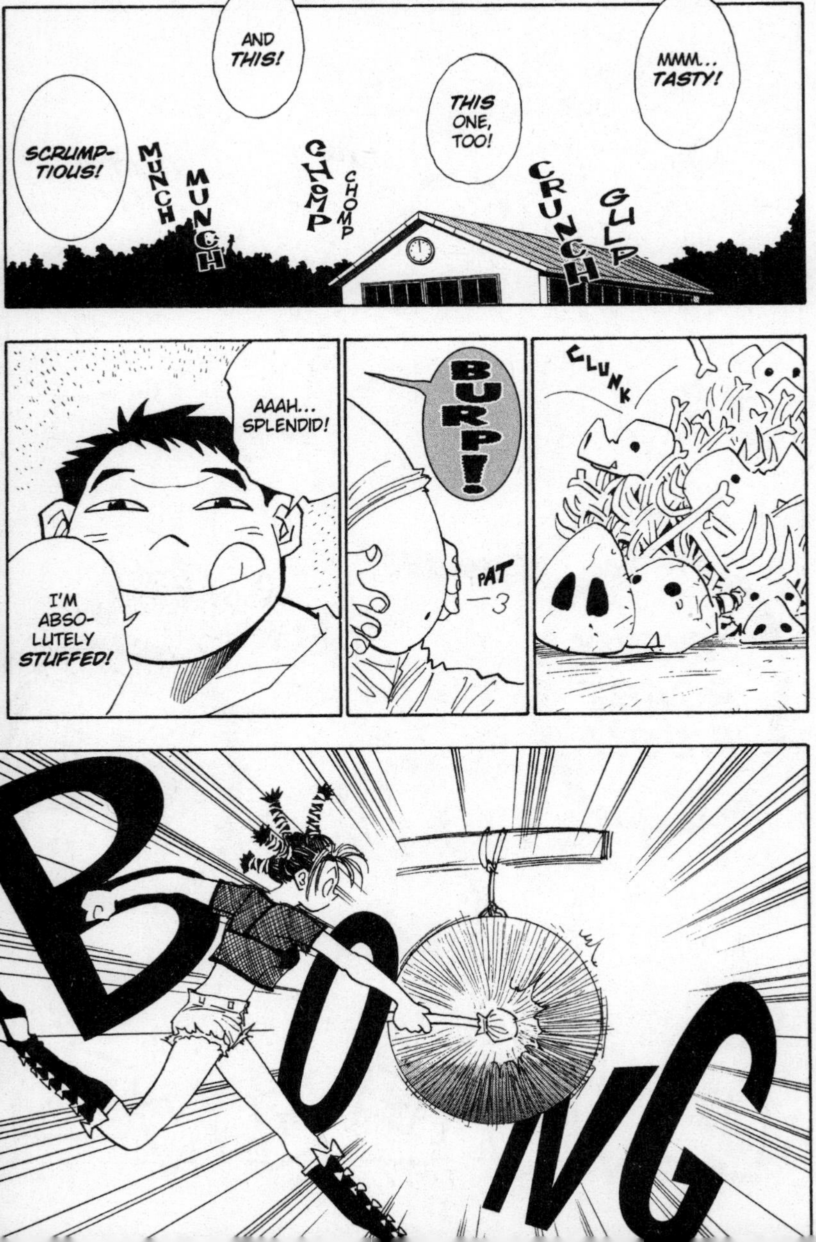
MMM... TASTY!
GULP
CRUNCH
THIS ONE, TOO!
AND THIS!
CHOMP CHOMP
MUNCH MUNCH
SCRUMPTIOUS!
CLUNK
BURP!
PAT
AAAH... SPLENDID!
I'M ABSOLUTELY STUFFED!
BOONG

Chapter 11
The Inevitable Outcome

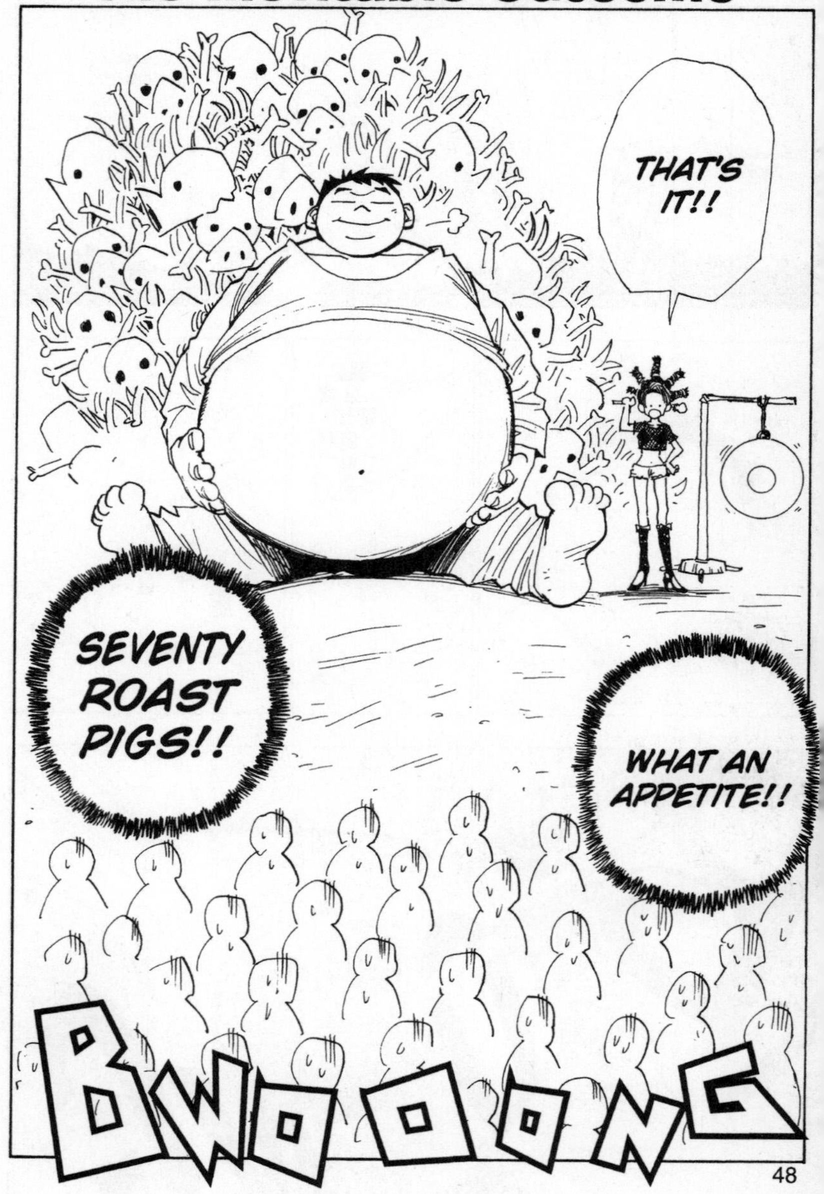
THAT'S IT!!
SEVENTY ROAST PIGS!!
WHAT AN APPETITE!!
BWOOONG

READ THIS WAY

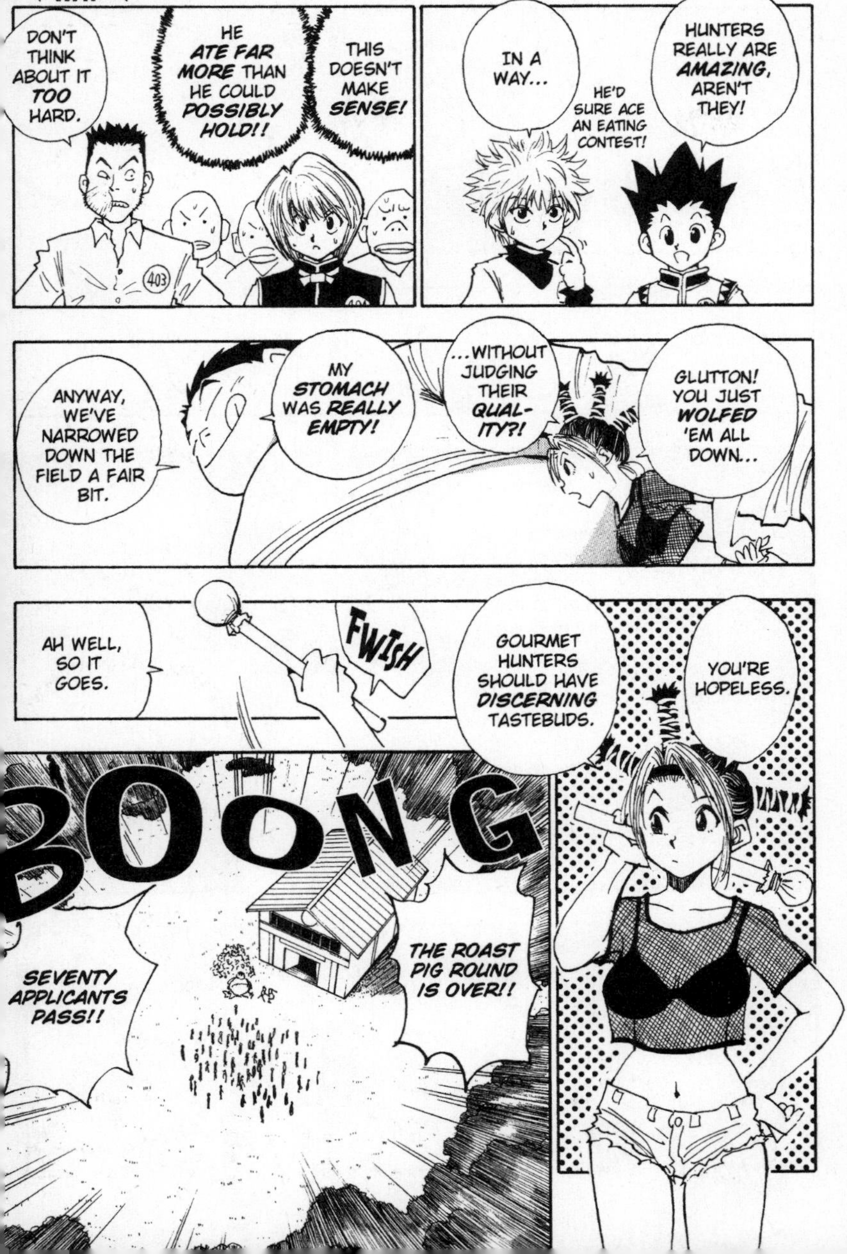

HUNTERS REALLY ARE AMAZING, AREN'T THEY!
IN A WAY...
HE'D SURE ACE AN EATING CONTEST!
THIS DOESN'T MAKE SENSE!
HE ATE FAR MORE THAN HE COULD POSSIBLY HOLD!!
DON'T THINK ABOUT IT TOO HARD.
GLUTTON! YOU JUST WOLFED 'EM ALL DOWN...
...WITHOUT JUDGING THEIR QUAL-ITY?!
MY STOMACH WAS REALLY EMPTY!
ANYWAY, WE'VE NARROWED DOWN THE FIELD A FAIR BIT.
YOU'RE HOPELESS.
GOURMET HUNTERS SHOULD HAVE DISCERNING TASTEBUDS.
FWISH
AH WELL, SO IT GOES.
BOONG
THE ROAST PIG ROUND IS OVER!!
SEVENTY APPLICANTS PASS!!

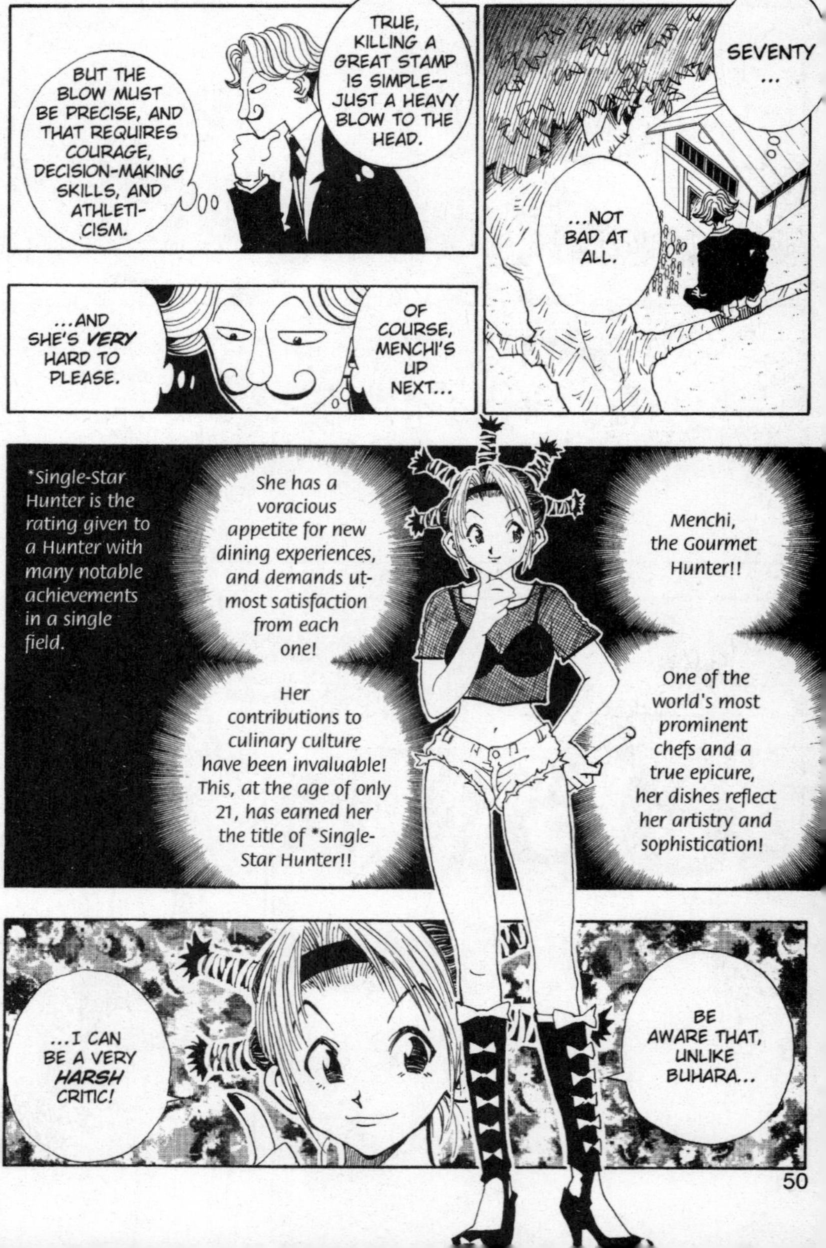
SEVENTY ...
...NOT BAD AT ALL.
TRUE, KILLING A GREAT STAMP IS SIMPLE-- JUST A HEAVY BLOW TO THE HEAD.
BUT THE BLOW MUST BE PRECISE, AND THAT REQUIRES COURAGE, DECISION-MAKING SKILLS, AND ATHLETICISM.
OF COURSE, MENCHI'S UP NEXT...
...AND SHE'S *VERY* HARD TO PLEASE.
Menchi, the Gourmet Hunter!!
One of the world's most prominent chefs and a true epicure, her dishes reflect her artistry and sophistication!
She has a voracious appetite for new dining experiences, and demands utmost satisfaction from each one!
Her contributions to culinary culture have been invaluable! This, at the age of only 21, has earned her the title of *Single-Star Hunter!!
*Single-Star Hunter is the rating given to a Hunter with many notable achievements in a single field.
BE AWARE THAT, UNLIKE BUHARA...
...I CAN BE A VERY *HARSH* CRITIC!

READ THIS WAY

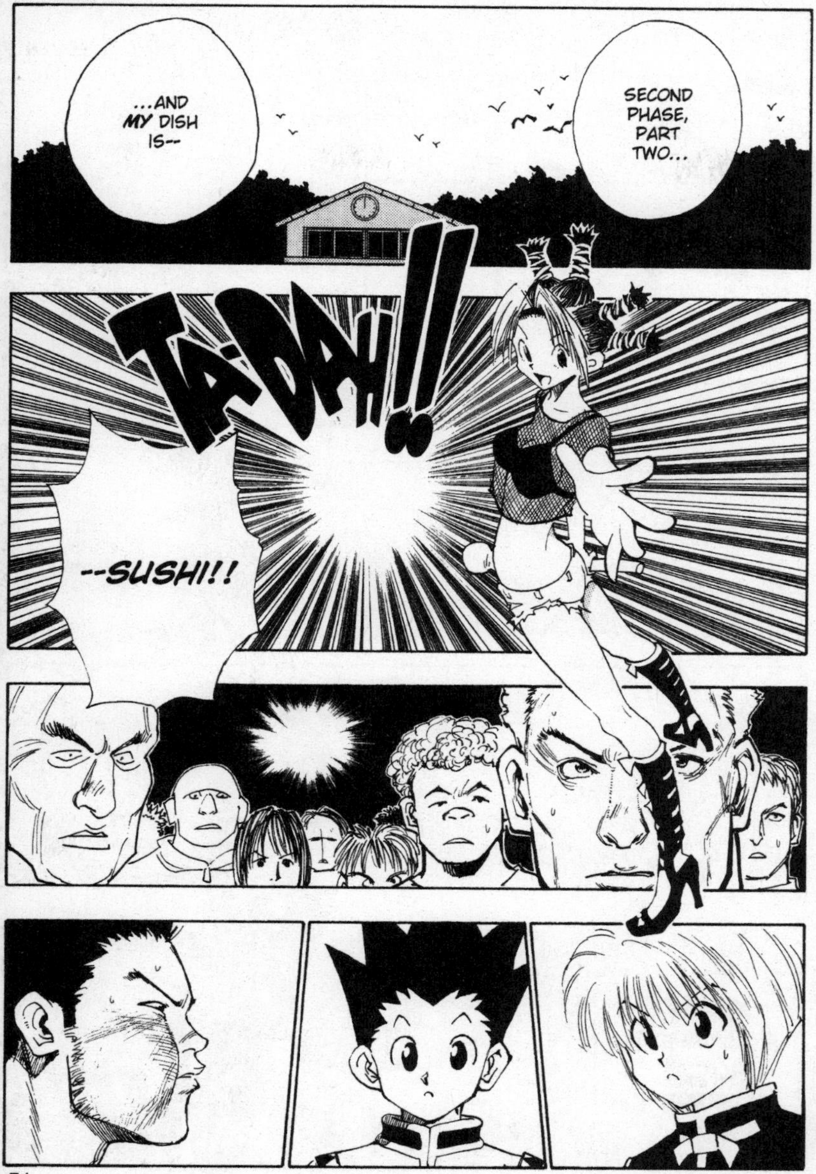

SECOND PHASE, PART TWO...
...AND MY DISH IS--
TA-DAH!!
--SUSHI!!

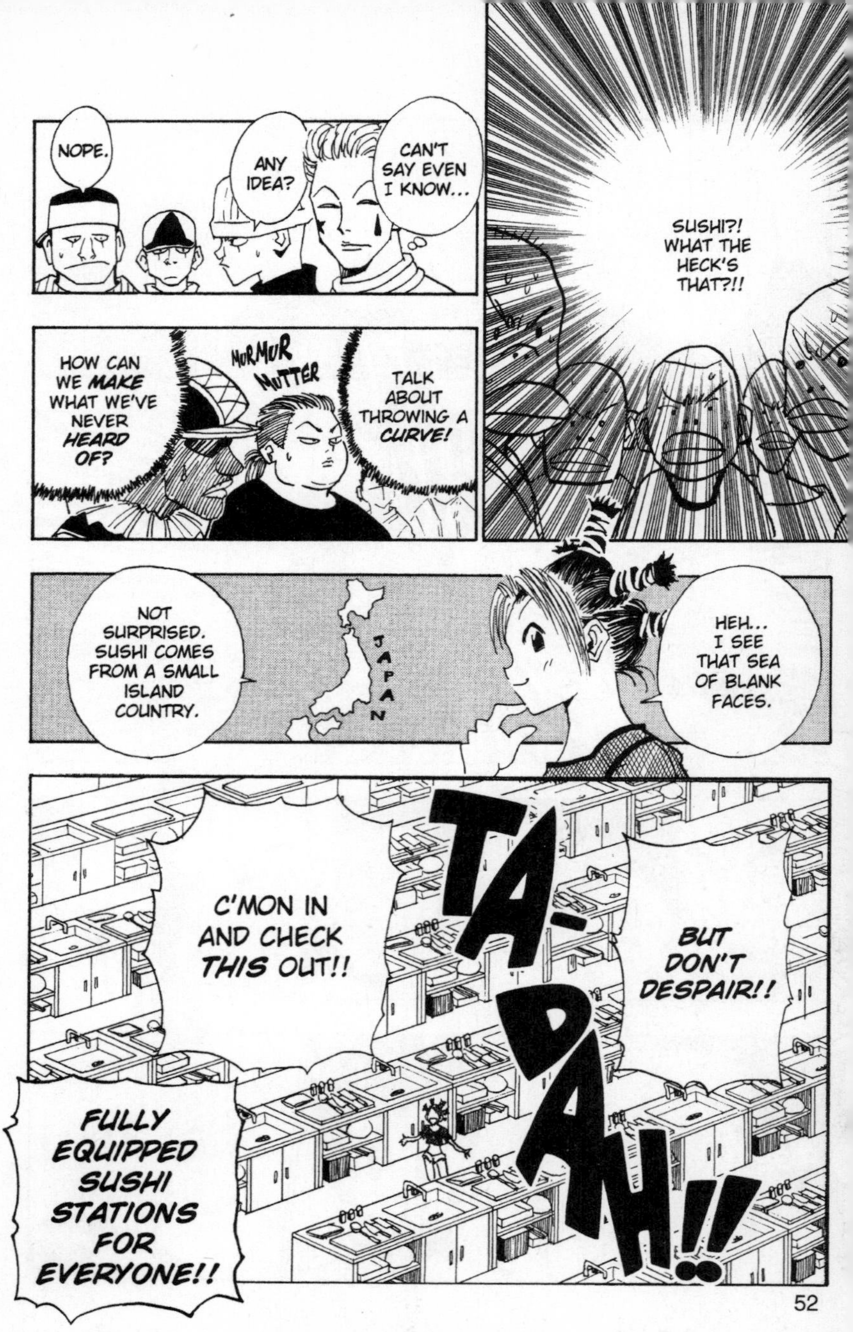
SUSHI?! WHAT THE HECK'S THAT?!!
CAN'T SAY EVEN I KNOW...
ANY IDEA?
NOPE.
TALK ABOUT THROWING A CURVE!
MURMUR
MUTTER
HOW CAN WE MAKE WHAT WE'VE NEVER HEARD OF?
HEH... I SEE THAT SEA OF BLANK FACES.
JAPAN
NOT SURPRISED. SUSHI COMES FROM A SMALL ISLAND COUNTRY.
BUT DON'T DESPAIR!!
TA-DAH!!
C'MON IN AND CHECK THIS OUT!!
FULLY EQUIPPED SUSHI STATIONS FOR EVERYONE!!

READ THIS WAY

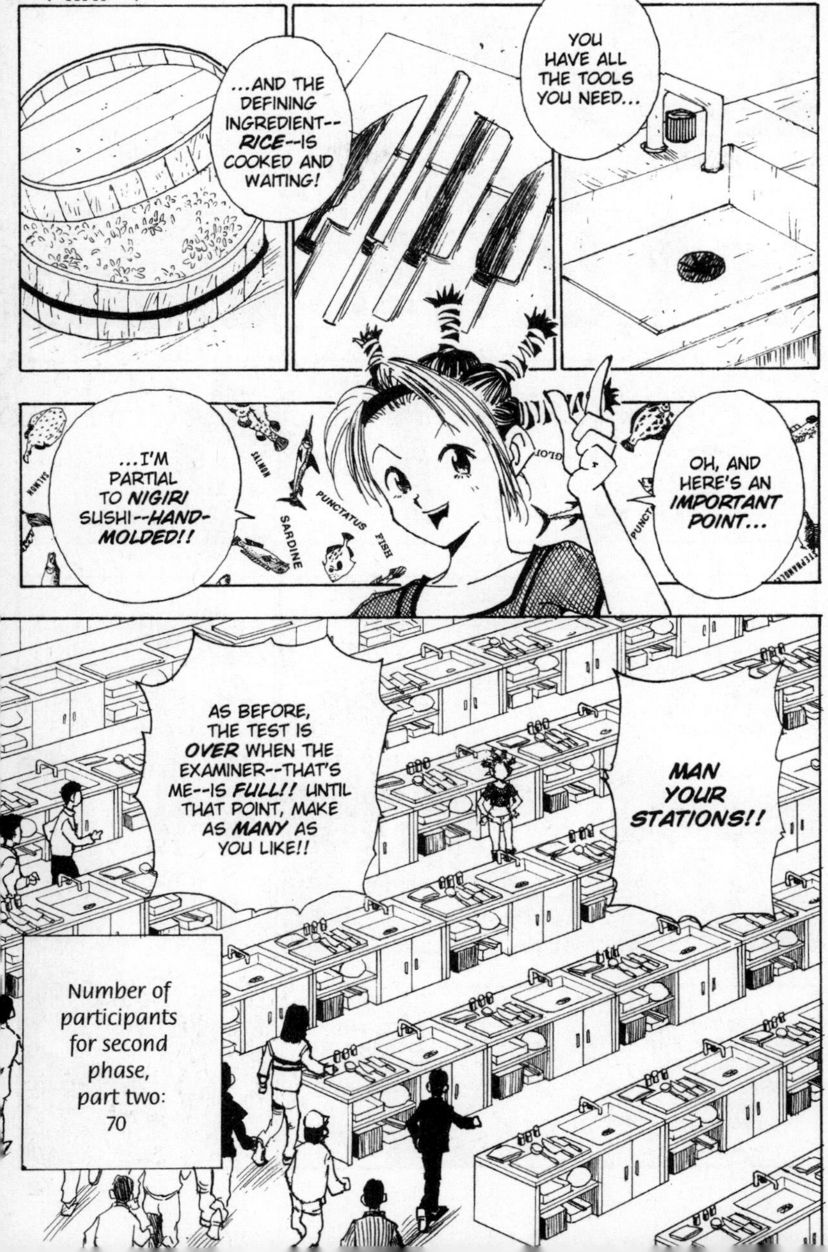
YOU HAVE ALL THE TOOLS YOU NEED...
...AND THE DEFINING INGREDIENT--RICE--IS COOKED AND WAITING!
OH, AND HERE'S AN IMPORTANT POINT...
...I'M PARTIAL TO NIGIRI SUSHI--HAND-MOLDED!!
SALMON
PUNCTATUS
FISH
SARDINE
MAN YOUR STATIONS!!
AS BEFORE, THE TEST IS OVER WHEN THE EXAMINER--THAT'S ME--IS FULL!! UNTIL THAT POINT, MAKE AS MANY AS YOU LIKE!!
Number of participants for second phase, part two: 70

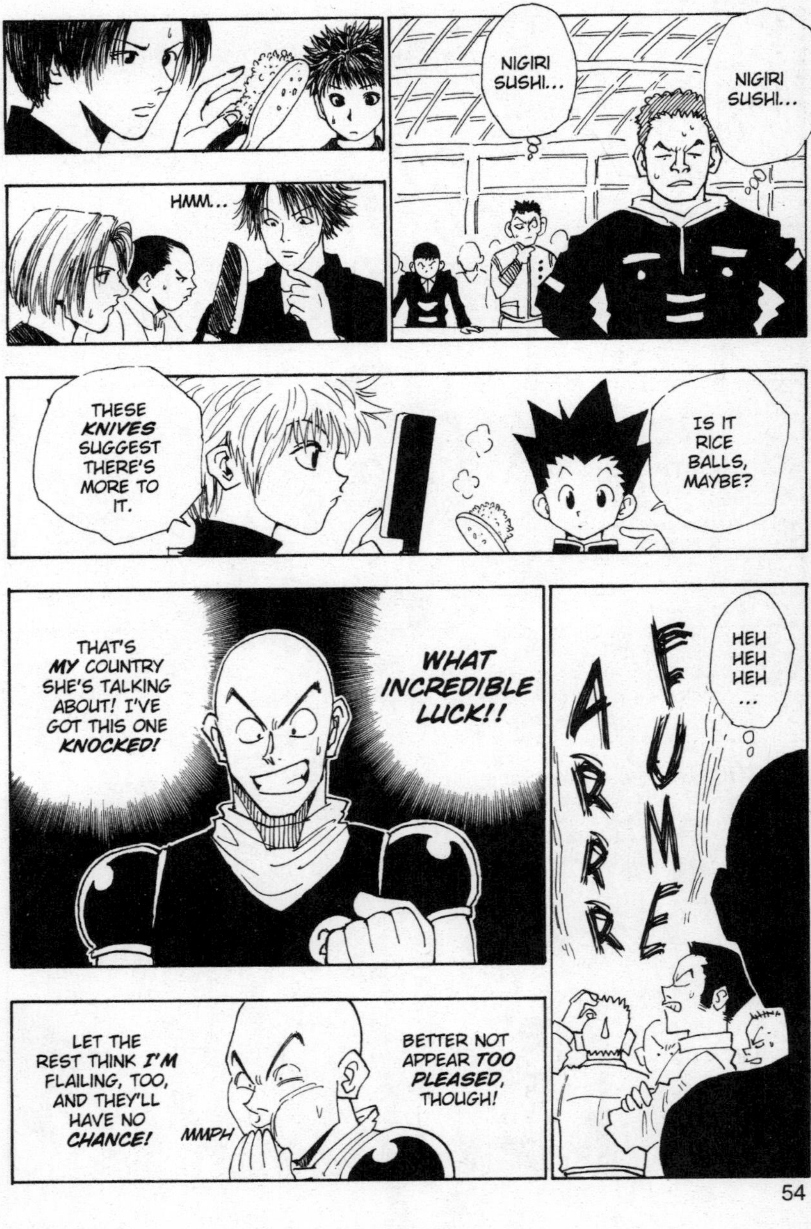
NIGIRI SUSHI...
NIGIRI SUSHI...
HMM...
IS IT RICE BALLS, MAYBE?
THESE KNIVES SUGGEST THERE'S MORE TO IT.
HEH HEH HEH ...
FUME
ARRR
WHAT INCREDIBLE LUCK!!
THAT'S MY COUNTRY SHE'S TALKING ABOUT! I'VE GOT THIS ONE KNOCKED!
BETTER NOT APPEAR TOO PLEASED, THOUGH!
MMPH
LET THE REST THINK I'M FLAILING, TOO, AND THEY'LL HAVE NO CHANCE!

READ THIS WAY

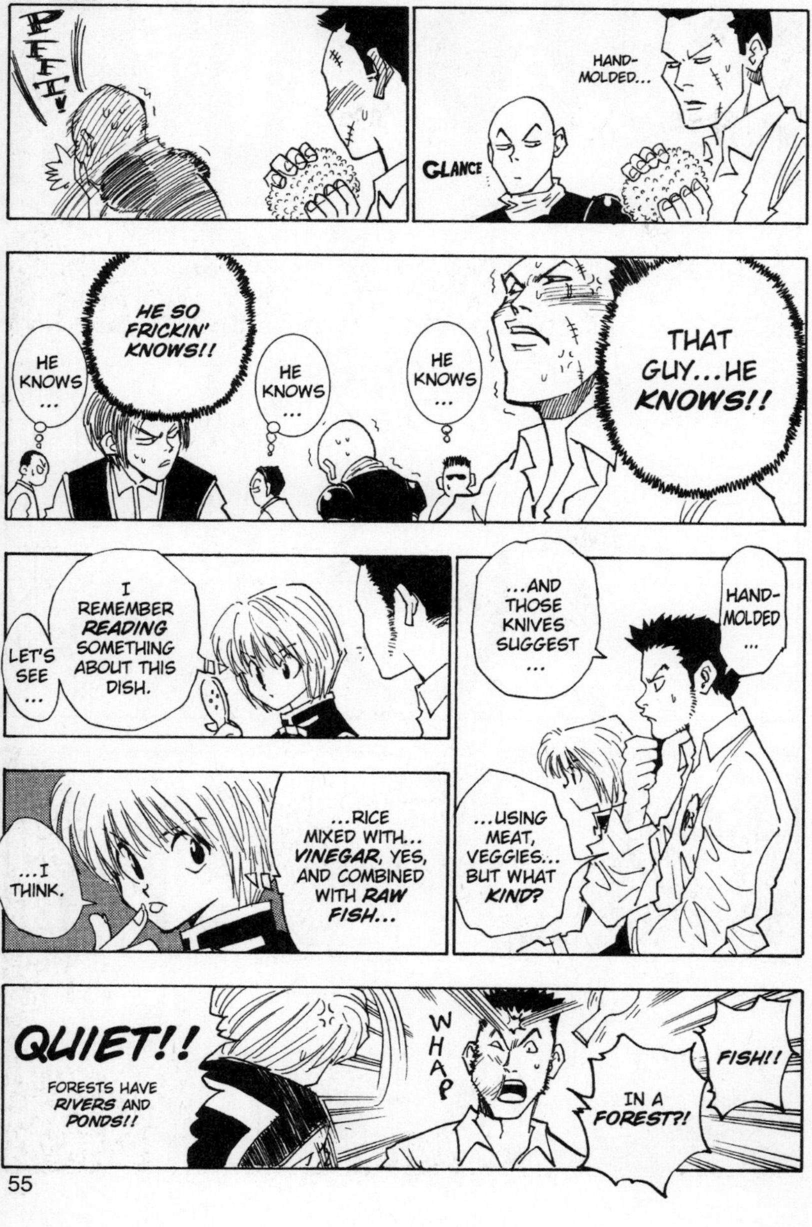
HAND-MOLDED...
GLANCE
PFFT!
THAT GUY...HE KNOWS!!
HE KNOWS ...
HE KNOWS ...
HE SO FRICKIN' KNOWS!!
HE KNOWS ...
HAND-MOLDED ...
...AND THOSE KNIVES SUGGEST ...
...USING MEAT, VEGGIES... BUT WHAT KIND?
I REMEMBER READING SOMETHING ABOUT THIS DISH.
LET'S SEE ...
...RICE MIXED WITH... VINEGAR, YES, AND COMBINED WITH RAW FISH...
...I THINK.
FISH!!
IN A FOREST?!
WHAP
QUIET!!
FORESTS HAVE RIVERS AND PONDS!!

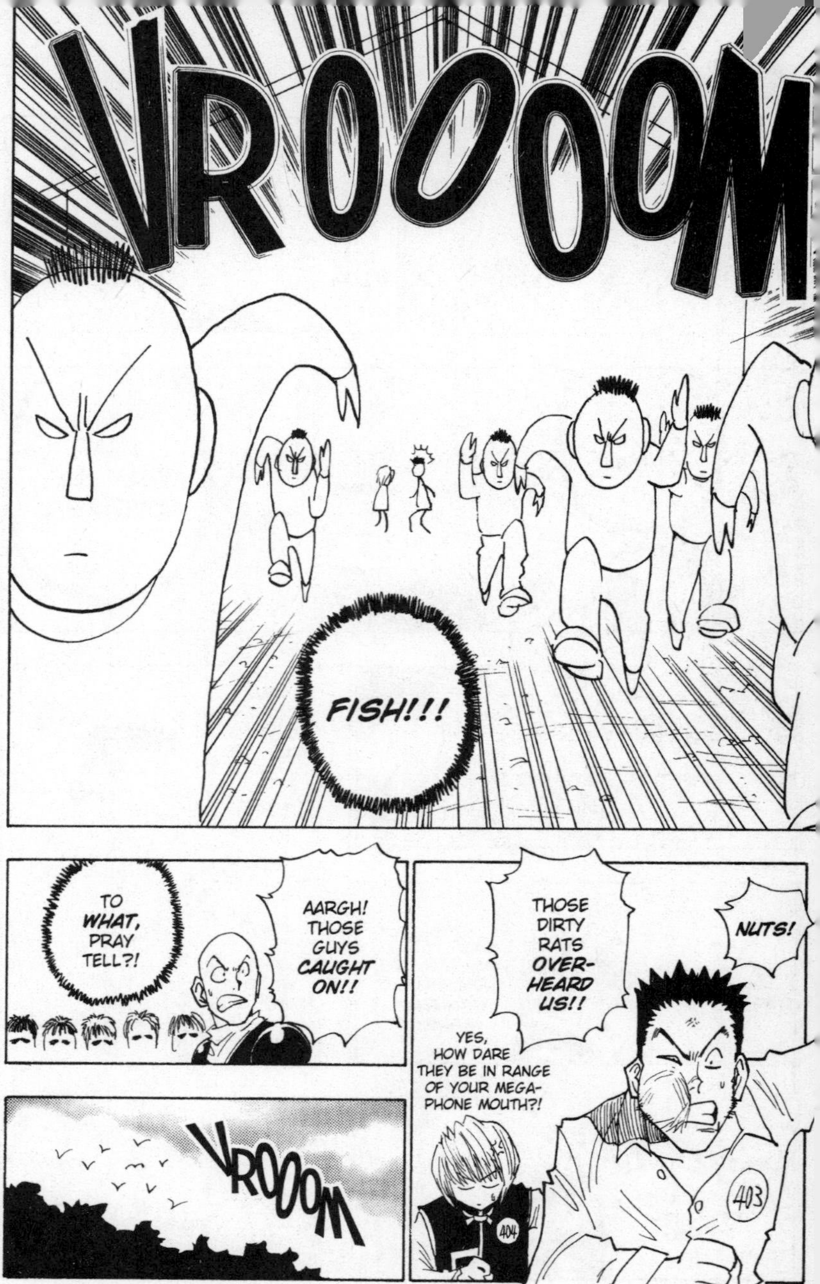
VROOOOM
FISH!!!
NUTS!
THOSE DIRTY RATS OVERHEARD US!!
YES, HOW DARE THEY BE IN RANGE OF YOUR MEGAPHONE MOUTH?!
AARGH! THOSE GUYS CAUGHT ON!!
TO WHAT, PRAY TELL?!
VROOOM

READ THIS WAY

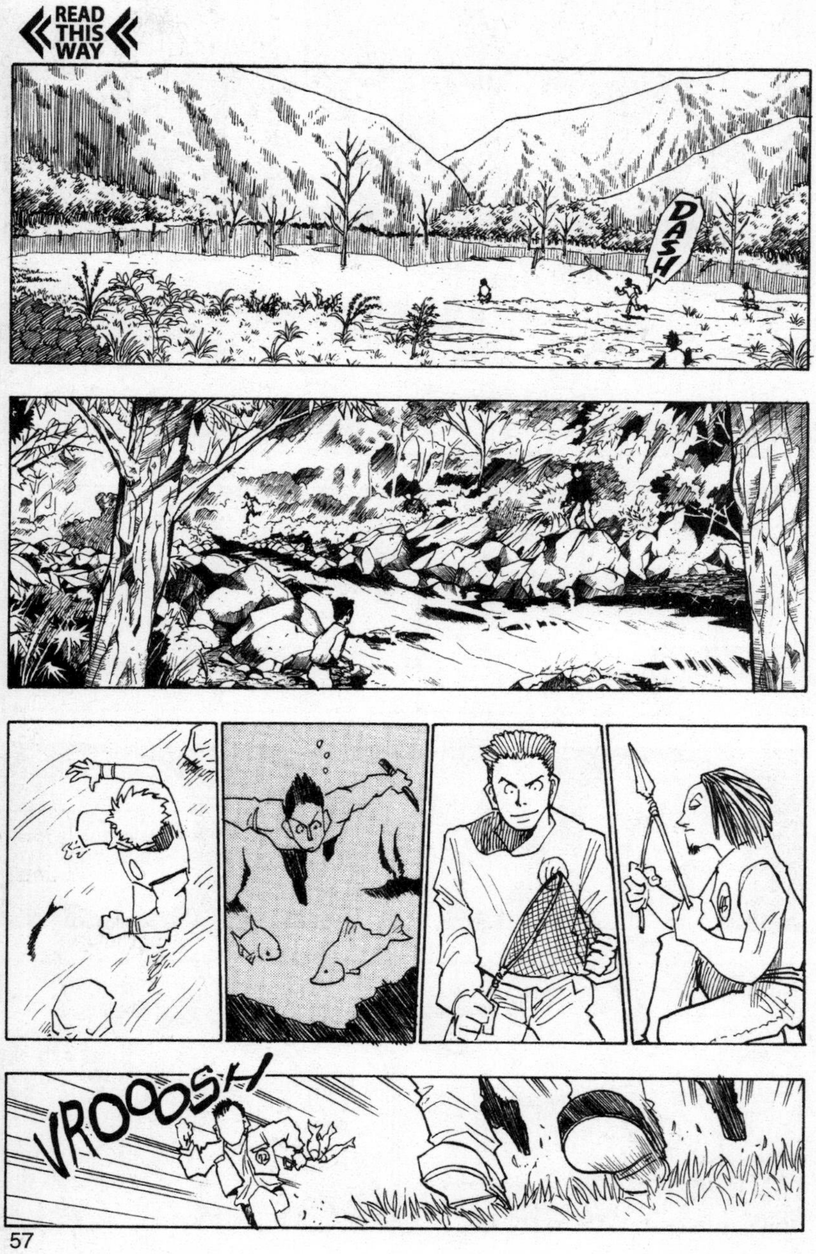
DASH
VROOOSH

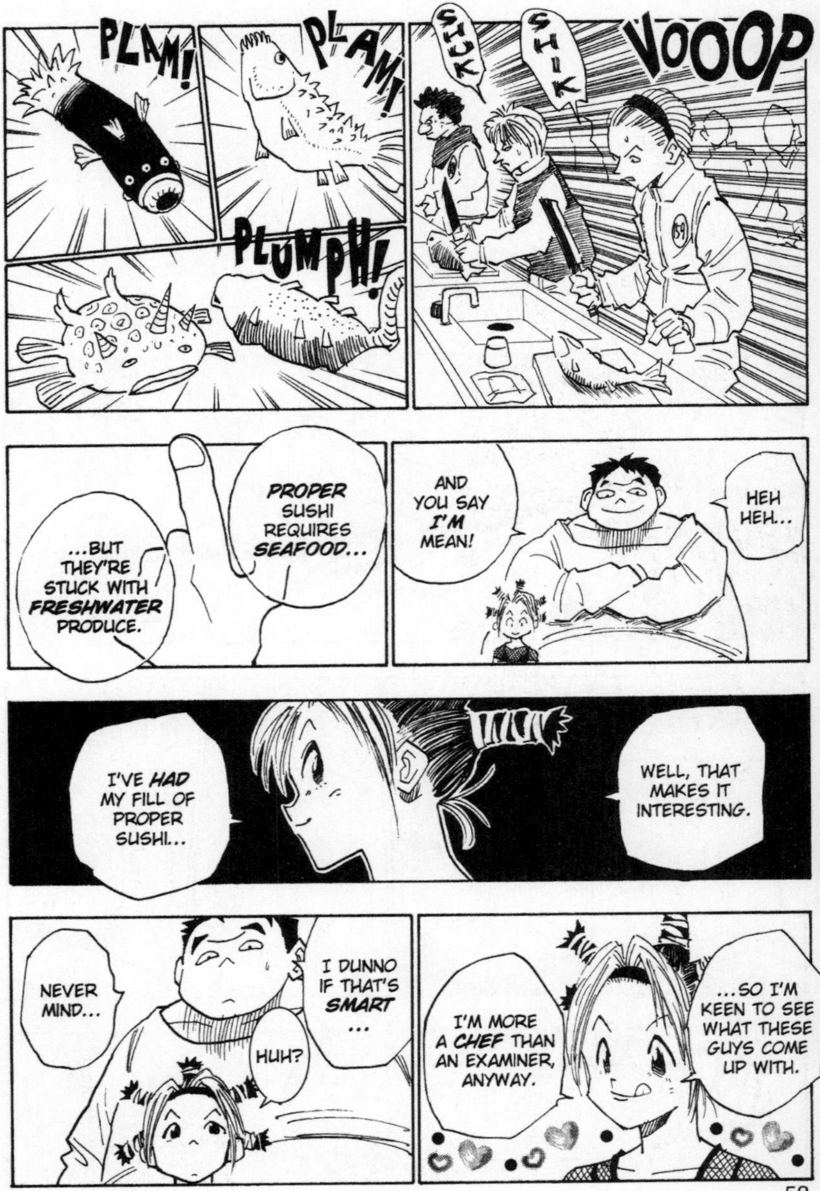
VOOOP
SHIK
SHUK
PLAM!
PLAM!
PLUMPH!
HEH HEH...
AND YOU SAY I'M MEAN!
PROPER SUSHI REQUIRES SEAFOOD...
...BUT THEY'RE STUCK WITH FRESHWATER PRODUCE.
WELL, THAT MAKES IT INTERESTING.
I'VE HAD MY FILL OF PROPER SUSHI...
I'M MORE A CHEF THAN AN EXAMINER, ANYWAY.
...SO I'M KEEN TO SEE WHAT THESE GUYS COME UP WITH.
I DUNNO IF THAT'S SMART...
HUH?
NEVER MIND...

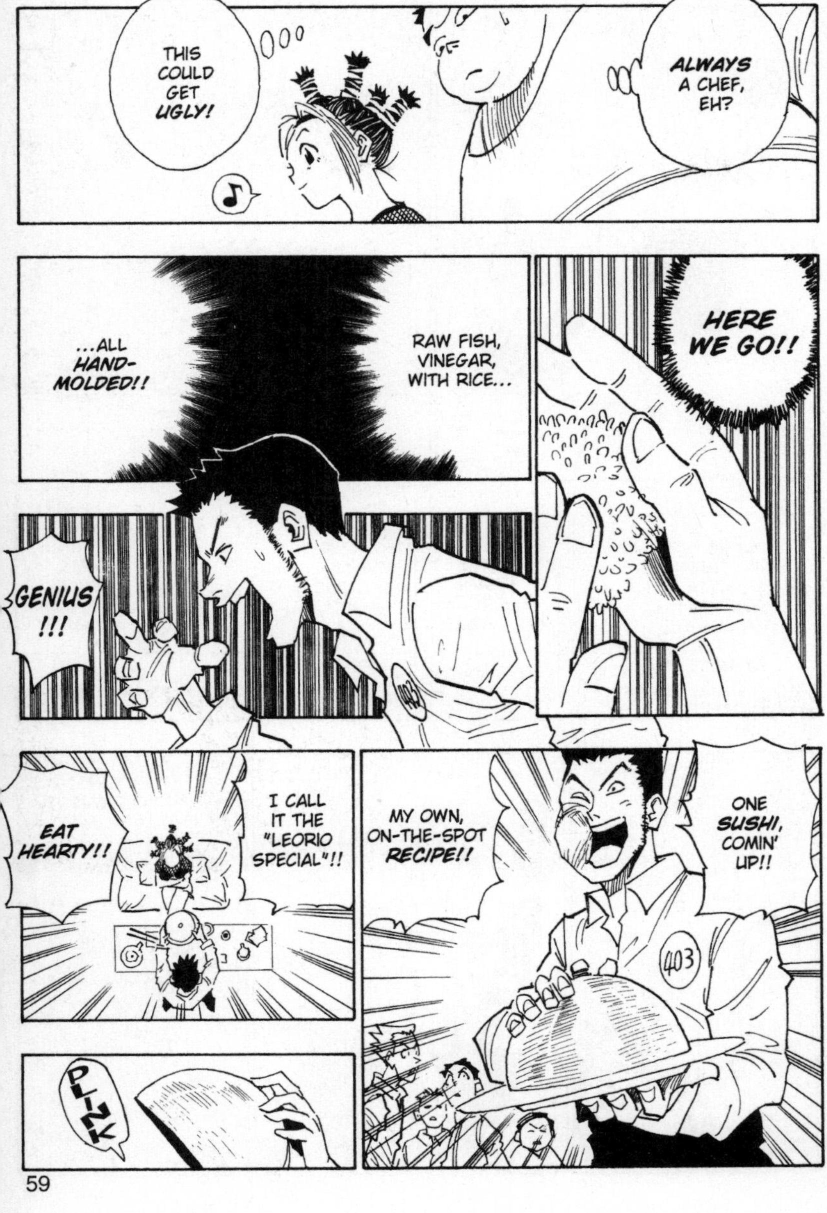
ALWAYS A CHEF, EH?
THIS COULD GET UGLY!
HERE WE GO!!
RAW FISH, VINEGAR, WITH RICE...
...ALL HAND-MOLDED!!
GENIUS !!!
ONE SUSHI, COMIN' UP!!
MY OWN, ON-THE-SPOT RECIPE!!
403
I CALL IT THE "LEORIO SPECIAL"!!
EAT HEARTY!!
PLINK

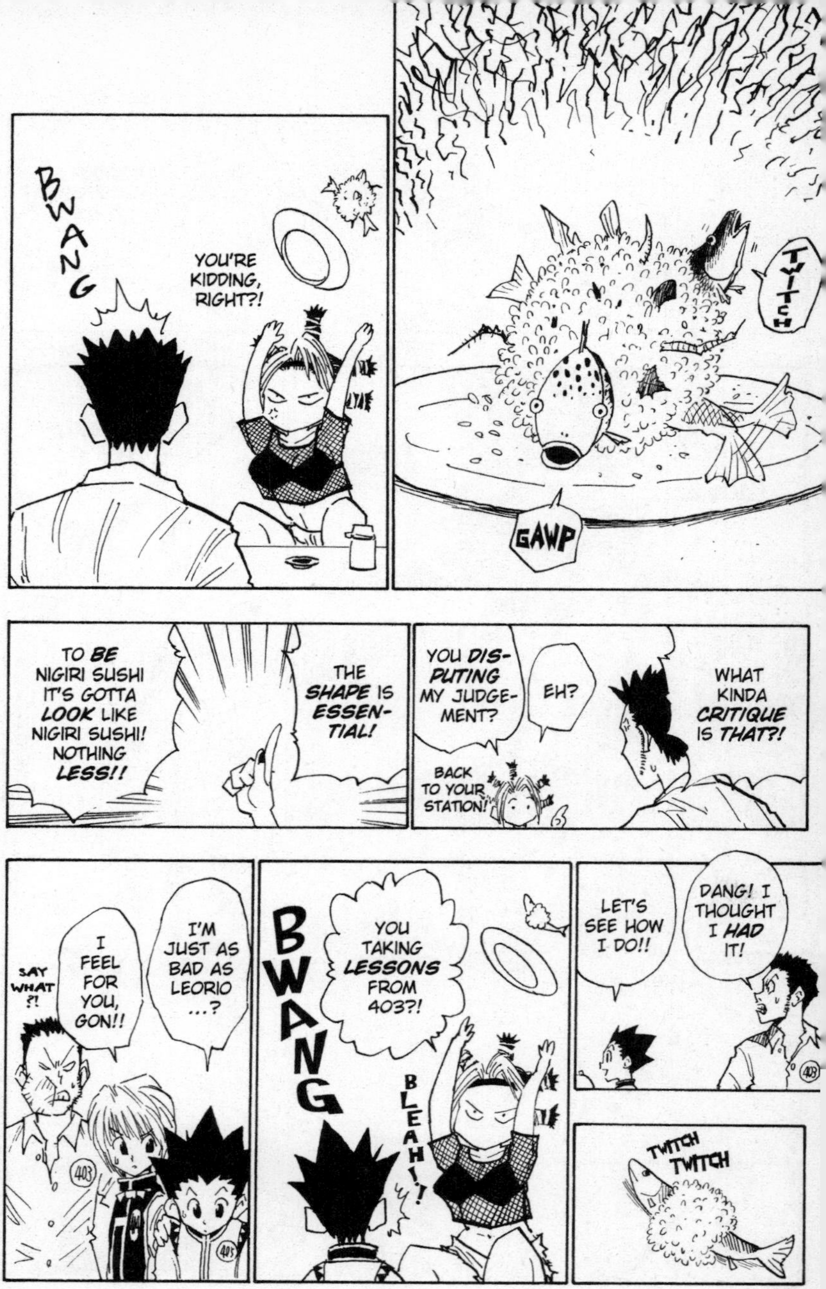
TWITCH
GAWP
YOU'RE KIDDING, RIGHT?!
BWANG
WHAT KINDA CRITIQUE IS THAT?!
EH?
YOU DISPUTING MY JUDGEMENT?
BACK TO YOUR STATION!
THE SHAPE IS ESSENTIAL!
TO BE NIGIRI SUSHI IT'S GOTTA LOOK LIKE NIGIRI SUSHI! NOTHING LESS!!
DANG! I THOUGHT I HAD IT!
LET'S SEE HOW I DO!!
TWITCH TWITCH
YOU TAKING LESSONS FROM 403?!
BWANG
BLEAH!!
I'M JUST AS BAD AS LEORIO...?
I FEEL FOR YOU, GON!!
SAY WHAT?!

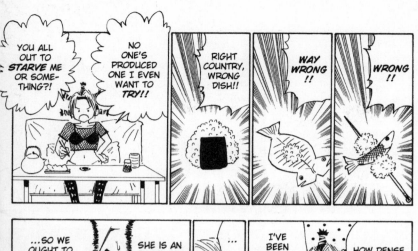

WRONG!!
WAY WRONG!!
RIGHT COUNTRY, WRONG DISH!!
NO ONE'S PRODUCED ONE I EVEN WANT TO TRY!!
YOU ALL OUT TO STARVE ME OR SOMETHING?!
HOW DENSE CAN THESE GUYS BE?
I'VE BEEN GIVING PLENTY OF HINTS.
FRET FRET
...
SHE IS AN EXAMINER, TESTING US...
...SO WE OUGHT TO BE ABLE TO FIGURE THIS OUT!!
...MAKE AS MANY AS YOU LIKE...
THE SHAPE IS ESSENTIAL!
THE SHAPE... SHOULD ALLOW US TO MAKE A LOT OF THEM FAIRLY QUICKLY. A FORMULA? MAKE ONE, PRODUCE MANY? DO SOMETHING WITH THE RICE AND FISH THAT CAN BE READILY DONE AGAIN AND AGAIN...IS THAT IT?
SHE'S HOLDING TWO STICKS AS IF THEY WERE UTENSILS...
...AND THERE'S A DISH OF SOME CONDIMENT.
IF SHE CAN HOLD AND DIP THE SUSHI WITH THOSE STICKS...
...ONE SUSHI MUST BE ONLY SO BIG!!
I HAVE IT!!

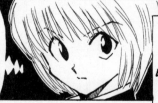

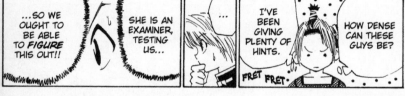

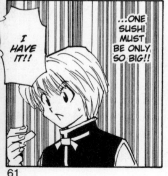

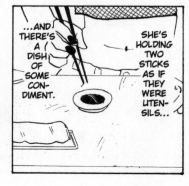

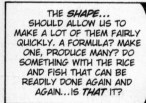

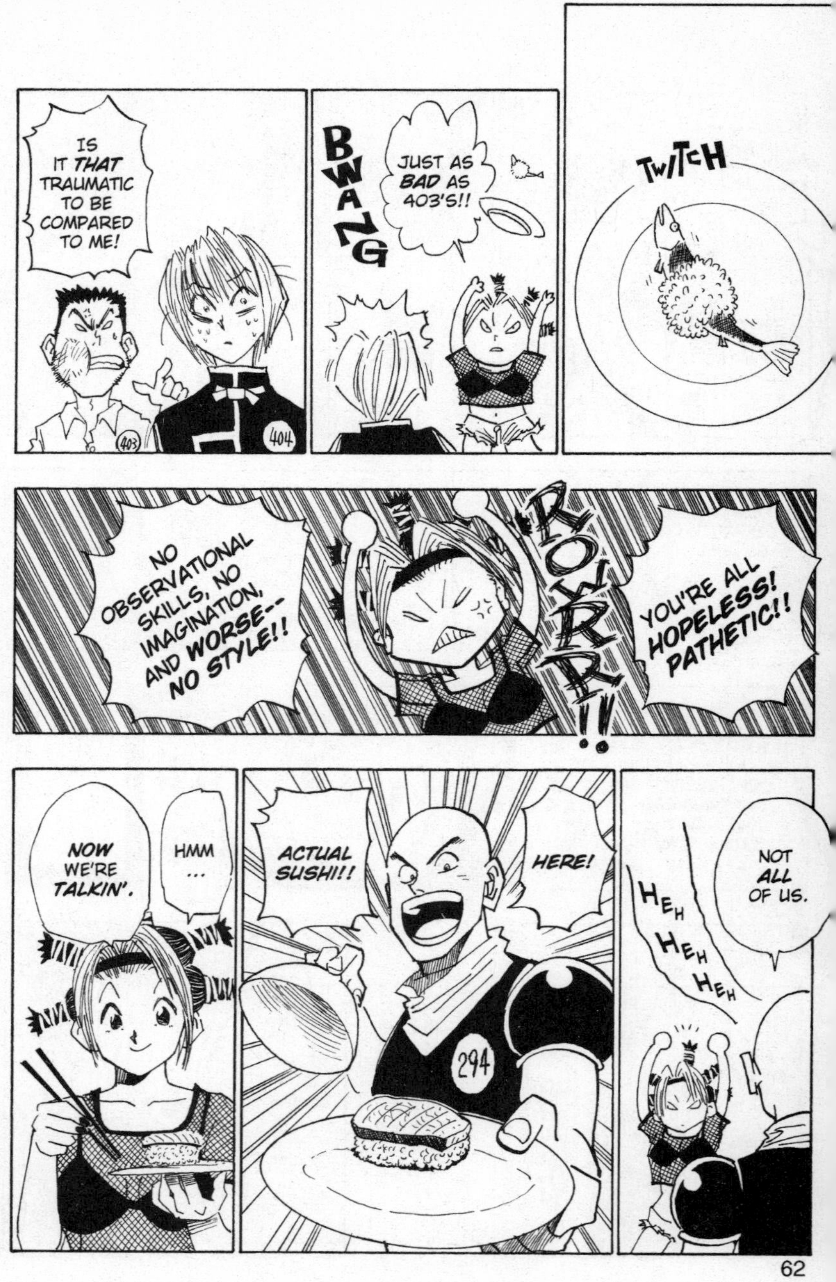
TWITCH
BWANG
JUST AS BAD AS 403'S!!
IS IT THAT TRAUMATIC TO BE COMPARED TO ME!
YOU'RE ALL HOPELESS! PATHETIC!!
ROWRR!!
NO OBSERVATIONAL SKILLS, NO IMAGINATION, AND WORSE-- NO STYLE!!
NOT ALL OF US.
HEH HEH HEH
HERE!
ACTUAL SUSHI!!
HMM ...
NOW WE'RE TALKIN'.

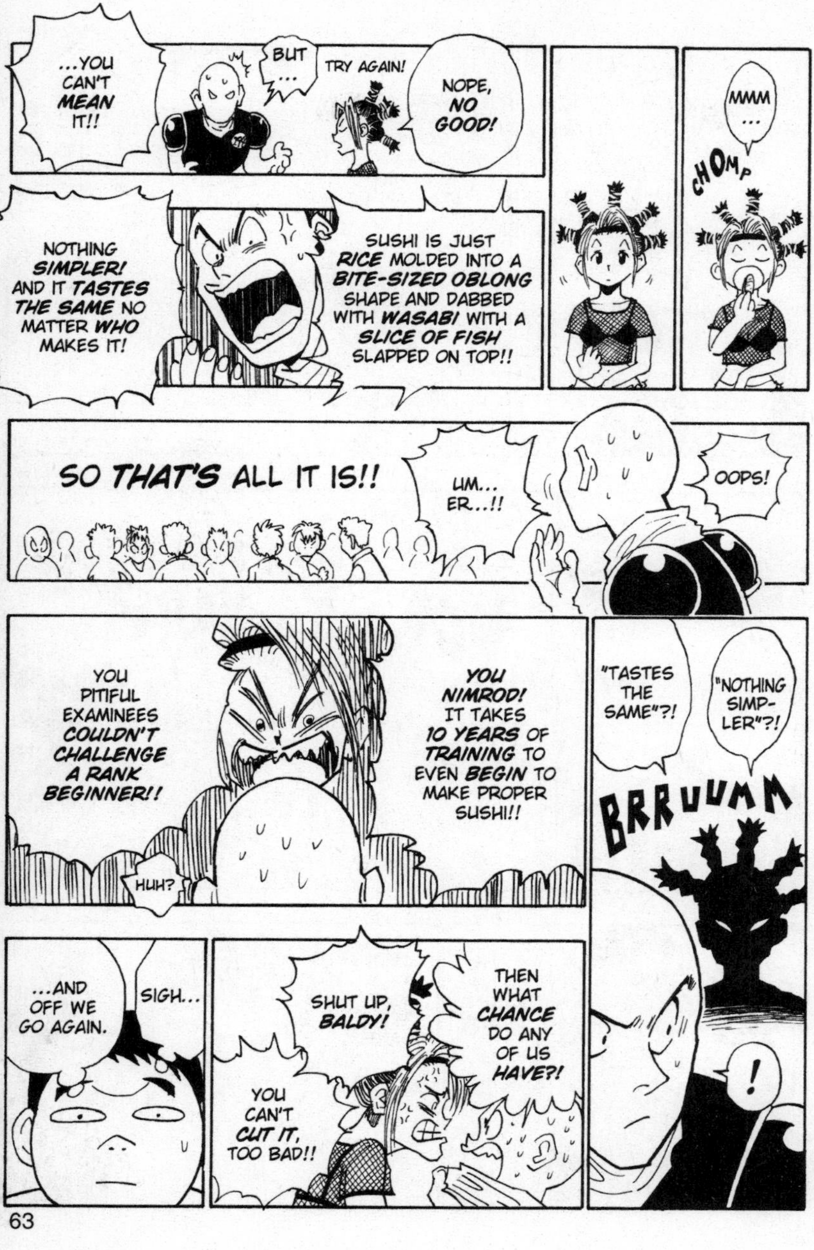
MMM...
CHOMP
NOPE, NO GOOD!
TRY AGAIN!
BUT...
...YOU CAN'T MEAN IT!!
SUSHI IS JUST RICE MOLDED INTO A BITE-SIZED OBLONG SHAPE AND DABBED WITH WASABI WITH A SLICE OF FISH SLAPPED ON TOP!!
NOTHING SIMPLER! AND IT TASTES THE SAME NO MATTER WHO MAKES IT!
OOPS!
UM... ER...!!
SO THAT'S ALL IT IS!!
"NOTHING SIMPLER"?!
"TASTES THE SAME"?!
BRRUUMM
!
YOU NIMROD! IT TAKES 10 YEARS OF TRAINING TO EVEN BEGIN TO MAKE PROPER SUSHI!!
YOU PITIFUL EXAMINEES COULDN'T CHALLENGE A RANK BEGINNER!!
HUH?
THEN WHAT CHANCE DO ANY OF US HAVE?!
SHUT UP, BALDY!
YOU CAN'T CUT IT, TOO BAD!!
SIGH...
...AND OFF WE GO AGAIN.

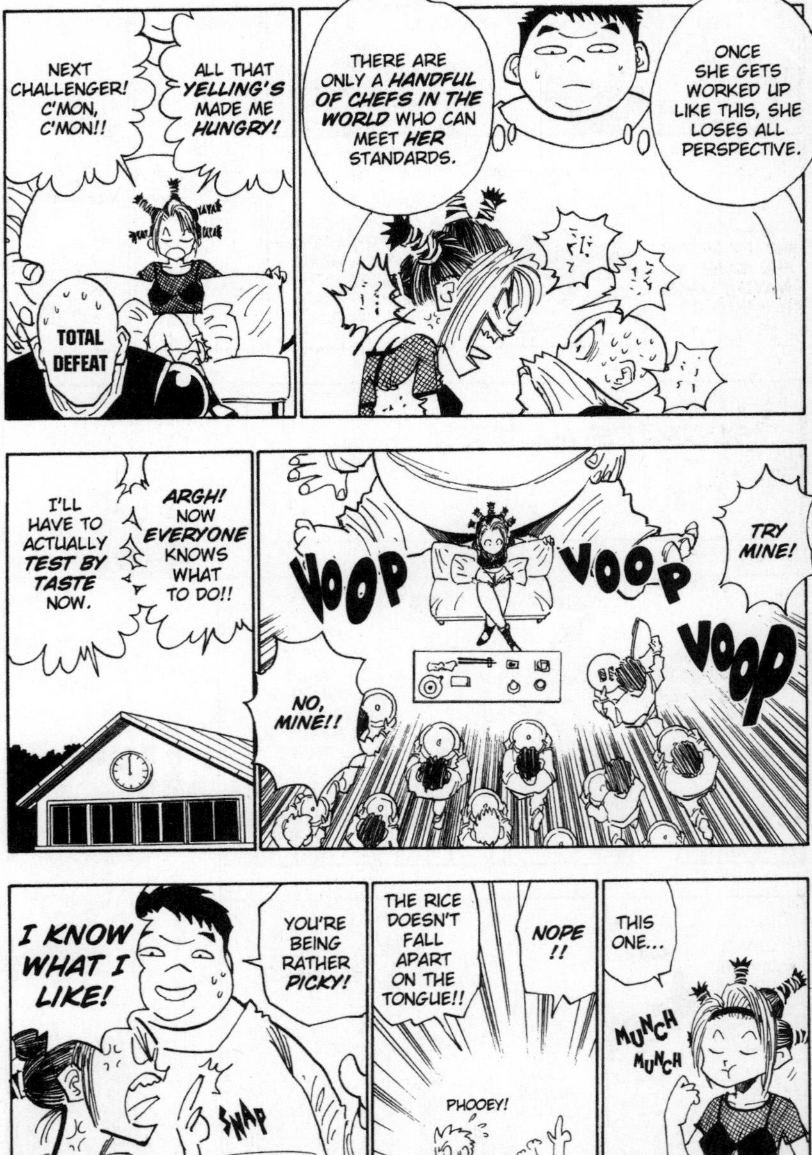
ONCE SHE GETS WORKED UP LIKE THIS, SHE LOSES ALL PERSPECTIVE.
THERE ARE ONLY A HANDFUL OF CHEFS IN THE WORLD WHO CAN MEET HER STANDARDS.
ALL THAT YELLING'S MADE ME HUNGRY!
NEXT CHALLENGER! C'MON, C'MON!!
TOTAL DEFEAT
TRY MINE!
VOOP
VOOP
VOOP
NO, MINE!!
ARGH! NOW EVERYONE KNOWS WHAT TO DO!!
I'LL HAVE TO ACTUALLY TEST BY TASTE NOW.
THIS ONE...
MUNCH
MUNCH
NOPE!!
THE RICE DOESN'T FALL APART ON THE TONGUE!!
PHOOEY!
YOU'RE BEING RATHER PICKY!
I KNOW WHAT I LIKE!
SNAP

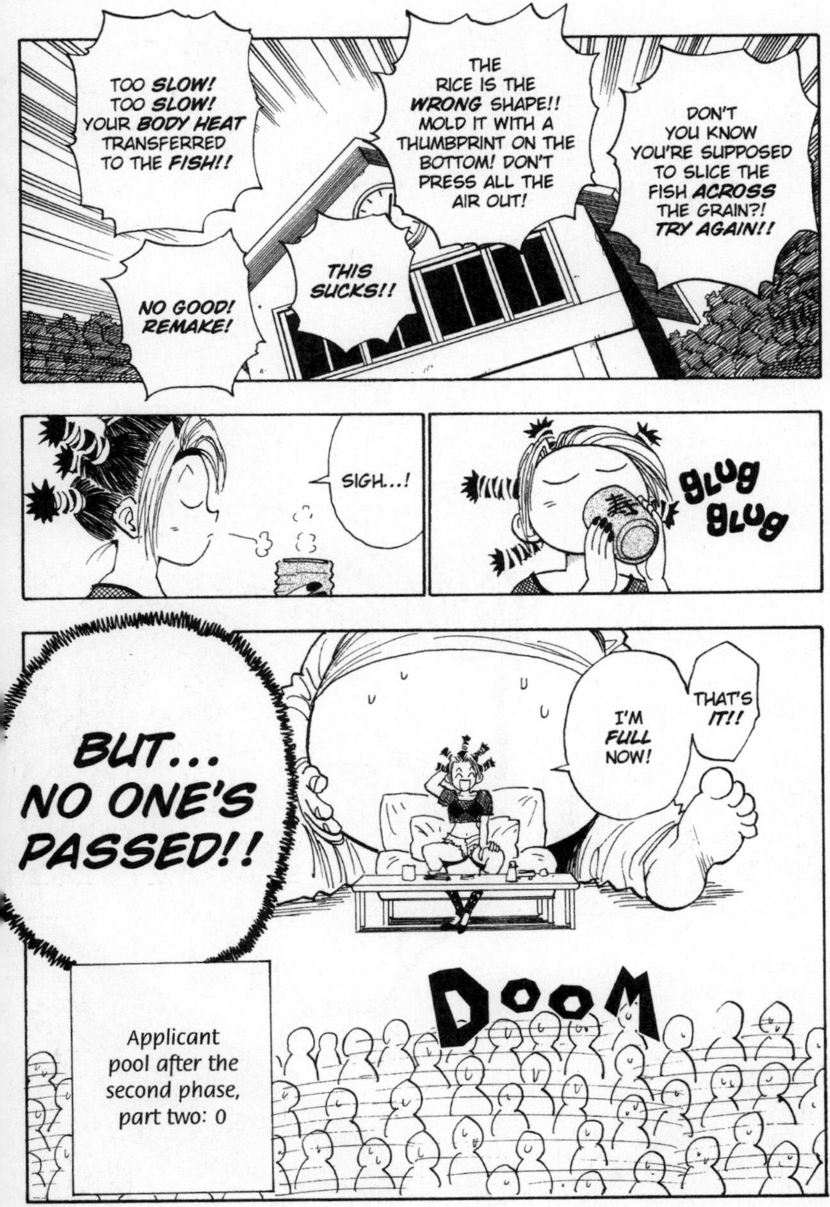
DON'T YOU KNOW YOU'RE SUPPOSED TO SLICE THE FISH ACROSS THE GRAIN?! TRY AGAIN!!
THE RICE IS THE WRONG SHAPE!! MOLD IT WITH A THUMBPRINT ON THE BOTTOM! DON'T PRESS ALL THE AIR OUT!
TOO SLOW! TOO SLOW! YOUR BODY HEAT TRANSFERRED TO THE FISH!!
THIS SUCKS!!
NO GOOD! REMAKE!
glug glug
SIGH...!
THAT'S IT!!
I'M FULL NOW!
BUT... NO ONE'S PASSED!!
DOOM
Applicant pool after the second phase, part two: 0

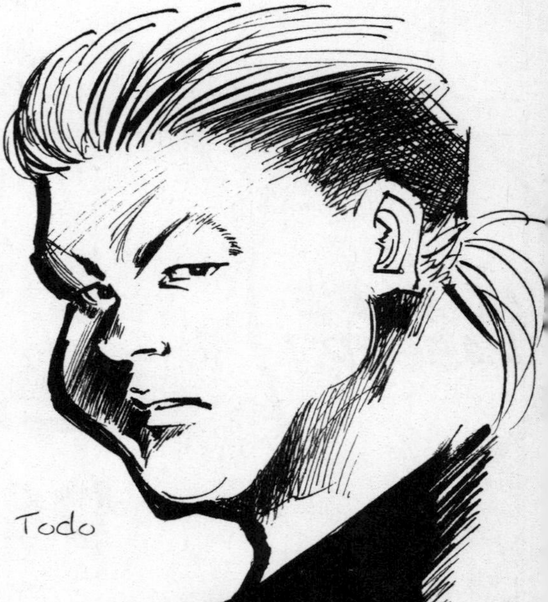
Todo

Chapter 12

The Chairman Arrives

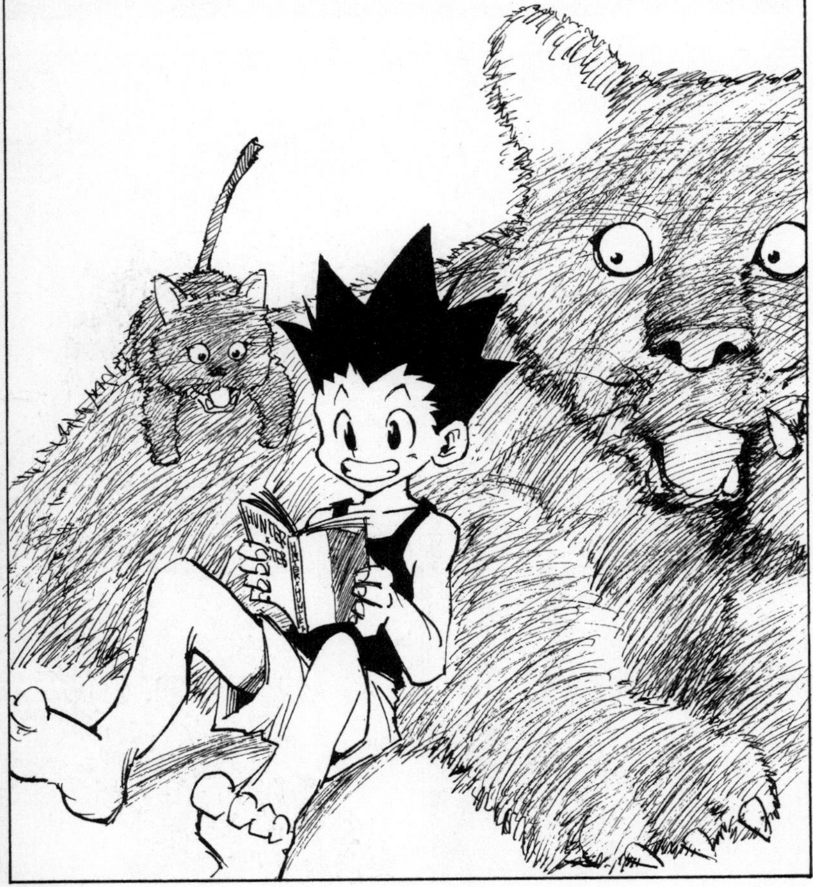

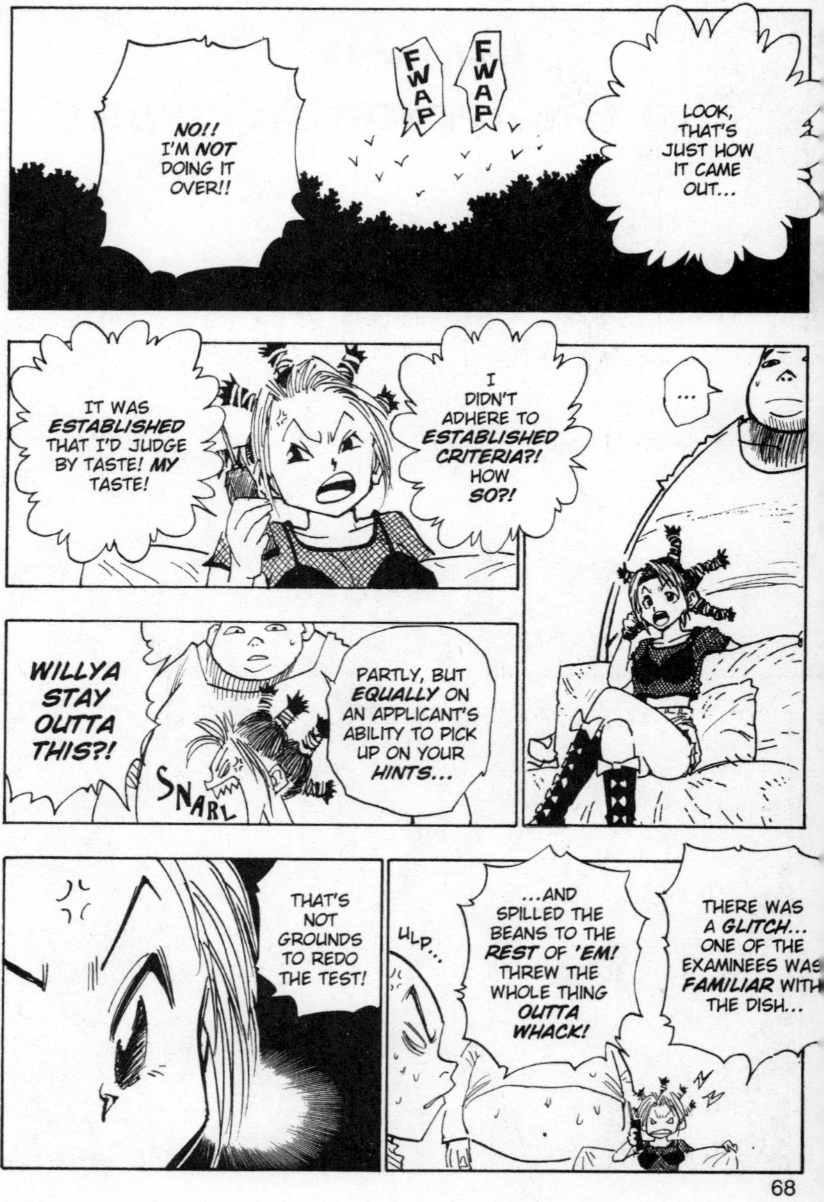
LOOK, THAT'S JUST HOW IT CAME OUT...
FWAP
FWAP
NO!! I'M NOT DOING IT OVER!!
...
I DIDN'T ADHERE TO ESTABLISHED CRITERIA?! HOW SO?!
IT WAS ESTABLISHED THAT I'D JUDGE BY TASTE! MY TASTE!
PARTLY, BUT EQUALLY ON AN APPLICANT'S ABILITY TO PICK UP ON YOUR HINTS...
SNARL
WILLYA STAY OUTTA THIS?!
THERE WAS A GLITCH... ONE OF THE EXAMINEES WAS FAMILIAR WITH THE DISH...
...AND SPILLED THE BEANS TO THE REST OF 'EM! THREW THE WHOLE THING OUTTA WHACK!
ULP...
THAT'S NOT GROUNDS TO REDO THE TEST!

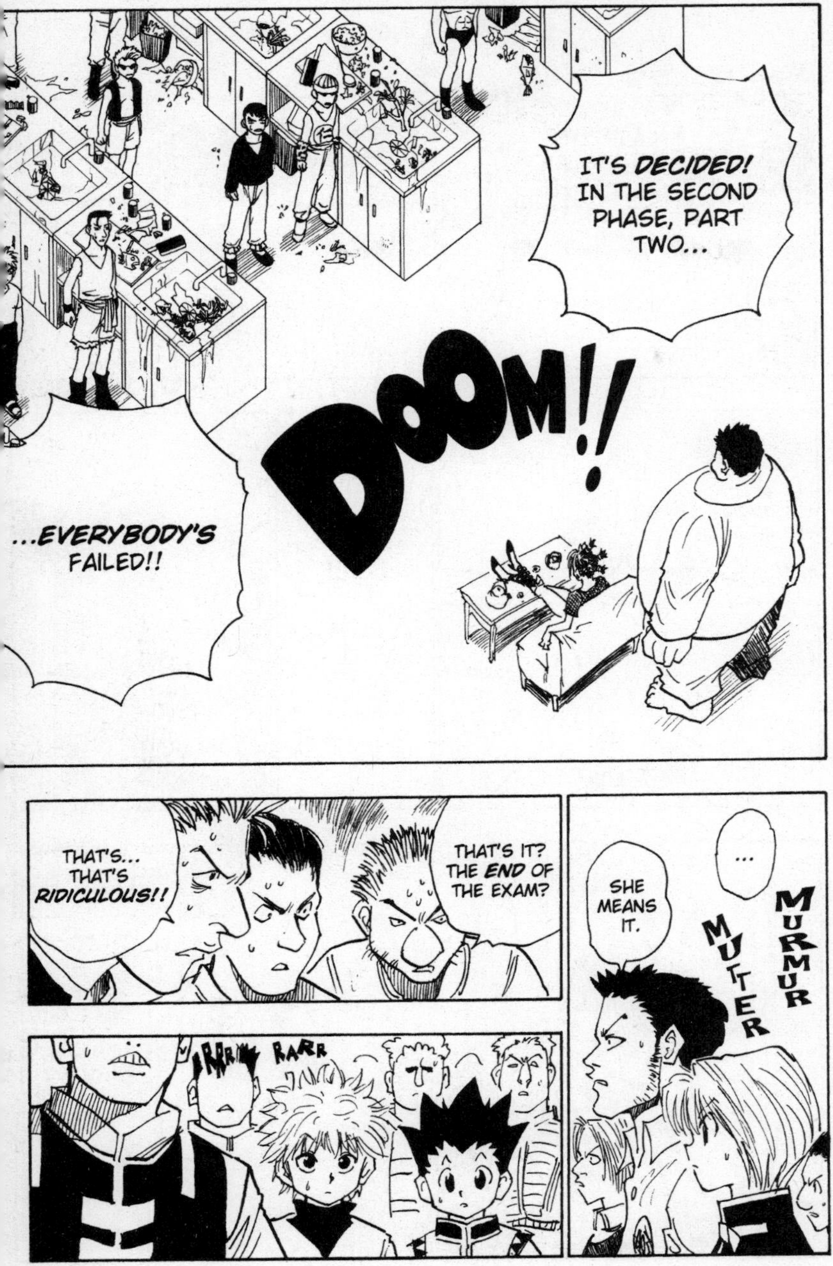
IT'S DECIDED! IN THE SECOND PHASE, PART TWO...
DOOM!!
...EVERYBODY'S FAILED!!
...
SHE MEANS IT.
MURMUR
MUTTER
THAT'S IT? THE END OF THE EXAM?
THAT'S... THAT'S RIDICULOUS!!
RARR

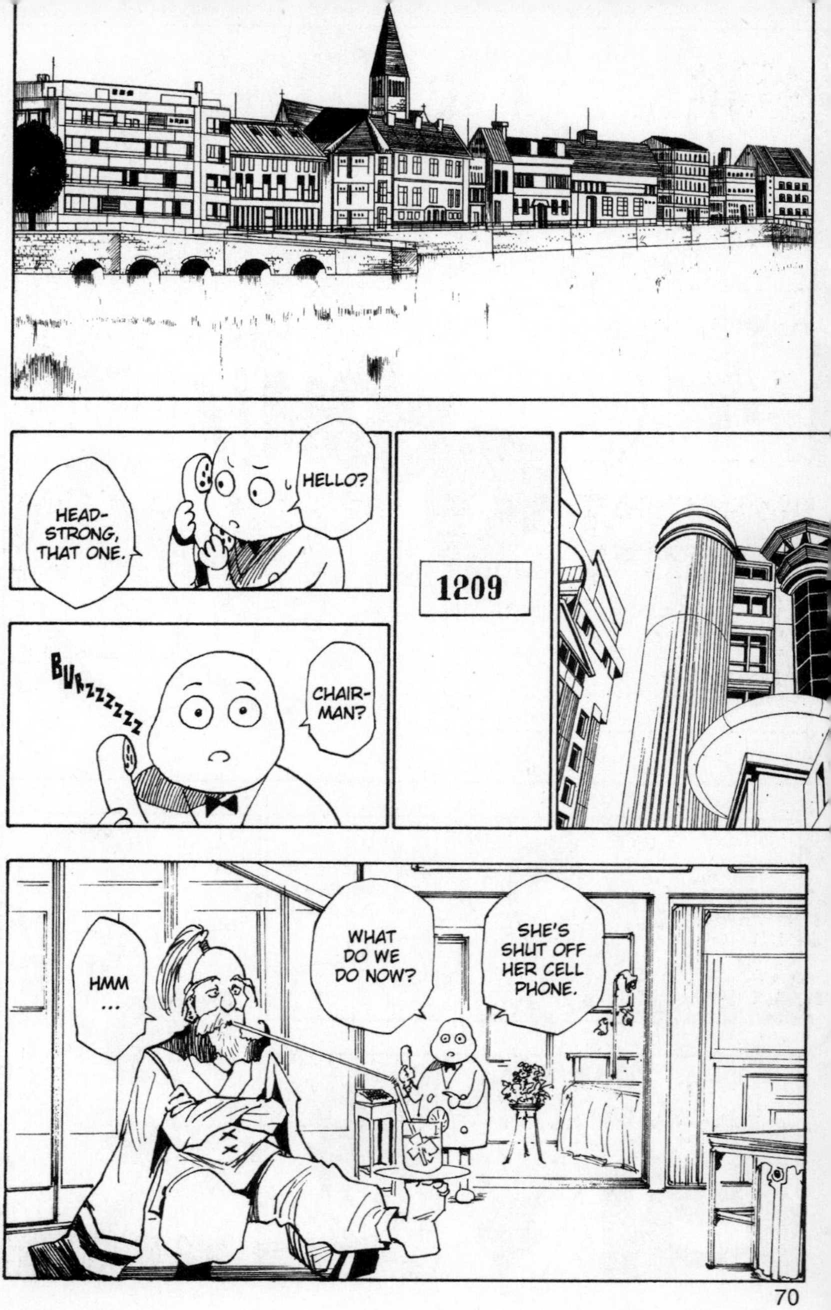
1209
HELLO?
HEAD-STRONG, THAT ONE.
CHAIR-MAN?
BURZZZZZZ
SHE'S SHUT OFF HER CELL PHONE.
WHAT DO WE DO NOW?
HMM ...

READ THIS WAY

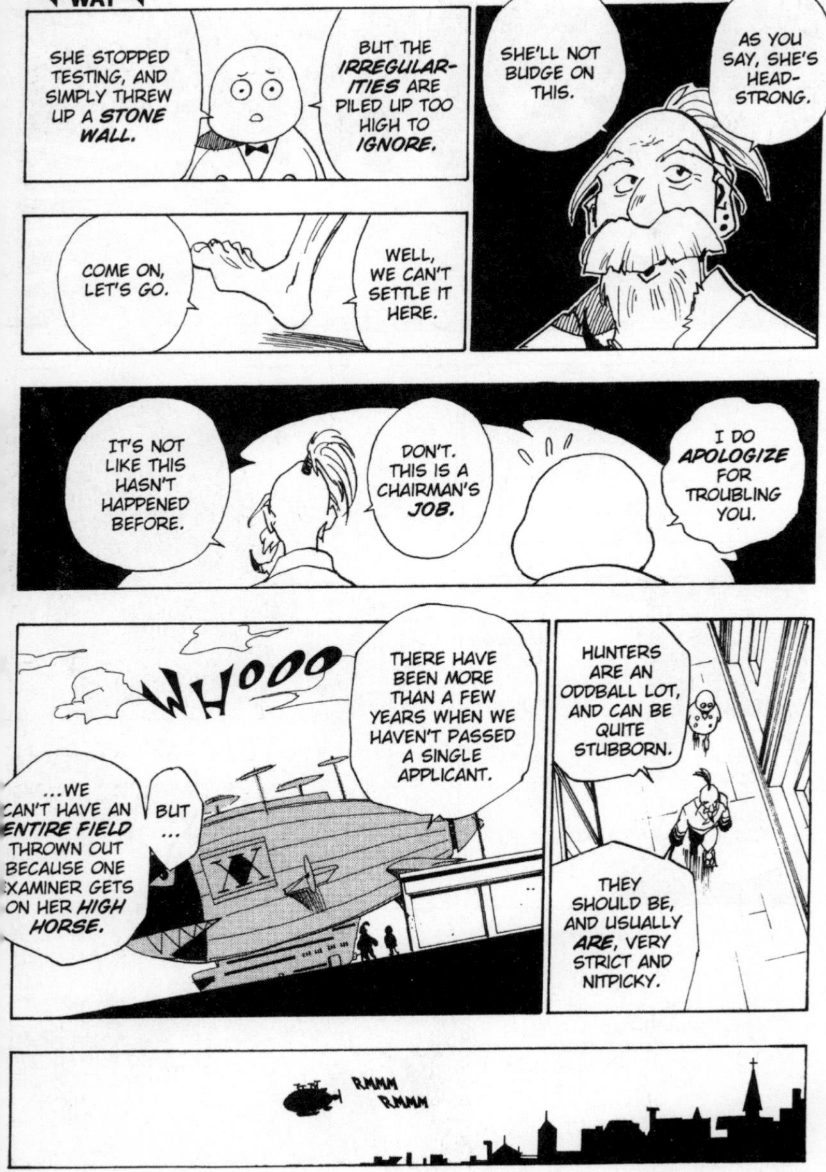
AS YOU SAY, SHE'S HEAD-STRONG.
SHE'LL NOT BUDGE ON THIS.
BUT THE *IRREGULARITIES* ARE PILED UP TOO HIGH TO *IGNORE.*
SHE STOPPED TESTING, AND SIMPLY THREW UP A *STONE WALL.*
WELL, WE CAN'T SETTLE IT HERE.
COME ON, LET'S GO.
I DO *APOLOGIZE* FOR TROUBLING YOU.
DON'T. THIS IS A CHAIRMAN'S *JOB.*
IT'S NOT LIKE THIS HASN'T HAPPENED BEFORE.
HUNTERS ARE AN ODDBALL LOT, AND CAN BE QUITE STUBBORN.
THEY SHOULD BE, AND USUALLY *ARE*, VERY STRICT AND NITPICKY.
WHOOO
THERE HAVE BEEN MORE THAN A FEW YEARS WHEN WE HAVEN'T PASSED A SINGLE APPLICANT.
BUT ...
...WE CAN'T HAVE AN *ENTIRE FIELD* THROWN OUT BECAUSE ONE EXAMINER GETS ON HER *HIGH HORSE.*
RMMM RMMM

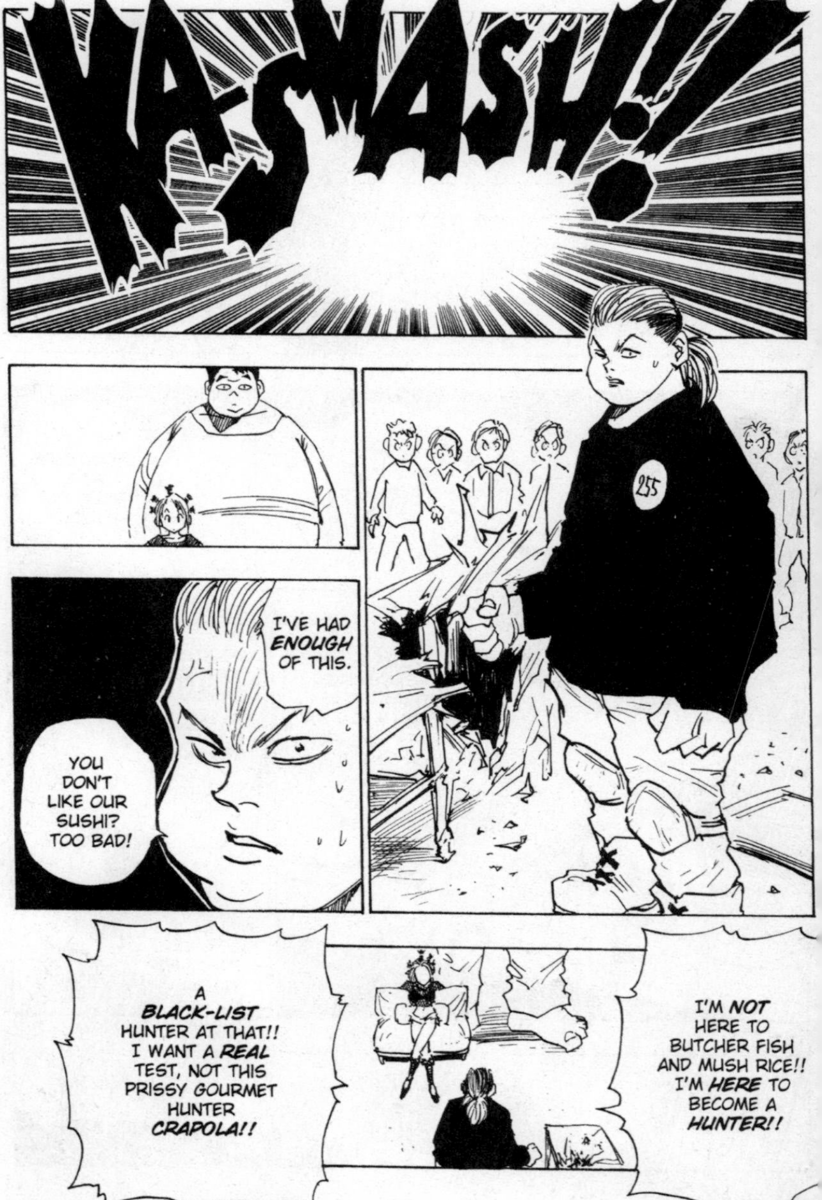
KA-SMASH!!
I'VE HAD ENOUGH OF THIS.
YOU DON'T LIKE OUR SUSHI? TOO BAD!
255
I'M NOT HERE TO BUTCHER FISH AND MUSH RICE!! I'M HERE TO BECOME A HUNTER!!
A BLACK-LIST HUNTER AT THAT!! I WANT A REAL TEST, NOT THIS PRISSY GOURMET HUNTER CRAPOLA!!

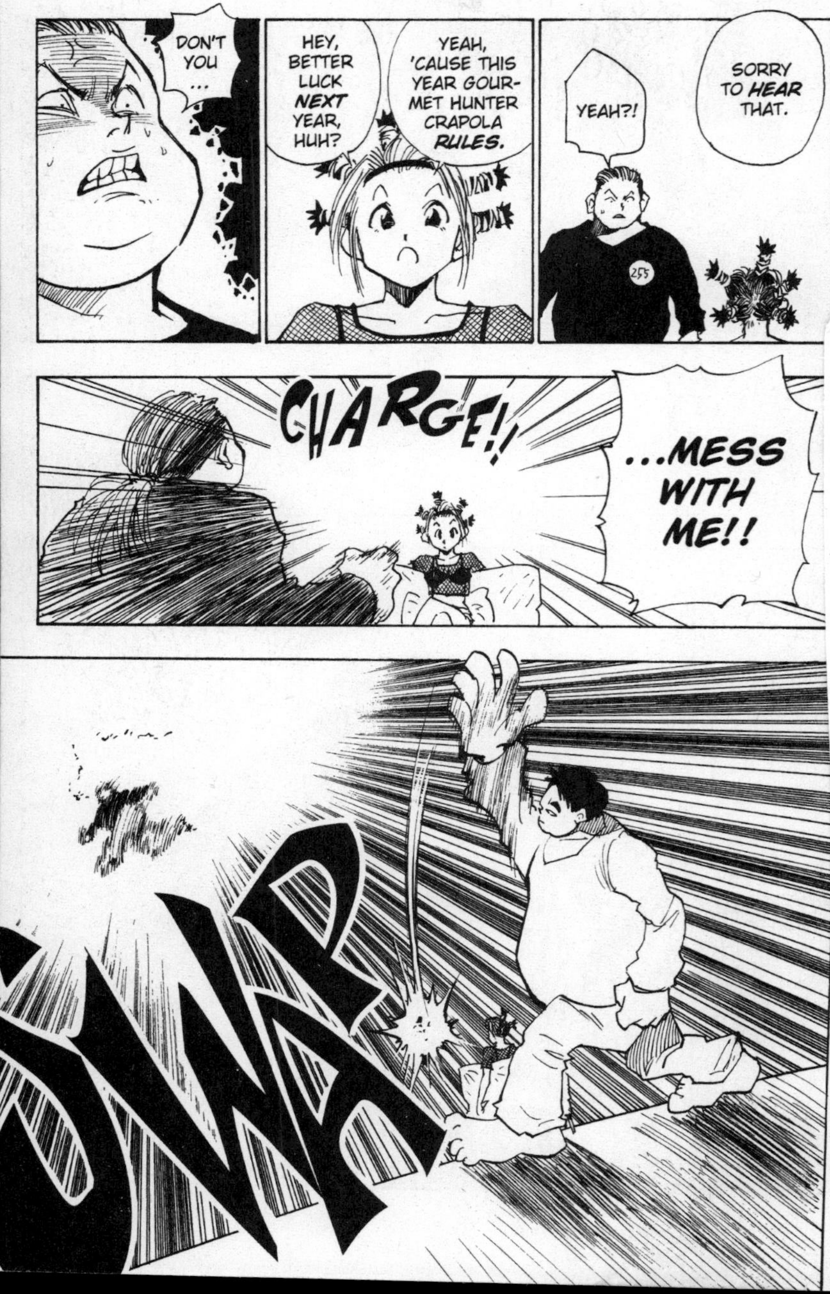
SORRY TO HEAR THAT.
YEAH?!
YEAH, 'CAUSE THIS YEAR GOURMET HUNTER CRAPOLA RULES.
HEY, BETTER LUCK NEXT YEAR, HUH?
DON'T YOU ...
...MESS WITH ME!!
CHARGE!!
WHAP

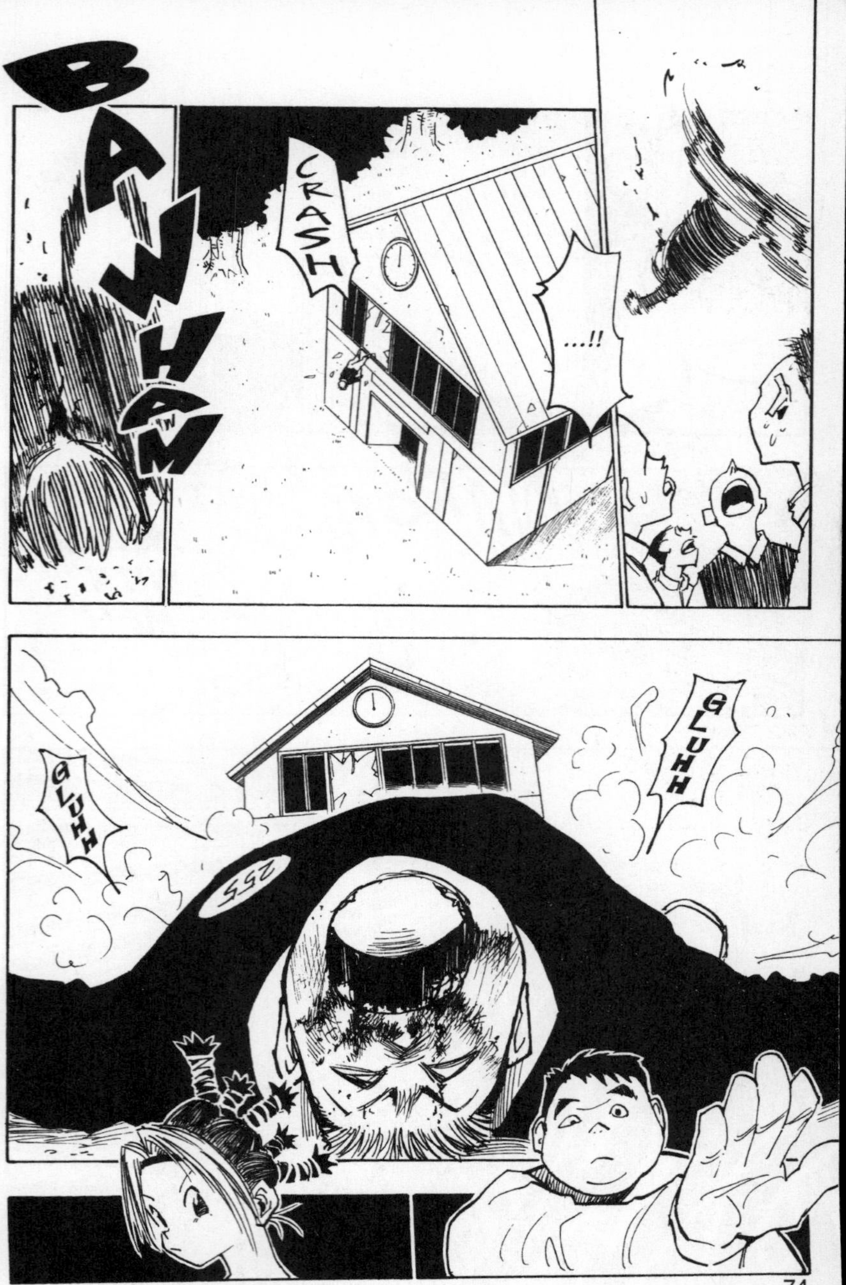
...!!
CRASH
BAWHAM
GLUHH
GLUHH

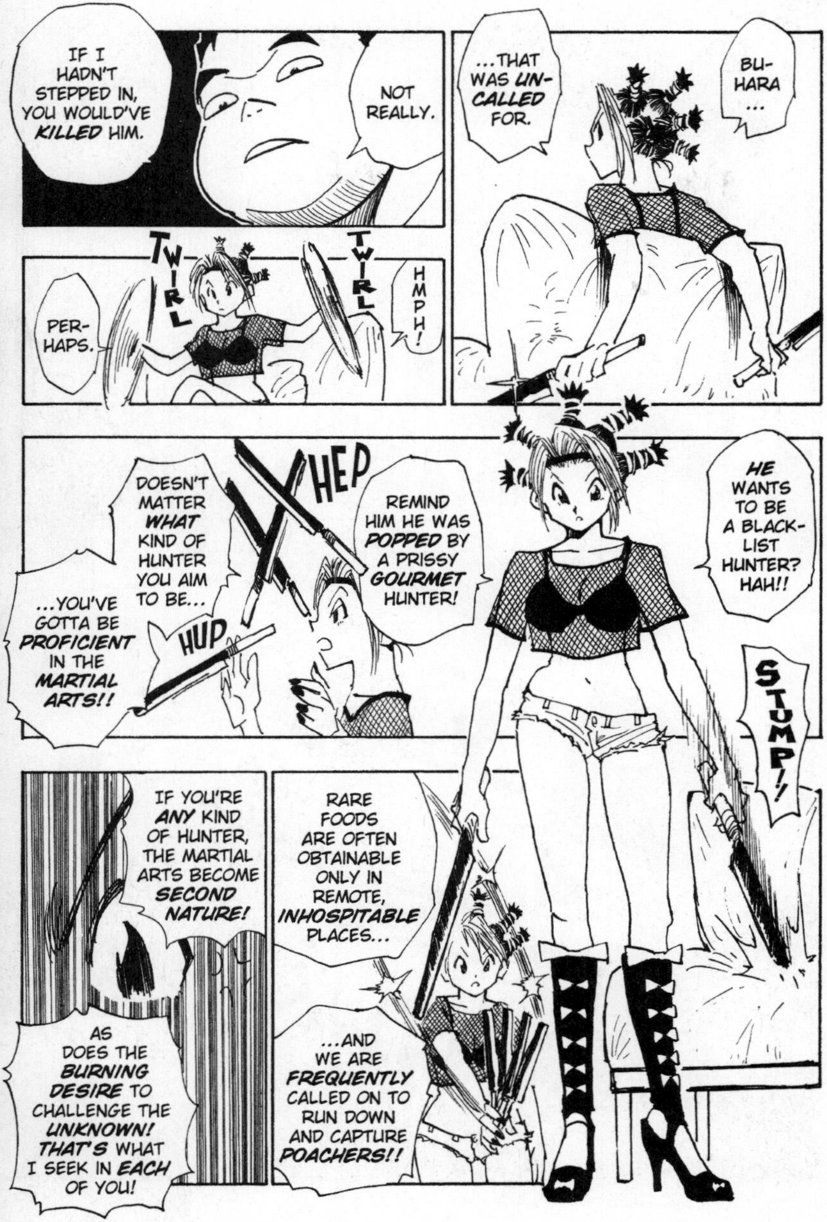
BU-HARA...
...THAT WAS UN-CALLED FOR.
NOT REALLY.
IF I HADN'T STEPPED IN, YOU WOULD'VE KILLED HIM.
HMPH!
TWIRL
TWIRL
PER-HAPS.
HE WANTS TO BE A BLACK-LIST HUNTER? HAH!!
STUMP!!
HEP
REMIND HIM HE WAS POPPED BY A PRISSY GOURMET HUNTER!
DOESN'T MATTER WHAT KIND OF HUNTER YOU AIM TO BE...
HUP
...YOU'VE GOTTA BE PROFICIENT IN THE MARTIAL ARTS!!
RARE FOODS ARE OFTEN OBTAINABLE ONLY IN REMOTE, INHOSPITABLE PLACES...
...AND WE ARE FREQUENTLY CALLED ON TO RUN DOWN AND CAPTURE POACHERS!!
IF YOU'RE ANY KIND OF HUNTER, THE MARTIAL ARTS BECOME SECOND NATURE!
AS DOES THE BURNING DESIRE TO CHALLENGE THE UNKNOWN! THAT'S WHAT I SEEK IN EACH OF YOU!

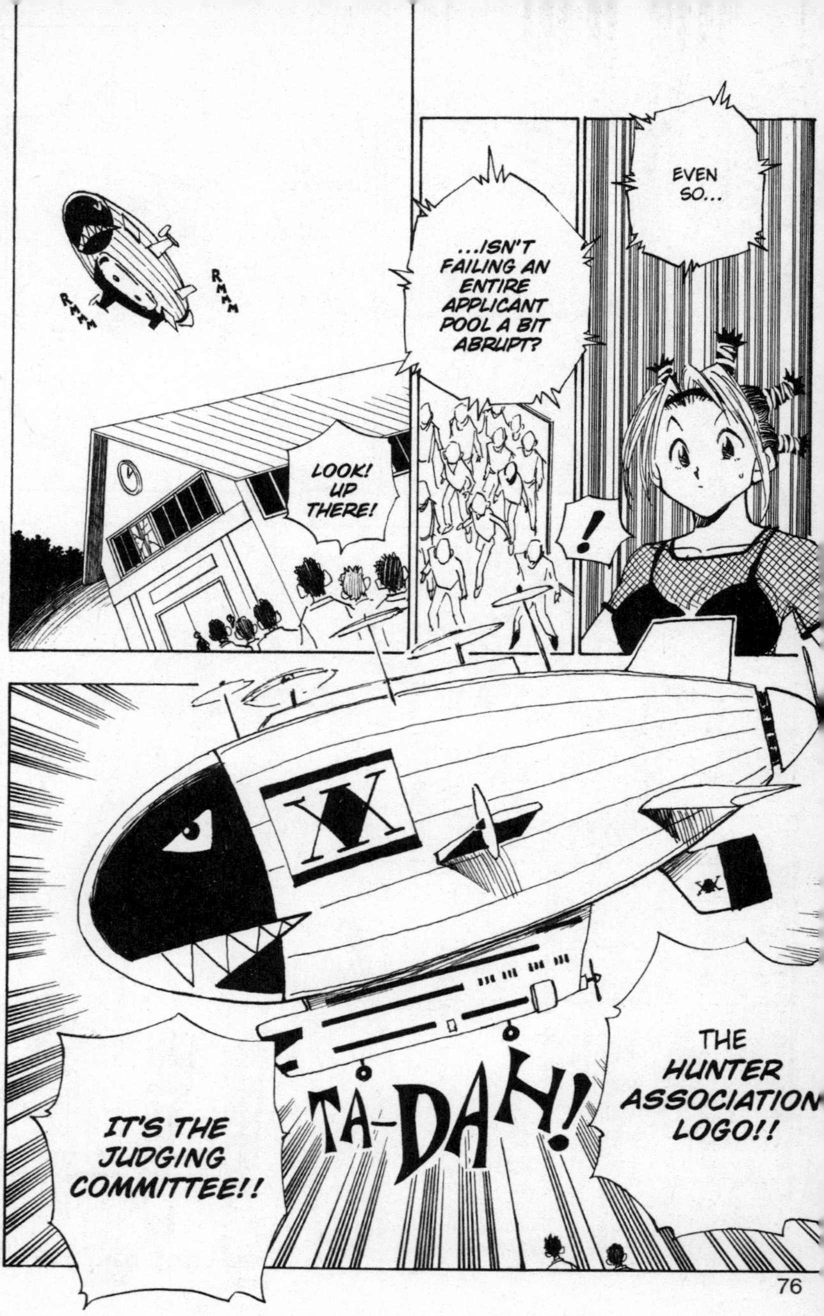
EVEN SO...
...ISN'T FAILING AN ENTIRE APPLICANT POOL A BIT ABRUPT?
!
RMMM
RMMM
LOOK! UP THERE!
THE HUNTER ASSOCIATION LOGO!!
TA-DAH!
IT'S THE JUDGING COMMITTEE!!

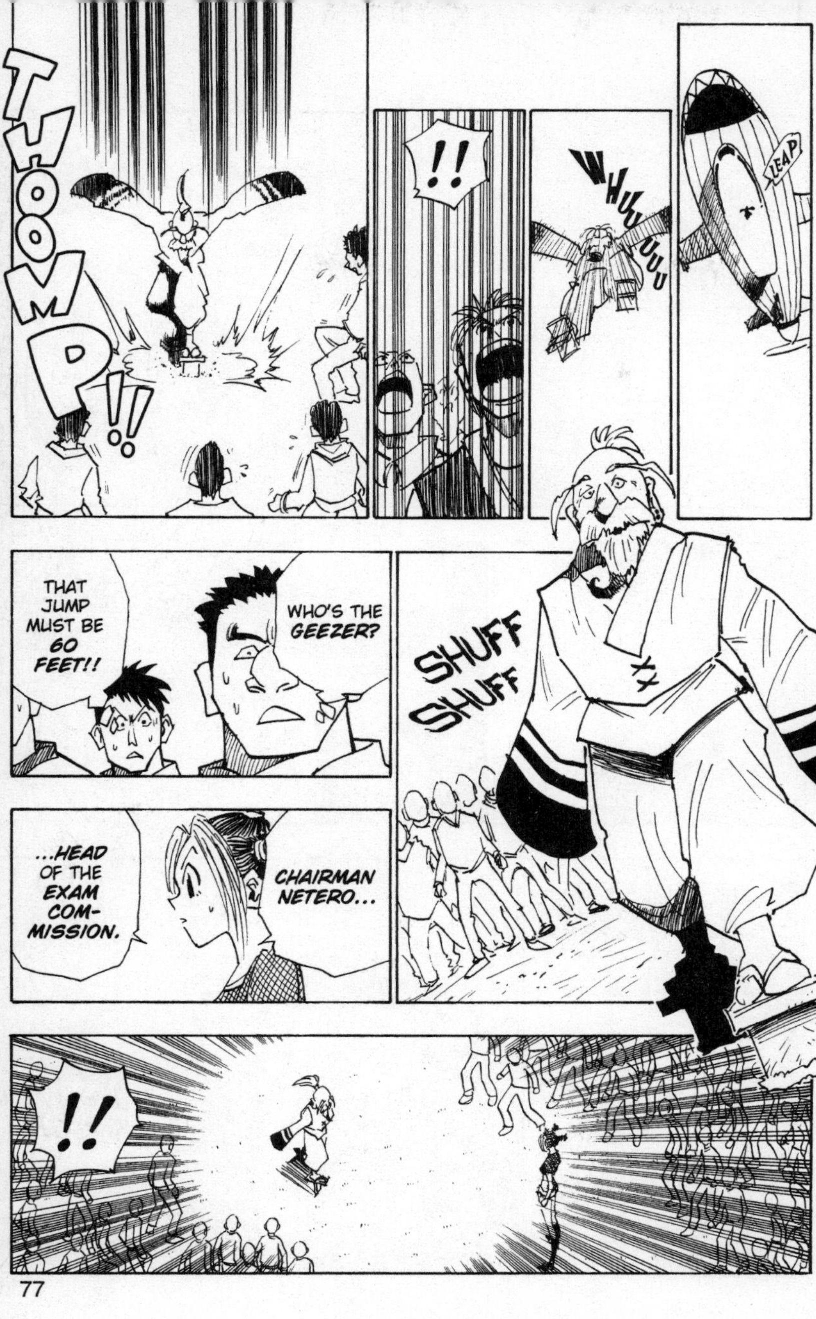

LEAP
WHUUUUUU
!!
THOOMP!!
SHUFF SHUFF
WHO'S THE GEEZER?
THAT JUMP MUST BE 60 FEET!!
CHAIRMAN NETERO...
...HEAD OF THE EXAM COM-MISSION.
!!

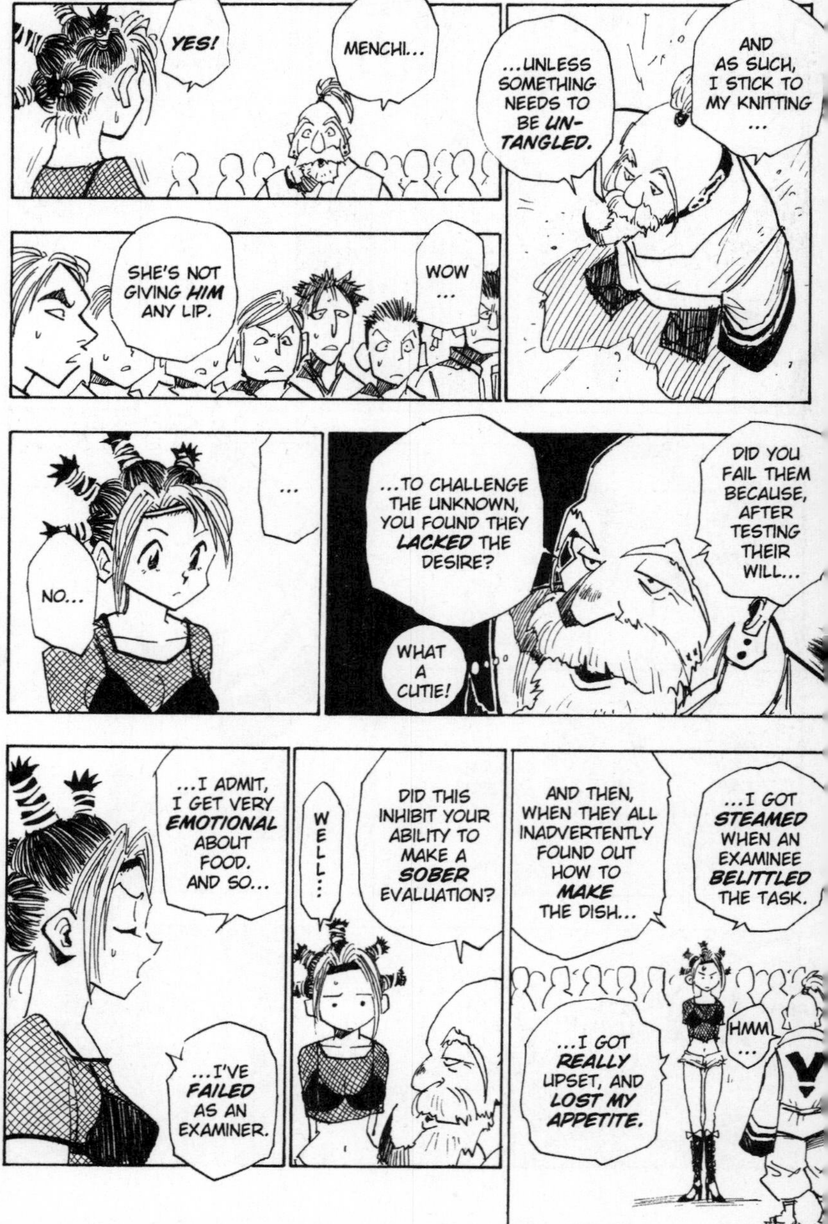
AND AS SUCH, I STICK TO MY KNITTING ...
...UNLESS SOMETHING NEEDS TO BE **UN-TANGLED.**
MENCHI...
YES!
WOW ...
SHE'S NOT GIVING **HIM** ANY LIP.
DID YOU FAIL THEM BECAUSE, AFTER TESTING THEIR WILL...
...TO CHALLENGE THE UNKNOWN, YOU FOUND THEY **LACKED** THE DESIRE?
WHAT A CUTIE!
...
NO...
...I GOT **STEAMED** WHEN AN EXAMINEE **BELITTLED** THE TASK.
AND THEN, WHEN THEY ALL INADVERTENTLY FOUND OUT HOW TO **MAKE** THE DISH...
HMM ...
...I GOT **REALLY** UPSET, AND **LOST MY APPETITE.**
DID THIS INHIBIT YOUR ABILITY TO MAKE A **SOBER** EVALUATION?
WELL...
...I ADMIT, I GET VERY **EMOTIONAL** ABOUT FOOD. AND SO...
...I'VE **FAILED** AS AN EXAMINER.

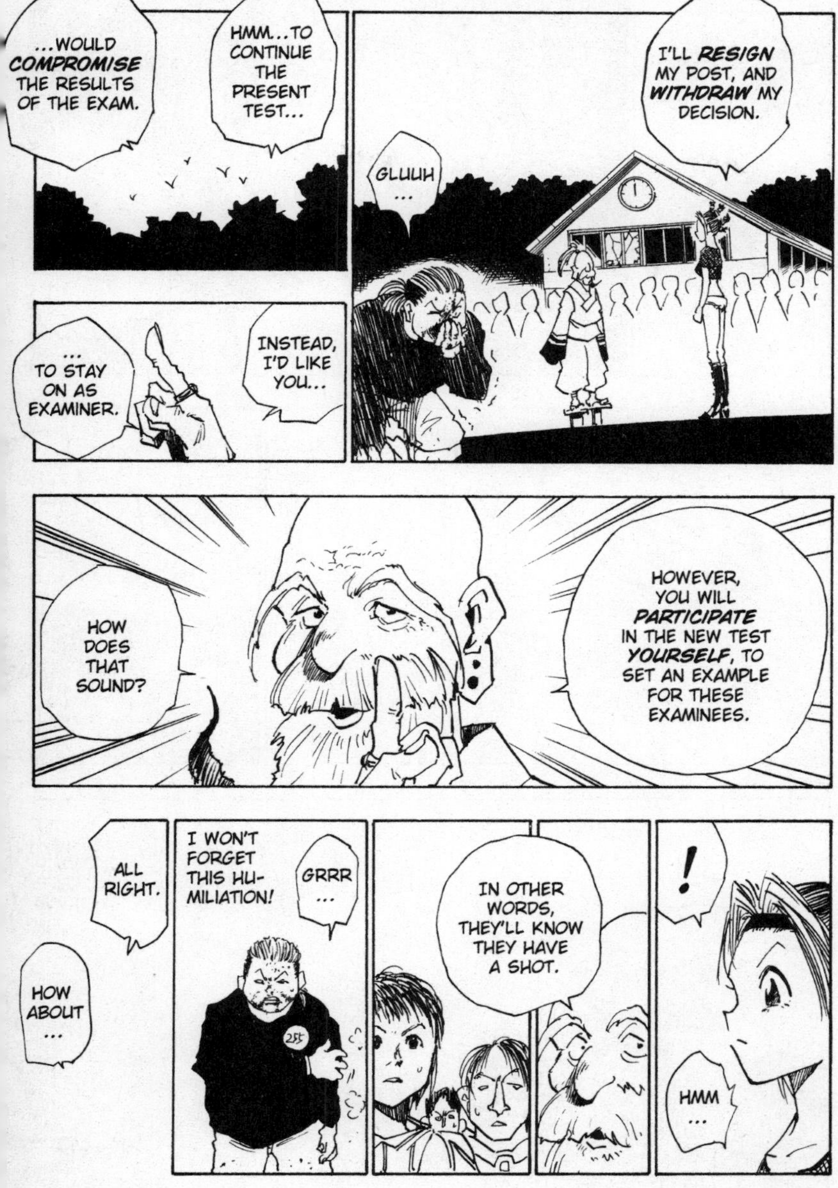
I'LL RESIGN MY POST, AND WITHDRAW MY DECISION.
GLUUH ...
HMM...TO CONTINUE THE PRESENT TEST...
...WOULD COMPROMISE THE RESULTS OF THE EXAM.
INSTEAD, I'D LIKE YOU...
... TO STAY ON AS EXAMINER.
HOWEVER, YOU WILL PARTICIPATE IN THE NEW TEST YOURSELF, TO SET AN EXAMPLE FOR THESE EXAMINEES.
HOW DOES THAT SOUND?
!
HMM ...
IN OTHER WORDS, THEY'LL KNOW THEY HAVE A SHOT.
GRRR ...
I WON'T FORGET THIS HU-MILIATION!
ALL RIGHT.
HOW ABOUT ...

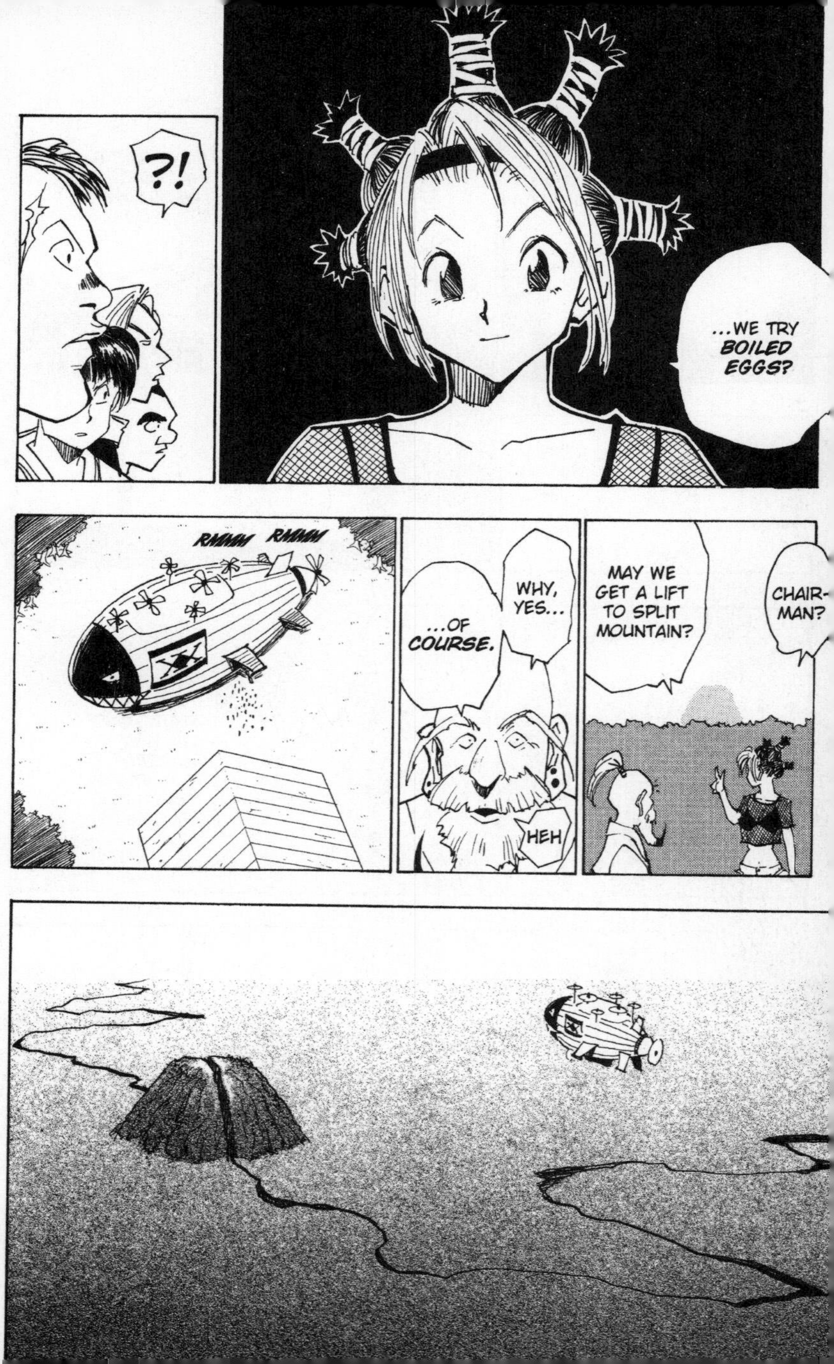
...WE TRY BOILED EGGS?
?!
CHAIR-MAN?
MAY WE GET A LIFT TO SPLIT MOUNTAIN?
WHY, YES...
...OF COURSE.
HEH
RMMM RMMM

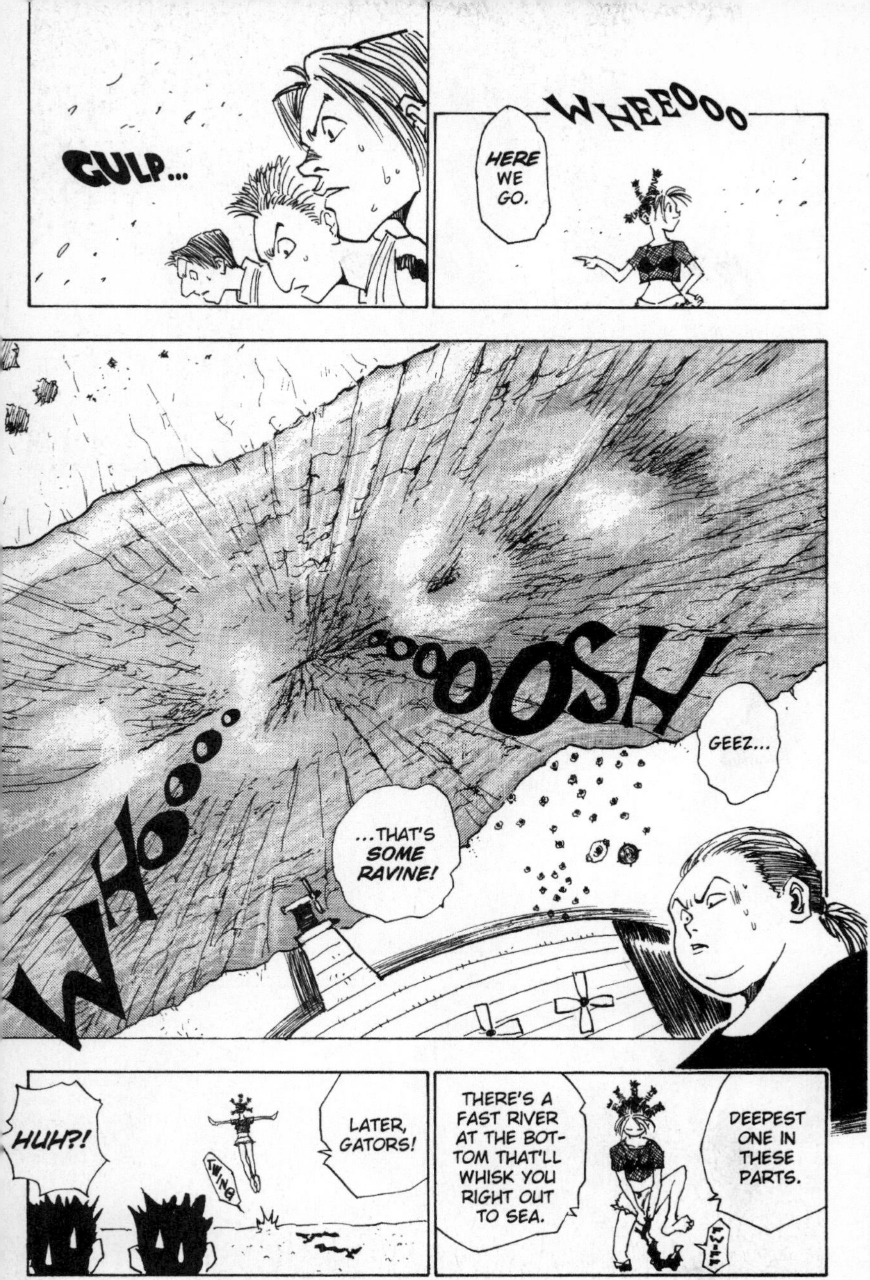

WHEEOOO
HERE WE GO.
GULP...
GEEZ...
...THAT'S SOME RAVINE!
WHOOOOOOOSH
DEEPEST ONE IN THESE PARTS.
THERE'S A FAST RIVER AT THE BOT-TOM THAT'LL WHISK YOU RIGHT OUT TO SEA.
FWIFF
LATER, GATORS!
TWING
HUH?!

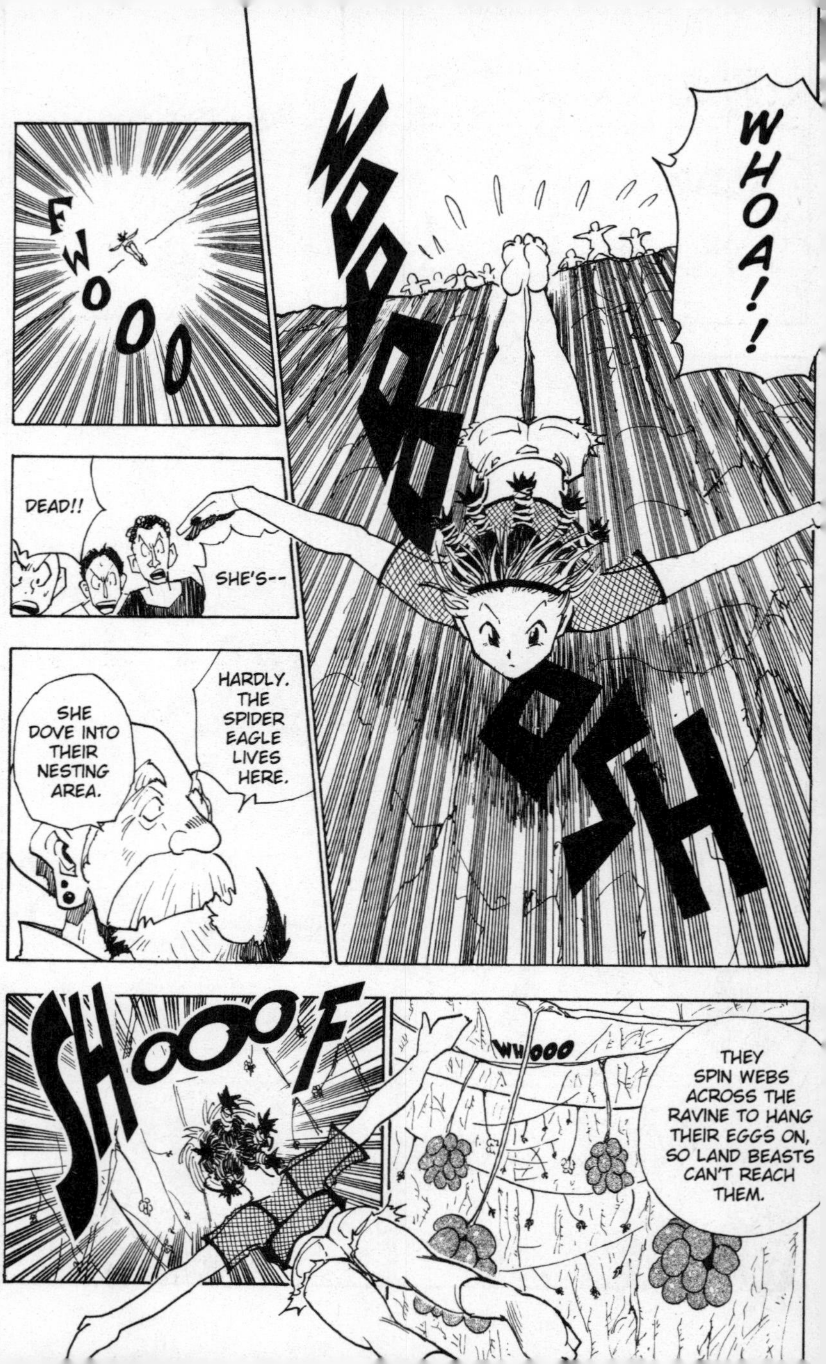
WHOA!!
WOOOSH
FWOOOO
SHE'S--
DEAD!!
HARDLY. THE SPIDER EAGLE LIVES HERE.
SHE DOVE INTO THEIR NESTING AREA.
WHOOO
THEY SPIN WEBS ACROSS THE RAVINE TO HANG THEIR EGGS ON, SO LAND BEASTS CAN'T REACH THEM.
SHOOOF

READ THIS WAY

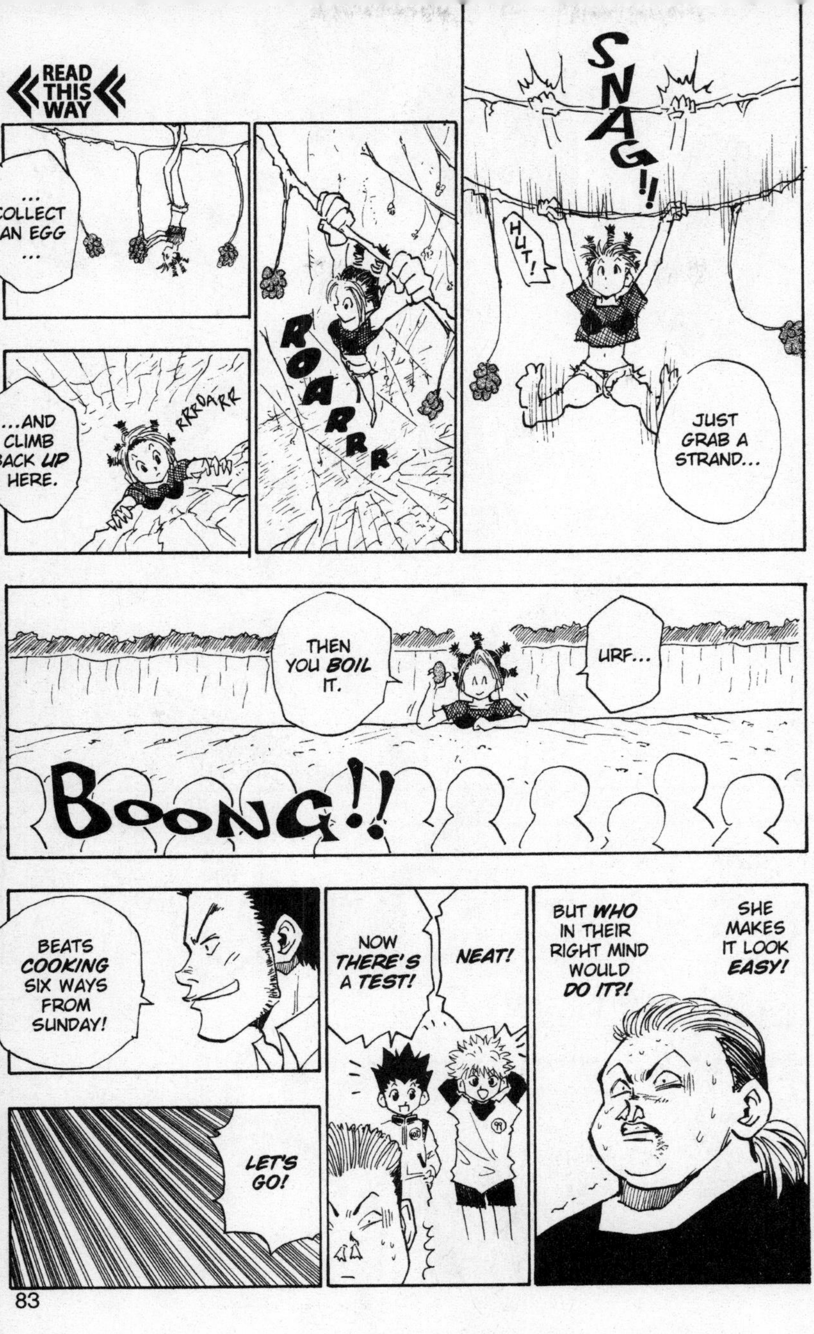

SNAG!!
HUT!
JUST GRAB A STRAND...
ROARRRR
...COLLECT AN EGG...
...AND CLIMB BACK UP HERE.
RRRDARR
URF...
THEN YOU BOIL IT.
BOONG!!
SHE MAKES IT LOOK EASY!
BUT WHO IN THEIR RIGHT MIND WOULD DO IT?!
NEAT!
NOW THERE'S A TEST!
BEATS COOKING SIX WAYS FROM SUNDAY!
LET'S GO!

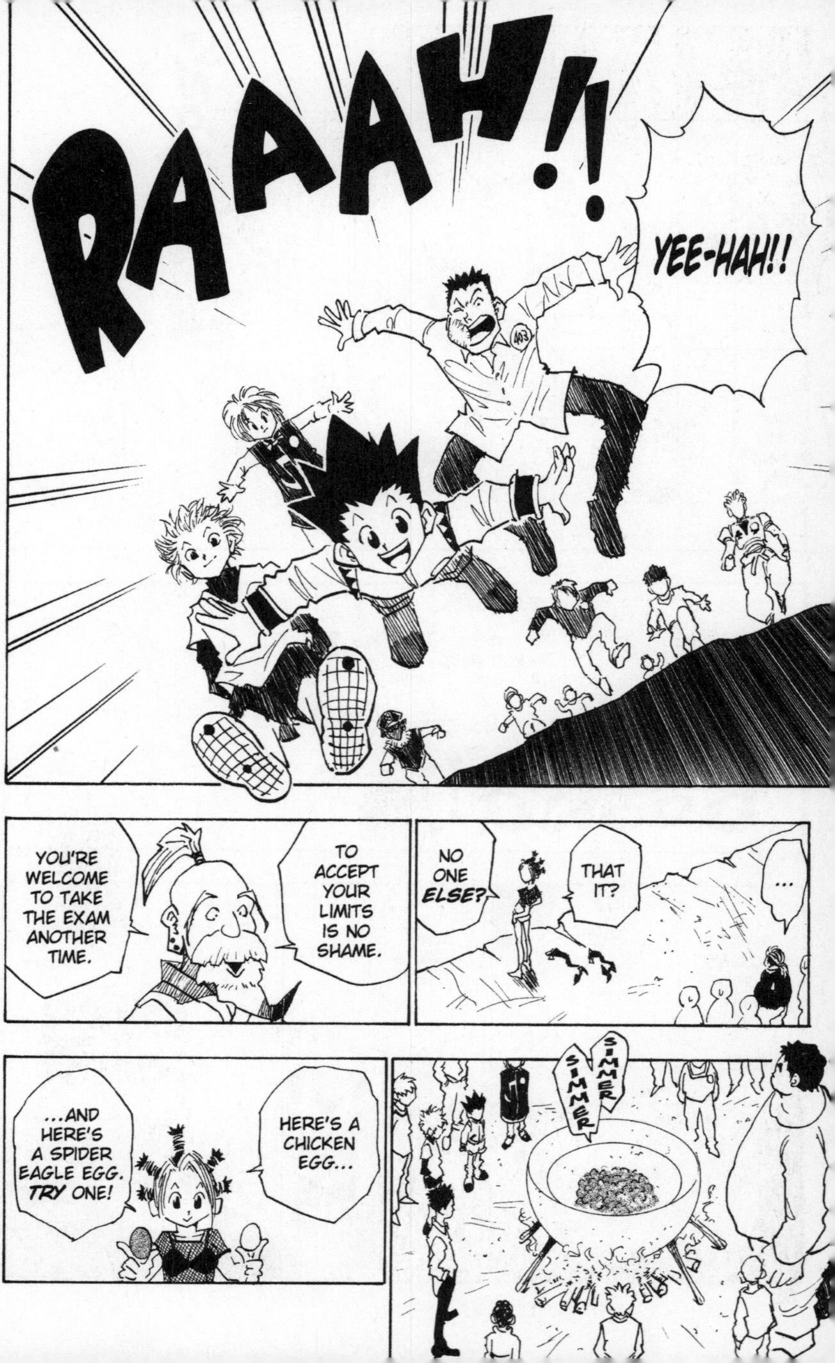
RAAAH!!
YEE-HAH!!
...
THAT IT?
NO ONE *ELSE*?
TO ACCEPT YOUR LIMITS IS NO SHAME.
YOU'RE WELCOME TO TAKE THE EXAM ANOTHER TIME.
SIMMER SIMMER
HERE'S A CHICKEN EGG...
...AND HERE'S A SPIDER EAGLE EGG. *TRY* ONE!

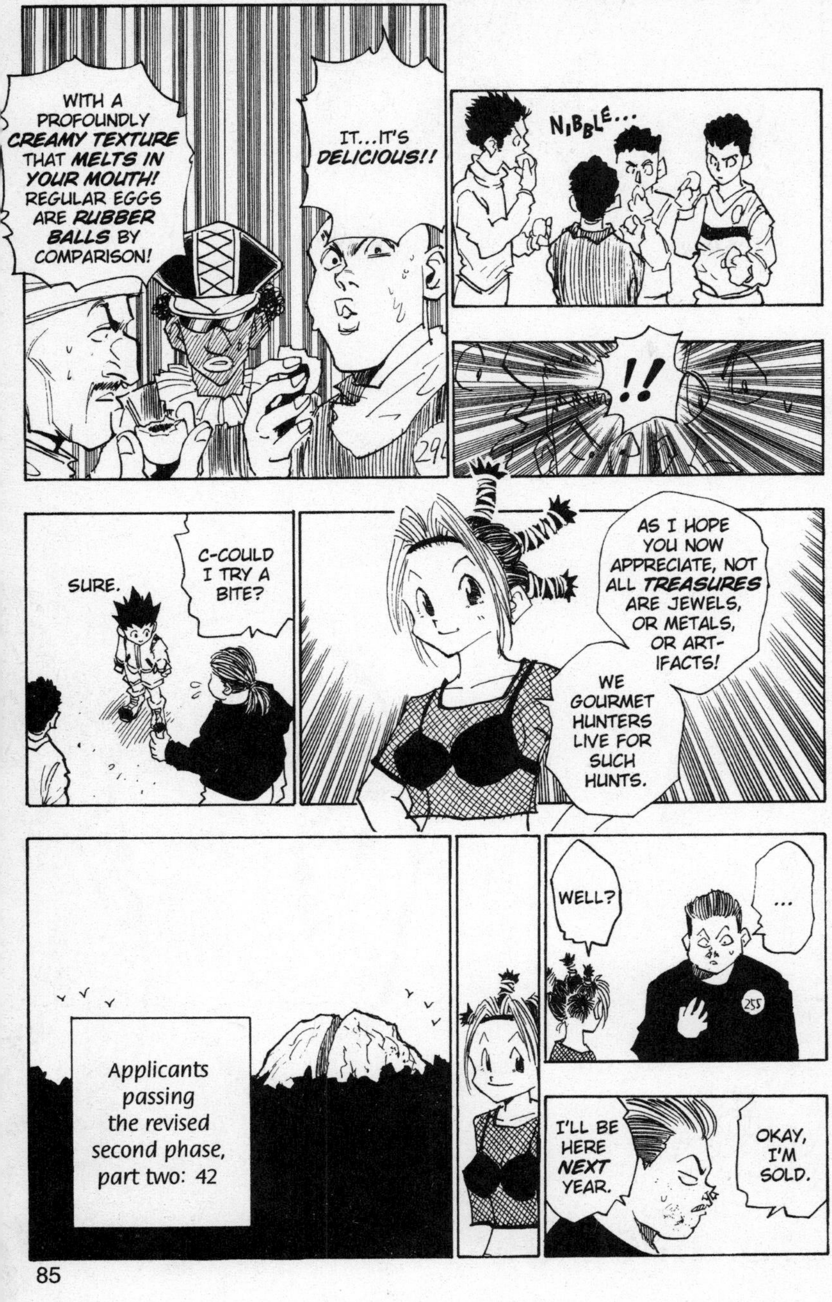
NIBBLE...
!!
IT...IT'S DELICIOUS!!
WITH A PROFOUNDLY CREAMY TEXTURE THAT MELTS IN YOUR MOUTH! REGULAR EGGS ARE RUBBER BALLS BY COMPARISON!
AS I HOPE YOU NOW APPRECIATE, NOT ALL TREASURES ARE JEWELS, OR METALS, OR ARTIFACTS!
WE GOURMET HUNTERS LIVE FOR SUCH HUNTS.
C-COULD I TRY A BITE?
SURE.
...
WELL?
OKAY, I'M SOLD.
I'LL BE HERE NEXT YEAR.
Applicants passing the revised second phase, part two: 42

Hanzo

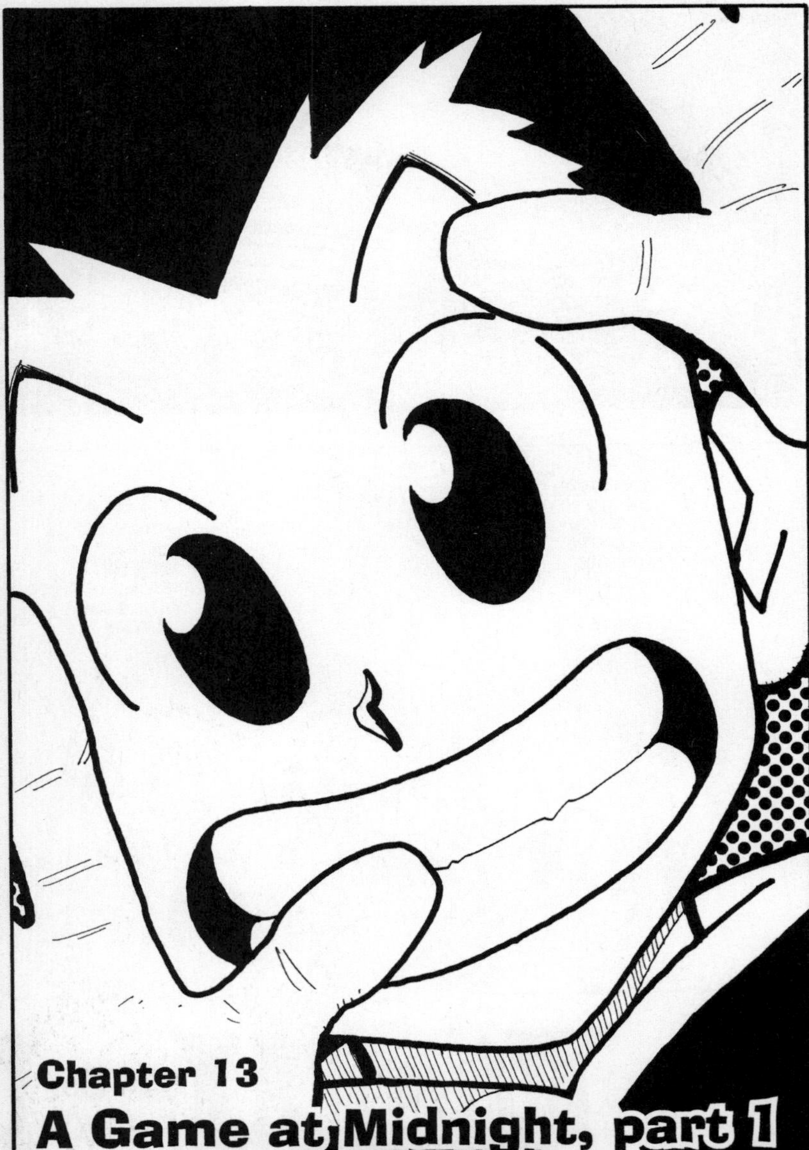

Chapter 13
A Game at Midnight, part 1

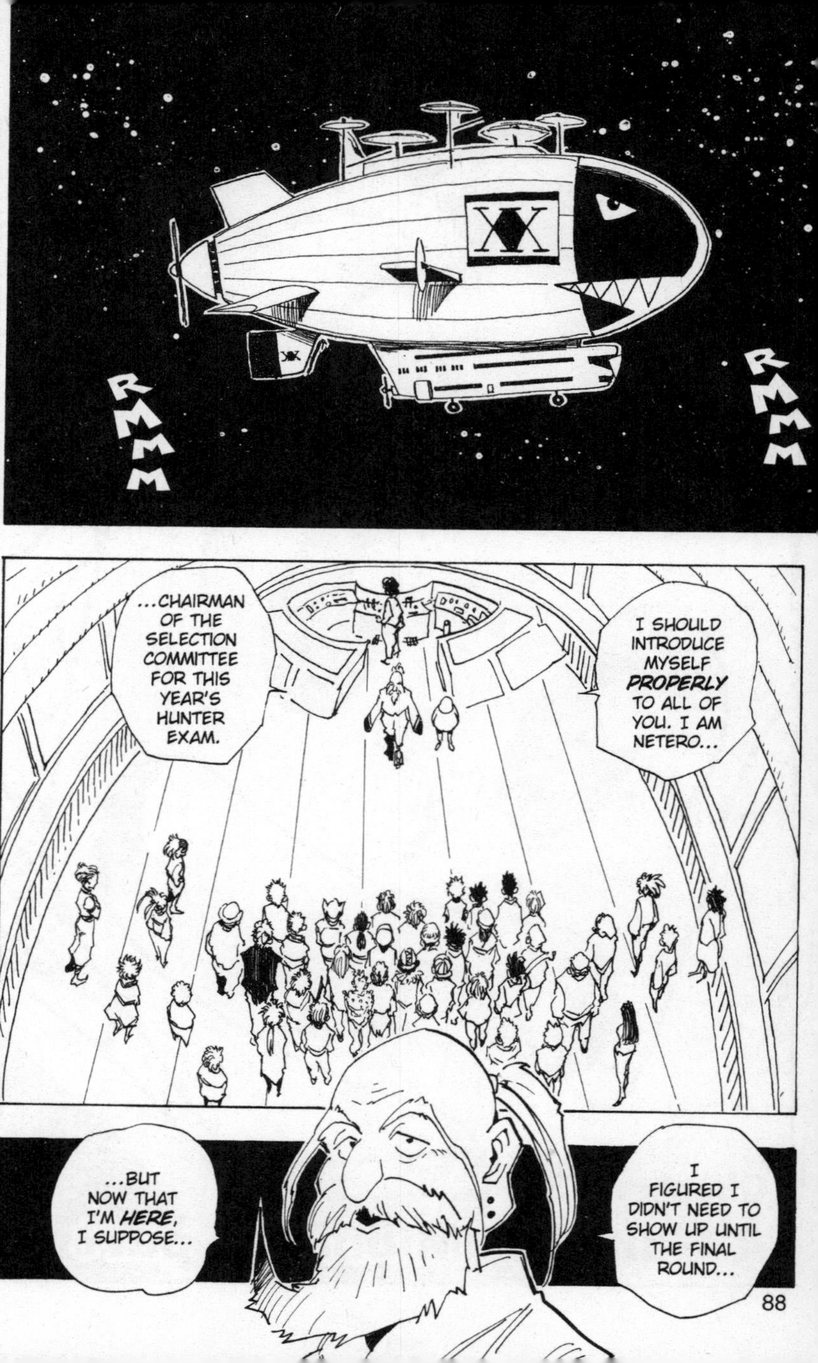
RMMM
RMMM
I SHOULD INTRODUCE MYSELF **PROPERLY** TO ALL OF YOU. I AM NETERO...
...CHAIRMAN OF THE SELECTION COMMITTEE FOR THIS YEAR'S HUNTER EXAM.
I FIGURED I DIDN'T NEED TO SHOW UP UNTIL THE FINAL ROUND...
...BUT NOW THAT I'M **HERE**, I SUPPOSE...

READ THIS WAY

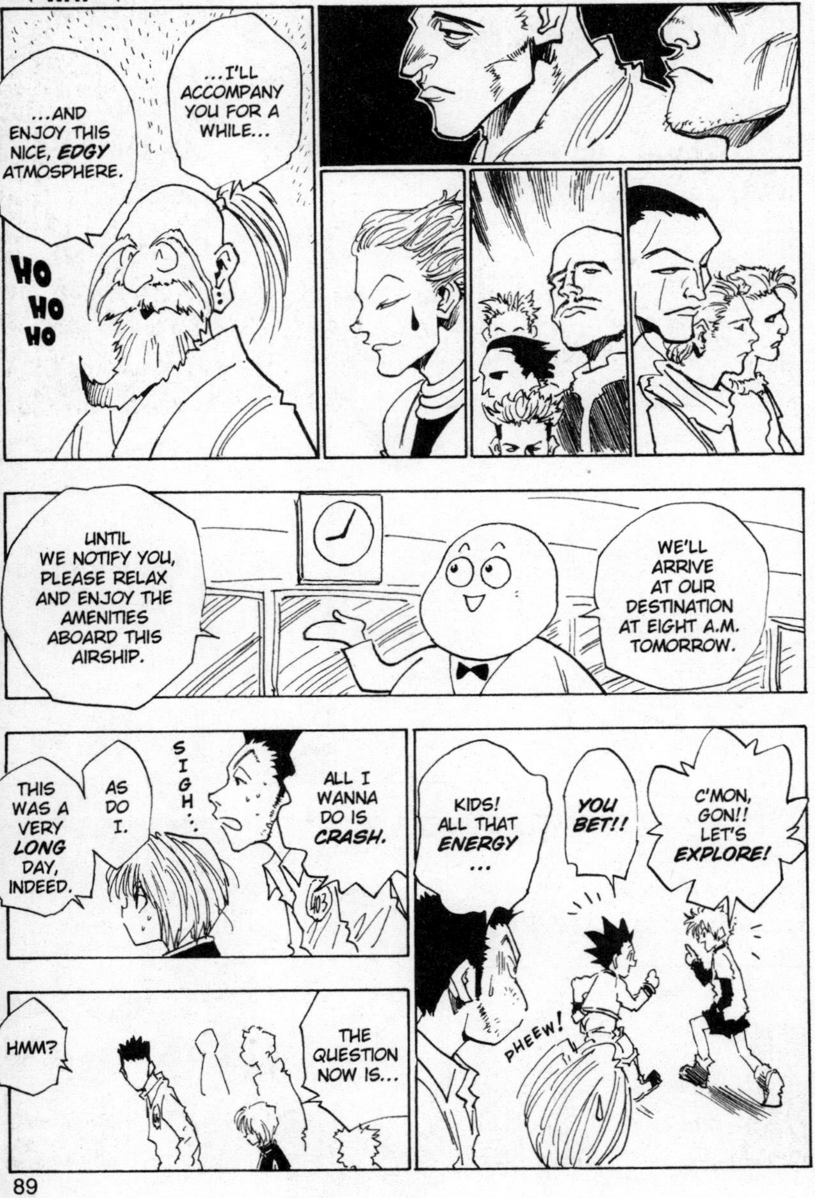
...I'LL ACCOMPANY YOU FOR A WHILE...
...AND ENJOY THIS NICE, EDGY ATMOSPHERE.
HO HO HO
WE'LL ARRIVE AT OUR DESTINATION AT EIGHT A.M. TOMORROW.
UNTIL WE NOTIFY YOU, PLEASE RELAX AND ENJOY THE AMENITIES ABOARD THIS AIRSHIP.
C'MON, GON!! LET'S EXPLORE!
YOU BET!!
KIDS! ALL THAT ENERGY ...
PHEEW!
ALL I WANNA DO IS CRASH.
SIGH...
AS DO I.
THIS WAS A VERY LONG DAY, INDEED.
THE QUESTION NOW IS...
HMM?

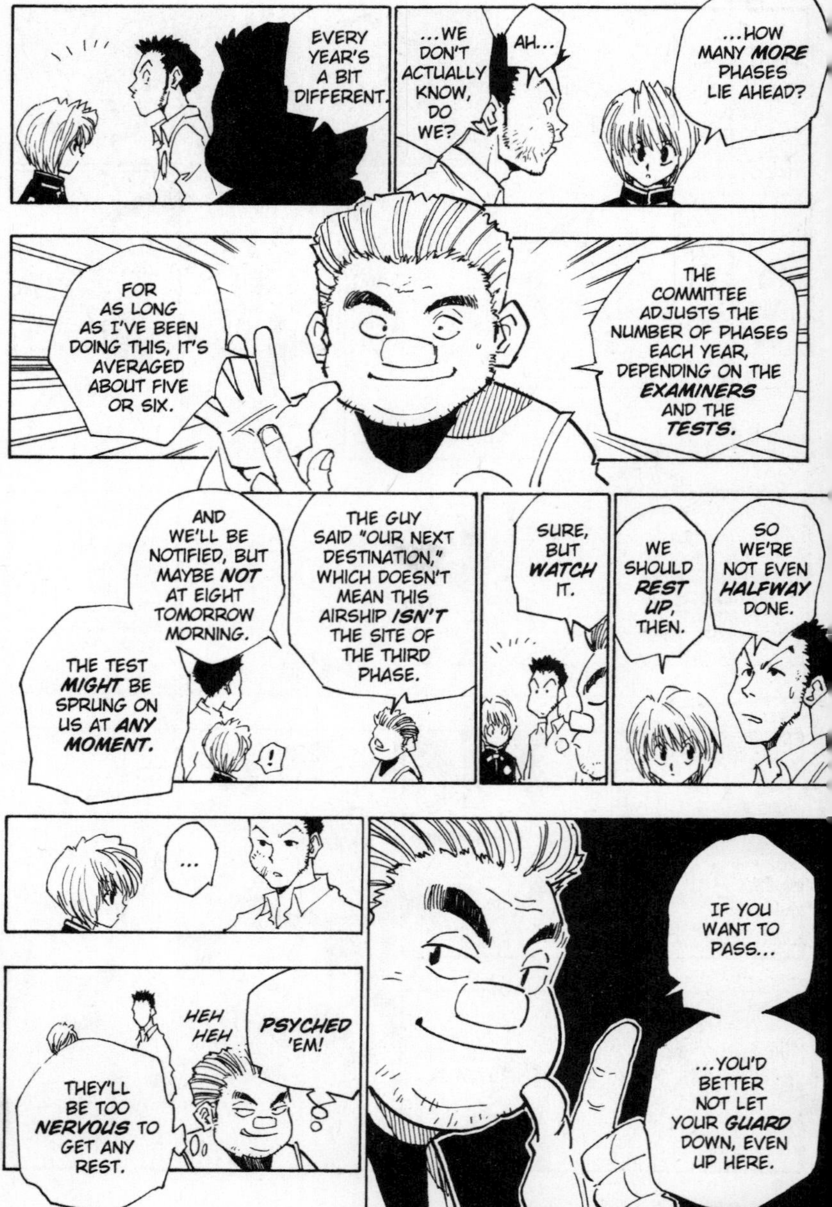
...HOW MANY MORE PHASES LIE AHEAD?
AH...
...WE DON'T ACTUALLY KNOW, DO WE?
EVERY YEAR'S A BIT DIFFERENT.
THE COMMITTEE ADJUSTS THE NUMBER OF PHASES EACH YEAR, DEPENDING ON THE EXAMINERS AND THE TESTS.
FOR AS LONG AS I'VE BEEN DOING THIS, IT'S AVERAGED ABOUT FIVE OR SIX.
SO WE'RE NOT EVEN HALFWAY DONE.
WE SHOULD REST UP, THEN.
SURE, BUT WATCH IT.
THE GUY SAID "OUR NEXT DESTINATION," WHICH DOESN'T MEAN THIS AIRSHIP ISN'T THE SITE OF THE THIRD PHASE.
AND WE'LL BE NOTIFIED, BUT MAYBE NOT AT EIGHT TOMORROW MORNING.
THE TEST MIGHT BE SPRUNG ON US AT ANY MOMENT.
!
IF YOU WANT TO PASS...
...YOU'D BETTER NOT LET YOUR GUARD DOWN, EVEN UP HERE.
...
PSYCHED 'EM!
HEH HEH
THEY'LL BE TOO NERVOUS TO GET ANY REST.

READ THIS WAY

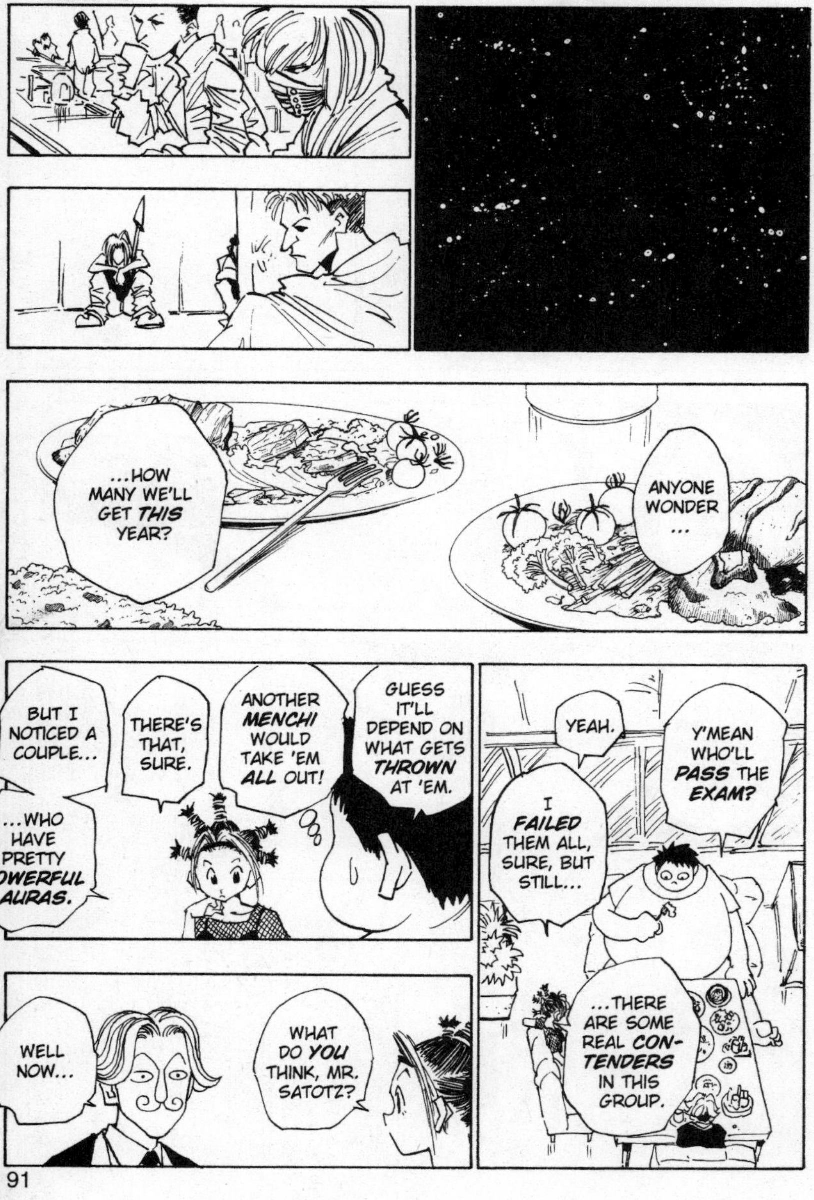

ANYONE WONDER ...
...HOW MANY WE'LL GET *THIS* YEAR?
Y'MEAN WHO'LL *PASS* THE *EXAM?*
YEAH.
I *FAILED* THEM ALL, SURE, BUT STILL...
...THERE ARE SOME REAL *CONTENDERS* IN THIS GROUP.
GUESS IT'LL DEPEND ON WHAT GETS *THROWN* AT 'EM.
ANOTHER *MENCHI* WOULD TAKE 'EM *ALL* OUT!
THERE'S THAT, SURE.
BUT I NOTICED A COUPLE...
...WHO HAVE PRETTY *POWERFUL AURAS.*
WHAT DO *YOU* THINK, MR. SATOTZ?
WELL NOW...

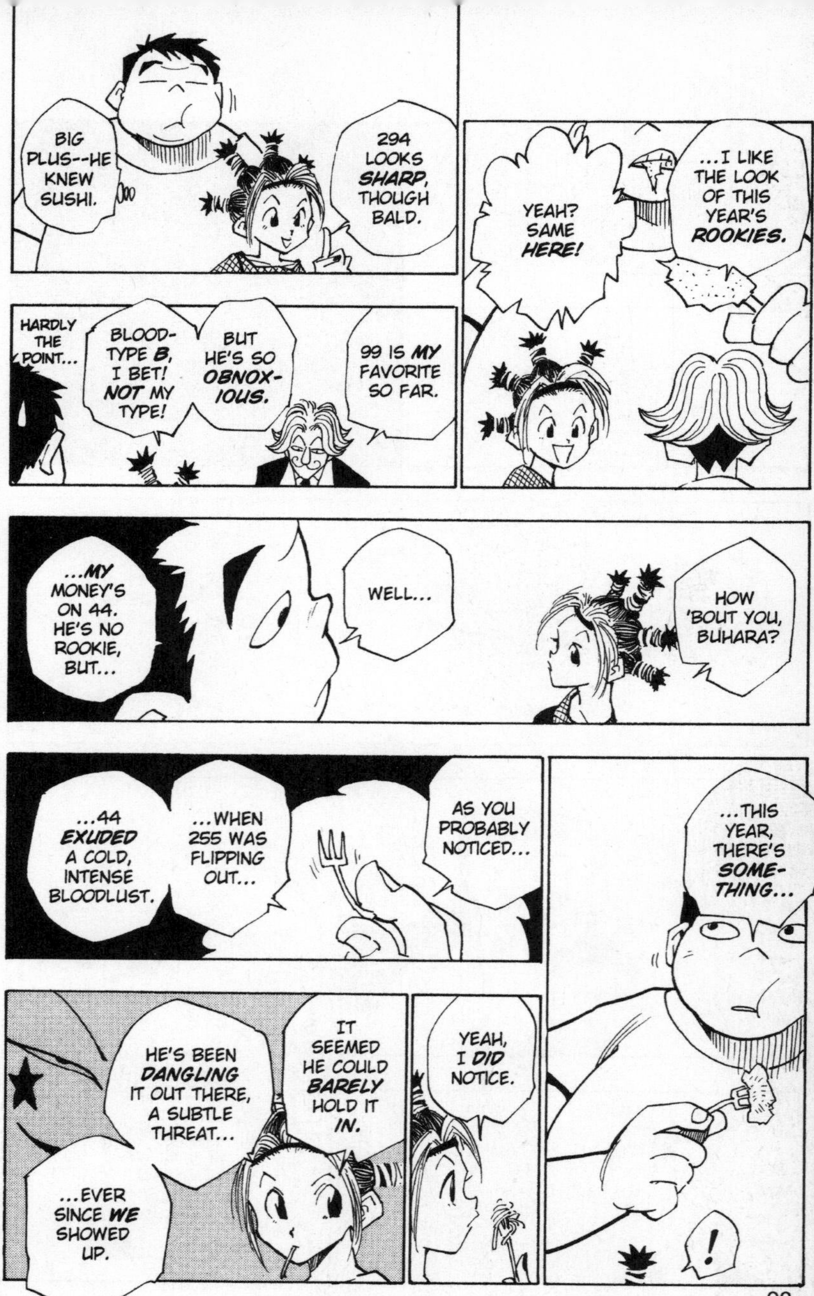
...I LIKE THE LOOK OF THIS YEAR'S ROOKIES.
YEAH? SAME HERE!
294 LOOKS SHARP, THOUGH BALD.
BIG PLUS--HE KNEW SUSHI.
99 IS MY FAVORITE SO FAR.
BUT HE'S SO OBNOXIOUS.
BLOOD-TYPE B, I BET! NOT MY TYPE!
HARDLY THE POINT...
HOW 'BOUT YOU, BUHARA?
WELL...
...MY MONEY'S ON 44. HE'S NO ROOKIE, BUT...
...THIS YEAR, THERE'S SOMETHING...
!
AS YOU PROBABLY NOTICED...
...WHEN 255 WAS FLIPPING OUT...
...44 EXUDED A COLD, INTENSE BLOODLUST.
YEAH, I DID NOTICE.
IT SEEMED HE COULD BARELY HOLD IT IN.
HE'S BEEN DANGLING IT OUT THERE, A SUBTLE THREAT...
...EVER SINCE WE SHOWED UP.

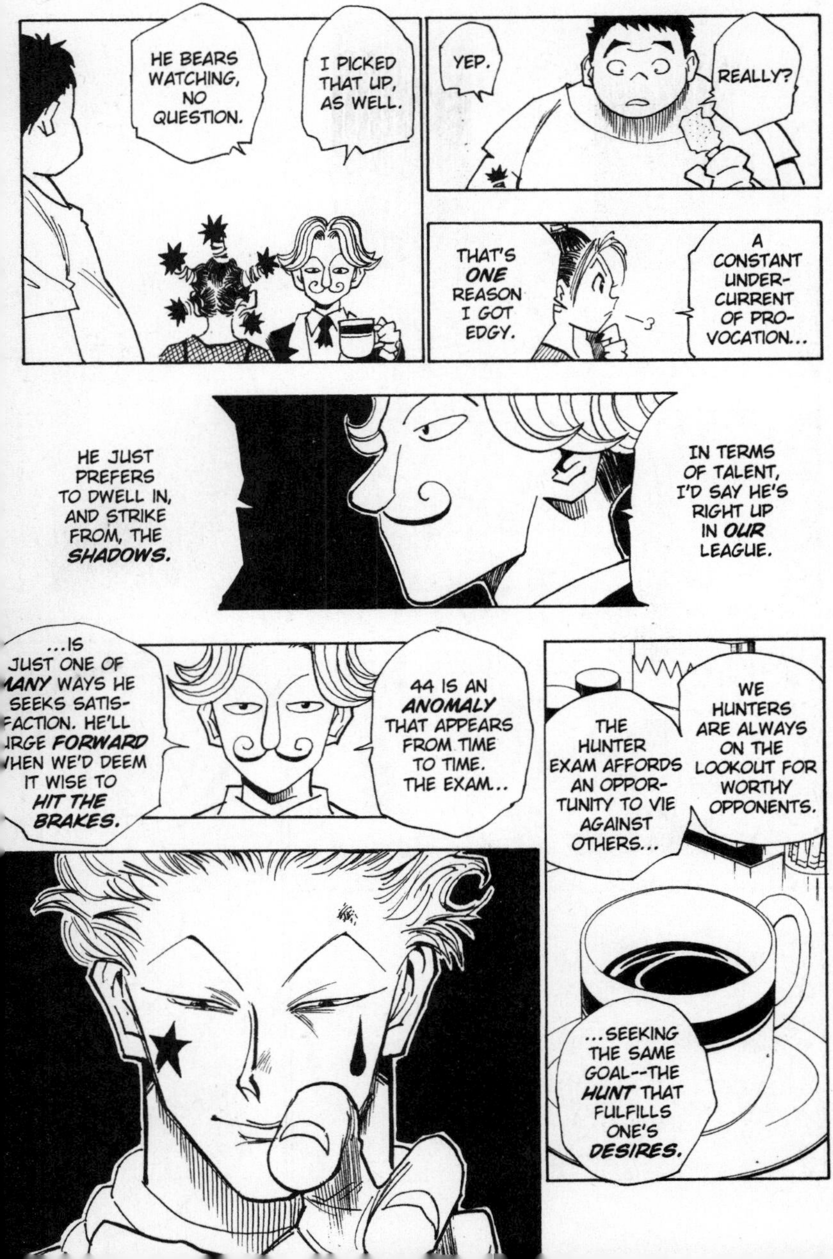
REALLY?
YEP.
A CONSTANT UNDER-CURRENT OF PRO-VOCATION...
THAT'S ONE REASON I GOT EDGY.
I PICKED THAT UP, AS WELL.
HE BEARS WATCHING, NO QUESTION.
IN TERMS OF TALENT, I'D SAY HE'S RIGHT UP IN OUR LEAGUE.
HE JUST PREFERS TO DWELL IN, AND STRIKE FROM, THE SHADOWS.
WE HUNTERS ARE ALWAYS ON THE LOOKOUT FOR WORTHY OPPONENTS.
THE HUNTER EXAM AFFORDS AN OPPOR-TUNITY TO VIE AGAINST OTHERS...
...SEEKING THE SAME GOAL--THE HUNT THAT FULFILLS ONE'S DESIRES.
44 IS AN ANOMALY THAT APPEARS FROM TIME TO TIME. THE EXAM...
...IS JUST ONE OF MANY WAYS HE SEEKS SATIS-FACTION. HE'LL URGE FORWARD WHEN WE'D DEEM IT WISE TO HIT THE BRAKES.

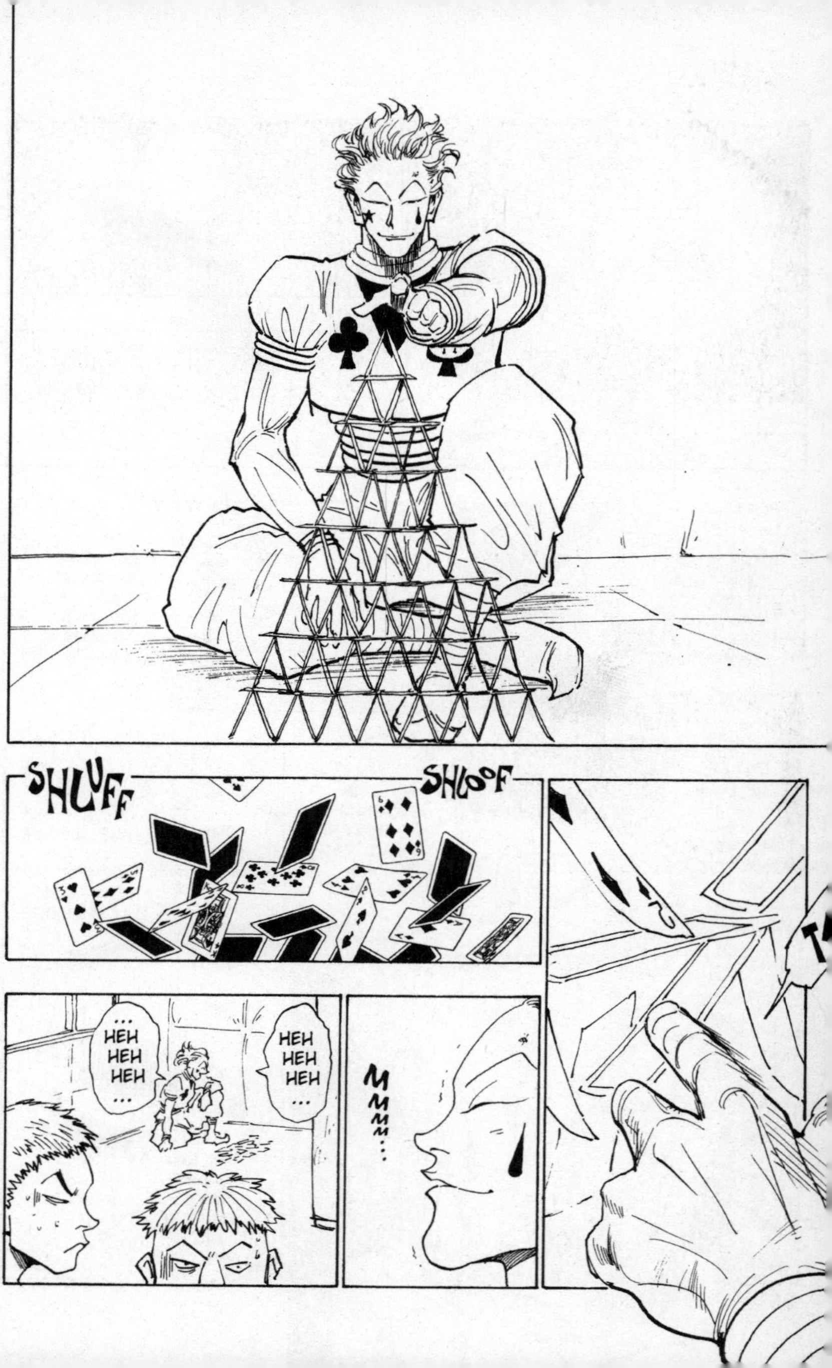
SHLOOF
SHLUFF
MMMM...
HEH HEH HEH ...
... HEH HEH HEH ...

READ THIS WAY

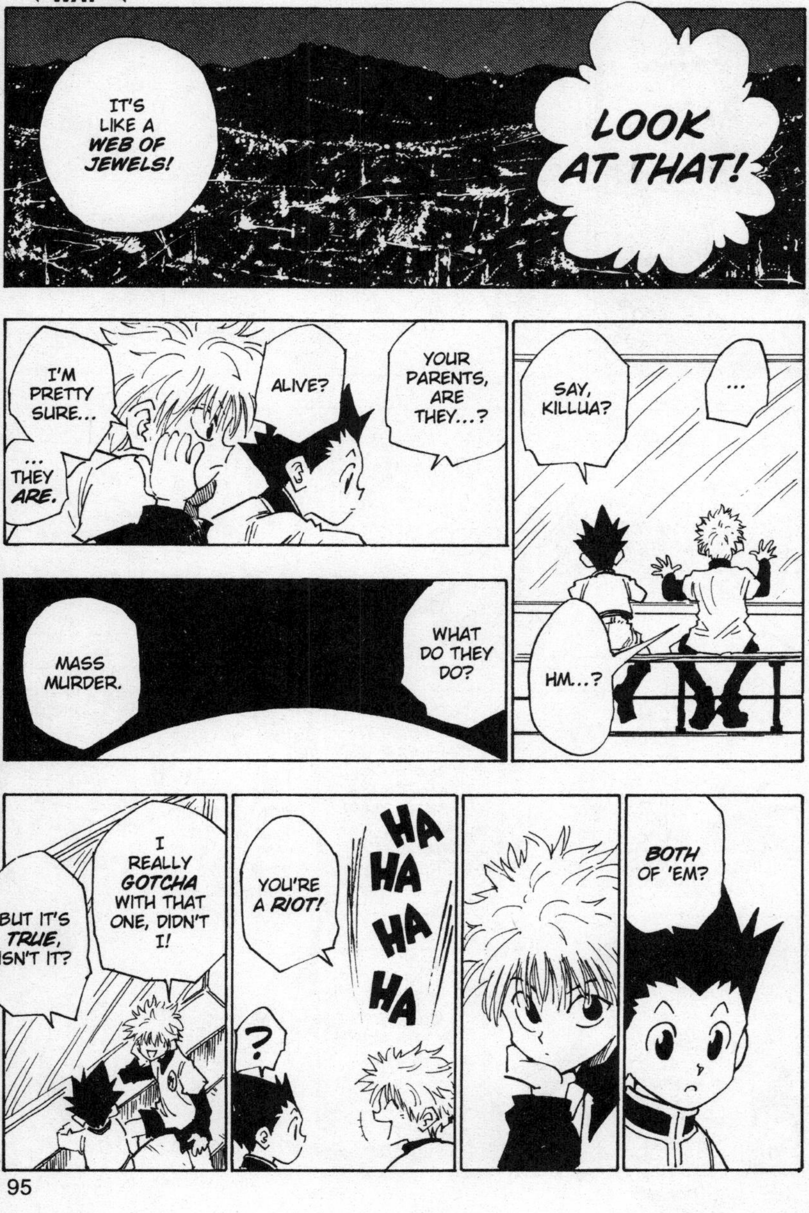
LOOK AT THAT!
IT'S LIKE A WEB OF JEWELS!
...
SAY, KILLUA?
HM...?
YOUR PARENTS, ARE THEY...?
ALIVE?
I'M PRETTY SURE...
...THEY ARE.
WHAT DO THEY DO?
MASS MURDER.
BOTH OF 'EM?
HA HA HA HA HA
YOU'RE A RIOT!
?
I REALLY GOTCHA WITH THAT ONE, DIDN'T I!
BUT IT'S TRUE, ISN'T IT?

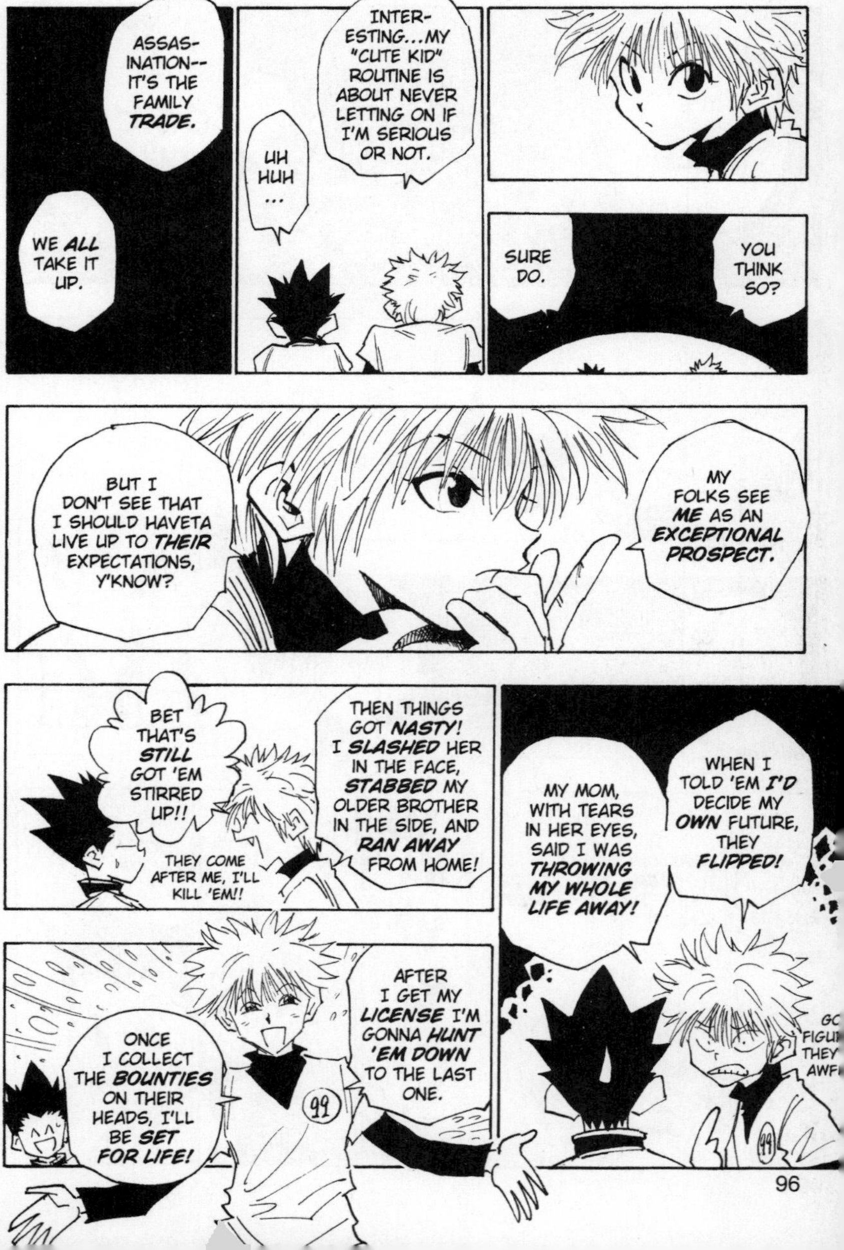
YOU THINK SO?
SURE DO.
INTER-ESTING... MY "CUTE KID" ROUTINE IS ABOUT NEVER LETTING ON IF I'M SERIOUS OR NOT.
UH HUH ...
ASSAS-INATION-- IT'S THE FAMILY TRADE.
WE ALL TAKE IT UP.
MY FOLKS SEE ME AS AN EXCEPTIONAL PROSPECT.
BUT I DON'T SEE THAT I SHOULD HAVETA LIVE UP TO THEIR EXPECTATIONS, Y'KNOW?
WHEN I TOLD 'EM I'D DECIDE MY OWN FUTURE, THEY FLIPPED!
MY MOM, WITH TEARS IN HER EYES, SAID I WAS THROWING MY WHOLE LIFE AWAY!
THEN THINGS GOT NASTY! I SLASHED HER IN THE FACE, STABBED MY OLDER BROTHER IN THE SIDE, AND RAN AWAY FROM HOME!
BET THAT'S STILL GOT 'EM STIRRED UP!!
THEY COME AFTER ME, I'LL KILL 'EM!!
AFTER I GET MY LICENSE I'M GONNA HUNT 'EM DOWN TO THE LAST ONE.
ONCE I COLLECT THE BOUNTIES ON THEIR HEADS, I'LL BE SET FOR LIFE!

READ THIS WAY

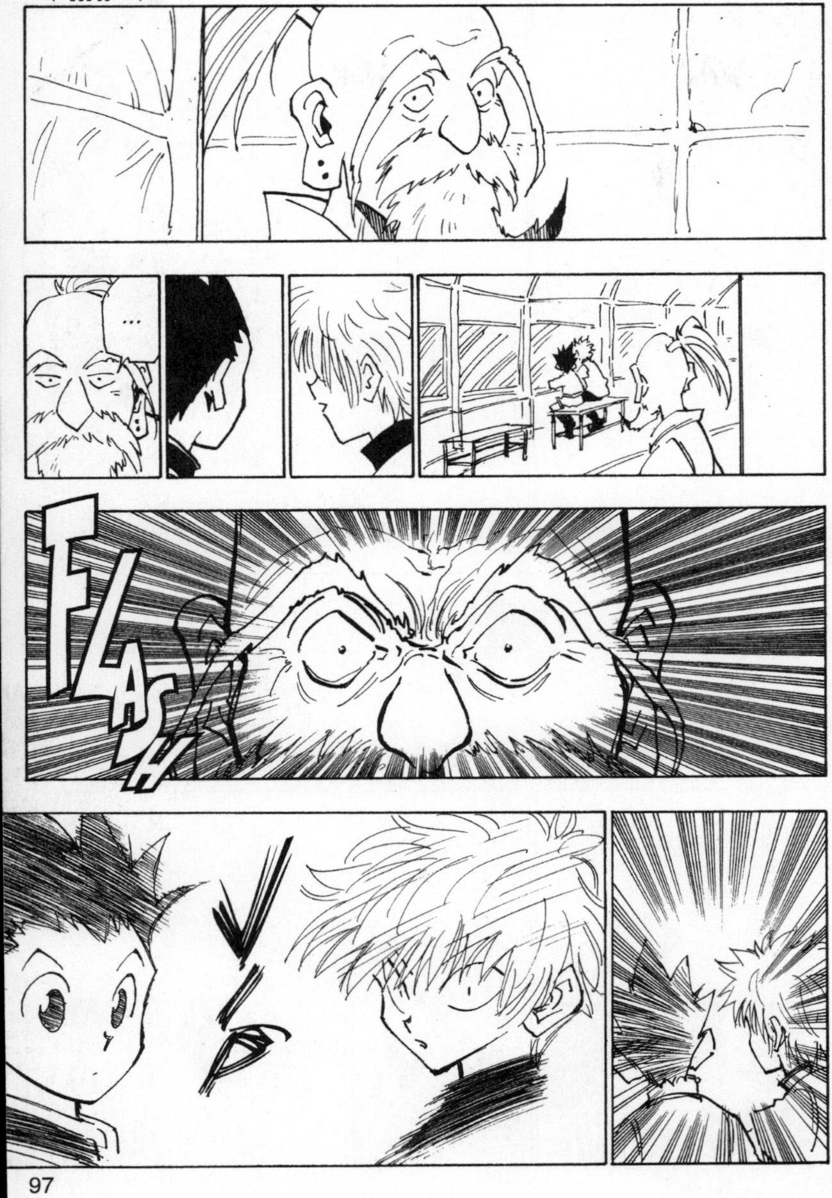
...
FLASH

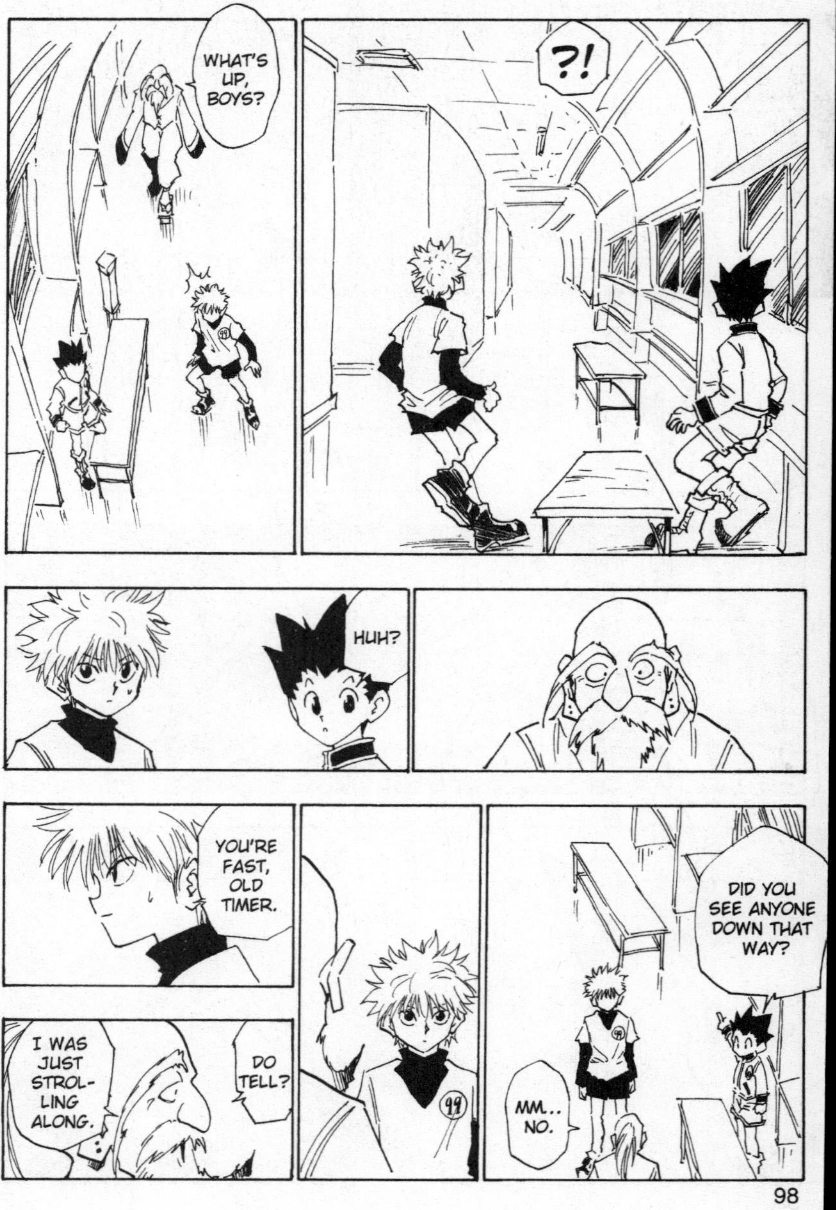
?!
WHAT'S UP, BOYS?
HUH?
DID YOU SEE ANYONE DOWN THAT WAY?
MM.. NO.
YOU'RE FAST, OLD TIMER.
DO TELL?
I WAS JUST STROL-LING ALONG.

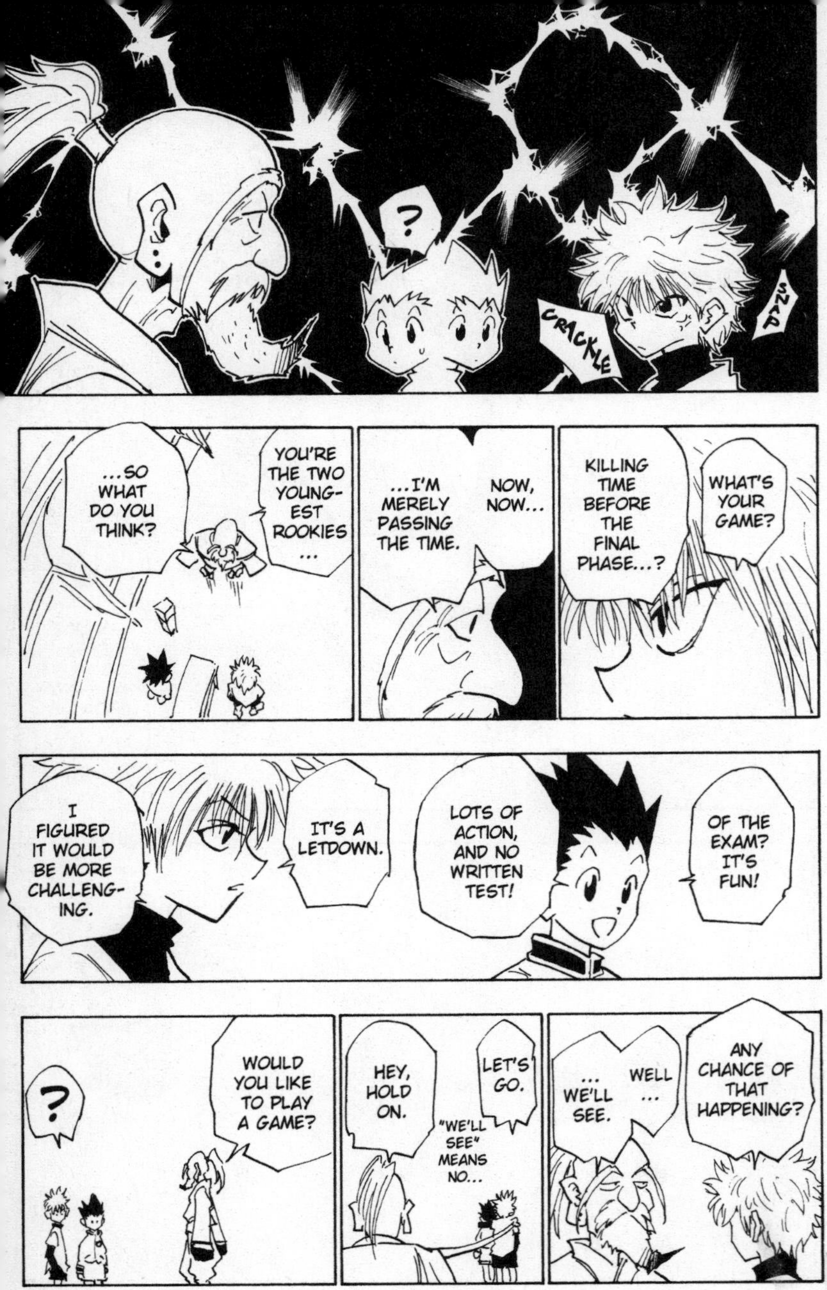
SNAP
CRACKLE
?
WHAT'S YOUR GAME?
KILLING TIME BEFORE THE FINAL PHASE...?
NOW, NOW...
...I'M MERELY PASSING THE TIME.
YOU'RE THE TWO YOUNG-EST ROOKIES...
...SO WHAT DO YOU THINK?
OF THE EXAM? IT'S FUN!
LOTS OF ACTION, AND NO WRITTEN TEST!
IT'S A LETDOWN.
I FIGURED IT WOULD BE MORE CHALLENG-ING.
ANY CHANCE OF THAT HAPPENING?
WELL...
...WE'LL SEE.
LET'S GO.
HEY, HOLD ON.
"WE'LL SEE" MEANS NO...
WOULD YOU LIKE TO PLAY A GAME?
?

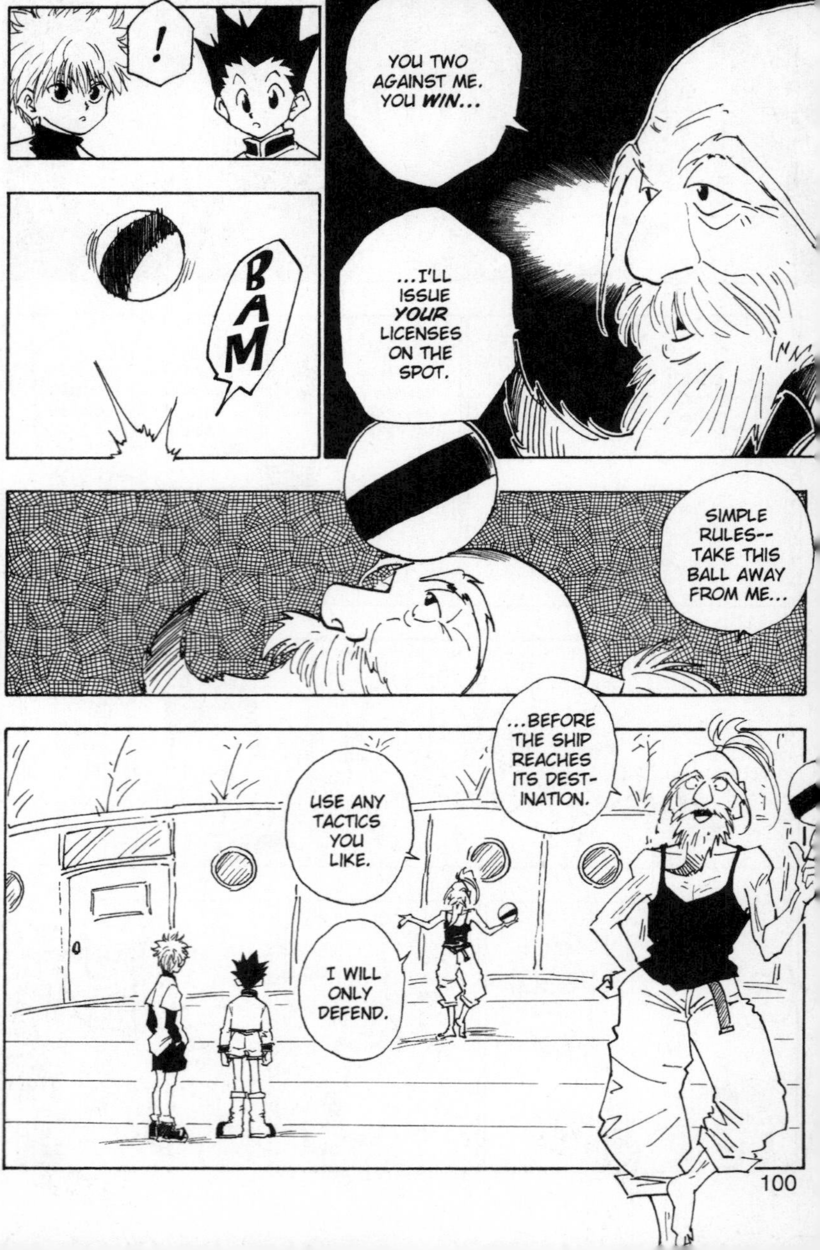
YOU TWO AGAINST ME. YOU WIN...
...I'LL ISSUE YOUR LICENSES ON THE SPOT.
!
BAM
SIMPLE RULES-- TAKE THIS BALL AWAY FROM ME...
...BEFORE THE SHIP REACHES ITS DEST-INATION.
USE ANY TACTICS YOU LIKE.
I WILL ONLY DEFEND.

READ THIS WAY

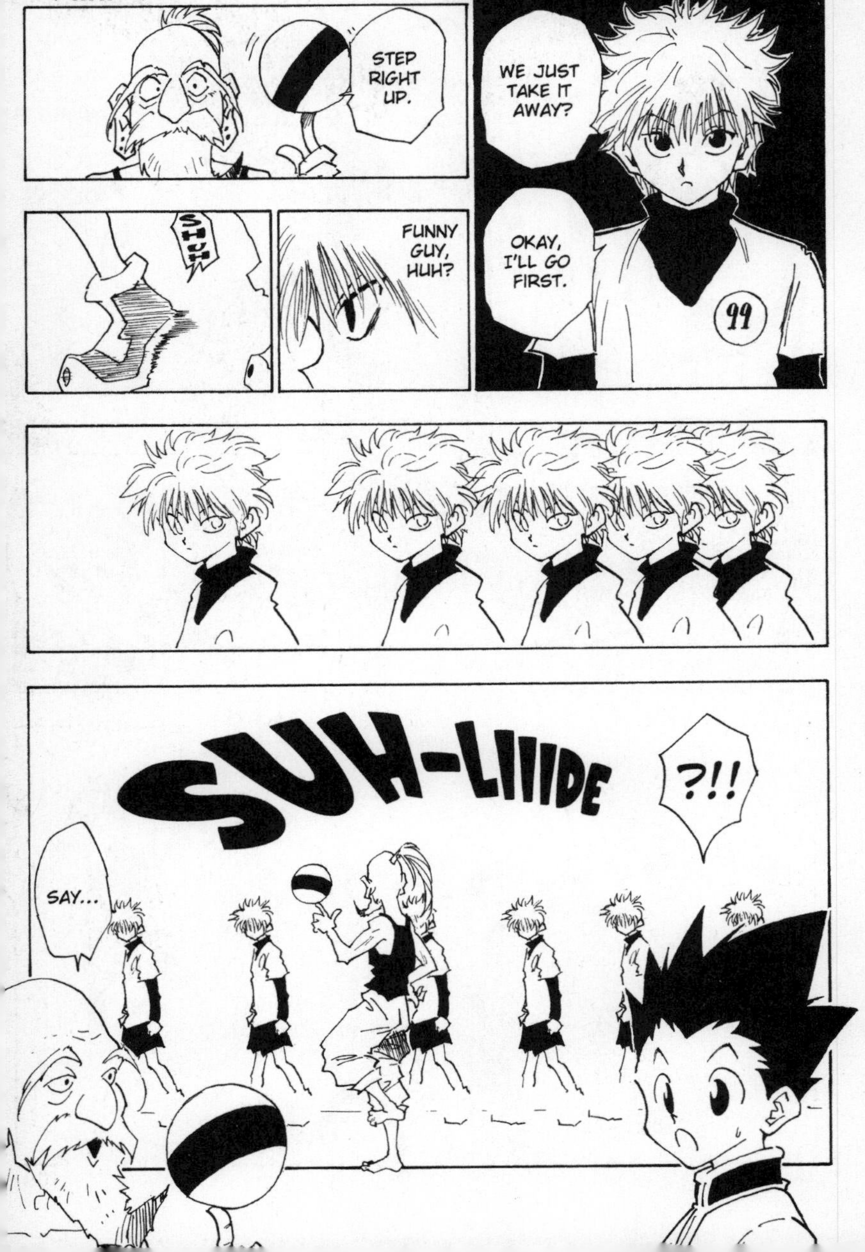
WE JUST TAKE IT AWAY?
OKAY, I'LL GO FIRST.
99
STEP RIGHT UP.
FUNNY GUY, HUH?
SHUH
?!!
SUH-LIIIDE
SAY...

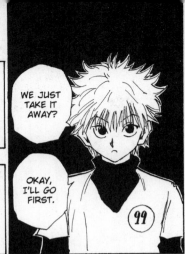

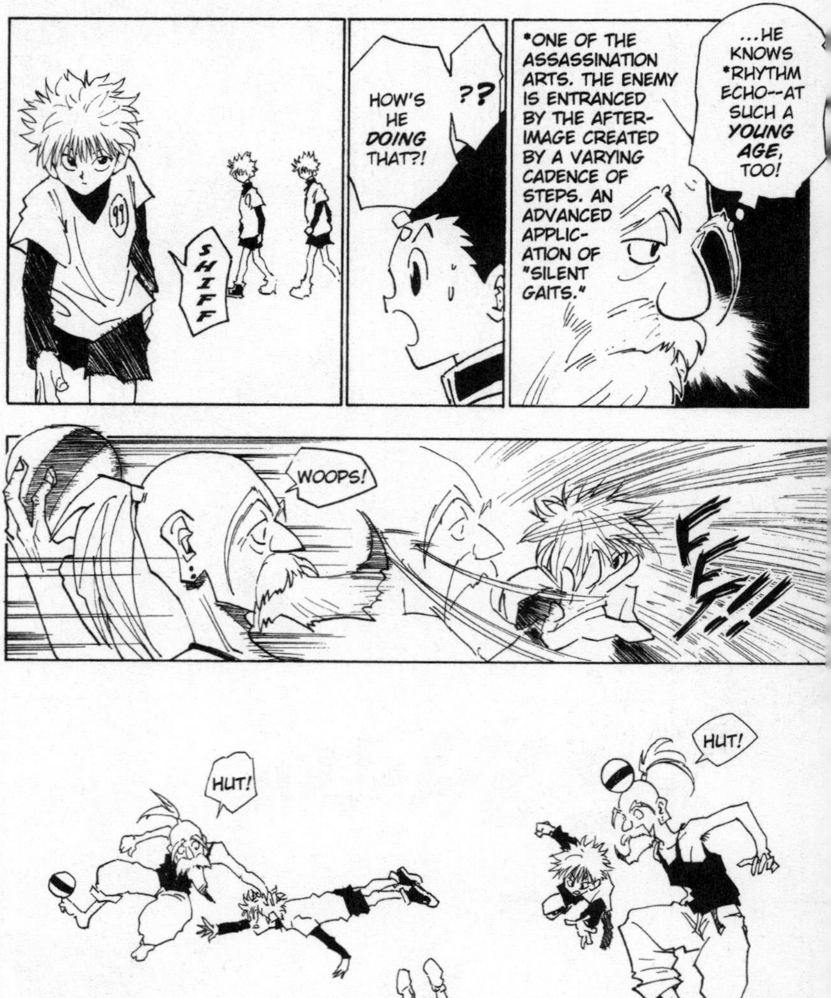
...HE KNOWS *RHYTHM ECHO--AT SUCH A YOUNG AGE, TOO!
*ONE OF THE ASSASSINATION ARTS. THE ENEMY IS ENTRANCED BY THE AFTER-IMAGE CREATED BY A VARYING CADENCE OF STEPS. AN ADVANCED APPLICATION OF "SILENT GAITS."
??
HOW'S HE DOING THAT?!
SHIFF
WOOPS!
HUT!
HUT!

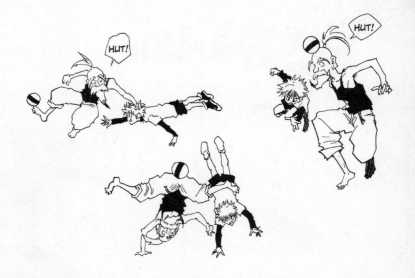

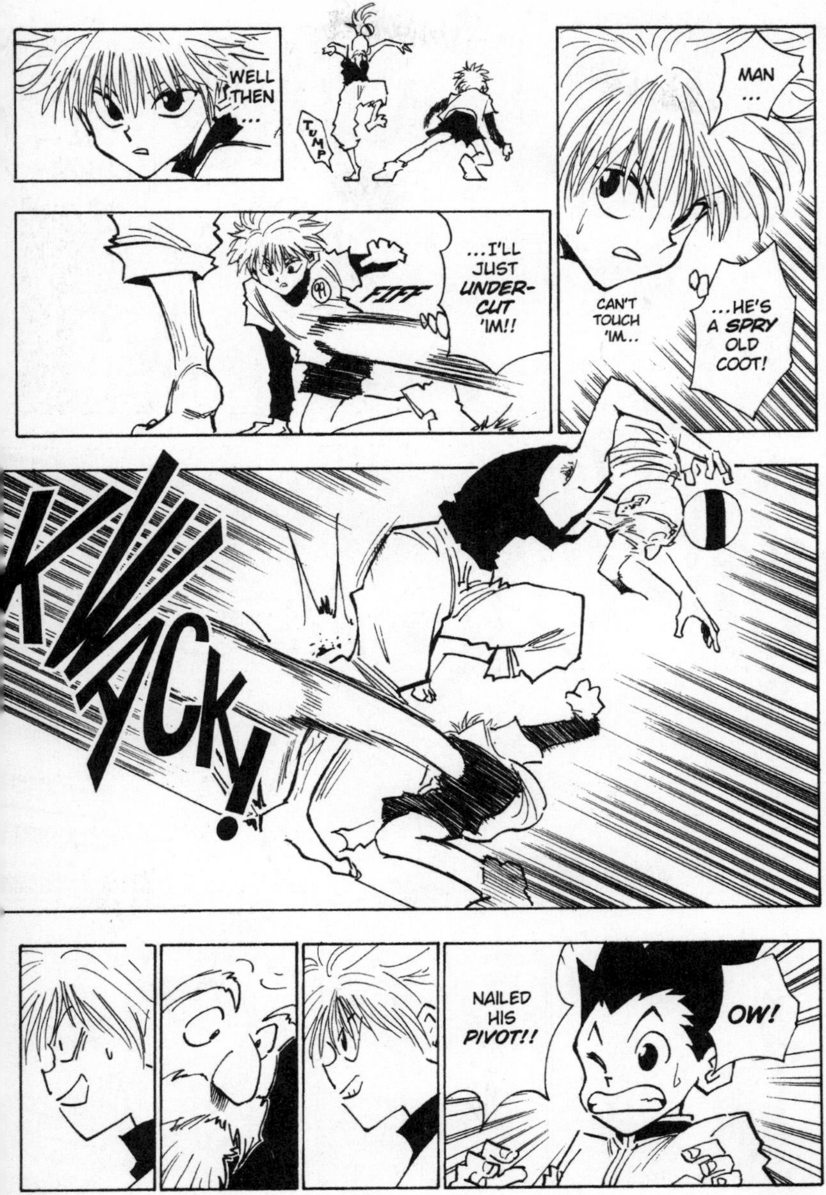
MAN ...
...HE'S A SPRY OLD COOT!
CAN'T TOUCH 'IM...
TUMP
WELL THEN ...
...I'LL JUST UNDER-CUT 'IM!!
FIFF
KWACK!
OW!
NAILED HIS PIVOT!!

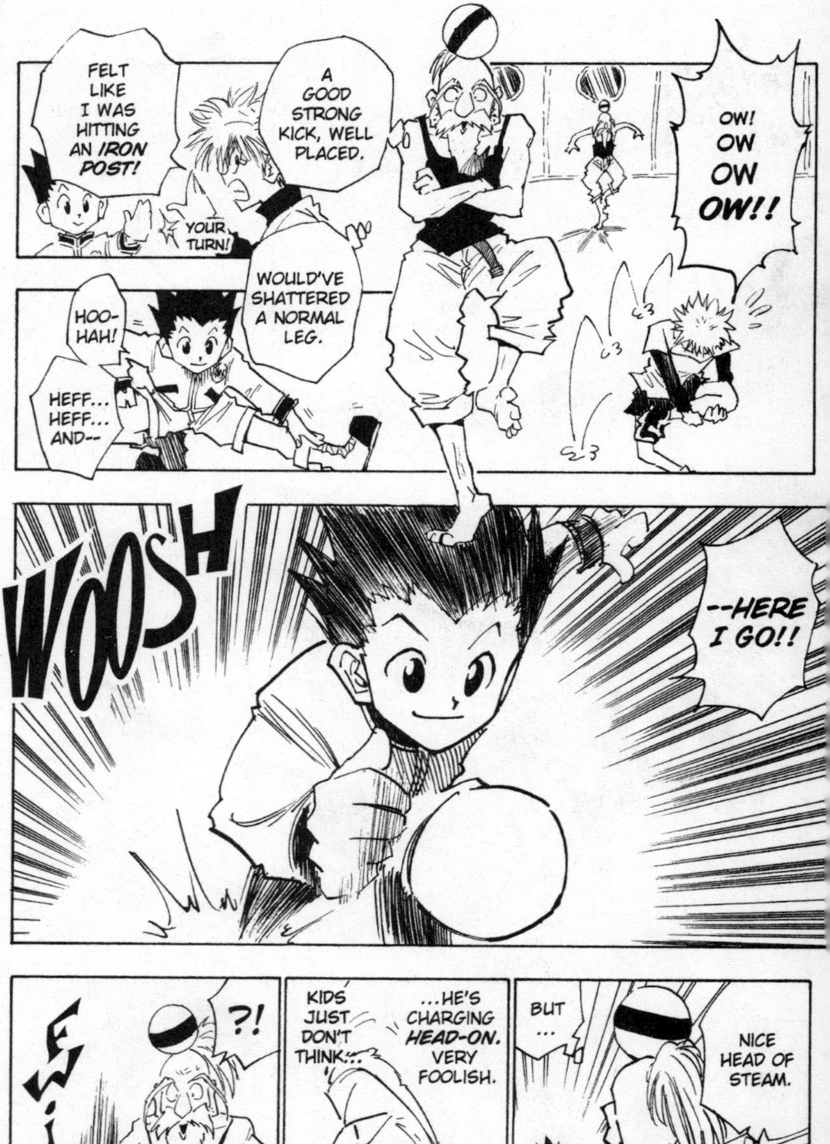
OW! OW OW OW!!
A GOOD STRONG KICK, WELL PLACED.
FELT LIKE I WAS HITTING AN *IRON POST!*
YOUR TURN!
WOULD'VE SHATTERED A NORMAL LEG.
HOO-HAH!
HEFF... HEFF... AND--
--HERE I GO!!
WOOSH
NICE HEAD OF STEAM.
BUT ...
...HE'S CHARGING *HEAD-ON.* VERY FOOLISH.
KIDS JUST DON'T THINK...
?!
FWIT

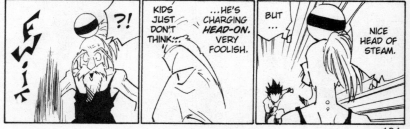

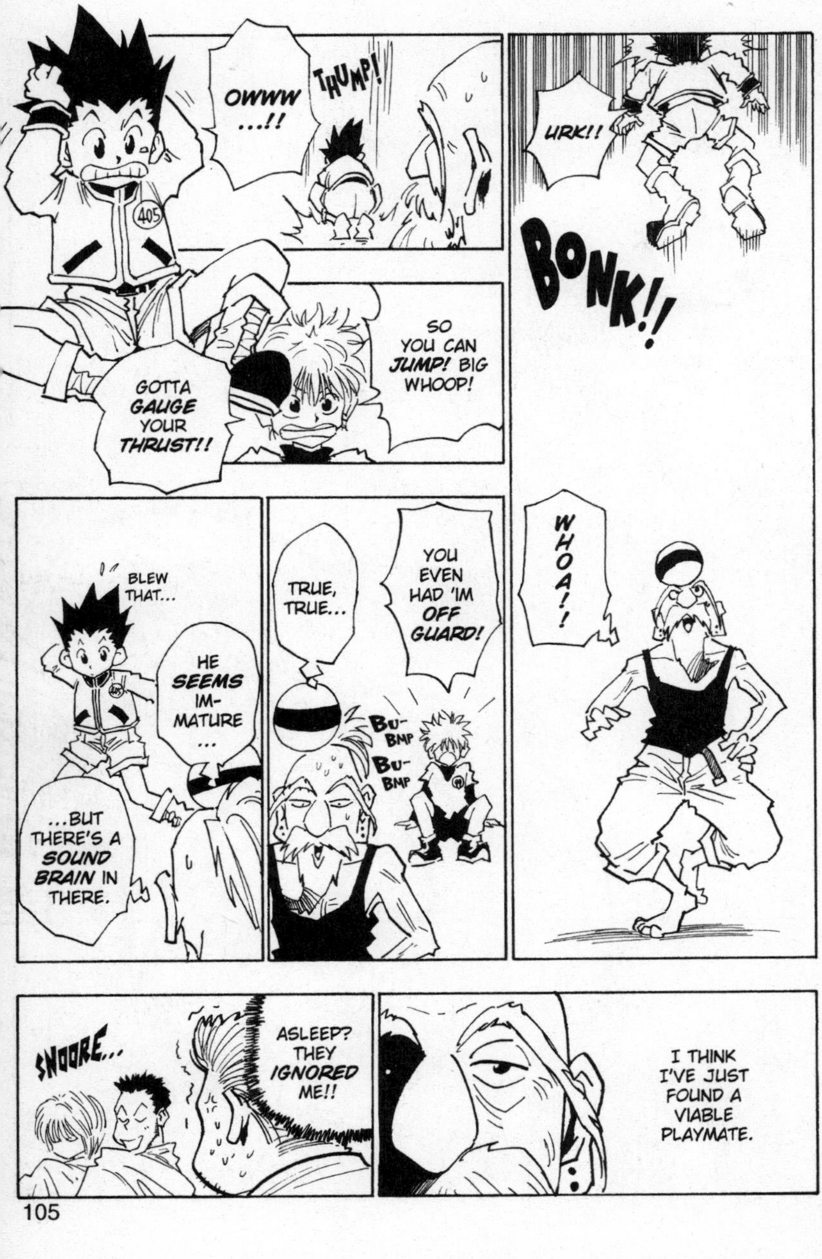
URK!!
BONK!!
WHOA!!
OWWW ...!!
THUMP!
SO YOU CAN JUMP! BIG WHOOP!
GOTTA GAUGE YOUR THRUST!!
YOU EVEN HAD 'IM OFF GUARD!
TRUE, TRUE...
BU-BMP
BU-BMP
BLEW THAT...
HE SEEMS IM-MATURE ...
...BUT THERE'S A SOUND BRAIN IN THERE.
I THINK I'VE JUST FOUND A VIABLE PLAYMATE.
ASLEEP? THEY IGNORED ME!!
SNOORE...

Netero

Chapter 14
A Game at Midnight, part 2

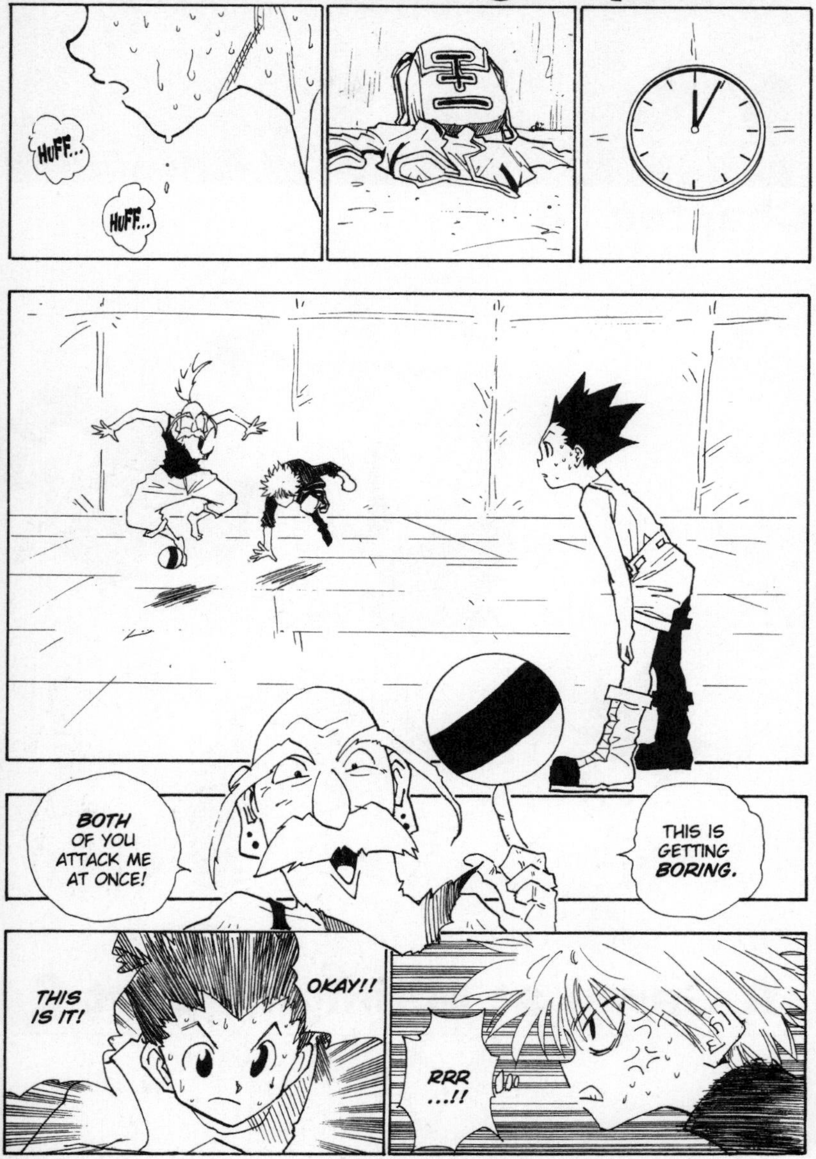
HUFF...
HUFF...
THIS IS GETTING BORING.
BOTH OF YOU ATTACK ME AT ONCE!
RRR ...!!
OKAY!!
THIS IS IT!

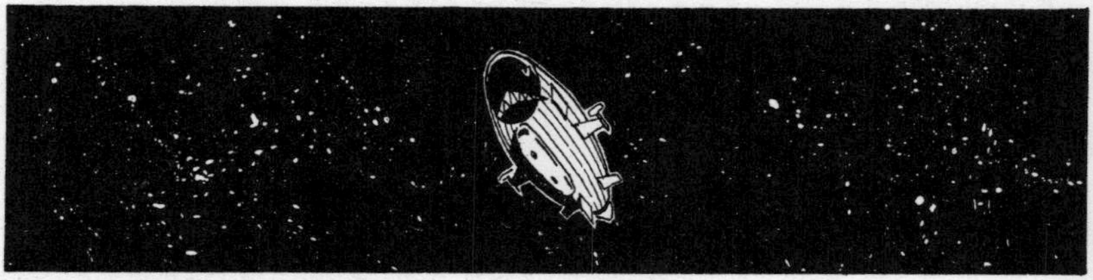

Chapter 14

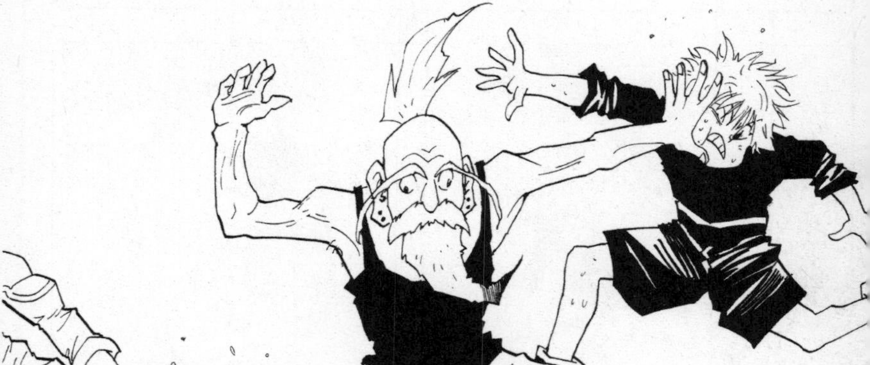

A Game at Midnight, part 2

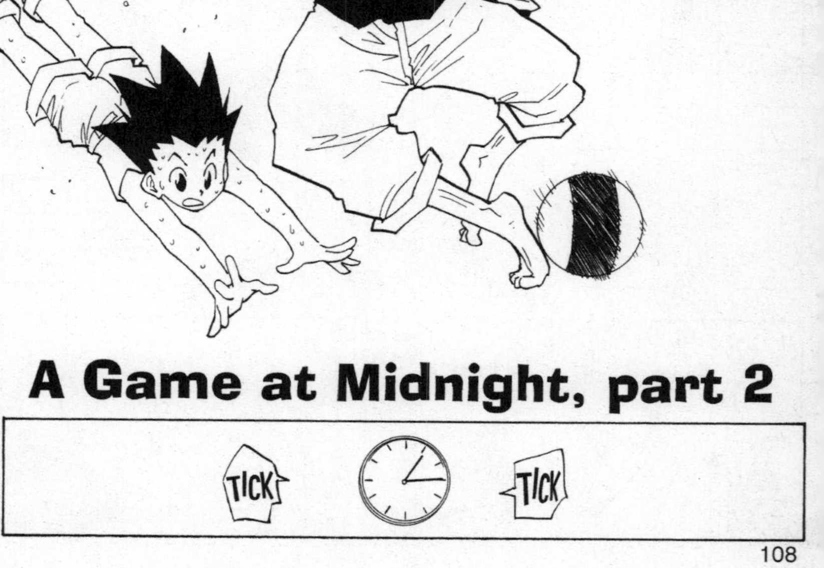
TICK
TICK

READ THIS WAY

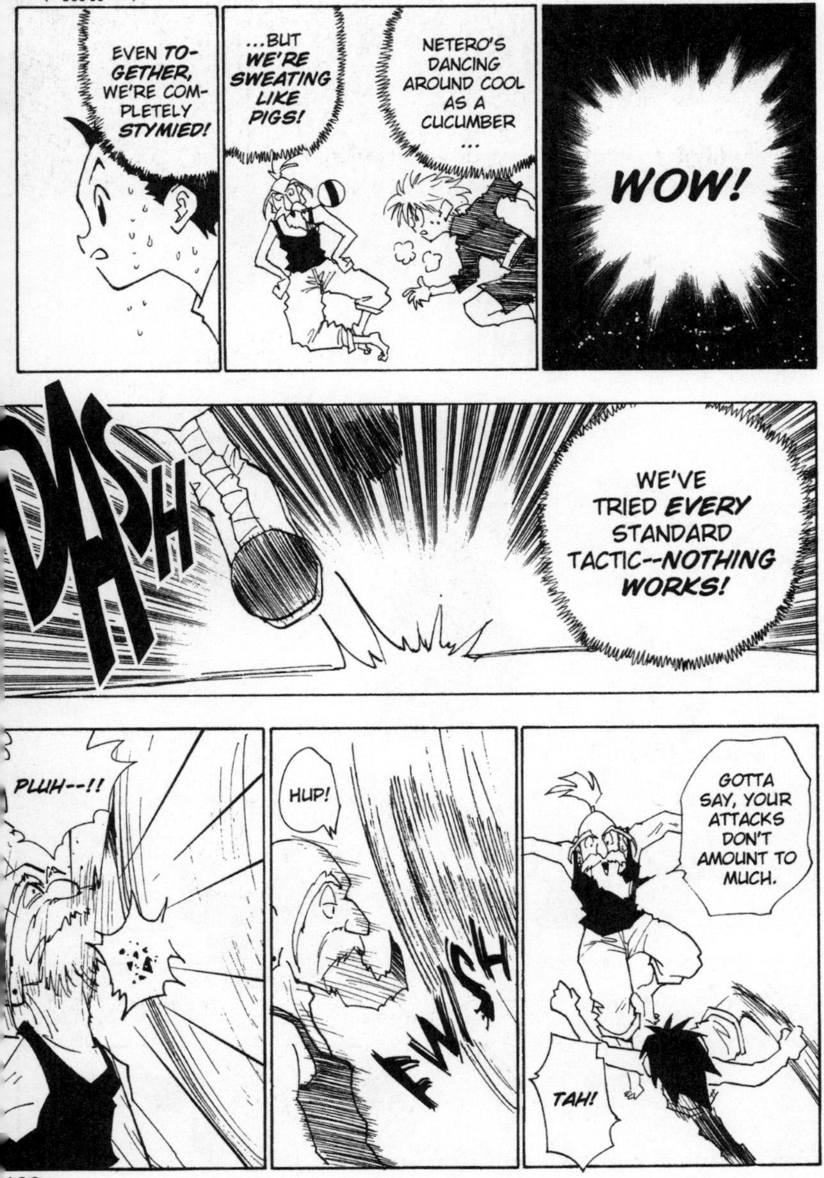
WOW!
NETERO'S DANCING AROUND COOL AS A CUCUMBER ...
...BUT WE'RE SWEATING LIKE PIGS!
EVEN TO-GETHER, WE'RE COM-PLETELY STYMIED!
WE'VE TRIED EVERY STANDARD TACTIC--NOTHING WORKS!
DASH
GOTTA SAY, YOUR ATTACKS DON'T AMOUNT TO MUCH.
TAH!
HUP!
FWSH
PLUH--!!

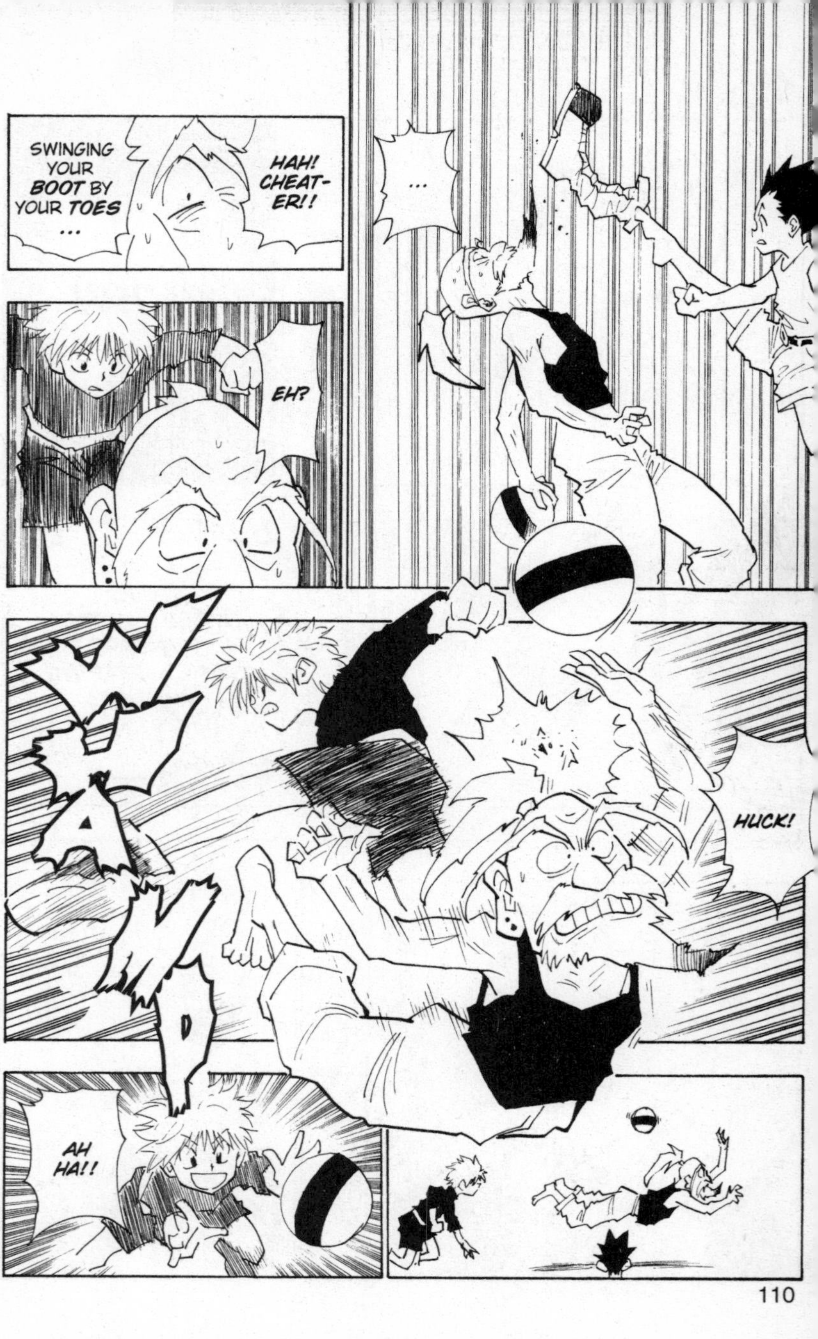
...
HAH! CHEATER!!
SWINGING YOUR BOOT BY YOUR TOES ...
EH?
HUCK!
AH HA!!

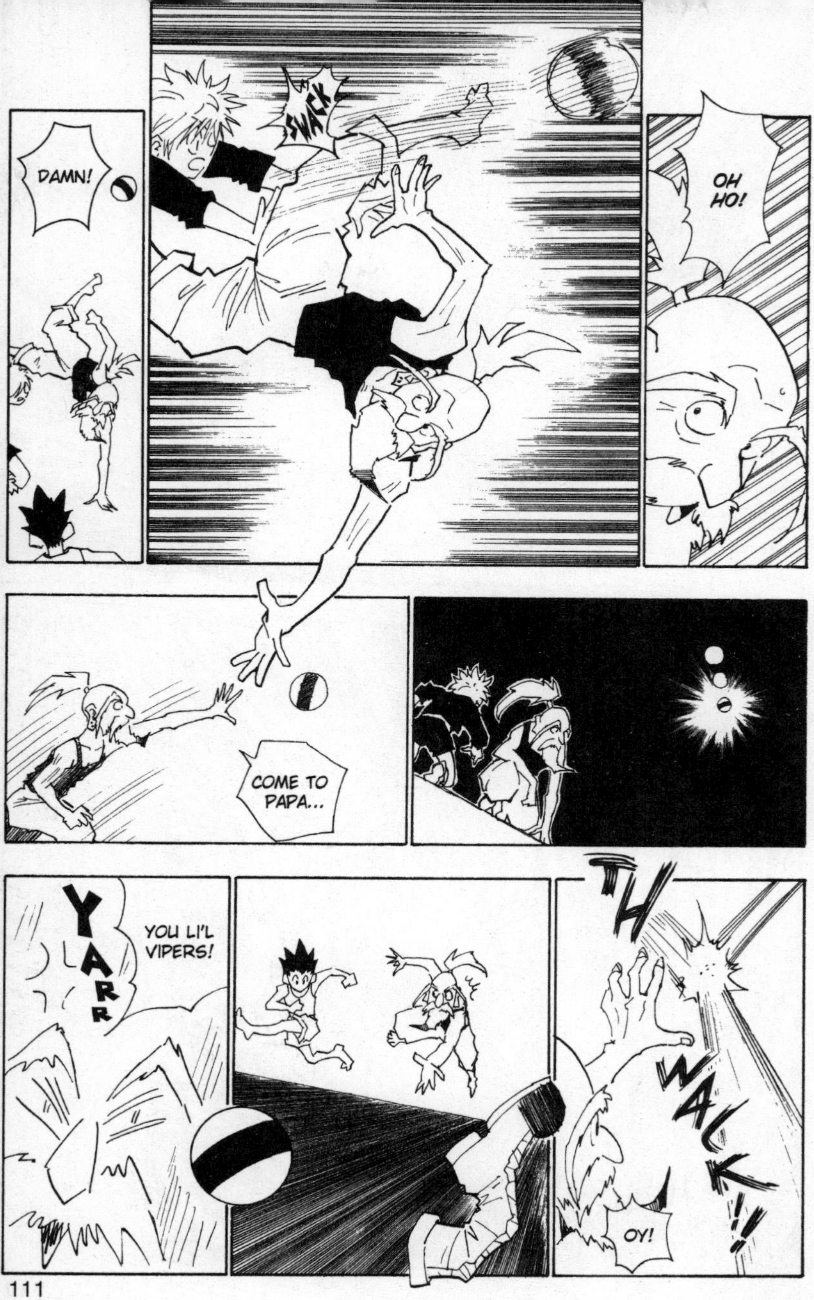

OH HO!
SWACK
DAMN!
COME TO PAPA...
THWACK!!
OY!
YARR
YOU LI'L VIPERS!

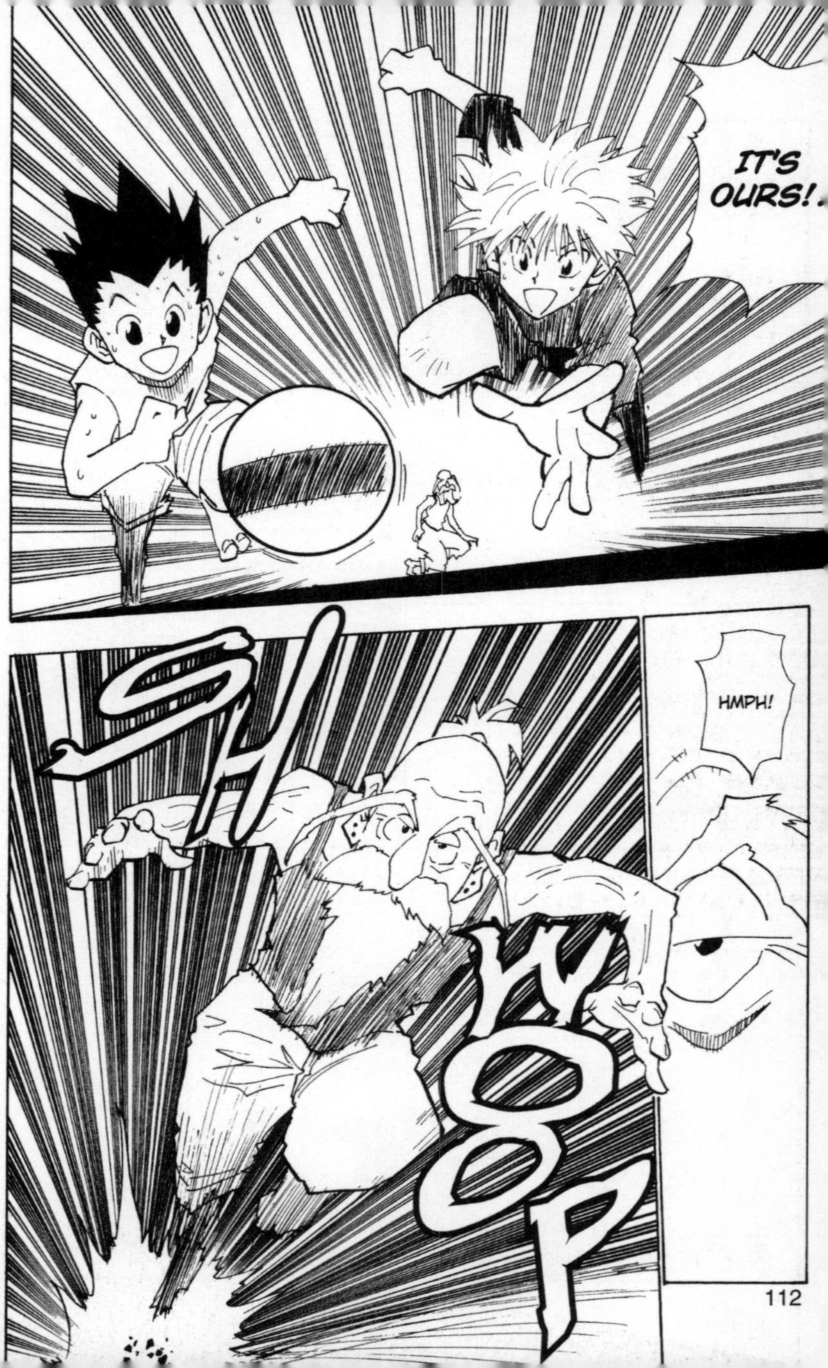
IT'S OURS!..
HMPH!
SH
WOOP

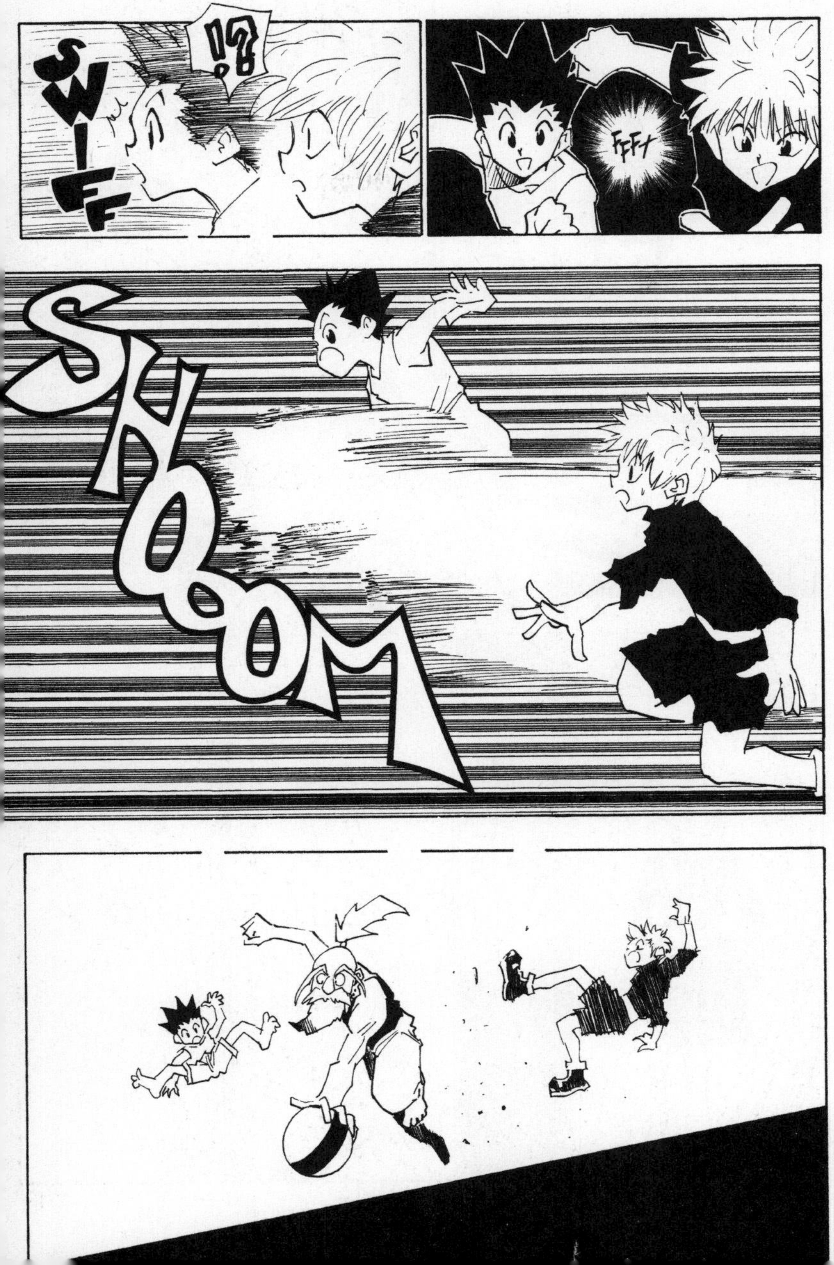
FFFT
!?
SWIFF
SHOOOM

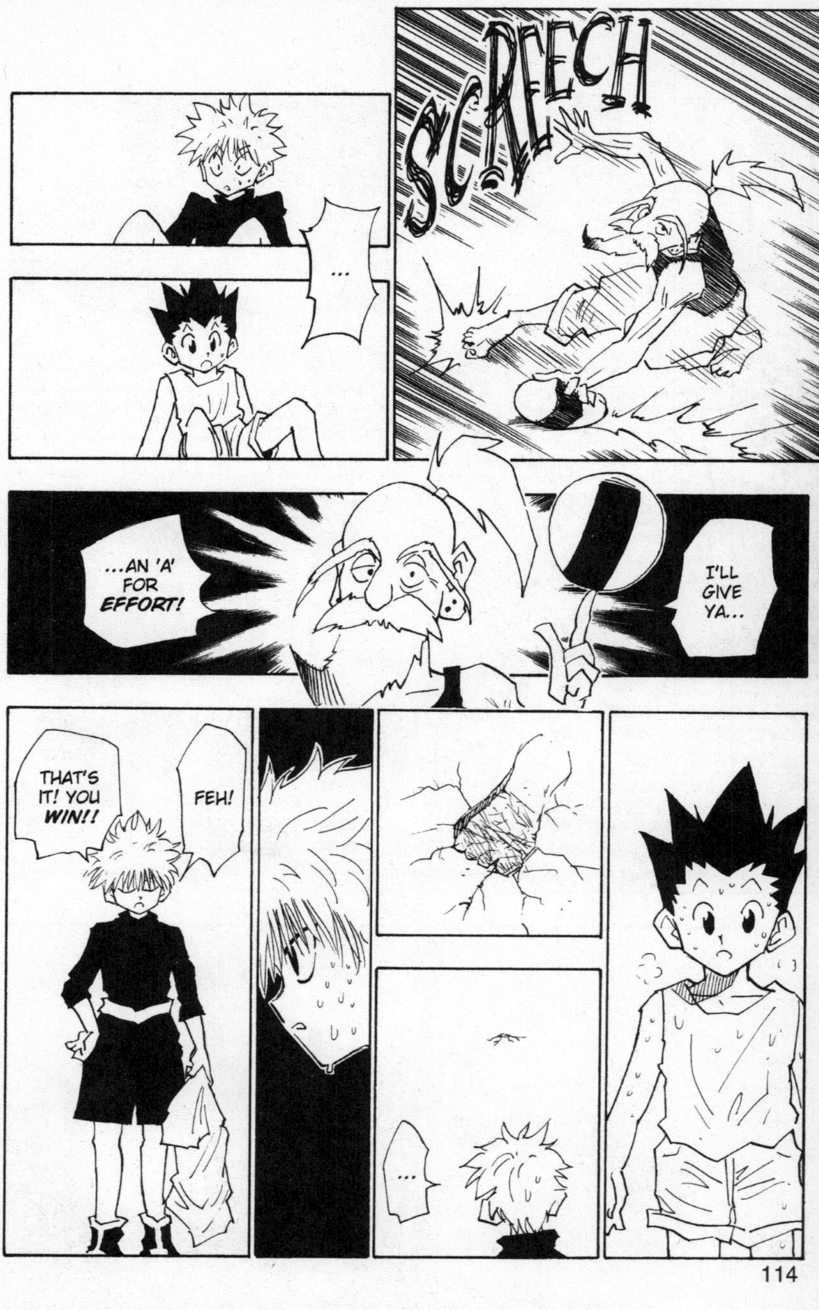
SCREECH
...
I'LL GIVE YA...
...AN 'A' FOR EFFORT!
...
FEH!
THAT'S IT! YOU WIN!!

READ THIS WAY

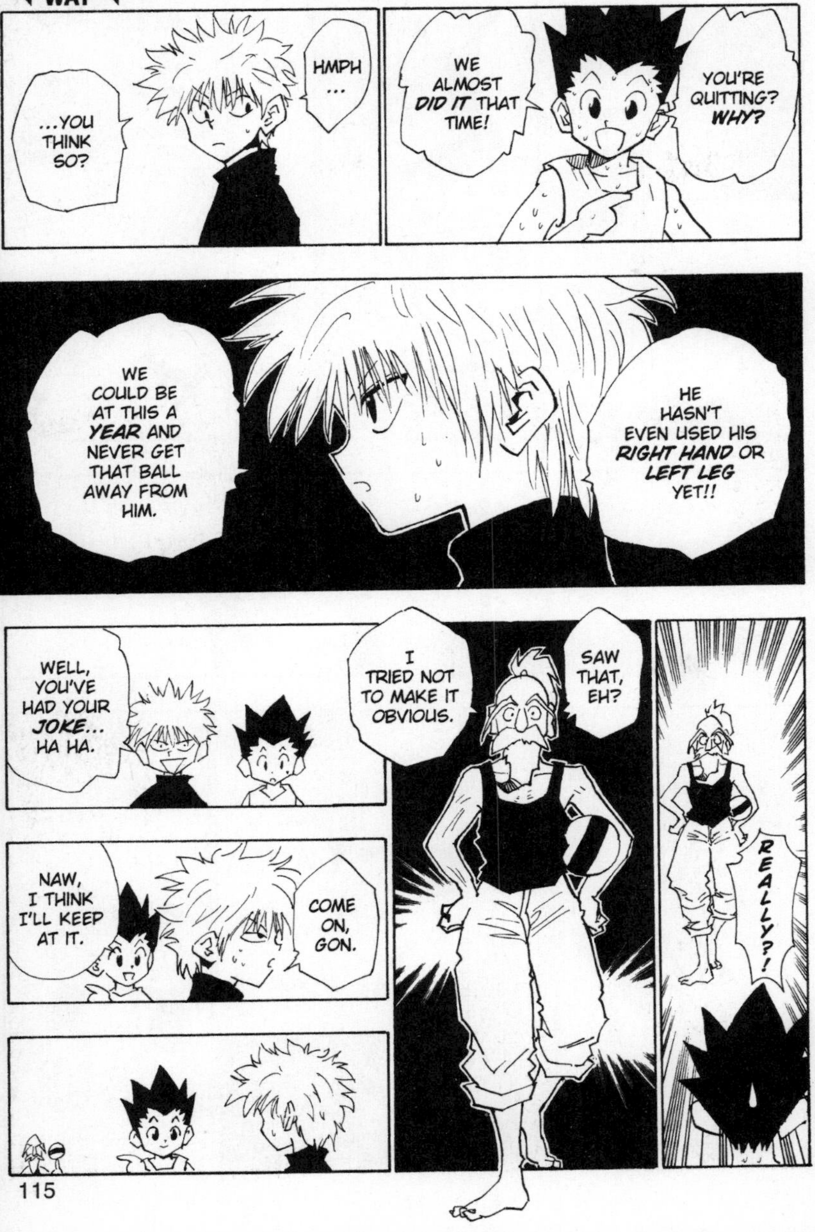
YOU'RE QUITTING? **WHY?**
WE ALMOST **DID IT** THAT TIME!
HMPH ...
...YOU THINK SO?
HE HASN'T EVEN USED HIS **RIGHT HAND** OR **LEFT LEG** YET!!
WE COULD BE AT THIS A **YEAR** AND NEVER GET THAT BALL AWAY FROM HIM.
REALLY?!
SAW THAT, EH?
I TRIED NOT TO MAKE IT OBVIOUS.
WELL, YOU'VE HAD YOUR **JOKE...** HA HA.
COME ON, GON.
NAW, I THINK I'LL KEEP AT IT.

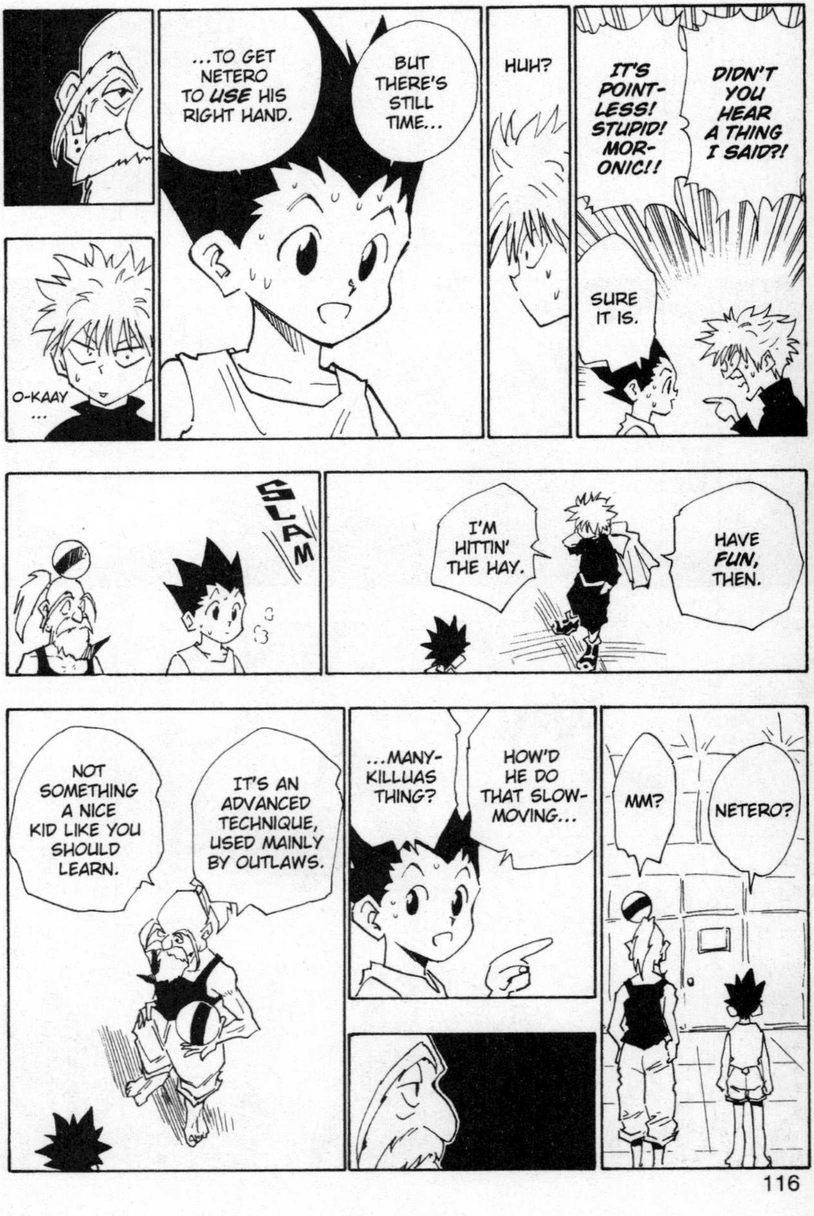
DIDN'T YOU HEAR A THING I SAID?!
IT'S POINTLESS! STUPID! MORONIC!!
SURE IT IS.
HUH?
BUT THERE'S STILL TIME...
...TO GET NETERO TO USE HIS RIGHT HAND.
O-KAAY ...
HAVE FUN, THEN.
I'M HITTIN' THE HAY.
SLAM
NETERO?
MM?
HOW'D HE DO THAT SLOW-MOVING...
...MANY-KILLUAS THING?
IT'S AN ADVANCED TECHNIQUE, USED MAINLY BY OUTLAWS.
NOT SOMETHING A NICE KID LIKE YOU SHOULD LEARN.

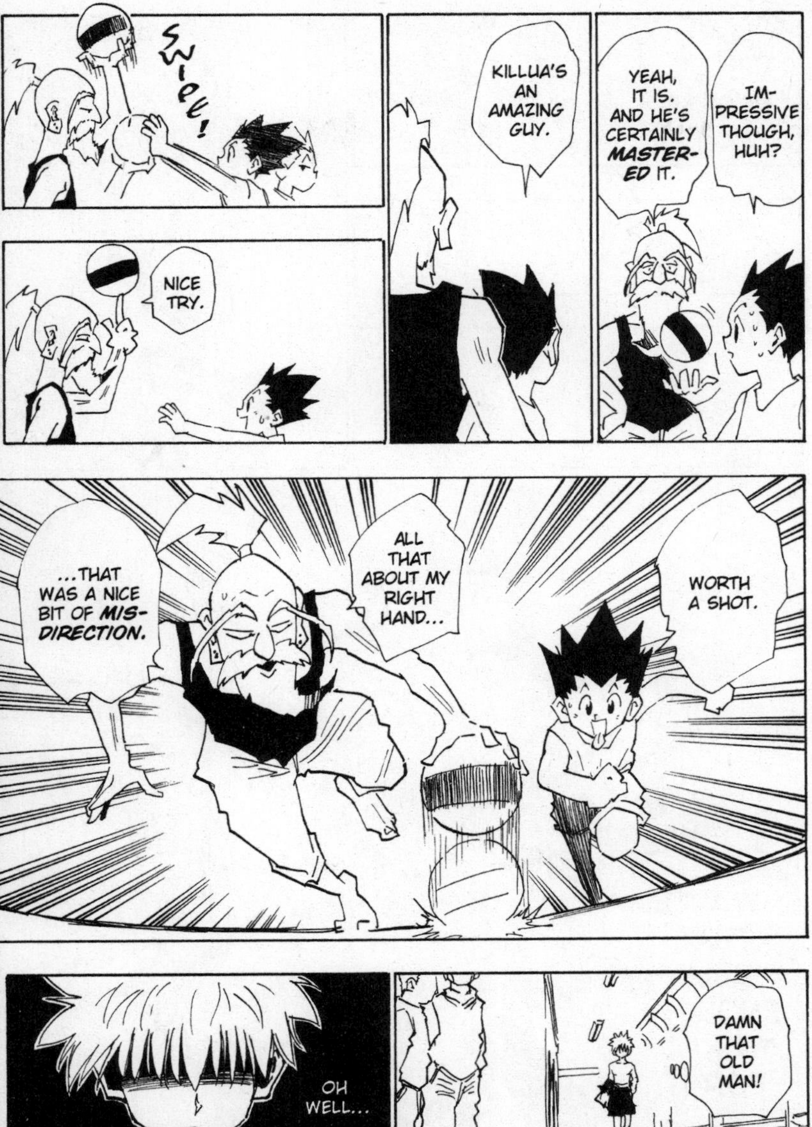

IM-PRESSIVE THOUGH, HUH?
YEAH, IT IS. AND HE'S CERTAINLY MASTER-ED IT.
KILLUA'S AN AMAZING GUY.
SWIPE!
NICE TRY.
WORTH A SHOT.
ALL THAT ABOUT MY RIGHT HAND...
...THAT WAS A NICE BIT OF MIS-DIRECTION.
DAMN THAT OLD MAN!
OH WELL...

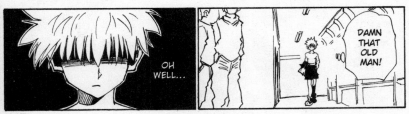

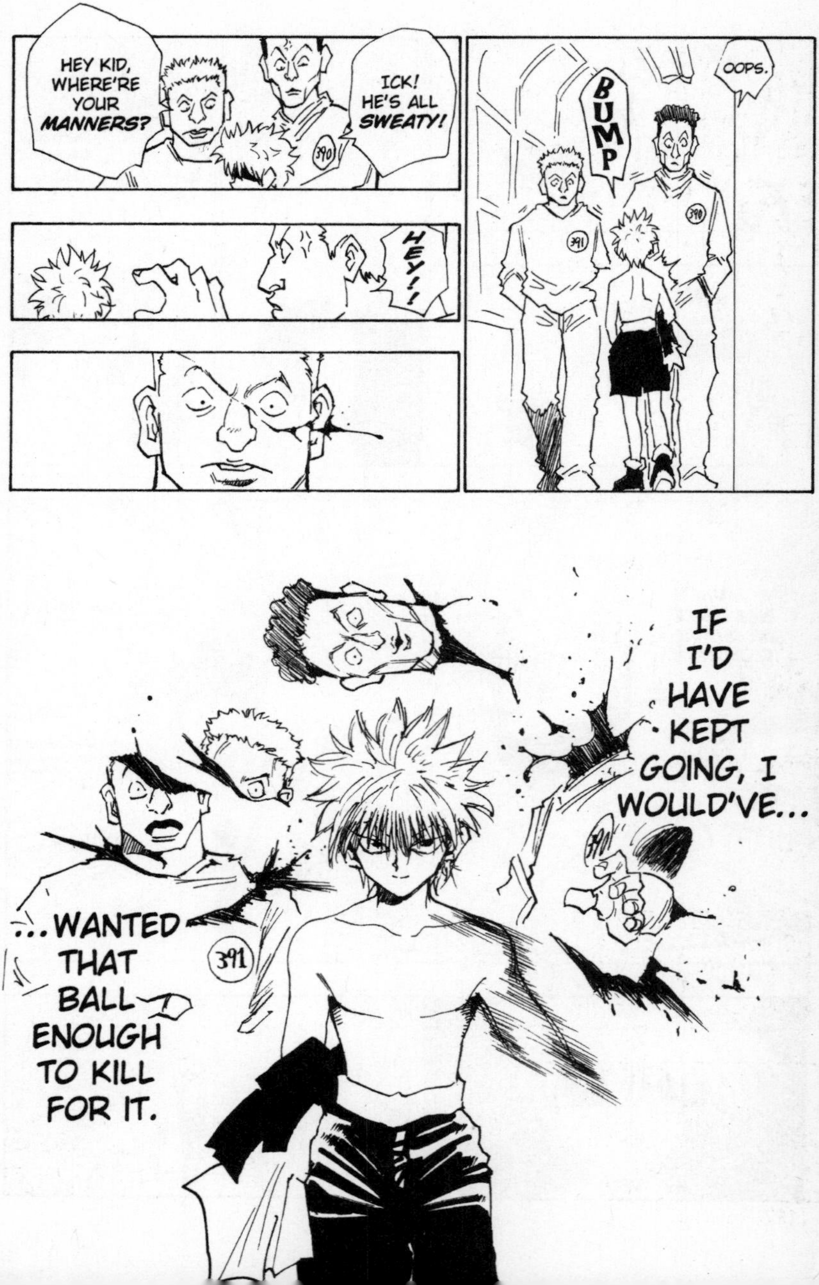
OOPS.
BUMP
ICK! HE'S ALL SWEATY!
HEY KID, WHERE'RE YOUR MANNERS?
HEY!!
IF I'D HAVE KEPT GOING, I WOULD'VE...
...WANTED THAT BALL ENOUGH TO KILL FOR IT.

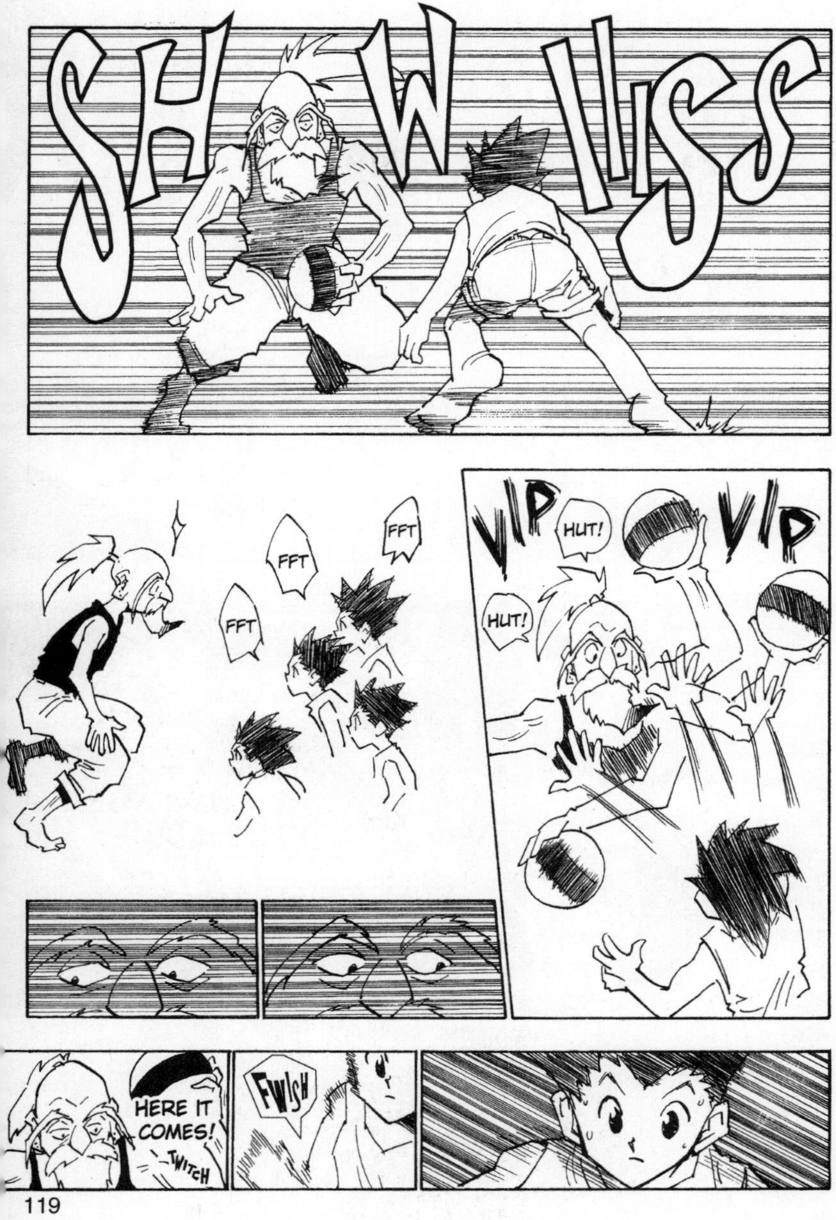
SHWISS
VIP
HUT!
VIP
HUT!
FFT
FFT
FFT
FWISH
HERE IT COMES!
TWITCH

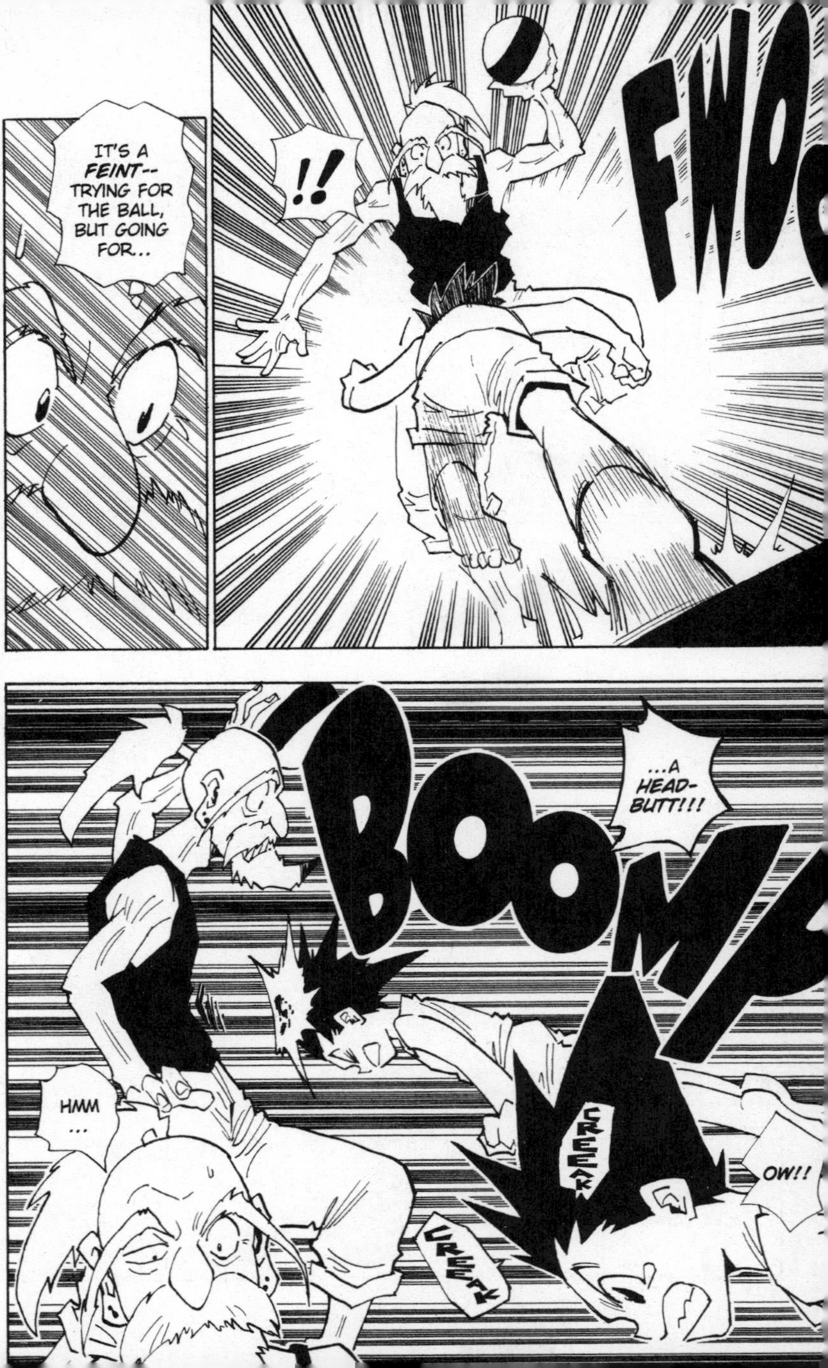
FWOO
!!
IT'S A FEINT-- TRYING FOR THE BALL, BUT GOING FOR...
...A HEAD-BUTT!!!
BOOM
OW!!
CREEAK
CREEAK
HMM ...

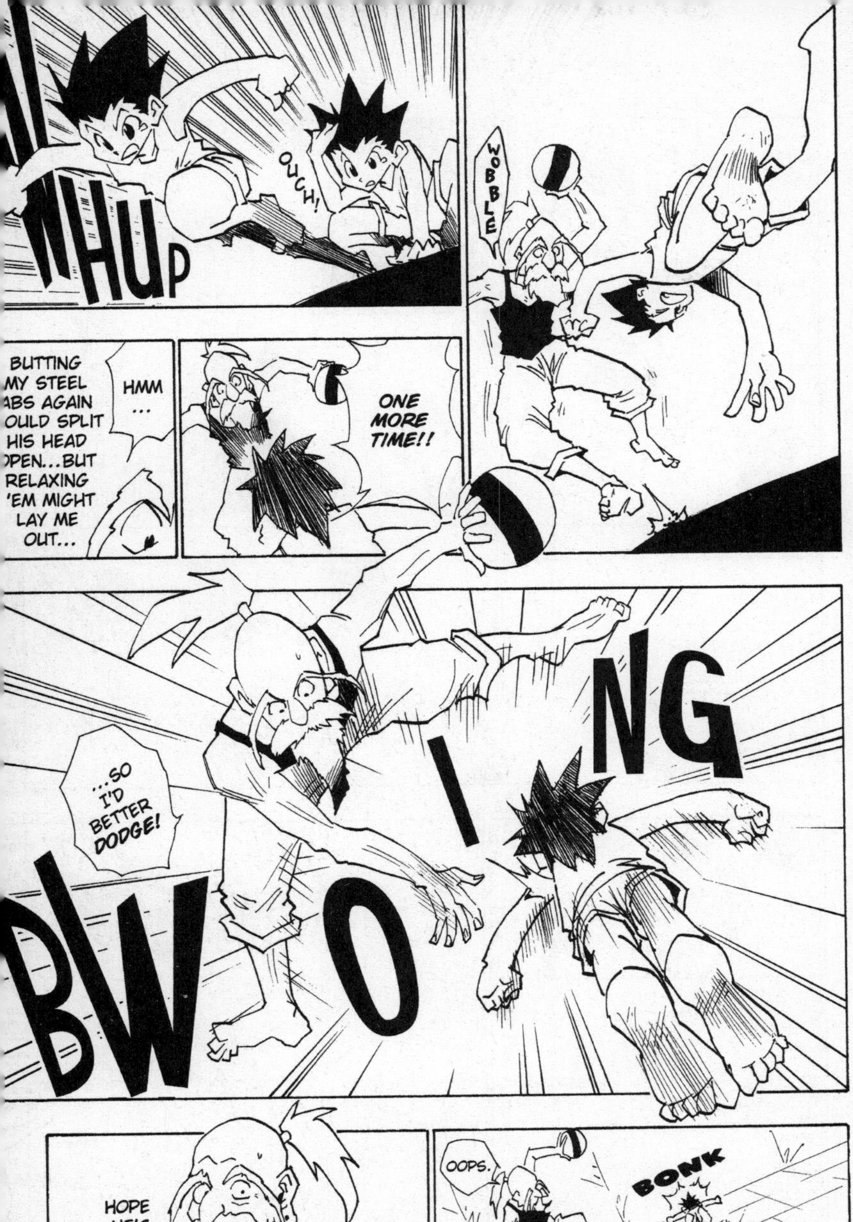

WOBBLE
WHUP
OUCH!
ONE MORE TIME!!
HMM ...
BUTTING MY STEEL ABS AGAIN OULD SPLIT HIS HEAD OPEN...BUT RELAXING 'EM MIGHT LAY ME OUT...
BWOING
...SO I'D BETTER DODGE!
OOPS.
BONK
HOPE HE'S OKAY...

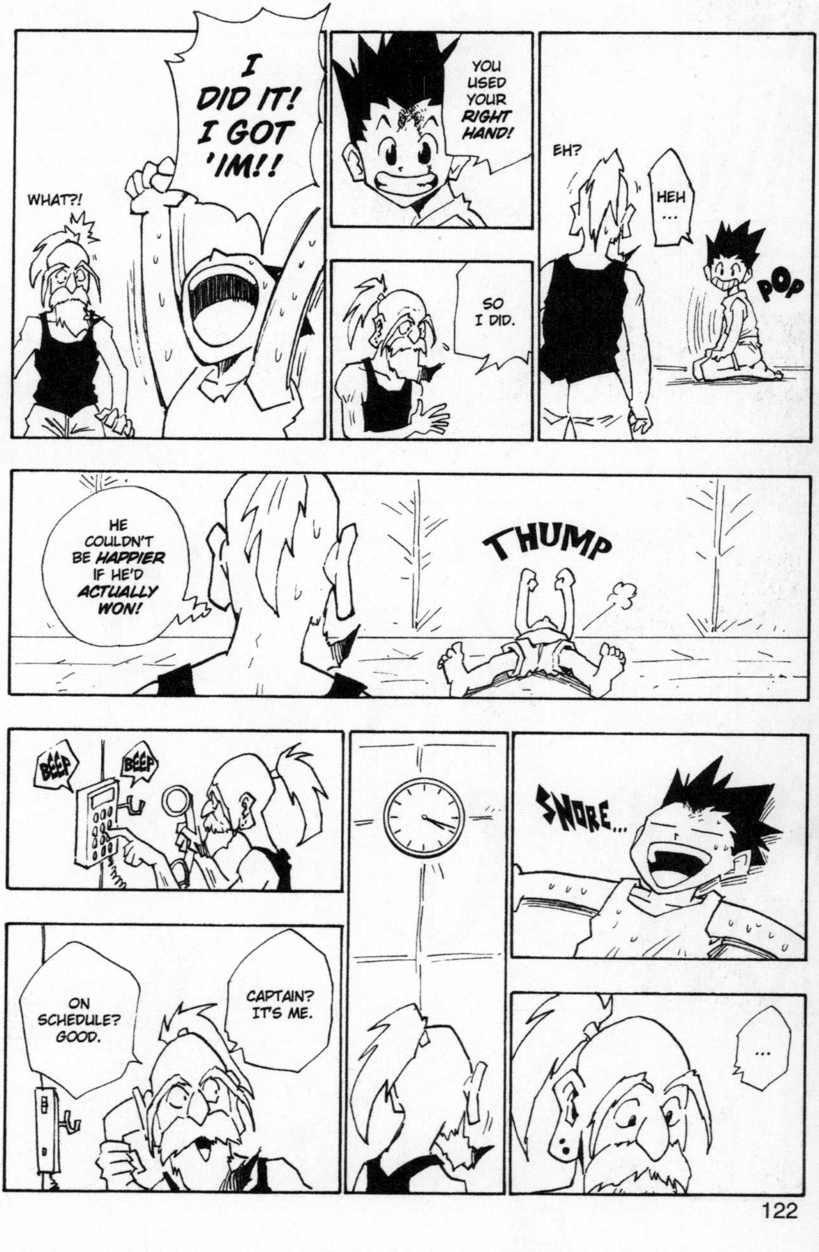

EH?
HEH...
POP
YOU USED YOUR RIGHT HAND!
SO I DID.
I DID IT! I GOT 'IM!!
WHAT?!
THUMP
HE COULDN'T BE HAPPIER IF HE'D ACTUALLY WON!
SNORE...
...
BEEP
BEEP
CAPTAIN? IT'S ME.
ON SCHEDULE? GOOD.

READ THIS WAY

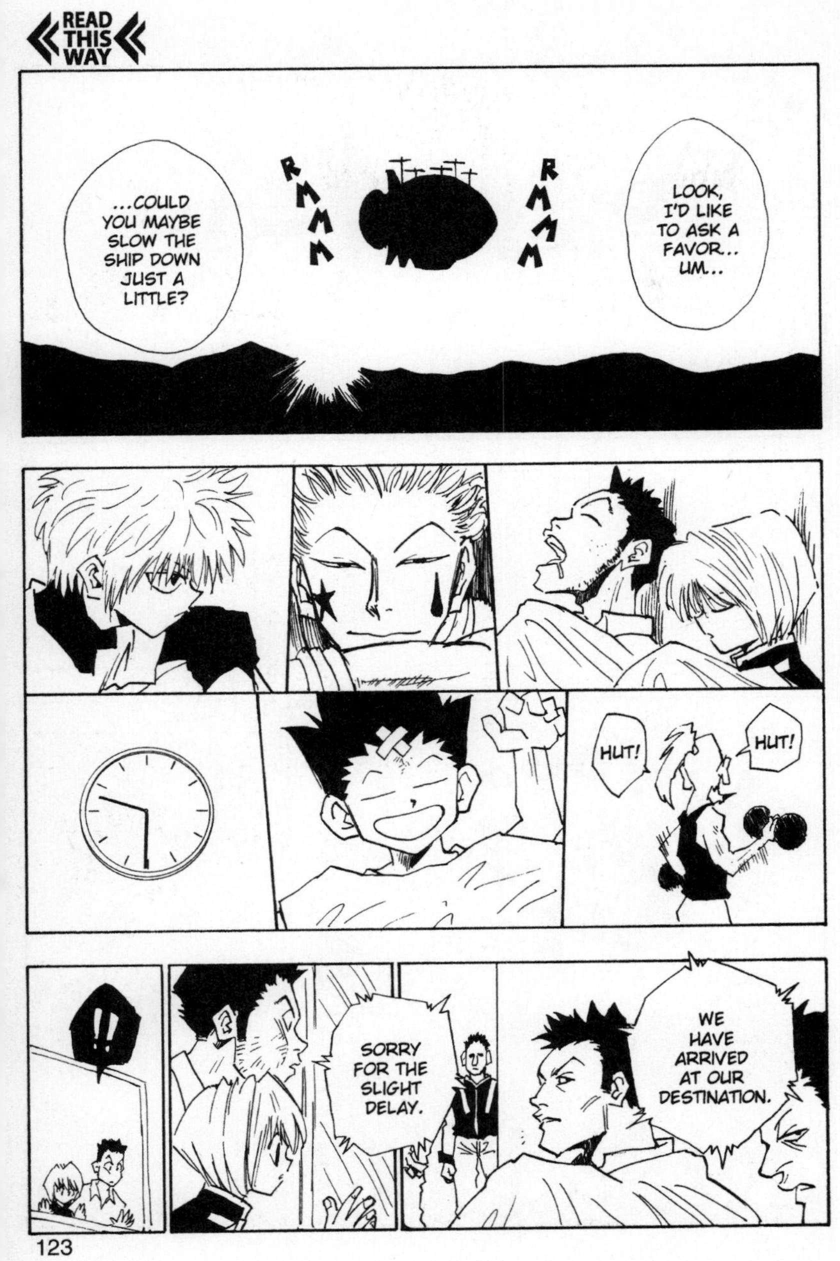
LOOK, I'D LIKE TO ASK A FAVOR... UM...
RMMM
RMMM
...COULD YOU MAYBE SLOW THE SHIP DOWN JUST A LITTLE?
HUT!
HUT!
WE HAVE ARRIVED AT OUR DESTINATION.
SORRY FOR THE SLIGHT DELAY.
!!

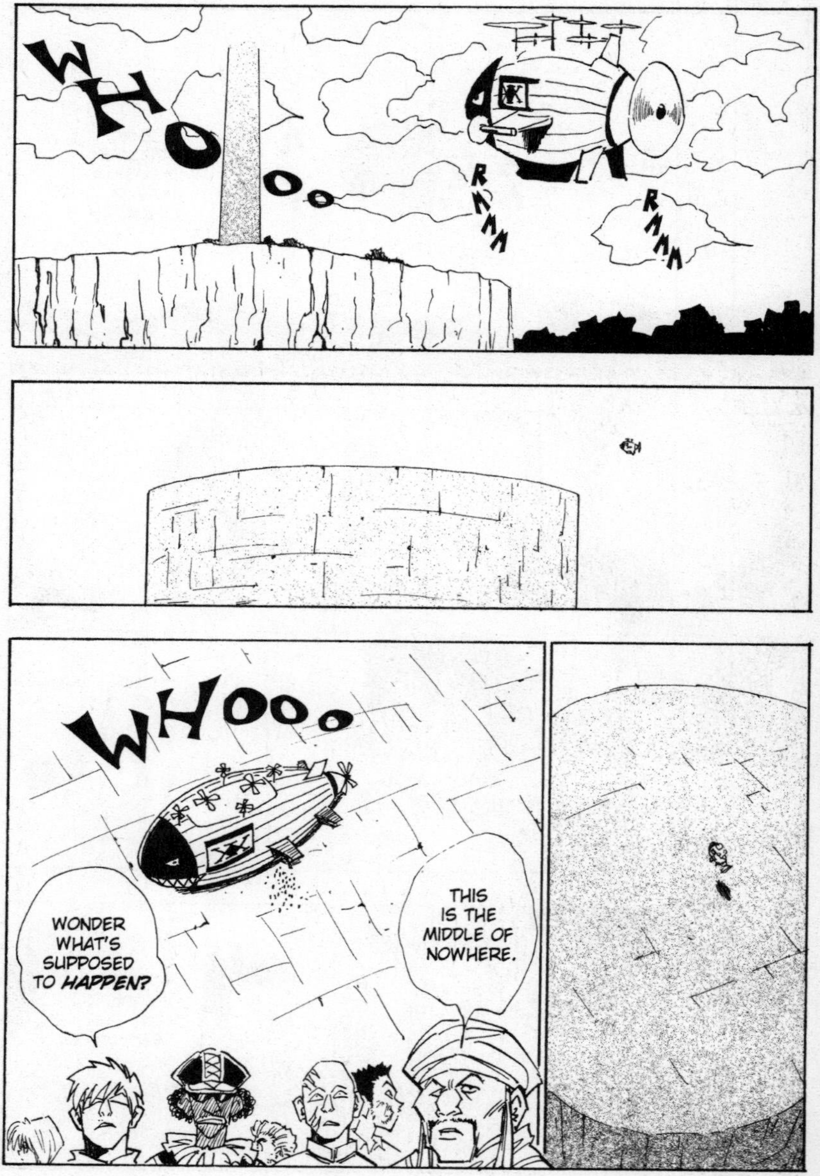
WHOOO
RMMM
RMMM
WHOOO
THIS IS THE MIDDLE OF NOWHERE.
WONDER WHAT'S SUPPOSED TO *HAPPEN?*

READ THIS WAY

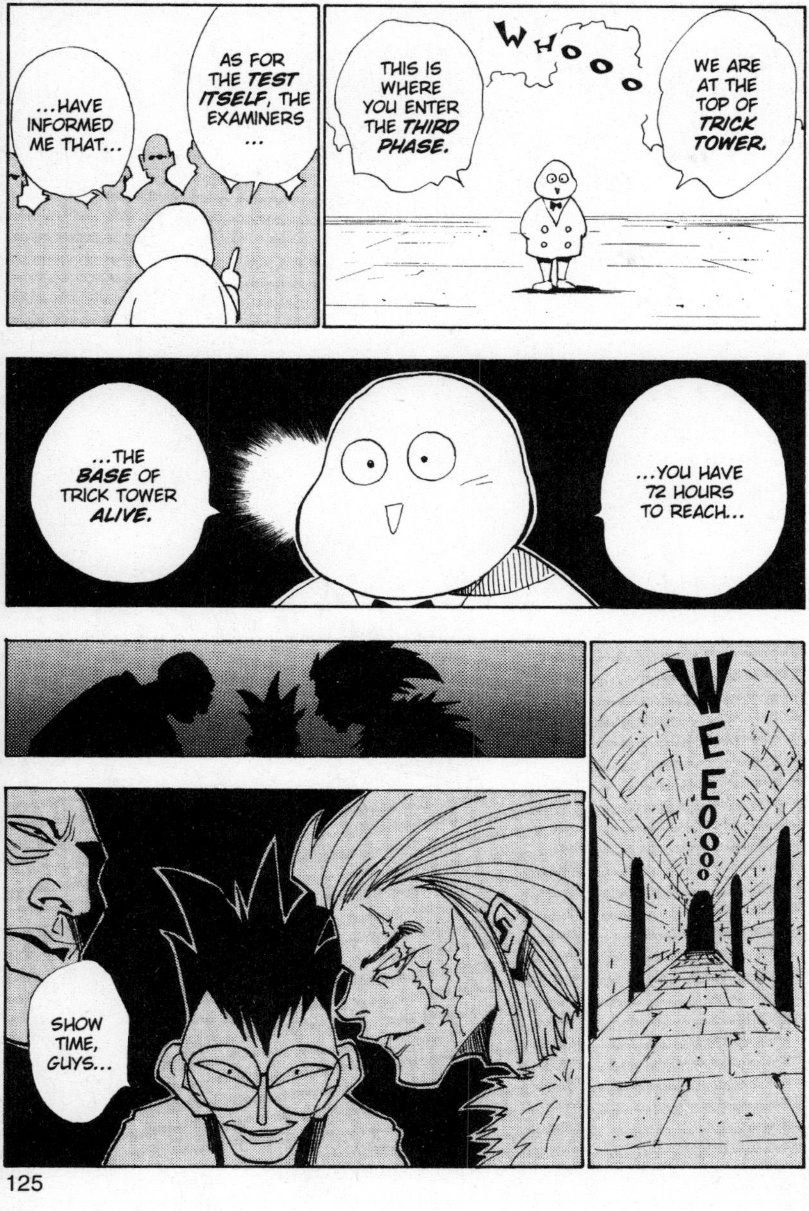

WE ARE AT THE TOP OF TRICK TOWER.
WHOOOO
THIS IS WHERE YOU ENTER THE THIRD PHASE.
AS FOR THE TEST ITSELF, THE EXAMINERS ...
...HAVE INFORMED ME THAT...
...YOU HAVE 72 HOURS TO REACH...
...THE BASE OF TRICK TOWER ALIVE.
WEEOOOO
SHOW TIME, GUYS...

Tonpa

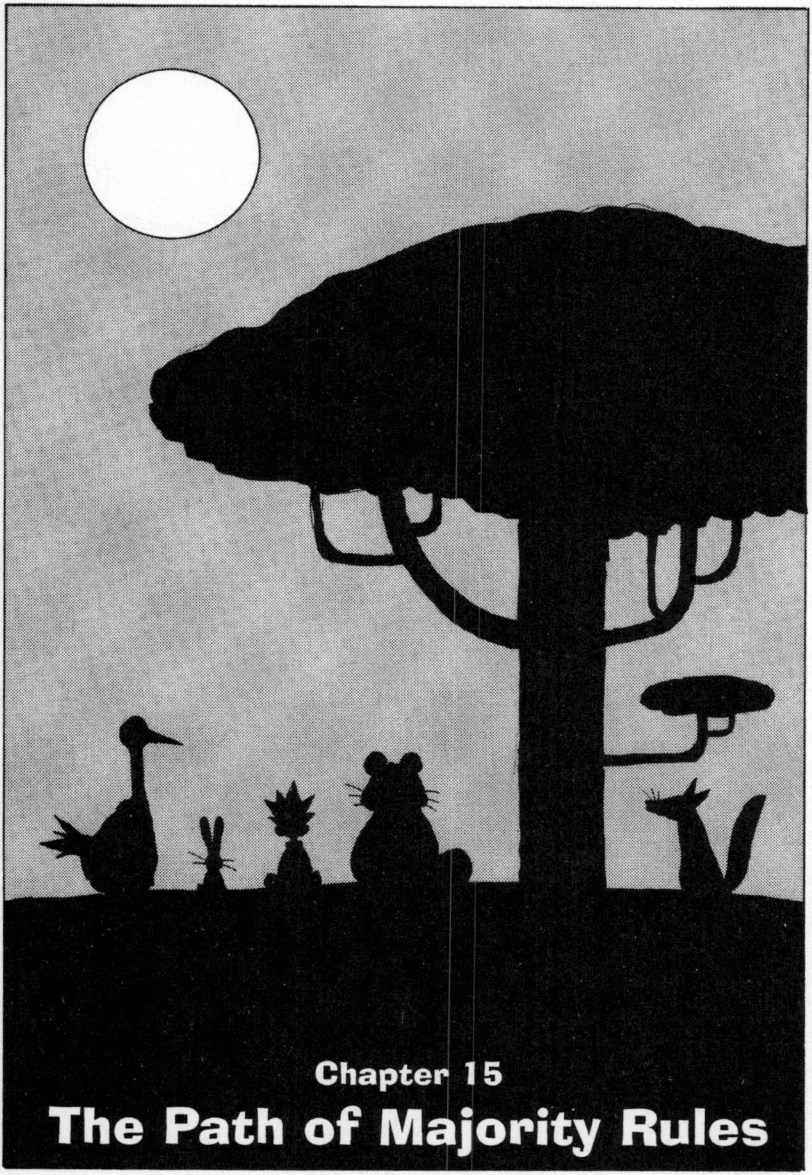

Chapter 15

The Path of Majority Rules

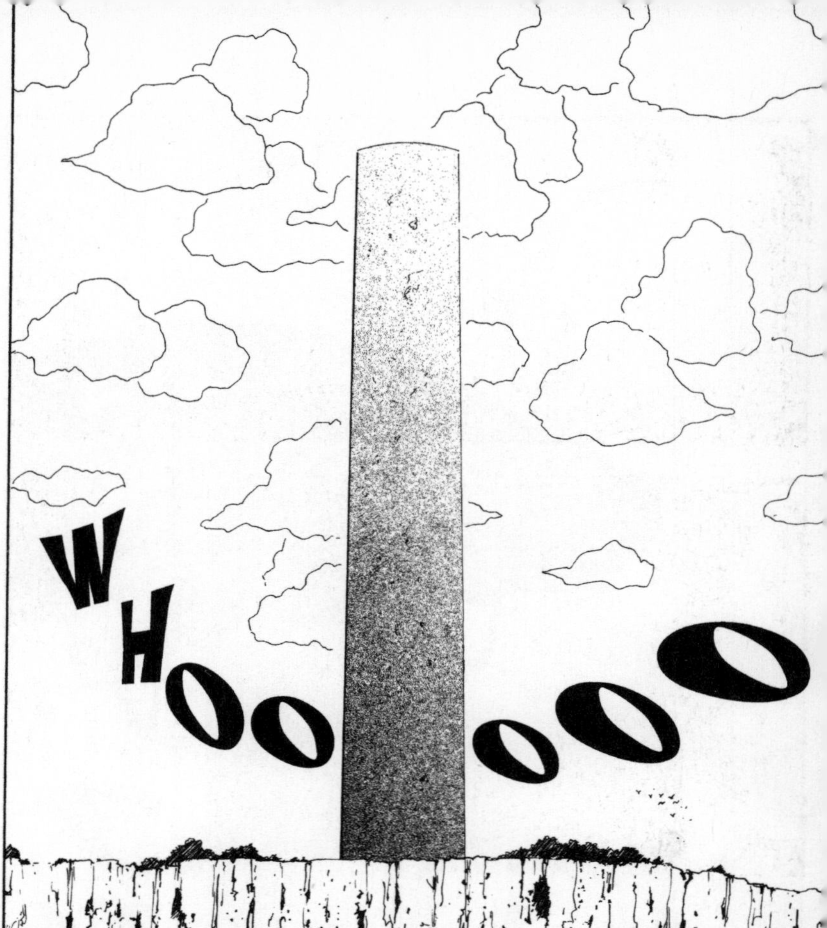
WHOOOOOO

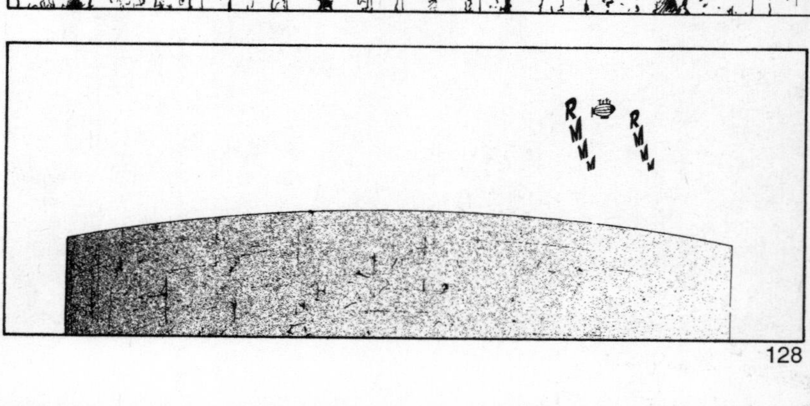
RMMM
RMMM

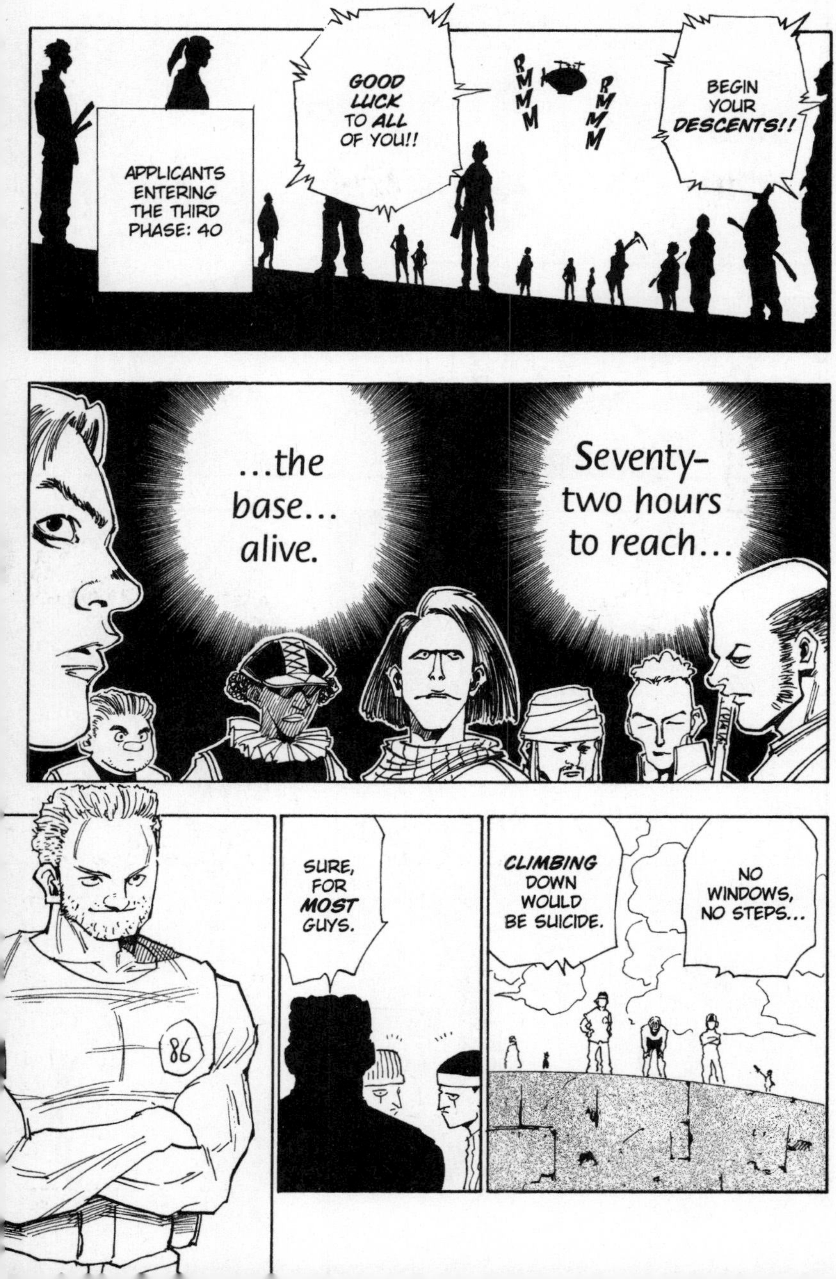
BEGIN YOUR DESCENTS!!
RMMM
RMMM
GOOD LUCK TO ALL OF YOU!!
APPLICANTS ENTERING THE THIRD PHASE: 40
Seventy-two hours to reach…
…the base… alive.
NO WINDOWS, NO STEPS…
CLIMBING DOWN WOULD BE SUICIDE.
SURE, FOR MOST GUYS.
86

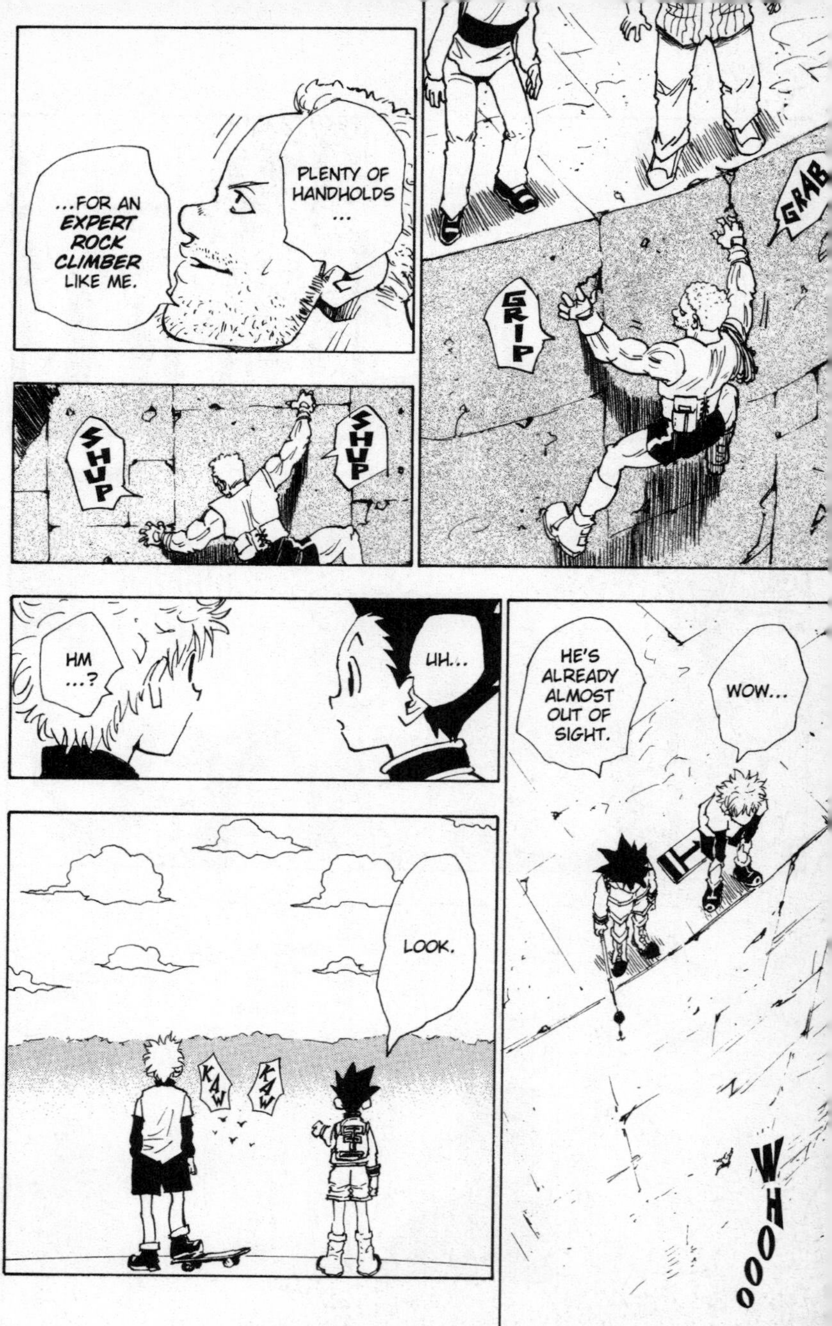
GRAB
GRIP
PLENTY OF HANDHOLDS ...
...FOR AN *EXPERT ROCK CLIMBER* LIKE ME.
SHUP
SHUP
WOW...
HE'S ALREADY ALMOST OUT OF SIGHT.
...WHOOOO
UH...
HM ...?
LOOK.
KAW
KAW

READ THIS WAY

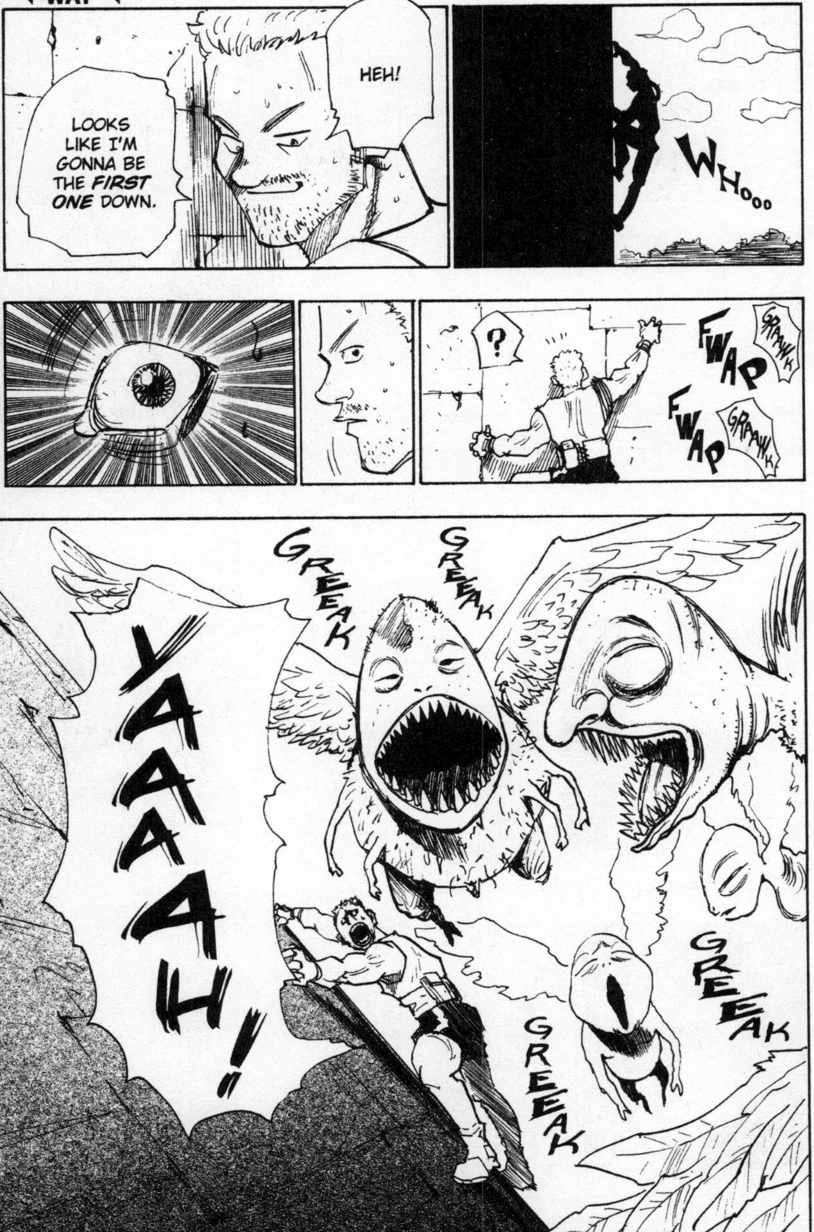
WHOooo
HEH!
LOOKS LIKE I'M GONNA BE THE *FIRST ONE* DOWN.
?
FWAP
GRAAWK
FWAP
GRAAWK
GREEAK
GREEAK
GREEAK
GREEAK
YAAAAH!

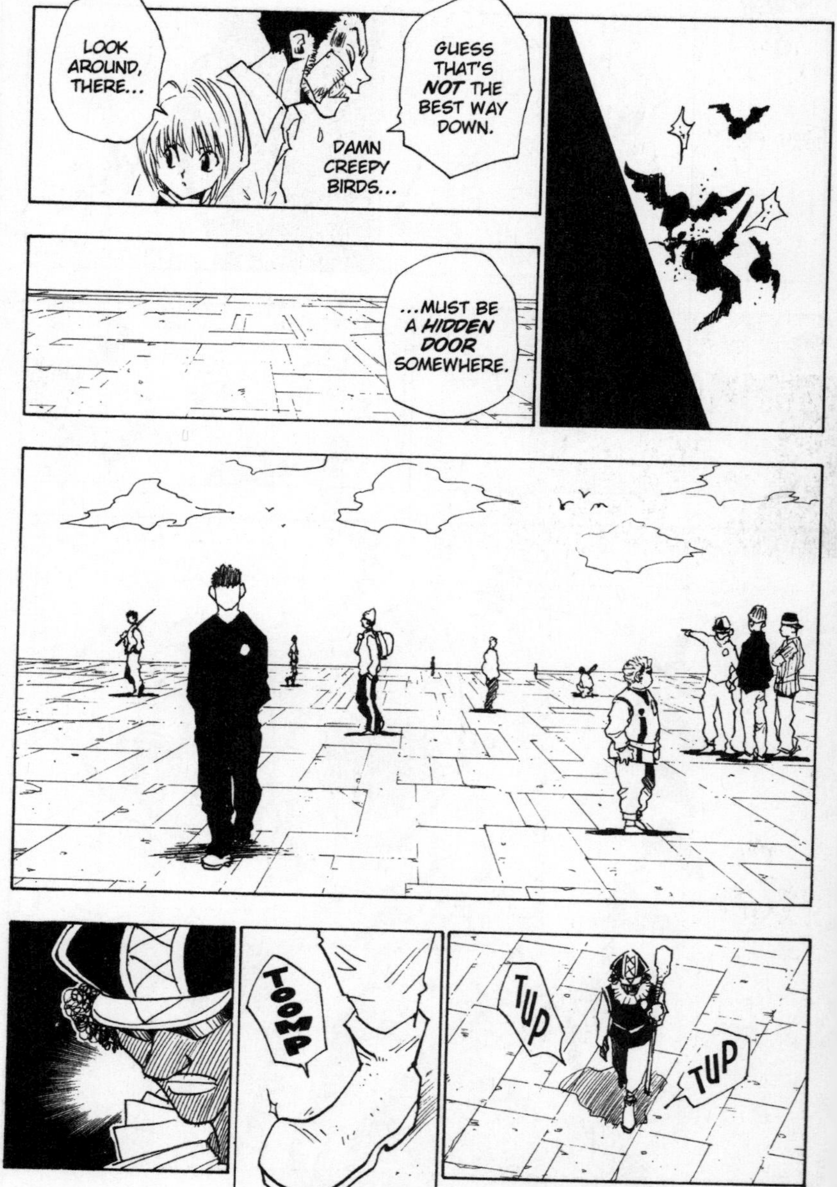
GUESS THAT'S NOT THE BEST WAY DOWN.
LOOK AROUND, THERE...
DAMN CREEPY BIRDS...
...MUST BE A HIDDEN DOOR SOMEWHERE.
TUP
TUP
TOOMP

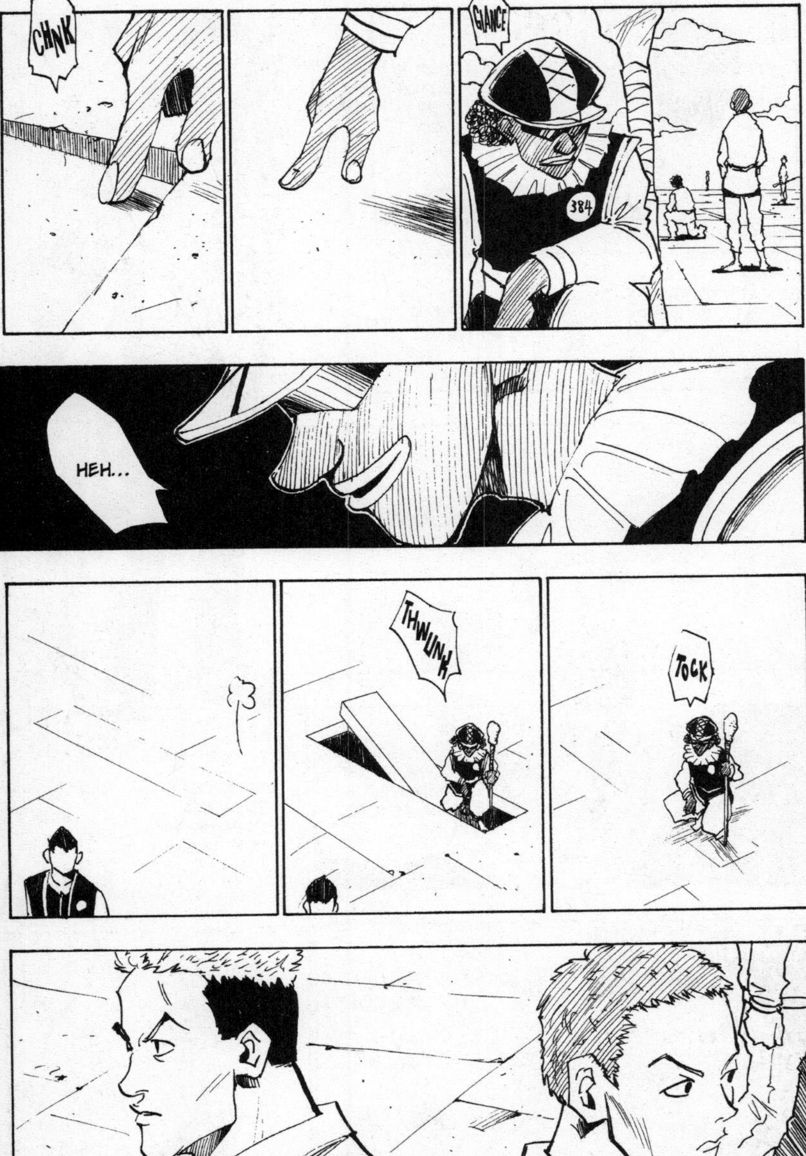
GLANCE
CHNK
HEH...
TOCK
THWUNK

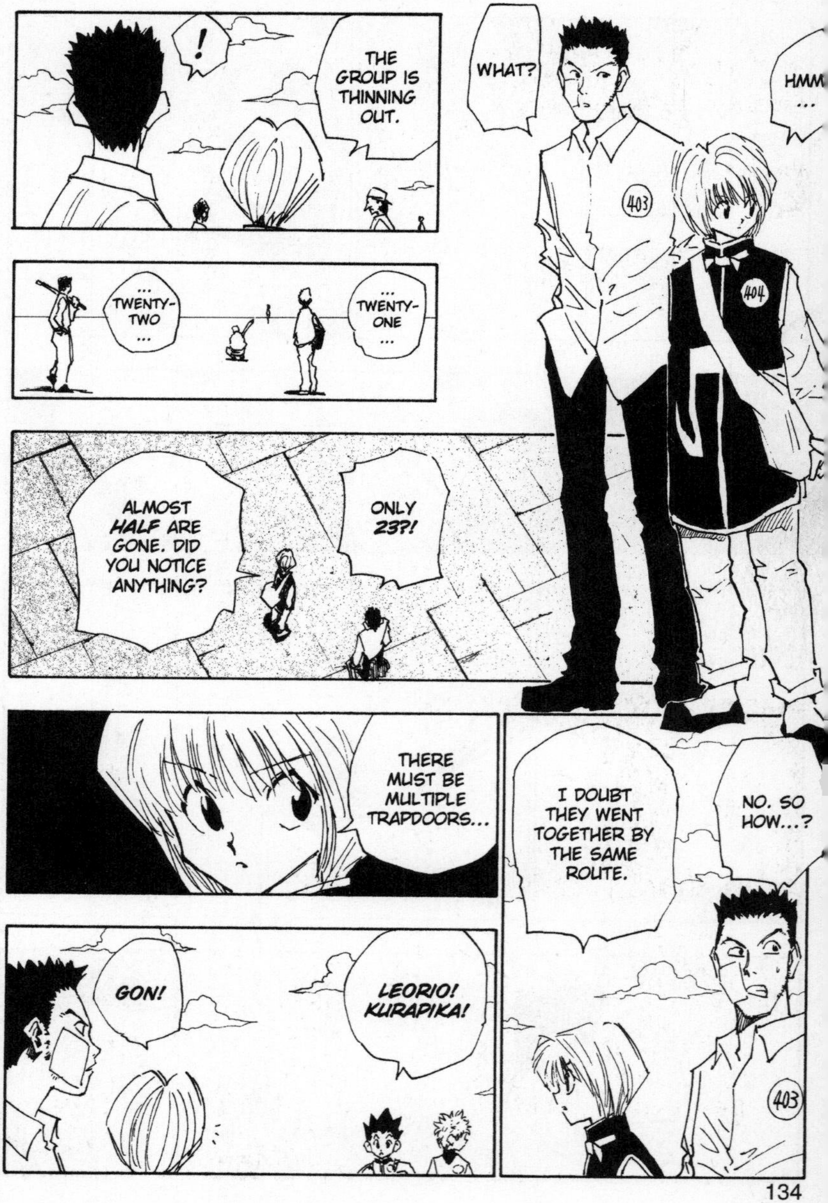
HMM...
WHAT?
THE GROUP IS THINNING OUT.
!
... TWENTY-ONE ...
... TWENTY-TWO ...
ONLY 23?!
ALMOST HALF ARE GONE. DID YOU NOTICE ANYTHING?
NO. SO HOW...?
I DOUBT THEY WENT TOGETHER BY THE SAME ROUTE.
THERE MUST BE MULTIPLE TRAPDOORS...
LEORIO! KURAPIKA!
GON!

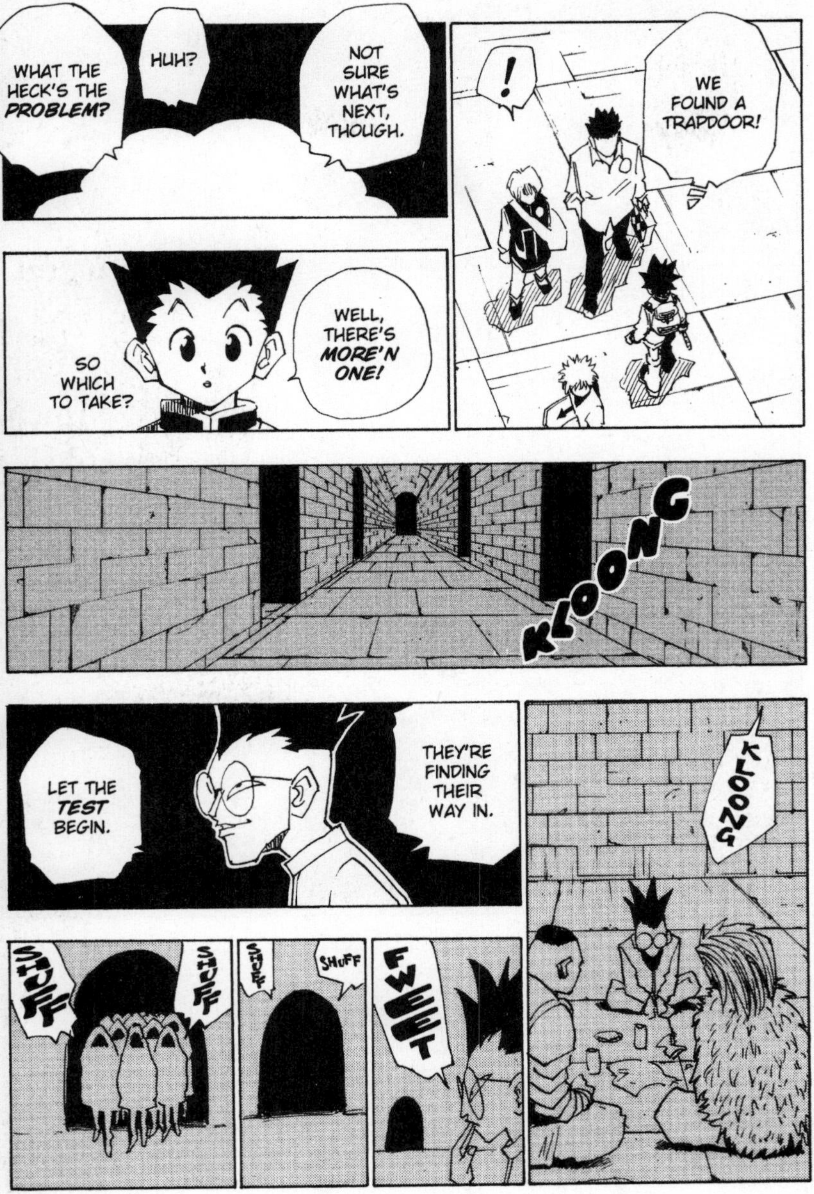
!
WE FOUND A TRAPDOOR!
NOT SURE WHAT'S NEXT, THOUGH.
HUH?
WHAT THE HECK'S THE *PROBLEM?*
WELL, THERE'S *MORE'N ONE!*
SO WHICH TO TAKE?
KLOONG
KLOONG
THEY'RE FINDING THEIR WAY IN.
LET THE *TEST* BEGIN.
FWEET
SHUFF
SHUFF
SHUFF
SHUFF

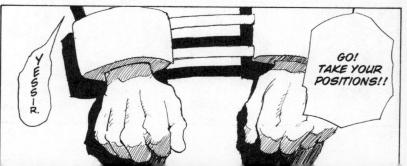

YESSIR.

GO! TAKE YOUR POSITIONS!!

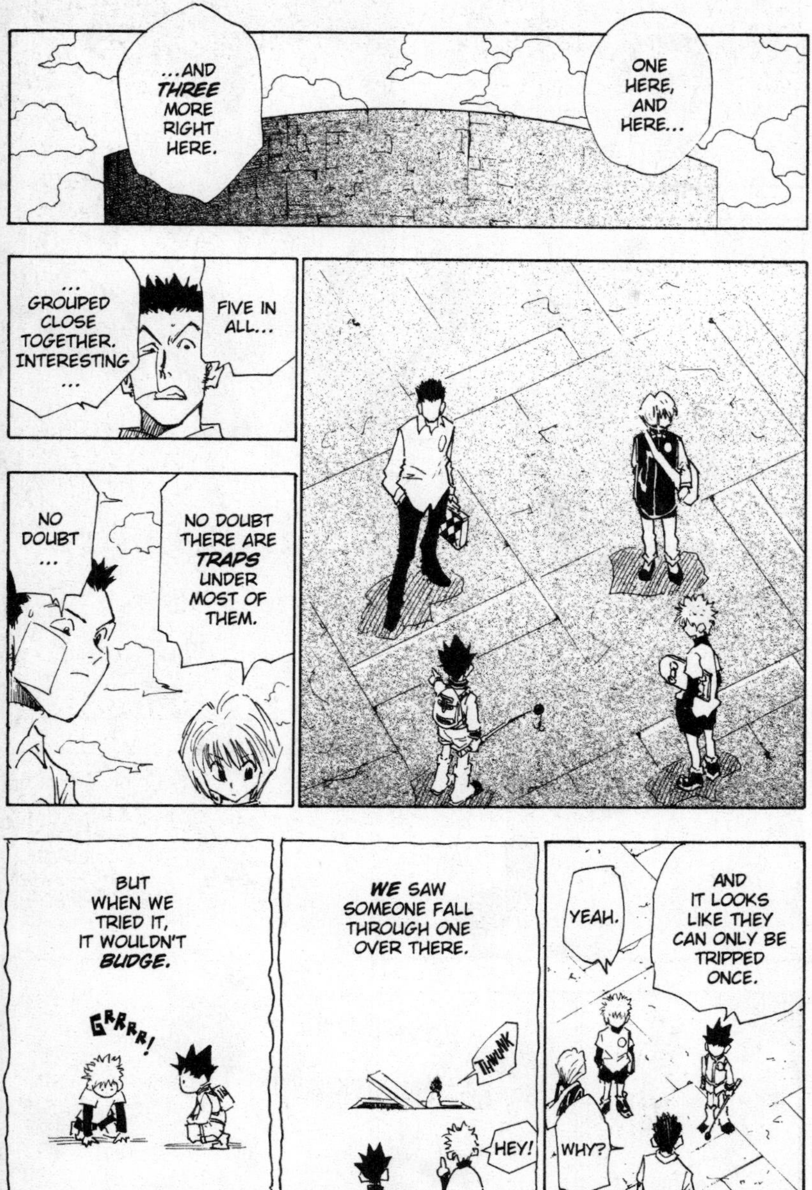
ONE HERE, AND HERE...
...AND THREE MORE RIGHT HERE.
FIVE IN ALL...
... GROUPED CLOSE TOGETHER. INTERESTING ...
NO DOUBT THERE ARE TRAPS UNDER MOST OF THEM.
NO DOUBT ...
AND IT LOOKS LIKE THEY CAN ONLY BE TRIPPED ONCE.
YEAH.
WHY?
WE SAW SOMEONE FALL THROUGH ONE OVER THERE.
THWUNK
HEY!
BUT WHEN WE TRIED IT, IT WOULDN'T BUDGE.
GRRRRR!

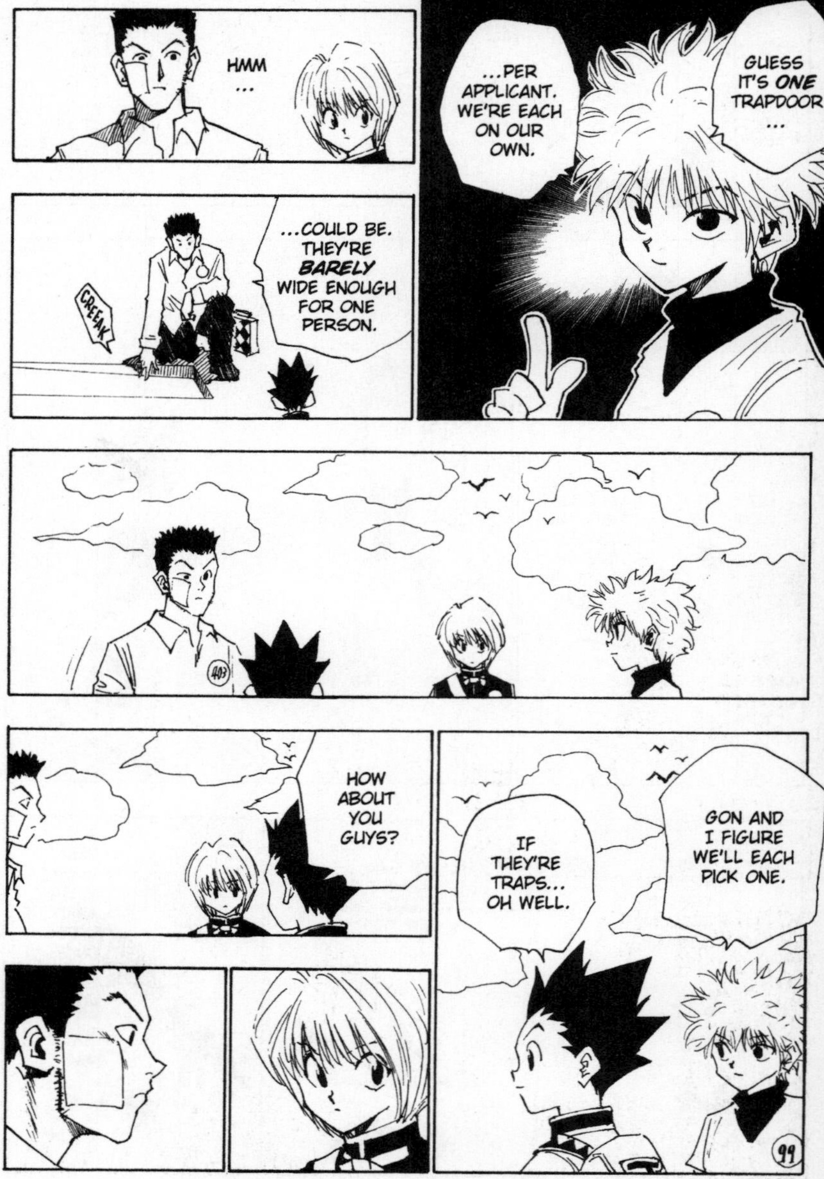
GUESS IT'S *ONE* TRAPDOOR ...
...PER APPLICANT. WE'RE EACH ON OUR OWN.
HMM ...
...COULD BE. THEY'RE *BARELY* WIDE ENOUGH FOR ONE PERSON.
CREEAK
GON AND I FIGURE WE'LL EACH PICK ONE.
IF THEY'RE TRAPS... OH WELL.
HOW ABOUT YOU GUYS?

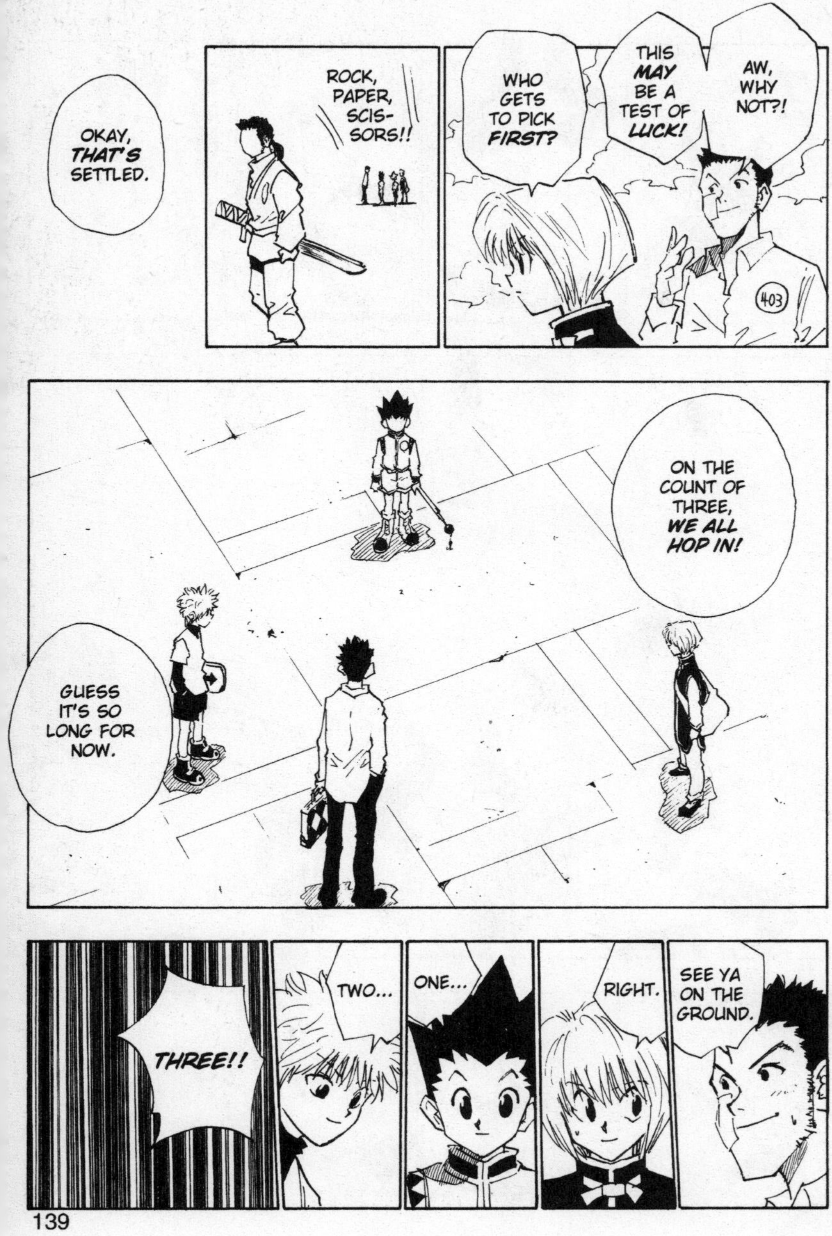
AW, WHY NOT?!
THIS *MAY* BE A TEST OF *LUCK!*
WHO GETS TO PICK *FIRST?*
ROCK, PAPER, SCIS-SORS!!
OKAY, *THAT'S* SETTLED.
ON THE COUNT OF THREE, *WE ALL HOP IN!*
GUESS IT'S SO LONG FOR NOW.
SEE YA ON THE GROUND.
RIGHT.
ONE...
TWO...
THREE!!

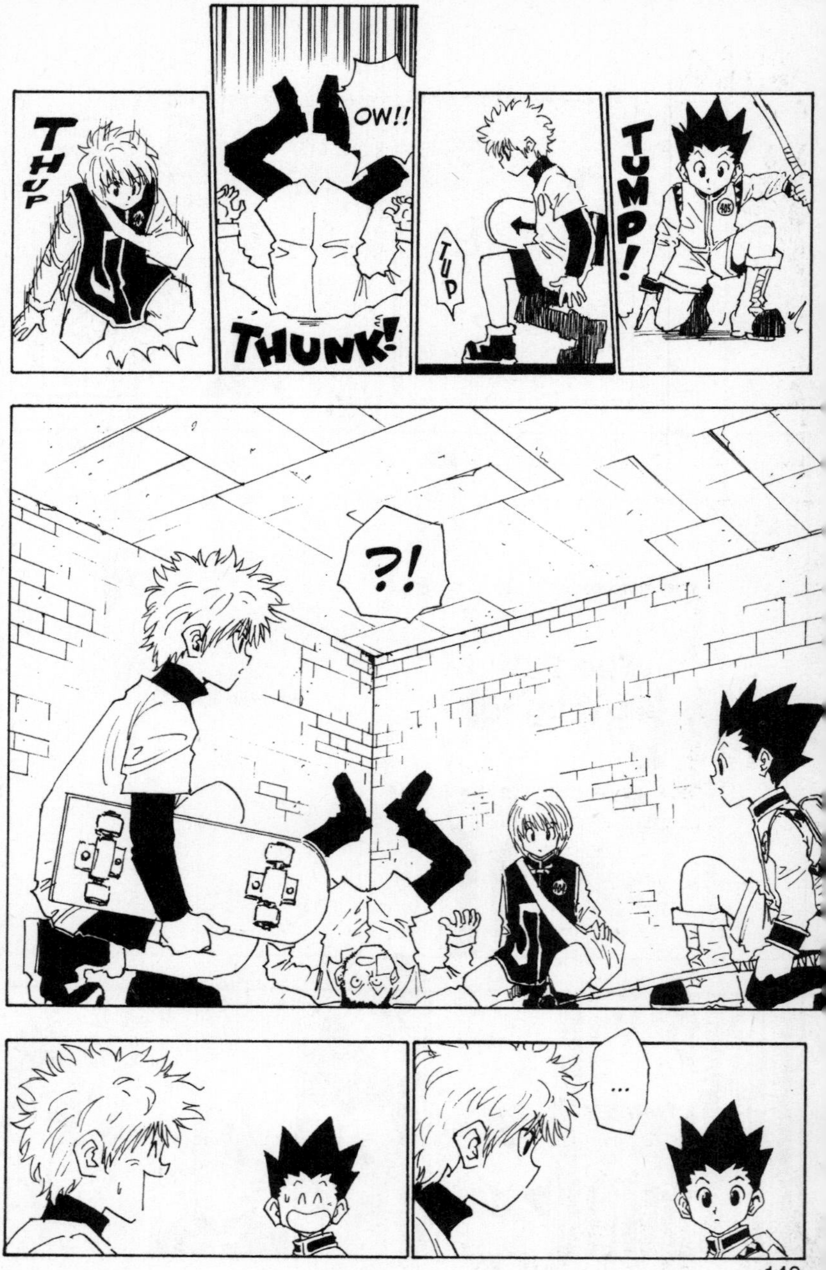
TUMP!
TUP
OW!!
THUNK!
THUP
?!
...

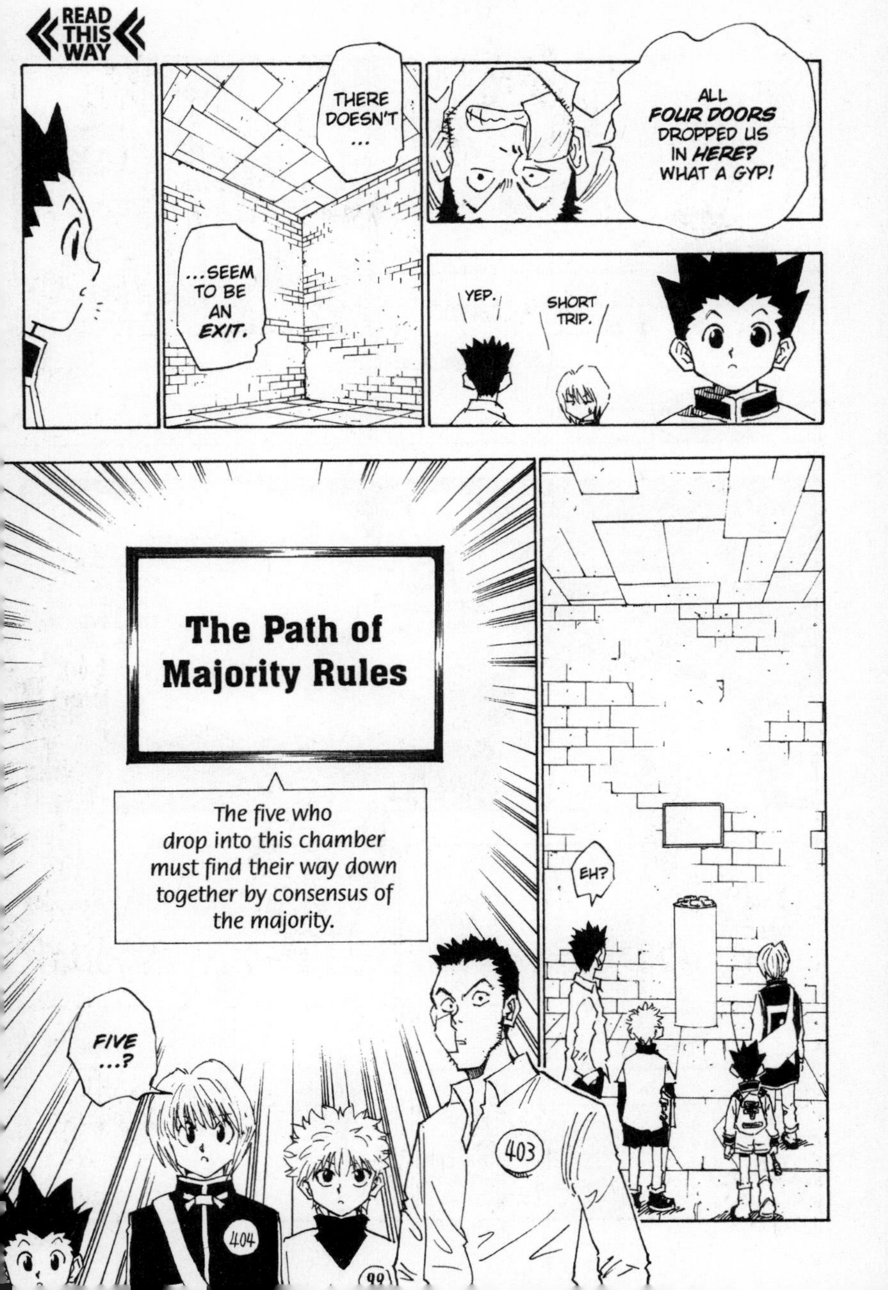
READ THIS WAY
ALL FOUR DOORS DROPPED US IN HERE? WHAT A GYP!
SHORT TRIP.
YEP.
THERE DOESN'T ...
...SEEM TO BE AN EXIT.
EH?
The Path of Majority Rules
The five who drop into this chamber must find their way down together by consensus of the majority.
FIVE ...?
403
404
99

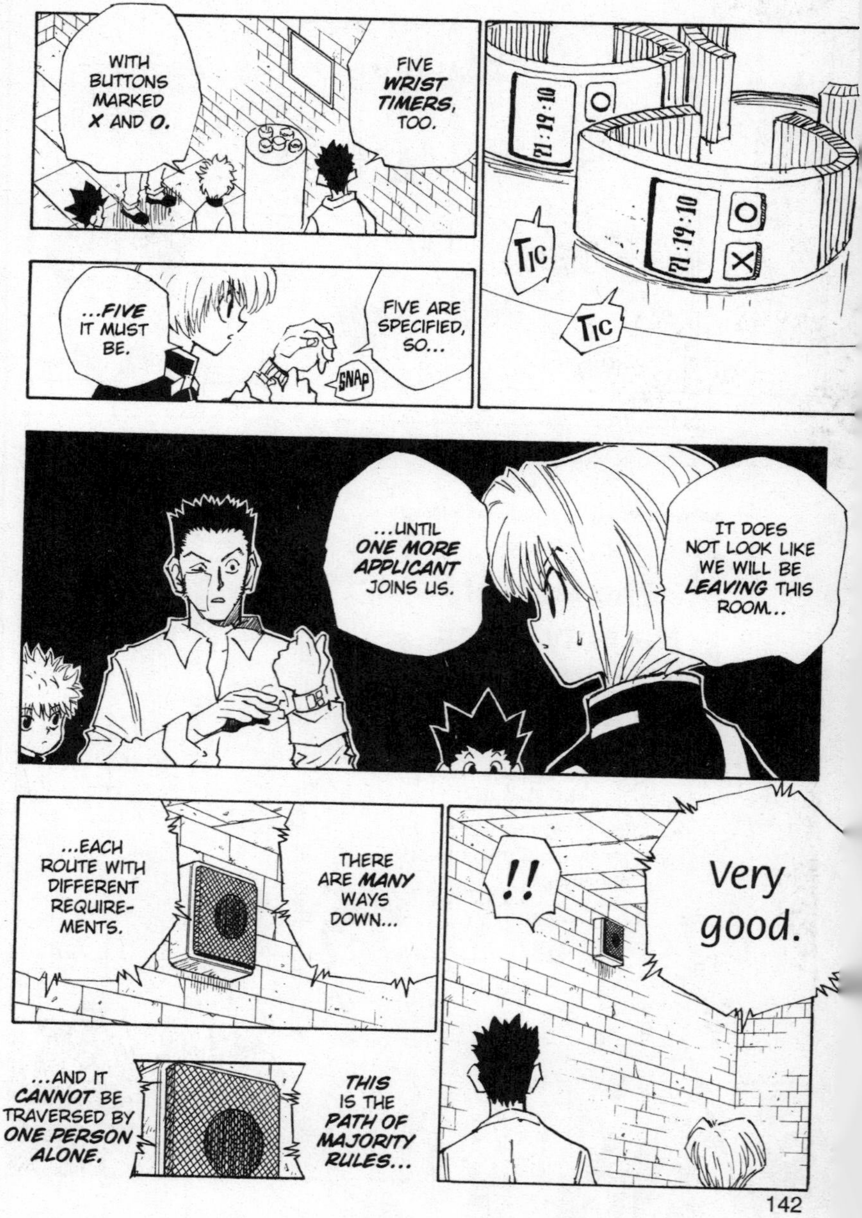
TIC
TIC
FIVE WRIST TIMERS, TOO.
WITH BUTTONS MARKED X AND O.
FIVE ARE SPECIFIED, SO...
SNAP
...FIVE IT MUST BE.
IT DOES NOT LOOK LIKE WE WILL BE LEAVING THIS ROOM...
...UNTIL ONE MORE APPLICANT JOINS US.
Very good.
!!
THERE ARE MANY WAYS DOWN...
...EACH ROUTE WITH DIFFERENT REQUIRE-MENTS.
THIS IS THE PATH OF MAJORITY RULES...
...AND IT CANNOT BE TRAVERSED BY ONE PERSON ALONE.

READ THIS WAY

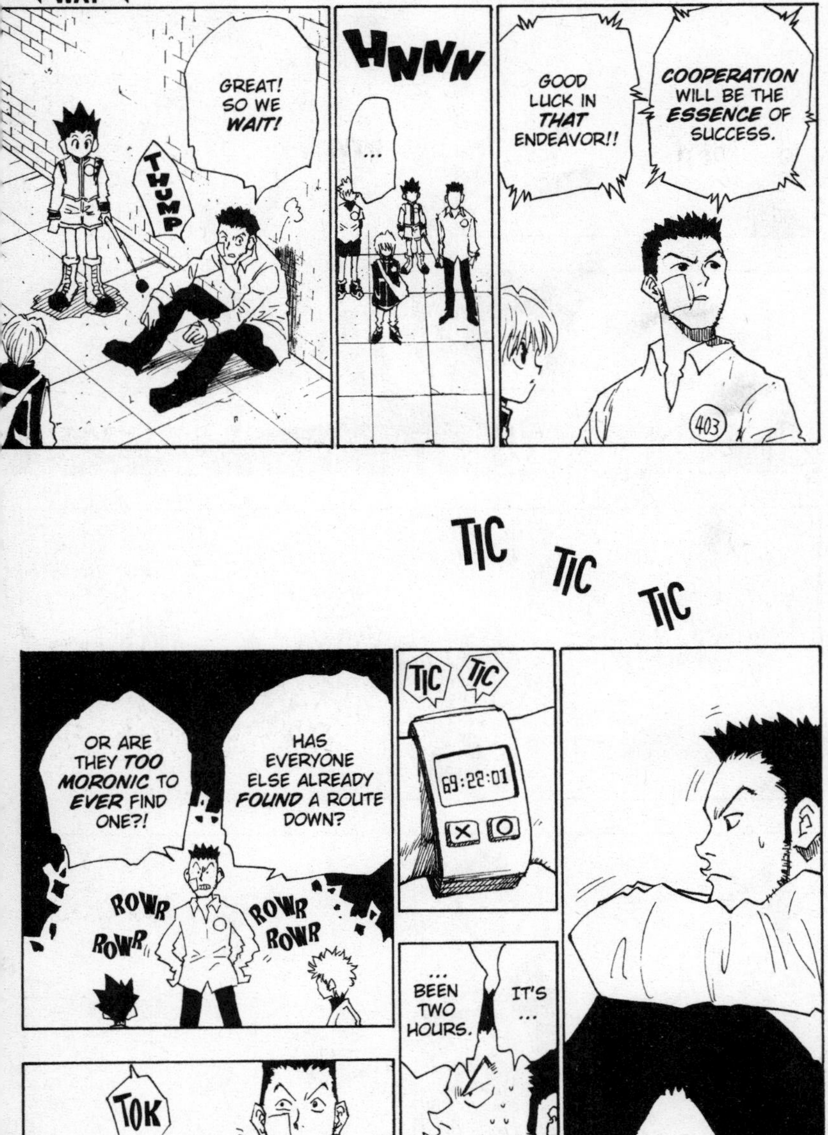
COOPERATION WILL BE THE ESSENCE OF SUCCESS.
GOOD LUCK IN THAT ENDEAVOR!!
HNNN
...
GREAT! SO WE WAIT!
THUMP
TIC
TIC
TIC
TIC
TIC
69:22:01
HAS EVERYONE ELSE ALREADY FOUND A ROUTE DOWN?
OR ARE THEY TOO MORONIC TO EVER FIND ONE?!
ROWR
ROWR
ROWR
ROWR
IT'S ...
... BEEN TWO HOURS.
TOK

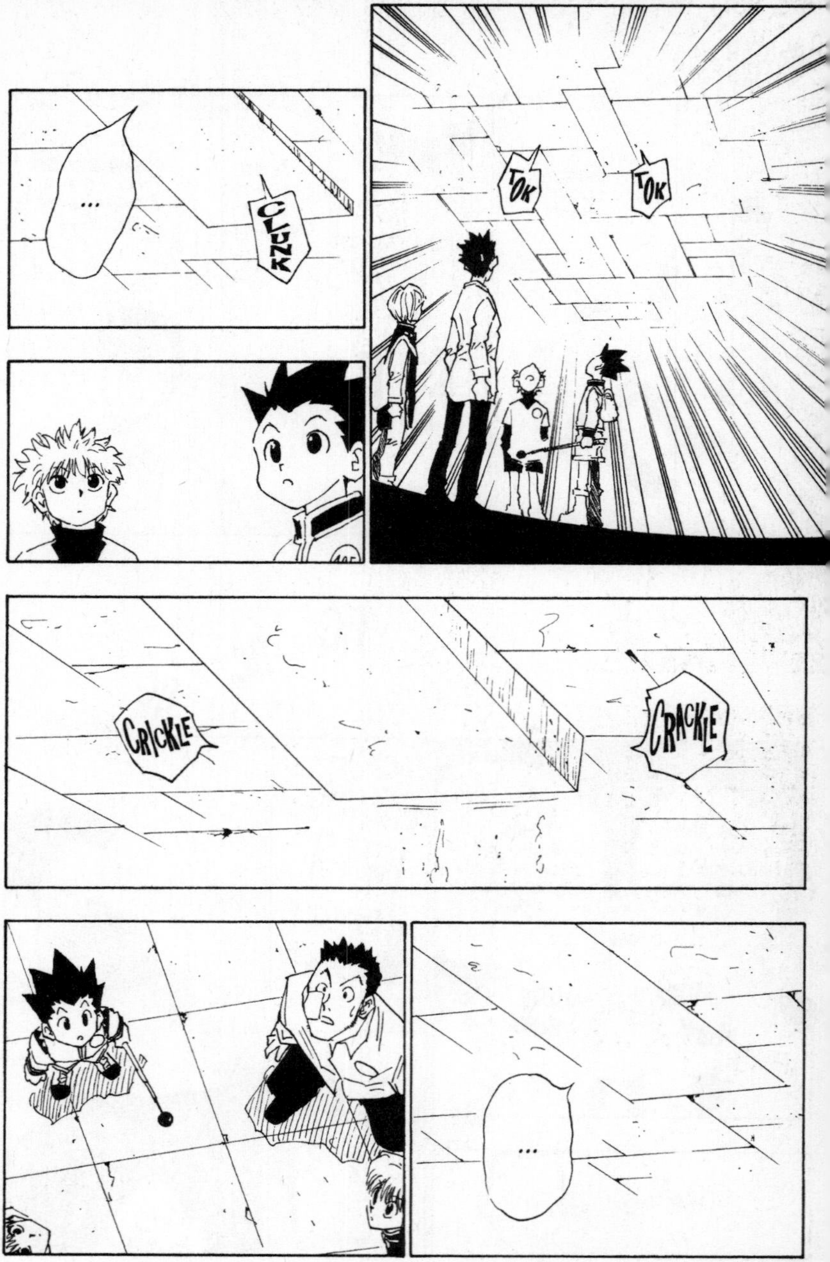
TOK
TOK
CLUNK
...
CRACKLE
CRICKLE
...

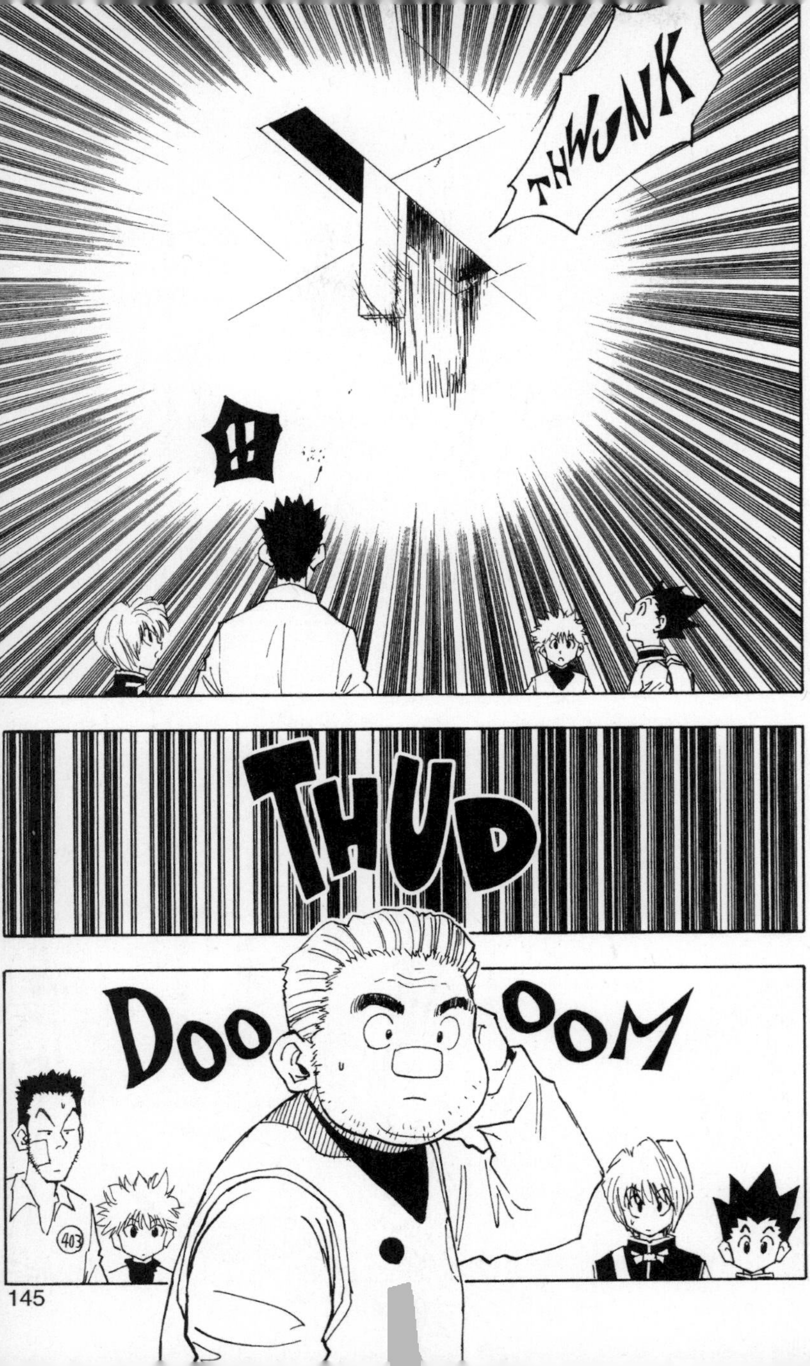
THWUNK
!!
THUD
DOO OOM

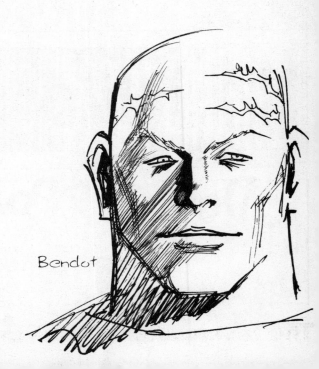

Bendot

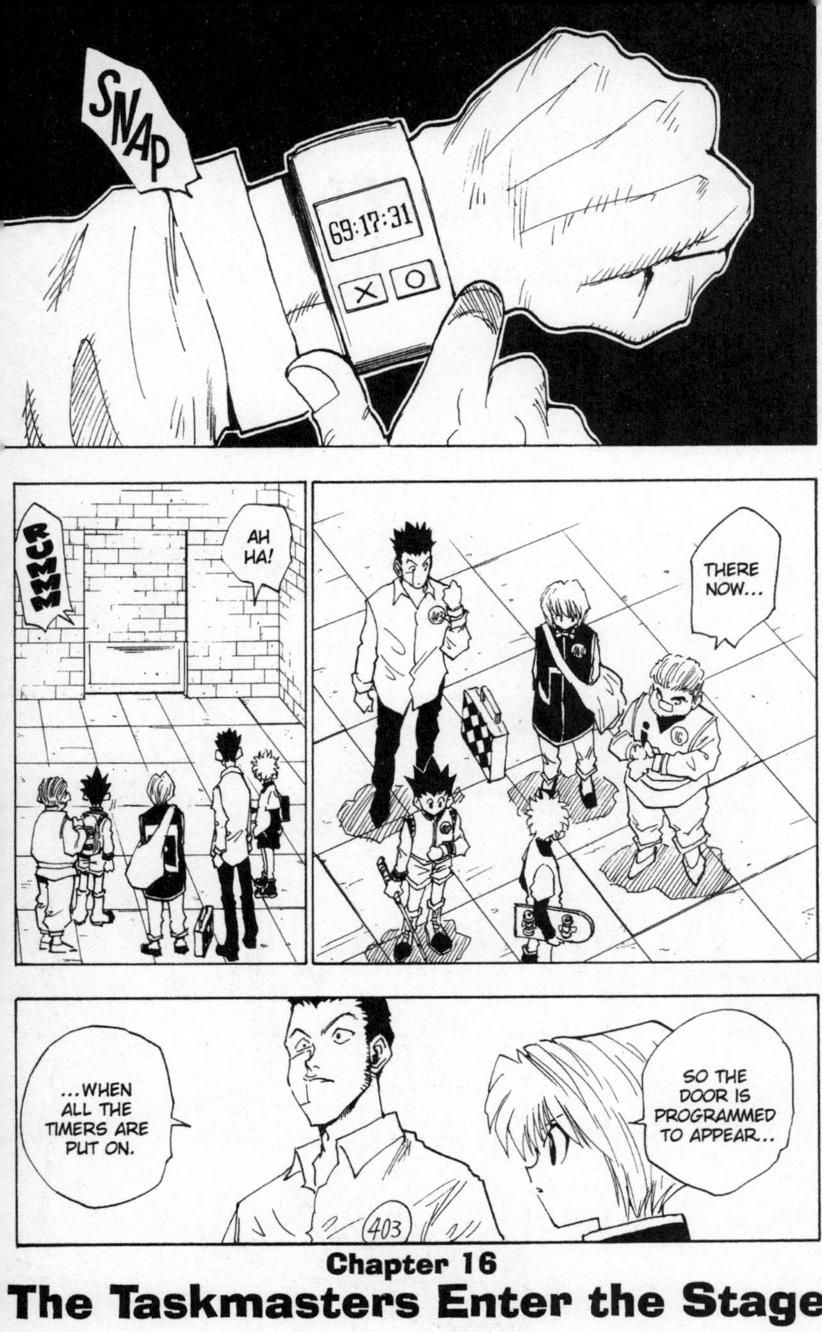
SNAP
69:17:31
THERE NOW...
AH HA!
RUMMM
SO THE DOOR IS PROGRAMMED TO APPEAR..
...WHEN ALL THE TIMERS ARE PUT ON.
403

Chapter 16

The Taskmasters Enter the Stage

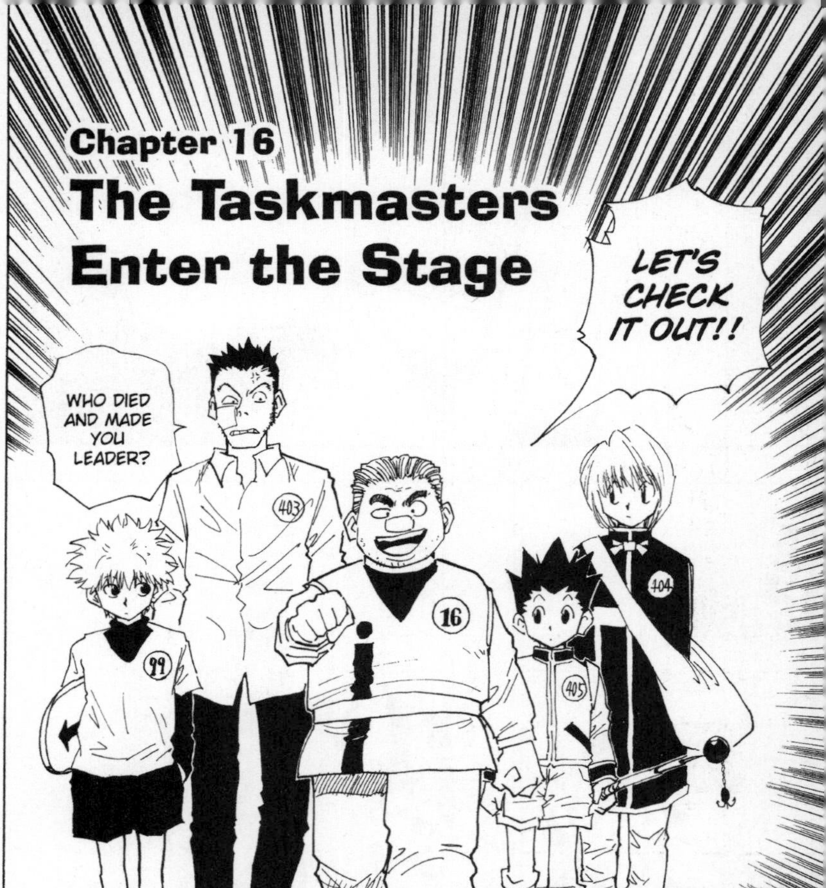
Chapter 16
The Taskmasters Enter the Stage
LET'S CHECK IT OUT!!
WHO DIED AND MADE YOU LEADER?
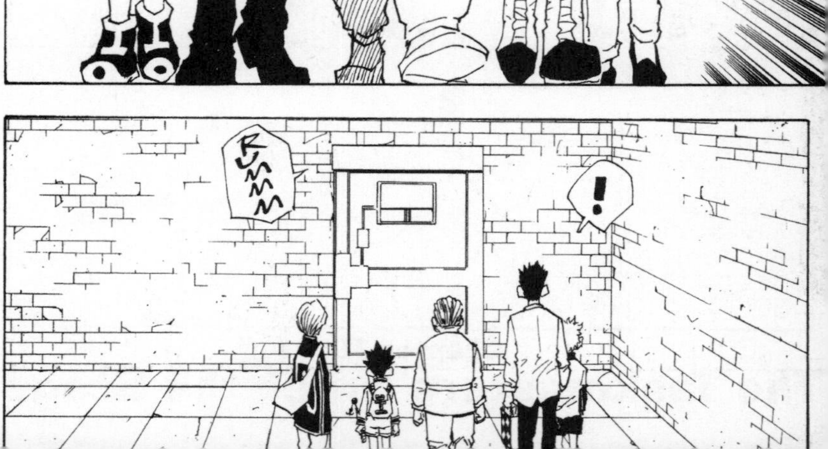
!
RUMMM

READ THIS WAY

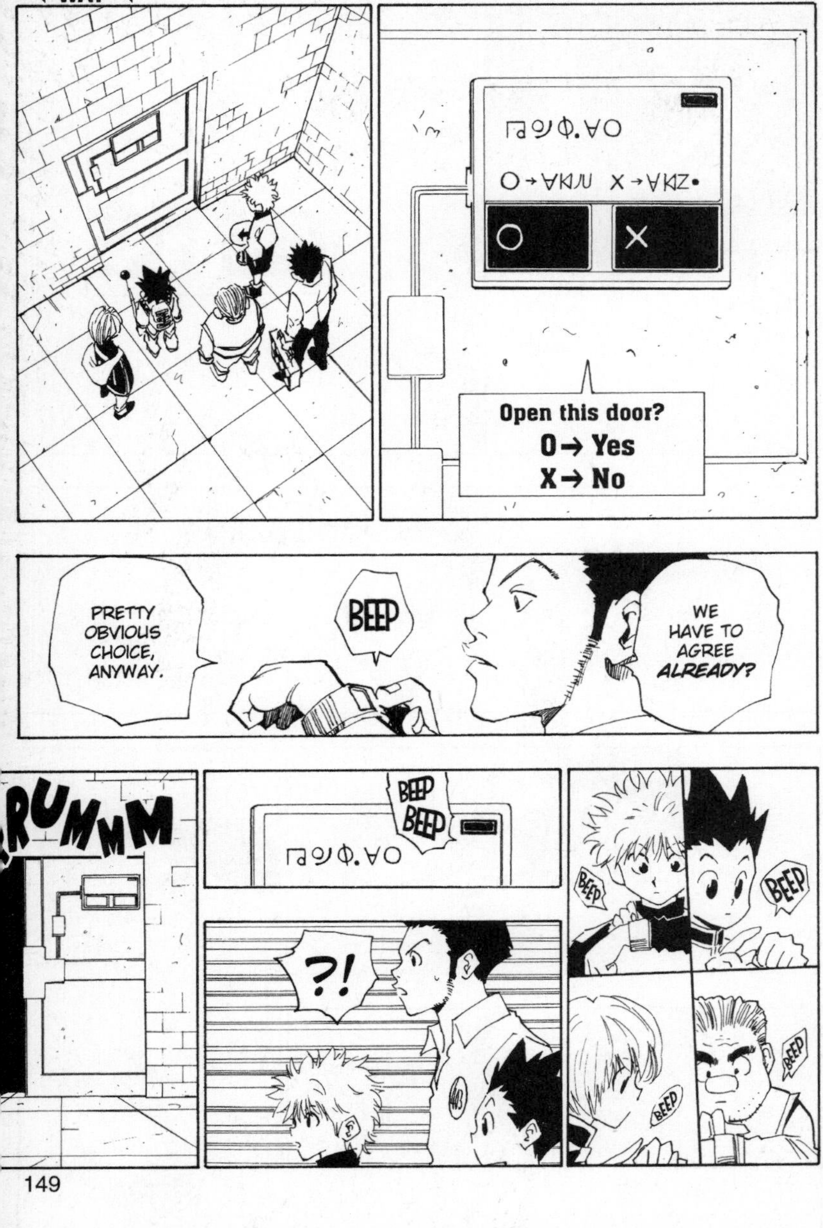
Open this door?
O→ Yes
X→ No
WE HAVE TO AGREE ALREADY?
BEEP
PRETTY OBVIOUS CHOICE, ANYWAY.
BEEP
BEEP
BEEP
BEEP
BEEP BEEP
?!
RUMMM

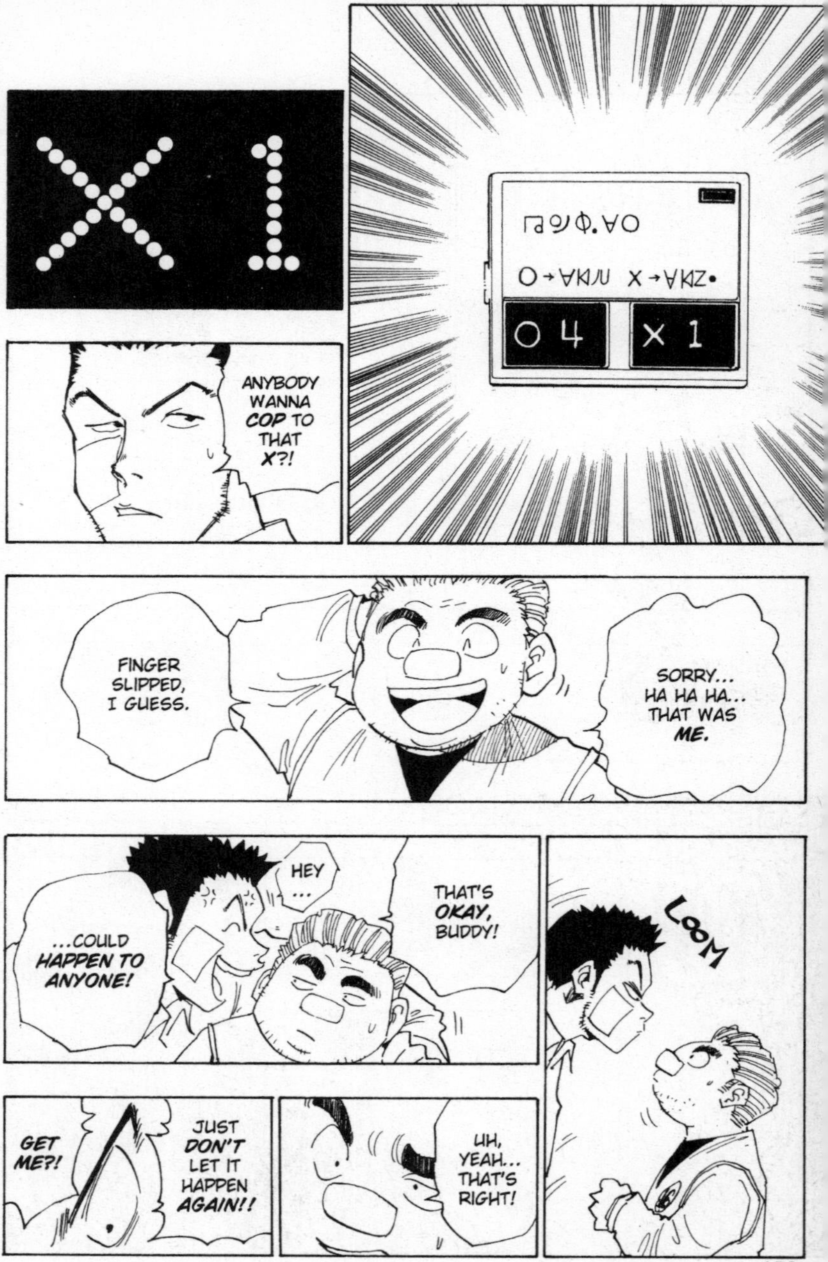
O 4
X 1
X 1
ANYBODY WANNA *COP* TO THAT *X*?!
SORRY... HA HA HA... THAT WAS *ME.*
FINGER SLIPPED, I GUESS.
LOOM
THAT'S *OKAY,* BUDDY!
HEY ...
...COULD *HAPPEN TO ANYONE!*
UH, YEAH... THAT'S RIGHT!
JUST *DON'T* LET IT HAPPEN *AGAIN!!*
GET ME?!

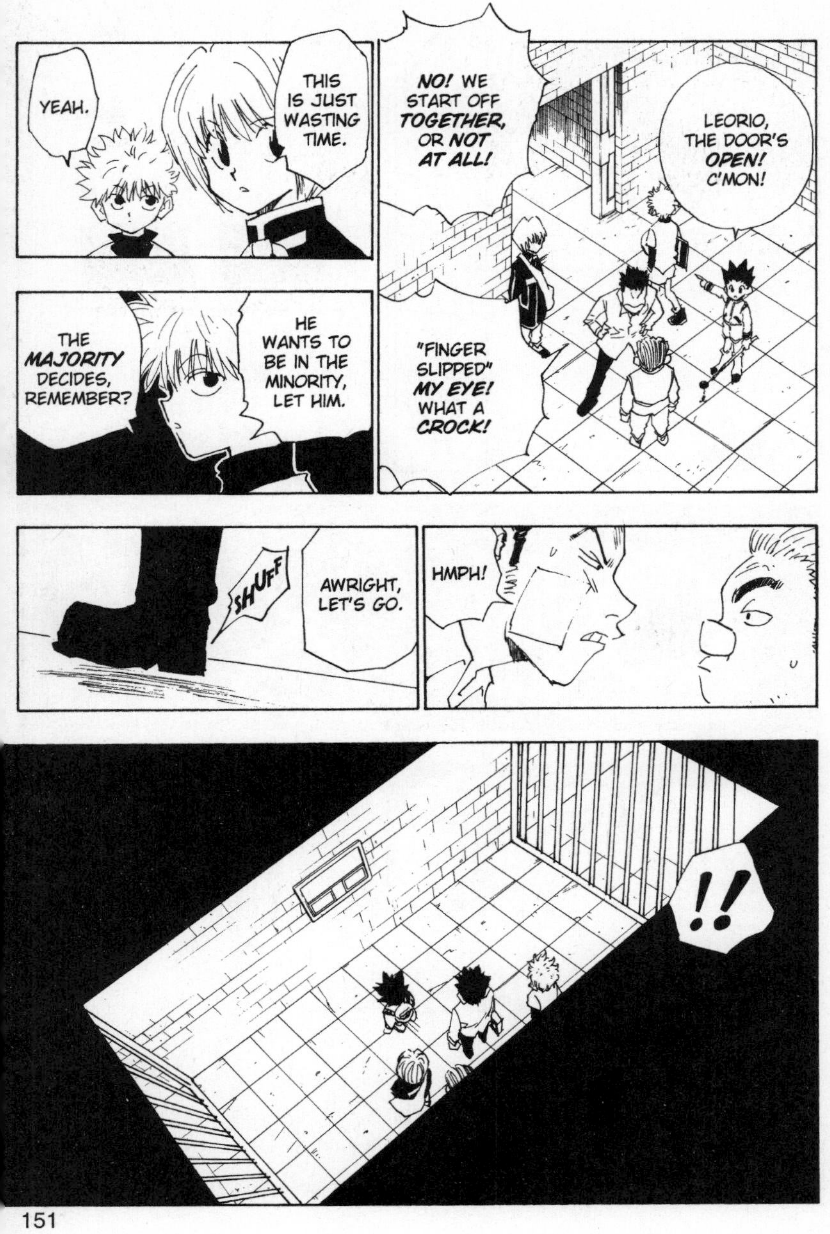
LEORIO, THE DOOR'S OPEN! C'MON!
NO! WE START OFF TOGETHER, OR NOT AT ALL!
"FINGER SLIPPED" MY EYE! WHAT A CROCK!
THIS IS JUST WASTING TIME.
YEAH.
HE WANTS TO BE IN THE MINORITY, LET HIM.
THE MAJORITY DECIDES, REMEMBER?
HMPH!
AWRIGHT, LET'S GO.
SHUFF
!!

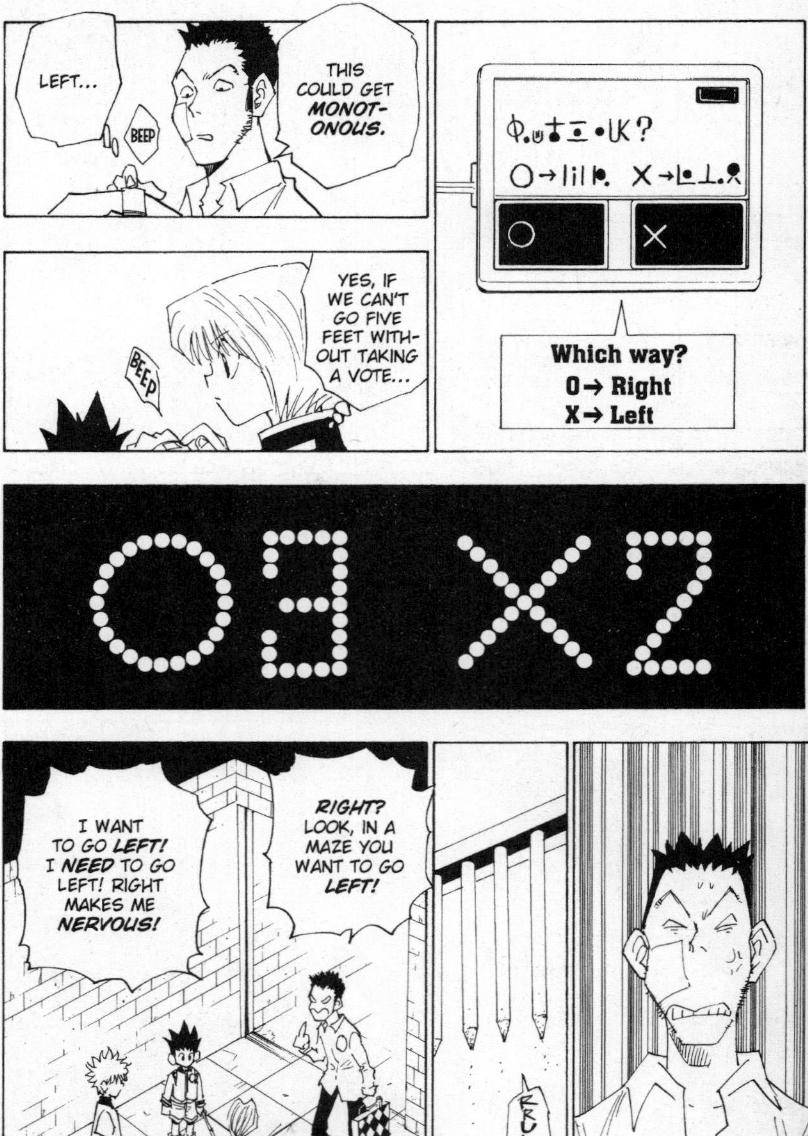
Which way?
O→ Right
X→ Left
THIS COULD GET MONOTONOUS.
LEFT...
BEEP
YES, IF WE CAN'T GO FIVE FEET WITHOUT TAKING A VOTE...
BEEP
RRUMM
403
RIGHT? LOOK, IN A MAZE YOU WANT TO GO LEFT!
I WANT TO GO LEFT! I NEED TO GO LEFT! RIGHT MAKES ME NERVOUS!

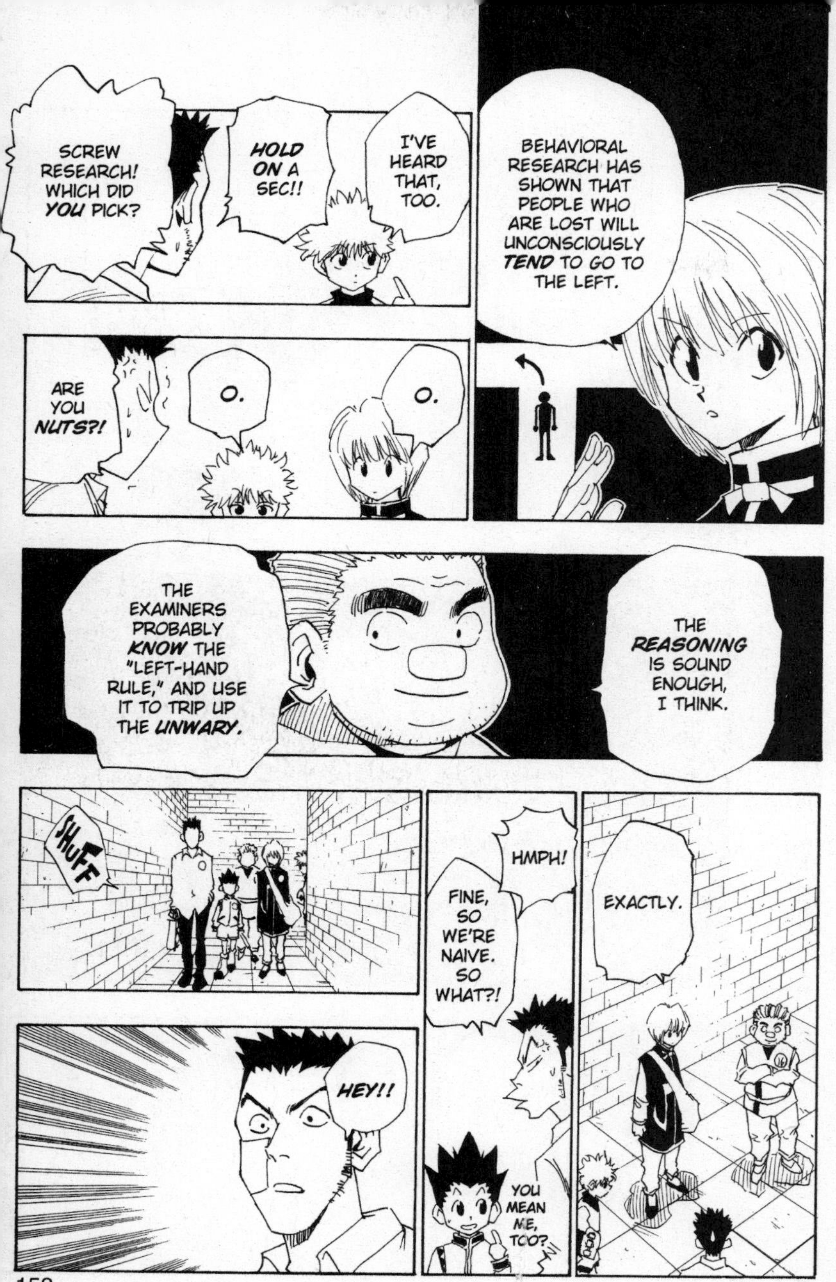
BEHAVIORAL RESEARCH HAS SHOWN THAT PEOPLE WHO ARE LOST WILL UNCONSCIOUSLY TEND TO GO TO THE LEFT.
I'VE HEARD THAT, TOO.
HOLD ON A SEC!!
SCREW RESEARCH! WHICH DID YOU PICK?
O.
O.
ARE YOU NUTS?!
THE REASONING IS SOUND ENOUGH, I THINK.
THE EXAMINERS PROBABLY KNOW THE "LEFT-HAND RULE," AND USE IT TO TRIP UP THE UNWARY.
EXACTLY.
HMPH!
FINE, SO WE'RE NAIVE. SO WHAT?!
YOU MEAN ME, TOO?
SHUFF
HEY!!

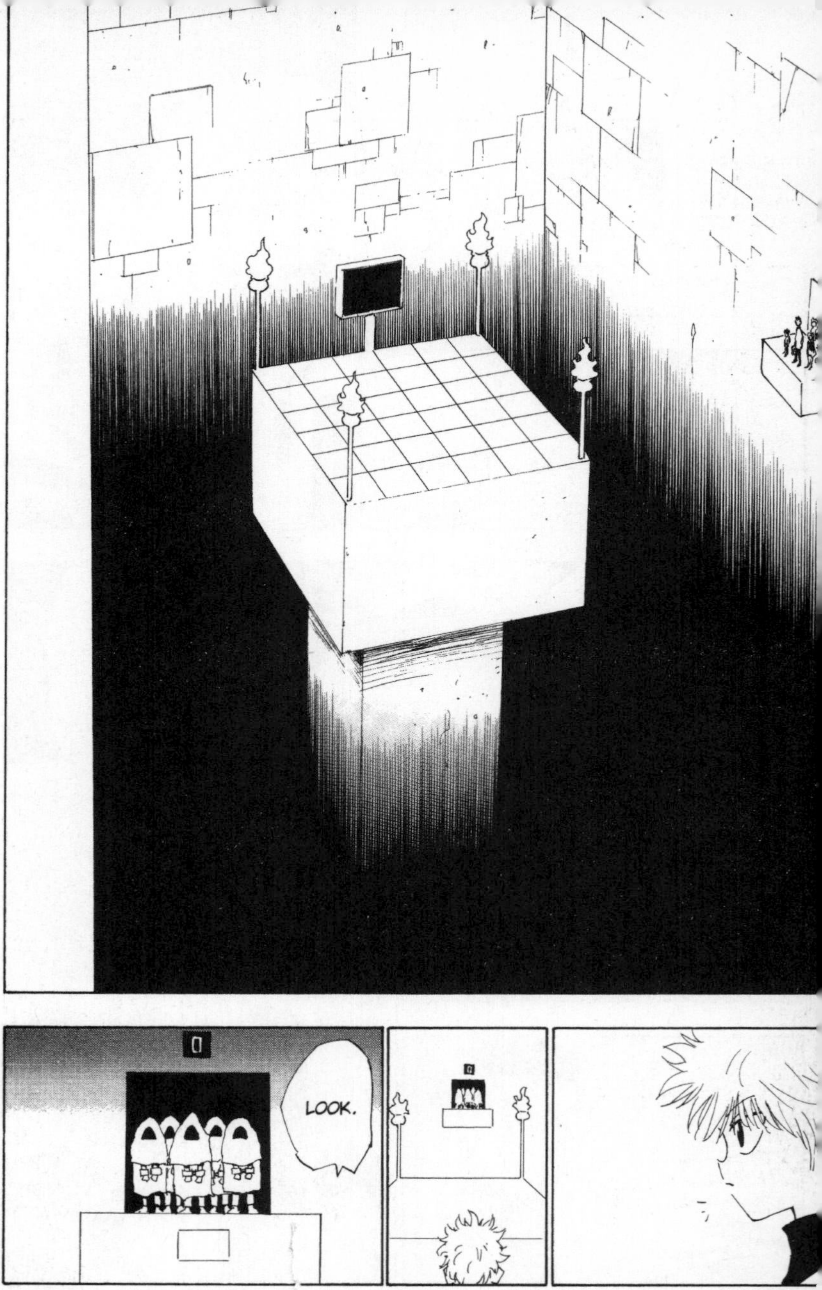
LOOK.

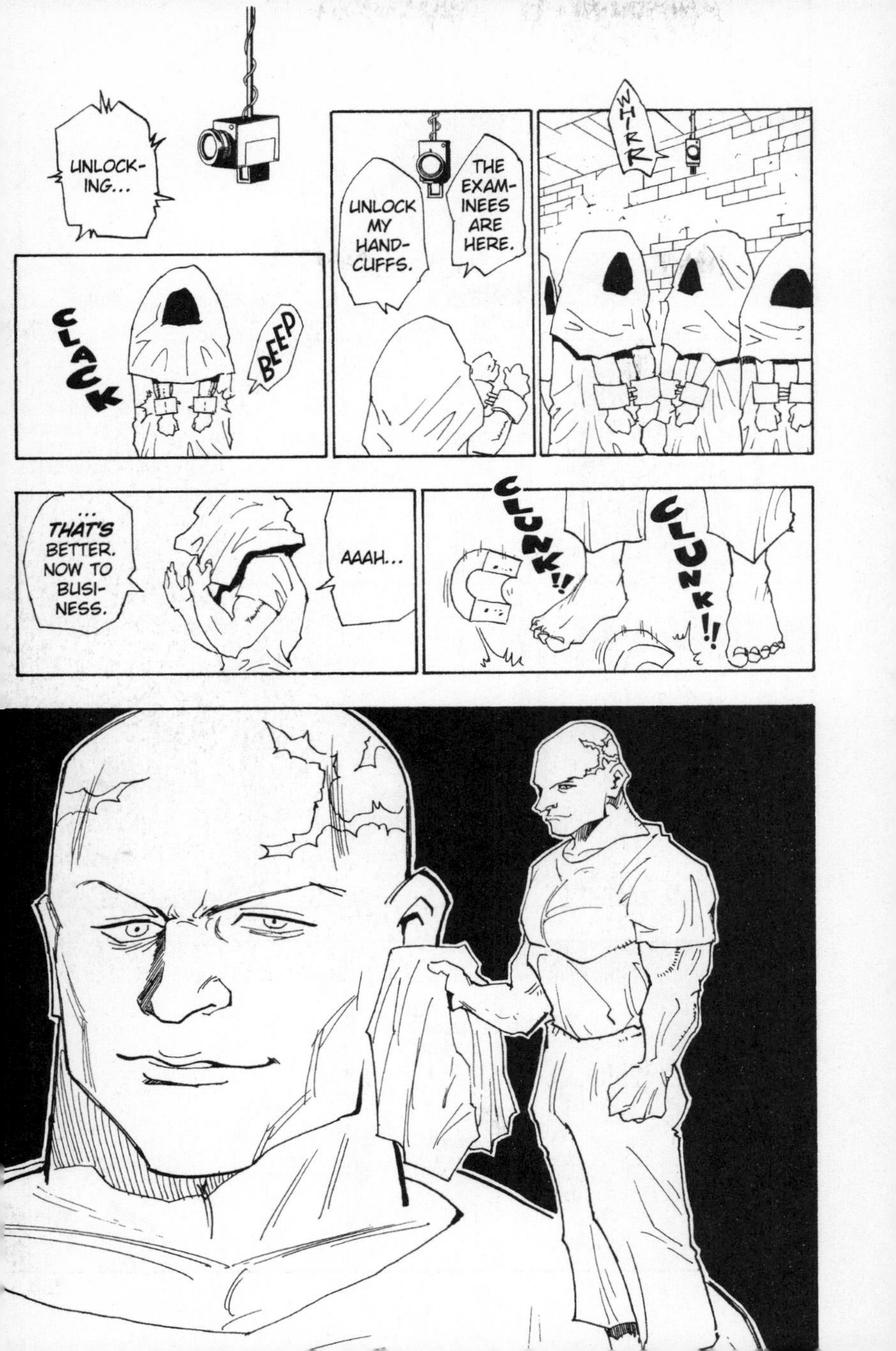
WHIRR
THE EXAMINEES ARE HERE.
UNLOCK MY HANDCUFFS.
UNLOCKING...
BEEP
CLACK
CLUNK!!
CLUNK!!
AAAH...
...THAT'S BETTER. NOW TO BUSINESS.

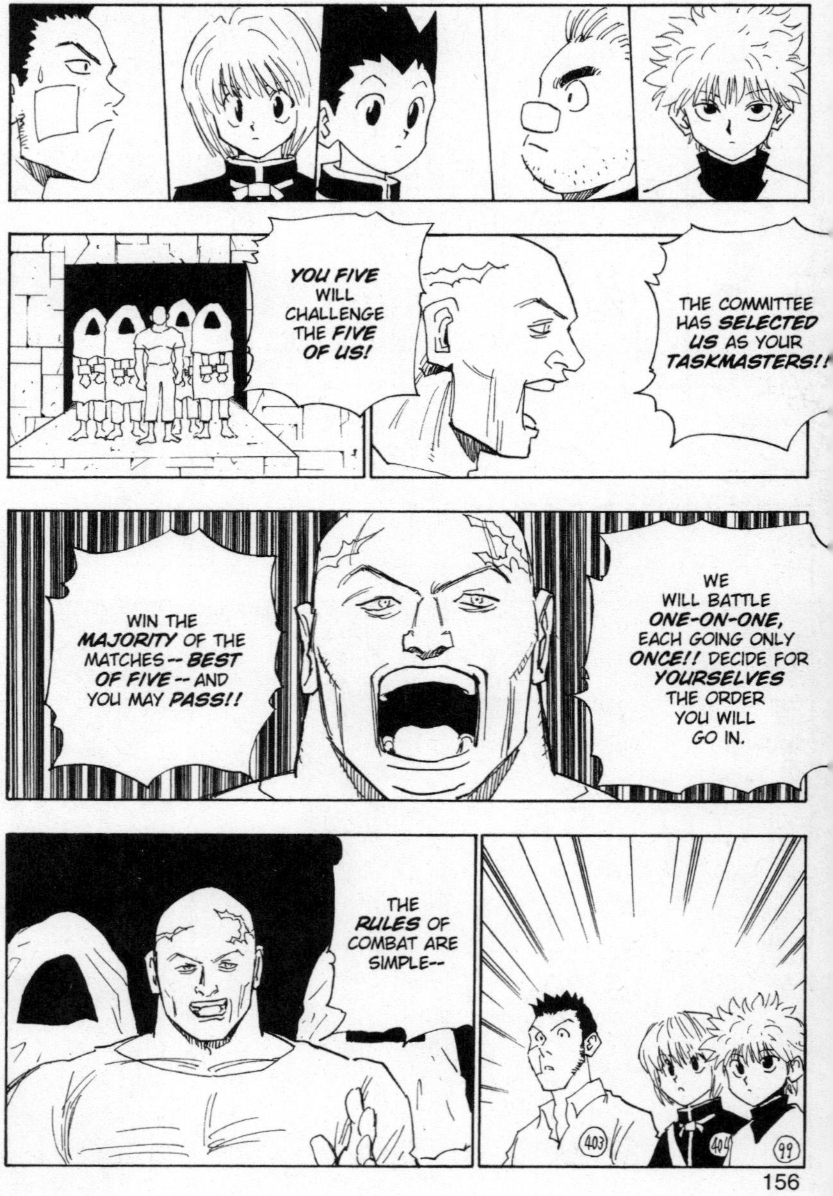
THE COMMITTEE HAS SELECTED US AS YOUR TASKMASTERS!!
YOU FIVE WILL CHALLENGE THE FIVE OF US!
WE WILL BATTLE ONE-ON-ONE, EACH GOING ONLY ONCE!! DECIDE FOR YOURSELVES THE ORDER YOU WILL GO IN.
WIN THE MAJORITY OF THE MATCHES -- BEST OF FIVE -- AND YOU MAY PASS!!
THE RULES OF COMBAT ARE SIMPLE--

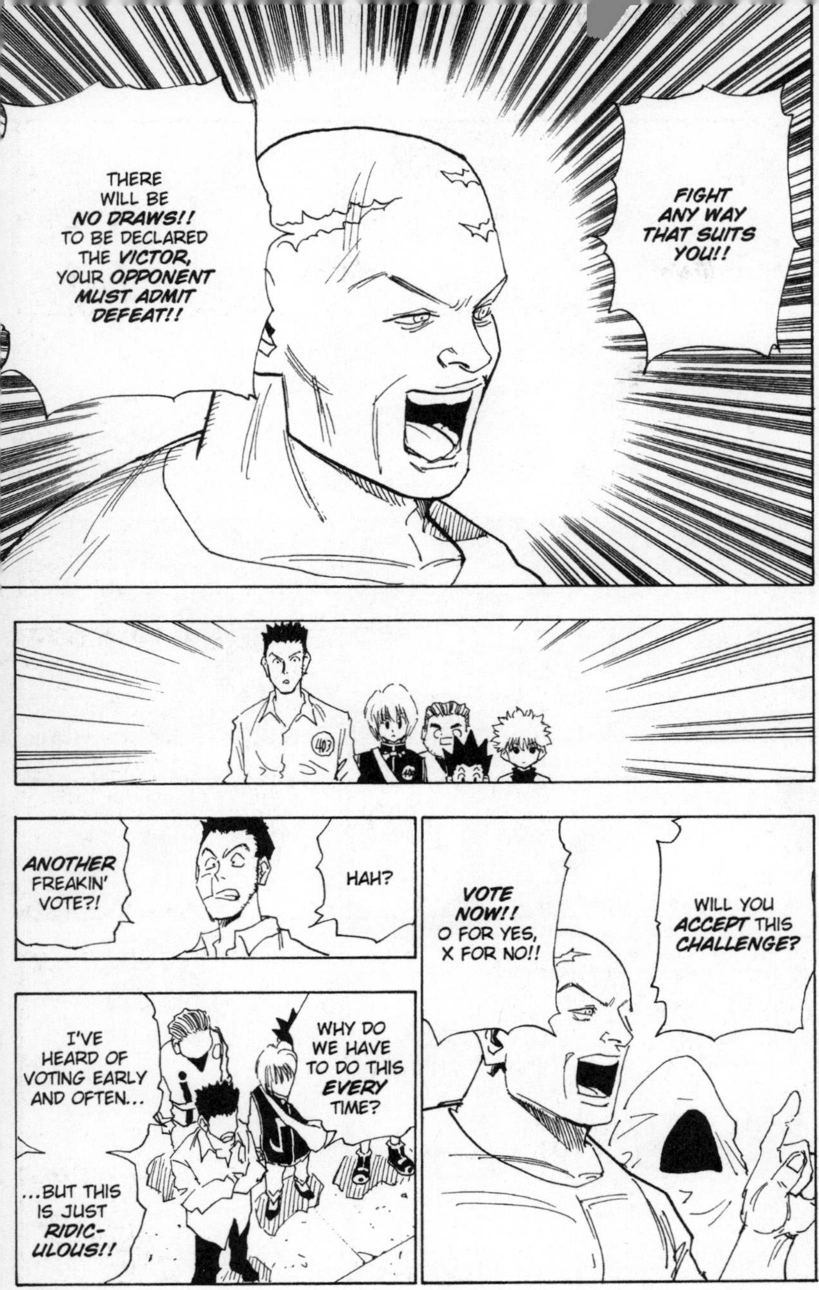
FIGHT ANY WAY THAT SUITS YOU!!
THERE WILL BE NO DRAWS!! TO BE DECLARED THE VICTOR, YOUR OPPONENT MUST ADMIT DEFEAT!!
WILL YOU ACCEPT THIS CHALLENGE?
VOTE NOW!! O FOR YES, X FOR NO!!
HAH?
ANOTHER FREAKIN' VOTE?!
WHY DO WE HAVE TO DO THIS EVERY TIME?
I'VE HEARD OF VOTING EARLY AND OFTEN...
...BUT THIS IS JUST RIDICULOUS!!

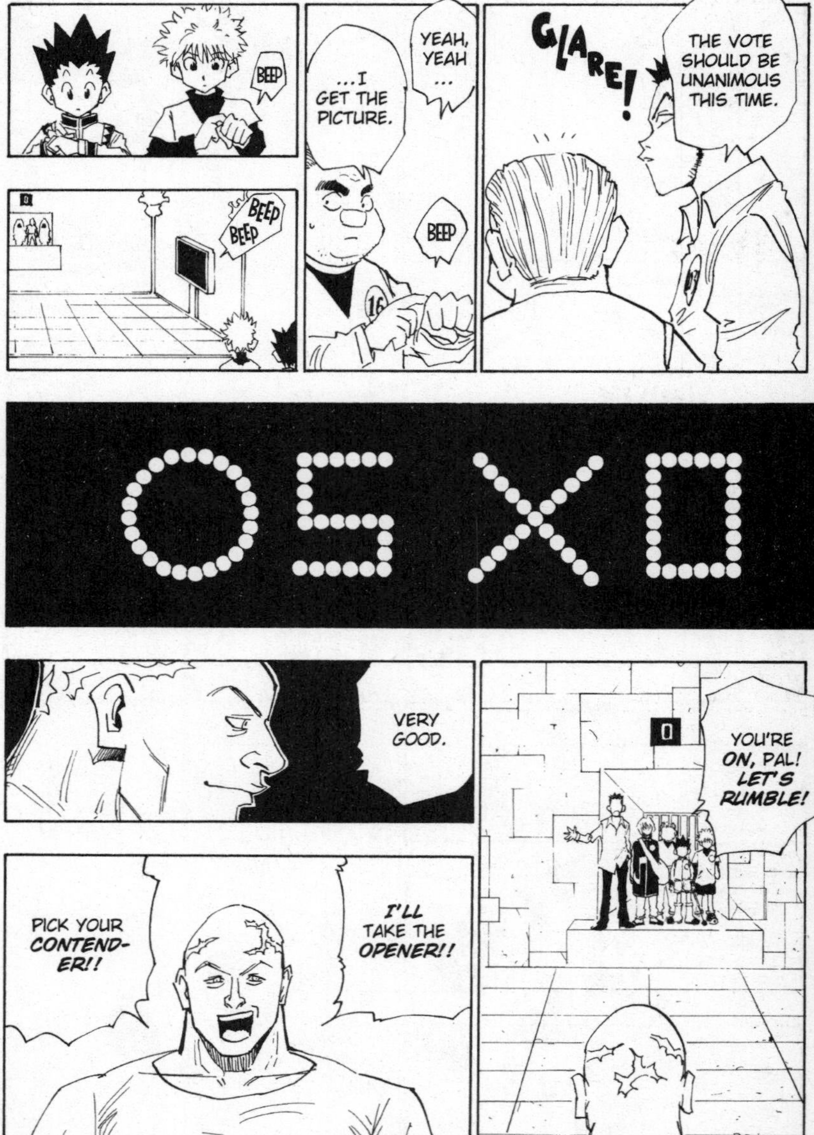
GLARE!
THE VOTE SHOULD BE UNANIMOUS THIS TIME.
YEAH, YEAH ...
...I GET THE PICTURE.
BEEP
BEEP
BEEP BEEP
05 X 0
YOU'RE ON, PAL! LET'S RUMBLE!
VERY GOOD.
I'LL TAKE THE OPENER!!
PICK YOUR CONTENDER!!

READ THIS WAY

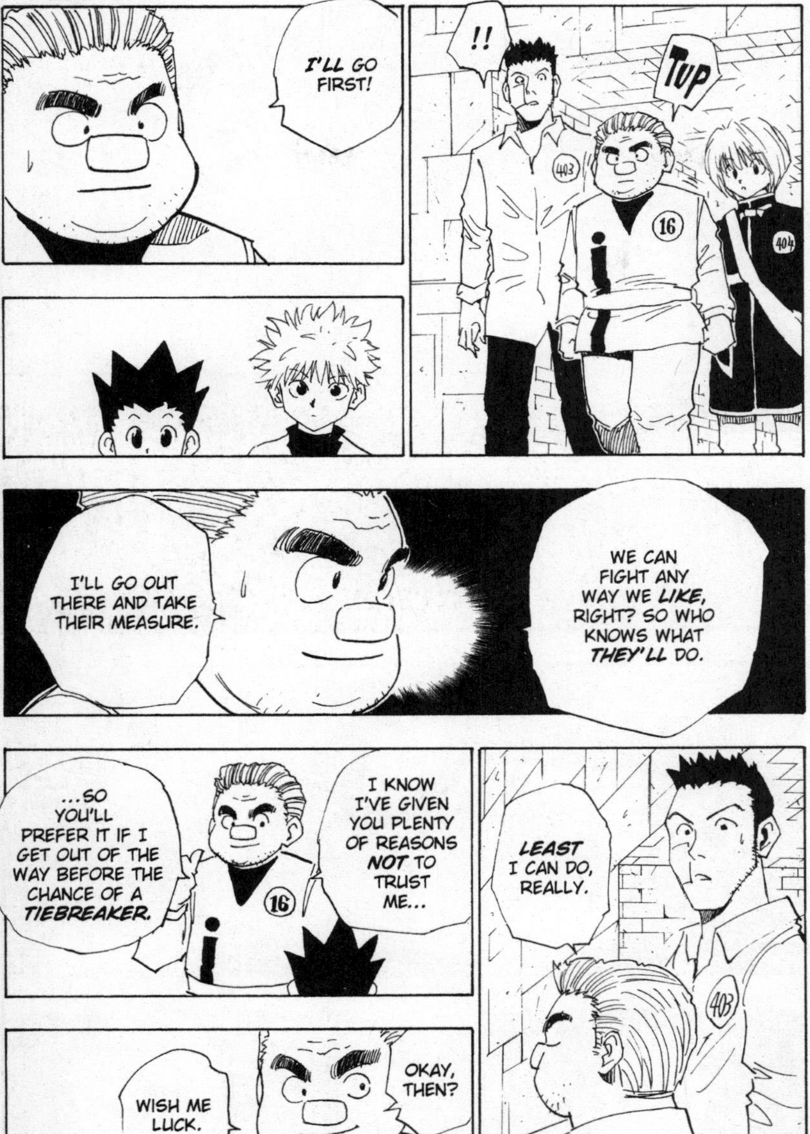
!!
TUP
I'LL GO FIRST!
WE CAN FIGHT ANY WAY WE *LIKE*, RIGHT? SO WHO KNOWS WHAT *THEY'LL* DO.
I'LL GO OUT THERE AND TAKE THEIR MEASURE.
LEAST I CAN DO, REALLY.
I KNOW I'VE GIVEN YOU PLENTY OF REASONS *NOT* TO TRUST ME...
...SO YOU'LL PREFER IT IF I GET OUT OF THE WAY BEFORE THE CHANCE OF A *TIEBREAKER*.
OKAY, THEN?
WISH ME LUCK.

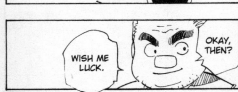

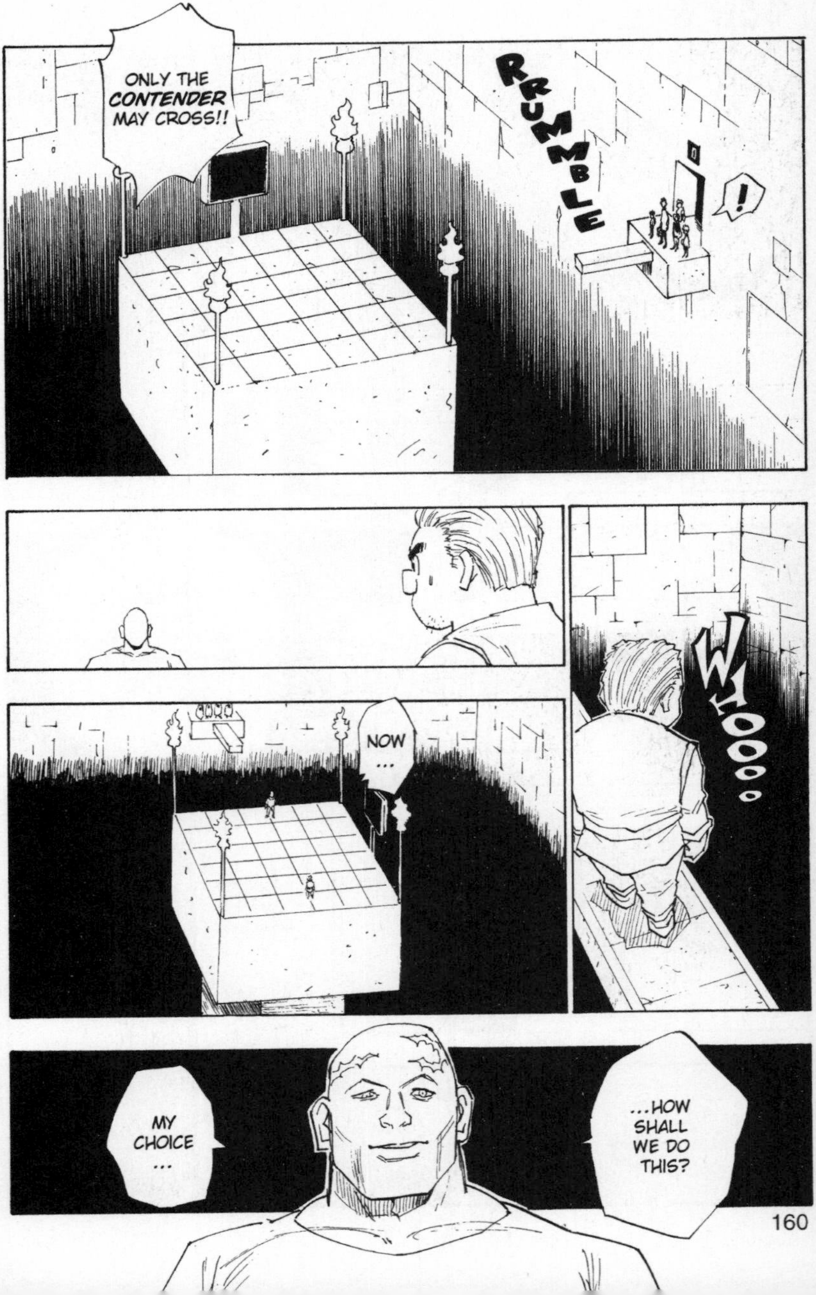
RRUMBLE
!
ONLY THE CONTENDER MAY CROSS!!
WHOOOO
NOW ...
...HOW SHALL WE DO THIS?
MY CHOICE ...

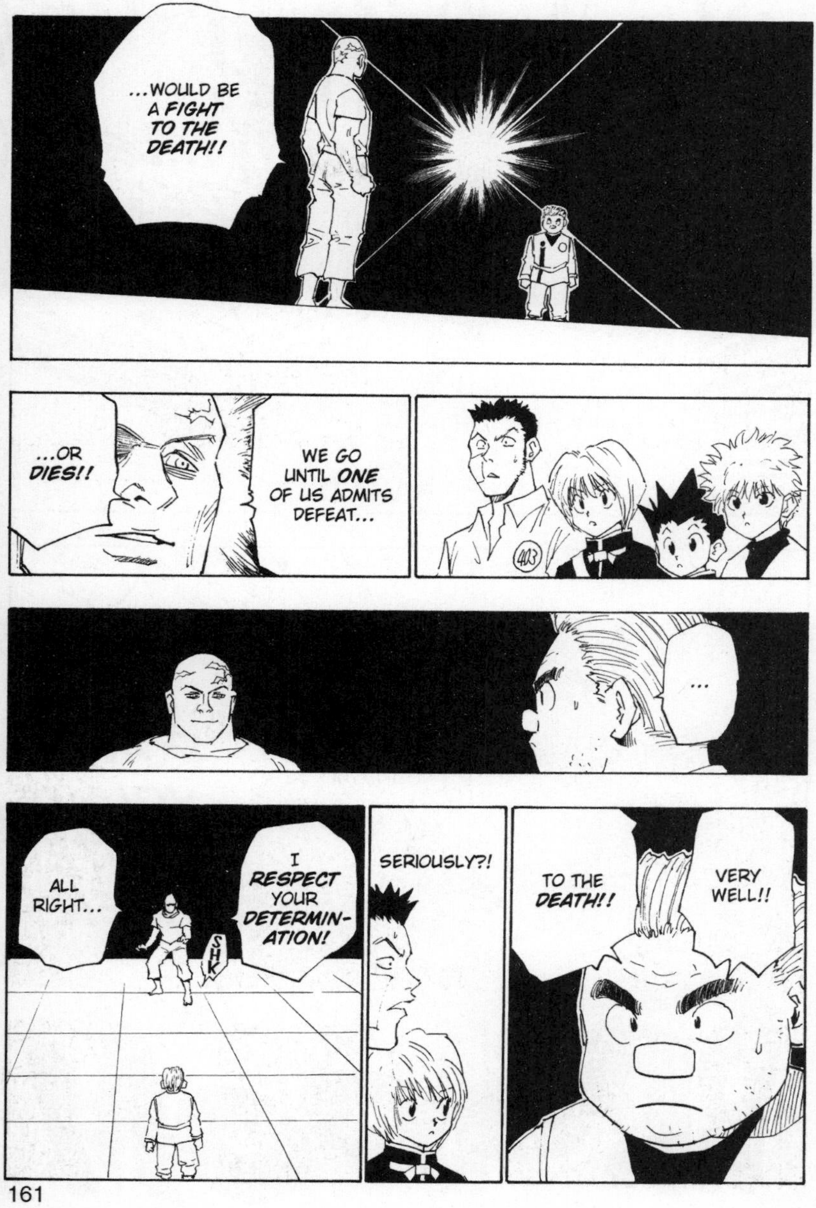
...WOULD BE A *FIGHT* *TO THE* *DEATH!!*
WE GO UNTIL *ONE* OF US ADMITS DEFEAT...
...OR *DIES!!*
...
VERY WELL!!
TO THE *DEATH!!*
SERIOUSLY?!
I *RESPECT* YOUR *DETERMIN-* *ATION!*
SHK
ALL RIGHT...

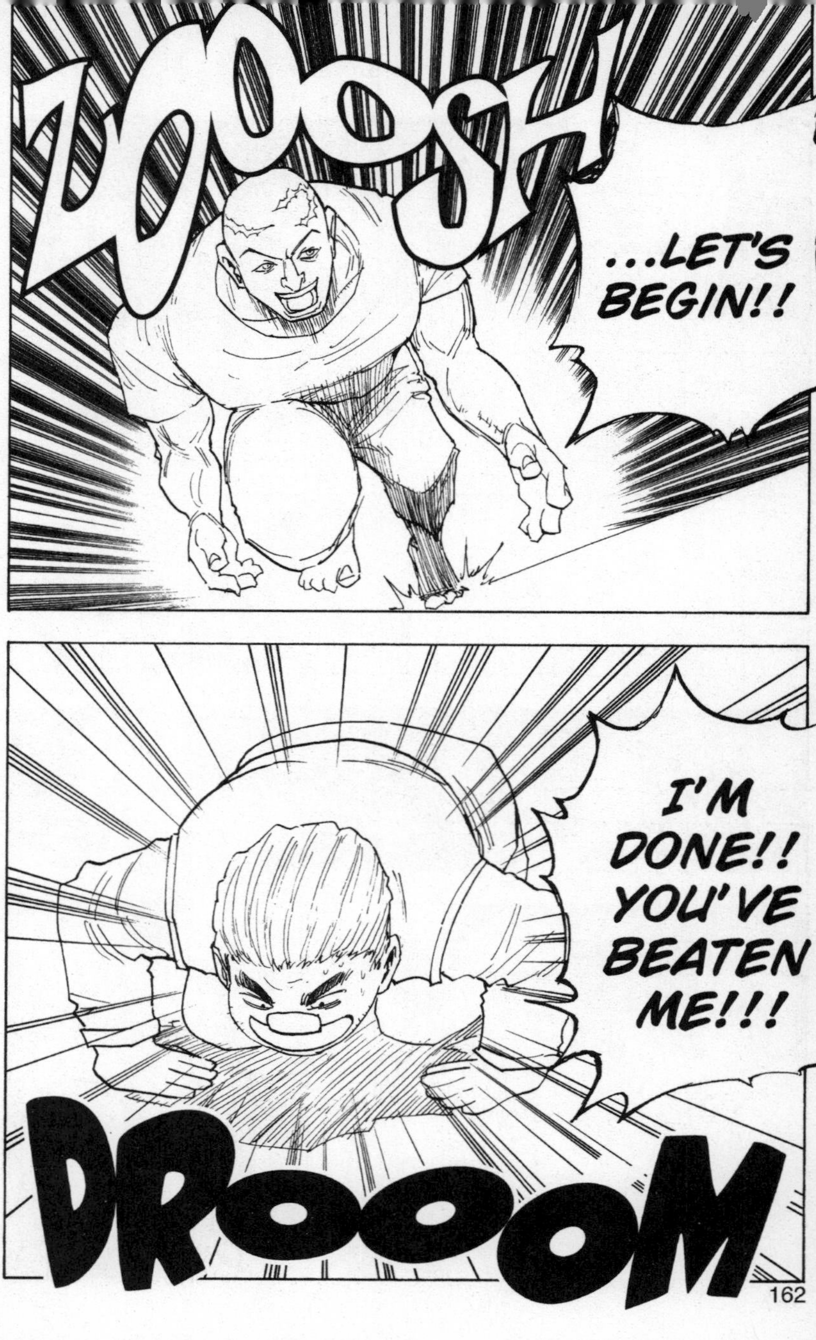
ZOOOSH
...LET'S BEGIN!!
I'M DONE!! YOU'VE BEATEN ME!!!
DROOOM

READ THIS WAY

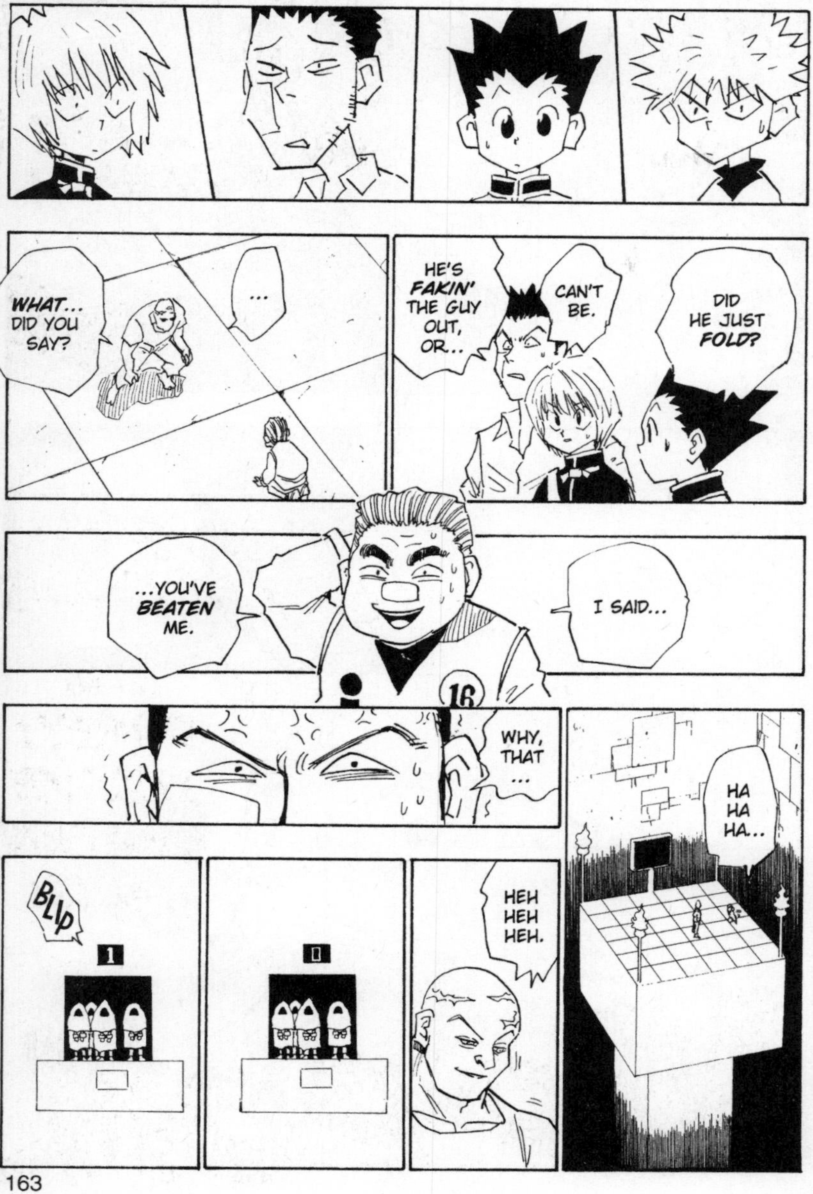
DID HE JUST FOLD?
CAN'T BE.
HE'S FAKIN' THE GUY OUT, OR...
...
WHAT... DID YOU SAY?
I SAID...
...YOU'VE BEATEN ME.
16
HA HA HA...
WHY, THAT ...
HEH HEH HEH.
0
BLIP
1

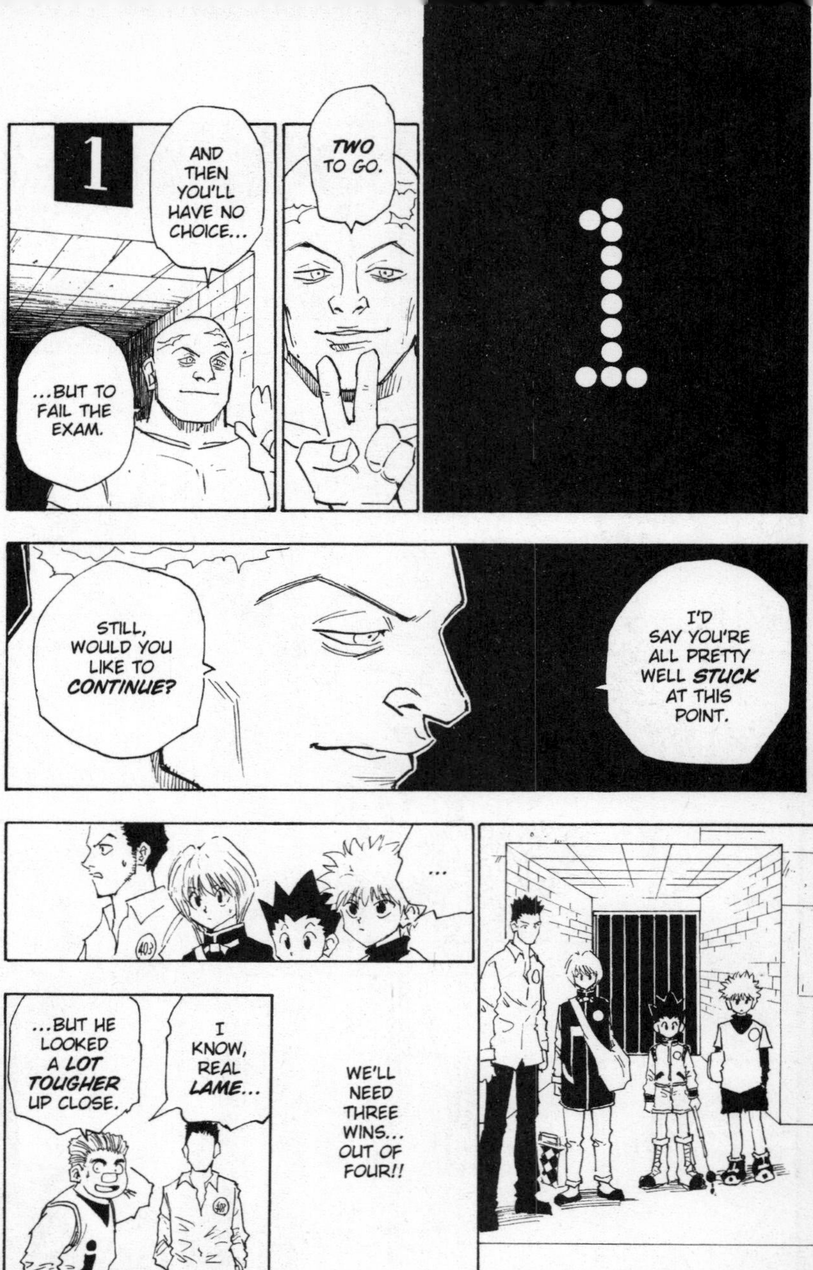
TWO TO GO.
1
AND THEN YOU'LL HAVE NO CHOICE...
...BUT TO FAIL THE EXAM.
I'D SAY YOU'RE ALL PRETTY WELL STUCK AT THIS POINT.
STILL, WOULD YOU LIKE TO CONTINUE?
...
WE'LL NEED THREE WINS... OUT OF FOUR!!
I KNOW, REAL LAME...
...BUT HE LOOKED A LOT TOUGHER UP CLOSE.

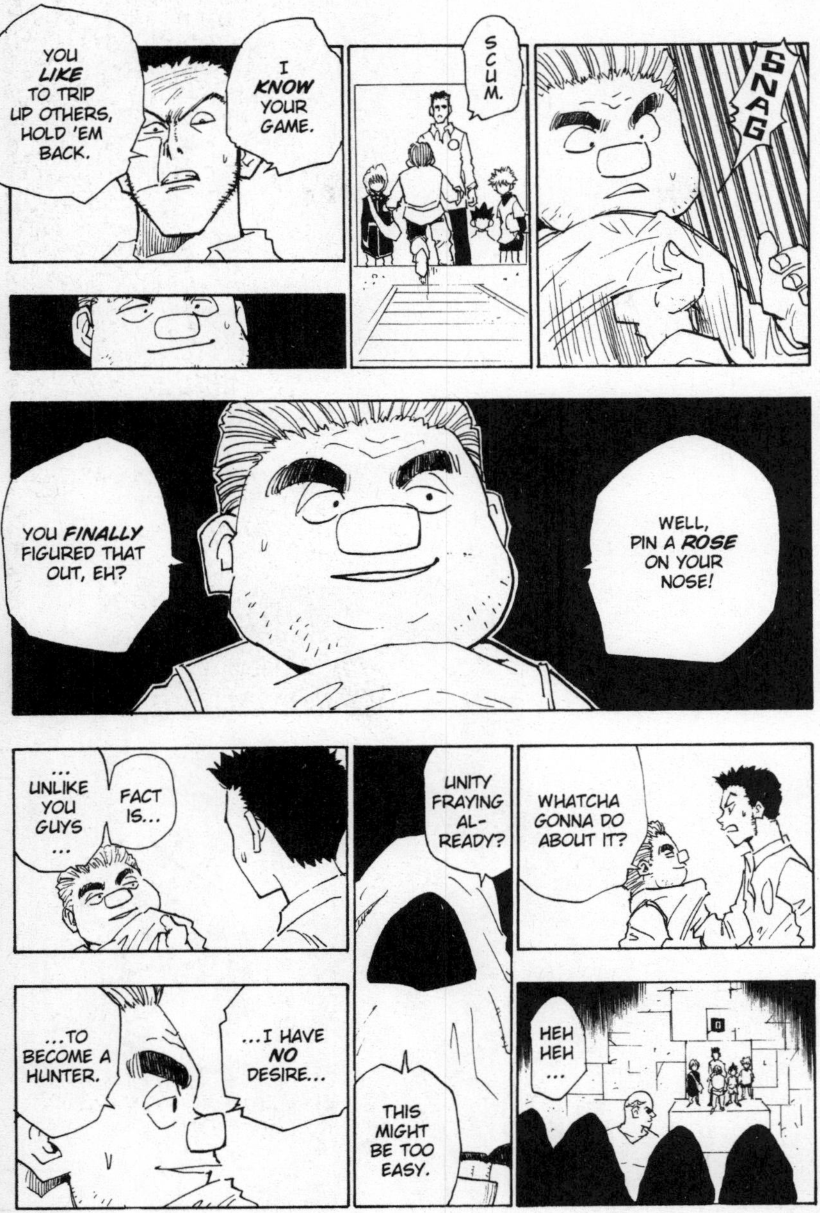
SNAG
SCUM.
I KNOW YOUR GAME.
YOU LIKE TO TRIP UP OTHERS, HOLD 'EM BACK.
WELL, PIN A ROSE ON YOUR NOSE!
YOU FINALLY FIGURED THAT OUT, EH?
WHATCHA GONNA DO ABOUT IT?
HEH HEH ...
UNITY FRAYING AL-READY?
THIS MIGHT BE TOO EASY.
FACT IS...
... UNLIKE YOU GUYS ...
...I HAVE NO DESIRE...
...TO BECOME A HUNTER.

Sedokan

Chapter 17
Disparate Choice

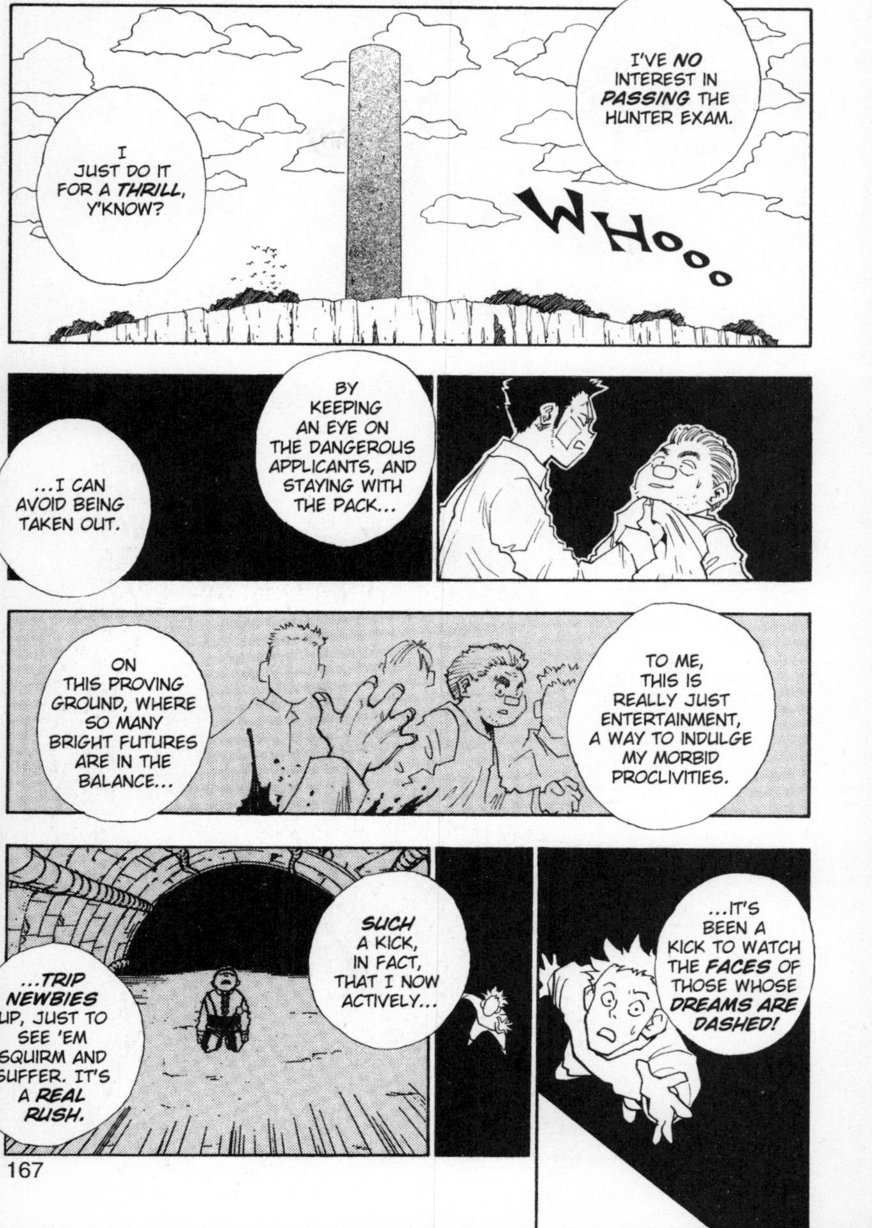
I'VE *NO* INTEREST IN *PASSING* THE HUNTER EXAM.
I JUST DO IT FOR A *THRILL*, Y'KNOW?
WHOOO
BY KEEPING AN EYE ON THE DANGEROUS APPLICANTS, AND STAYING WITH THE PACK...
...I CAN AVOID BEING TAKEN OUT.
TO ME, THIS IS REALLY JUST ENTERTAINMENT, A WAY TO INDULGE MY MORBID PROCLIVITIES.
ON THIS PROVING GROUND, WHERE SO MANY BRIGHT FUTURES ARE IN THE BALANCE...
...IT'S BEEN A KICK TO WATCH THE *FACES* OF THOSE WHOSE *DREAMS ARE DASHED!*
SUCH A KICK, IN FACT, THAT I NOW ACTIVELY...
...*TRIP NEWBIES* UP, JUST TO SEE 'EM SQUIRM AND SUFFER. IT'S A *REAL RUSH*.

Chapter 17

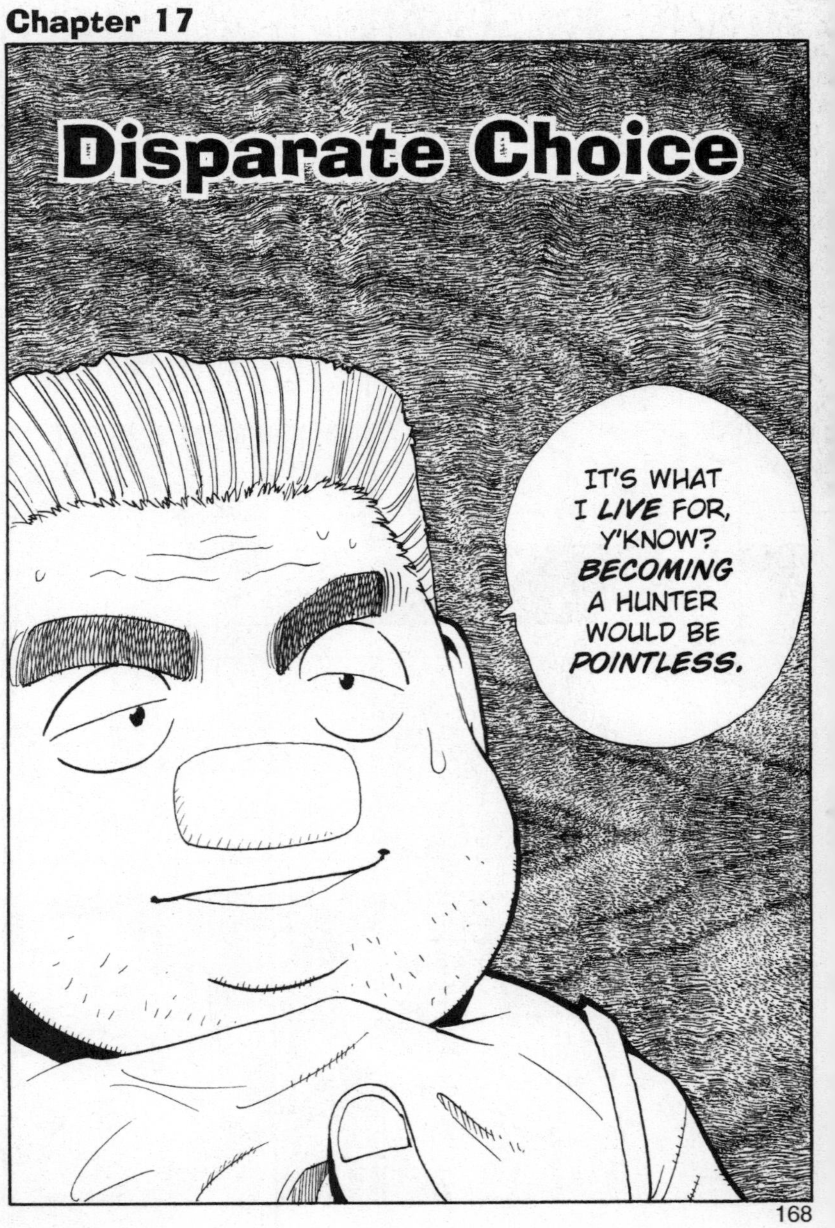
Disparate Choice
IT'S WHAT I *LIVE* FOR, Y'KNOW? *BECOMING* A HUNTER WOULD BE *POINTLESS.*

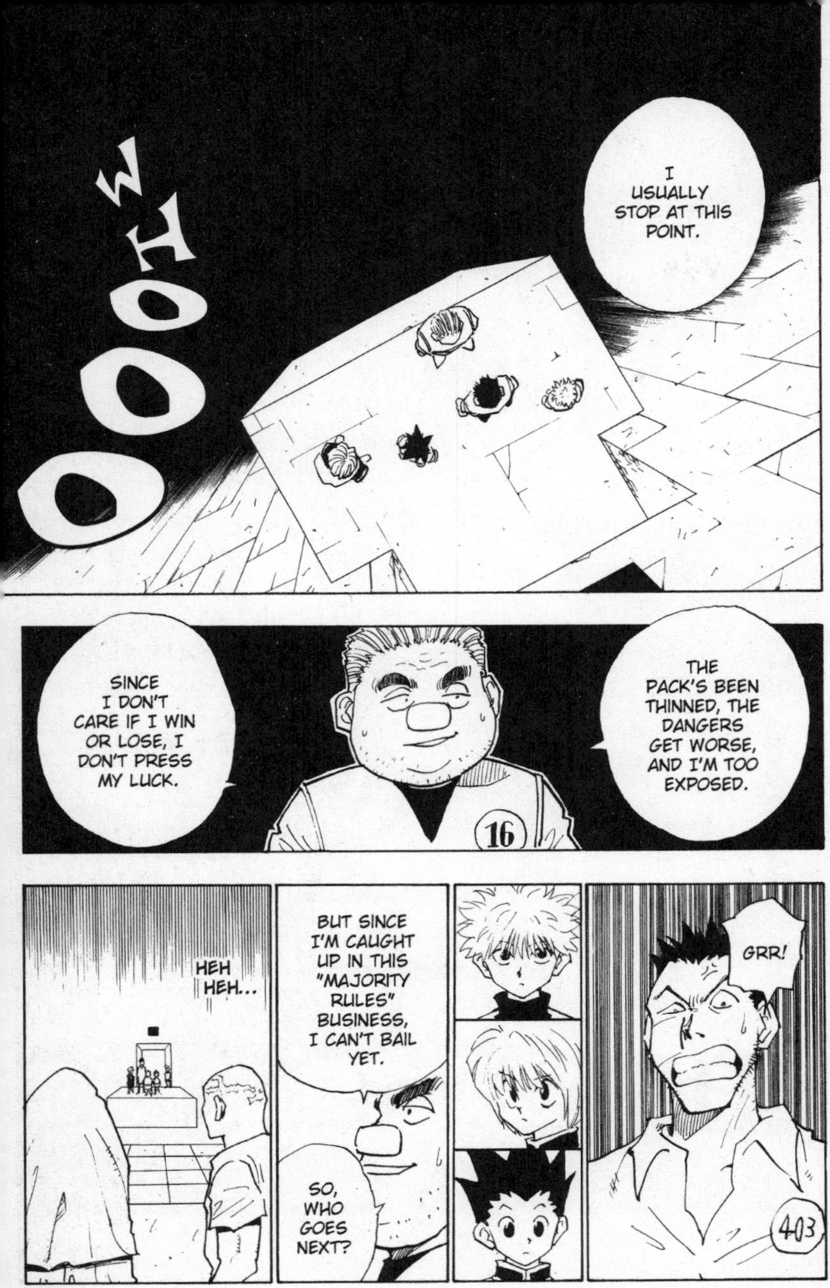
I USUALLY STOP AT THIS POINT.
WHOOO
THE PACK'S BEEN THINNED, THE DANGERS GET WORSE, AND I'M TOO EXPOSED.
SINCE I DON'T CARE IF I WIN OR LOSE, I DON'T PRESS MY LUCK.
16
GRR!
403
BUT SINCE I'M CAUGHT UP IN THIS "MAJORITY RULES" BUSINESS, I CAN'T BAIL YET.
SO, WHO GOES NEXT?
HEH HEH...

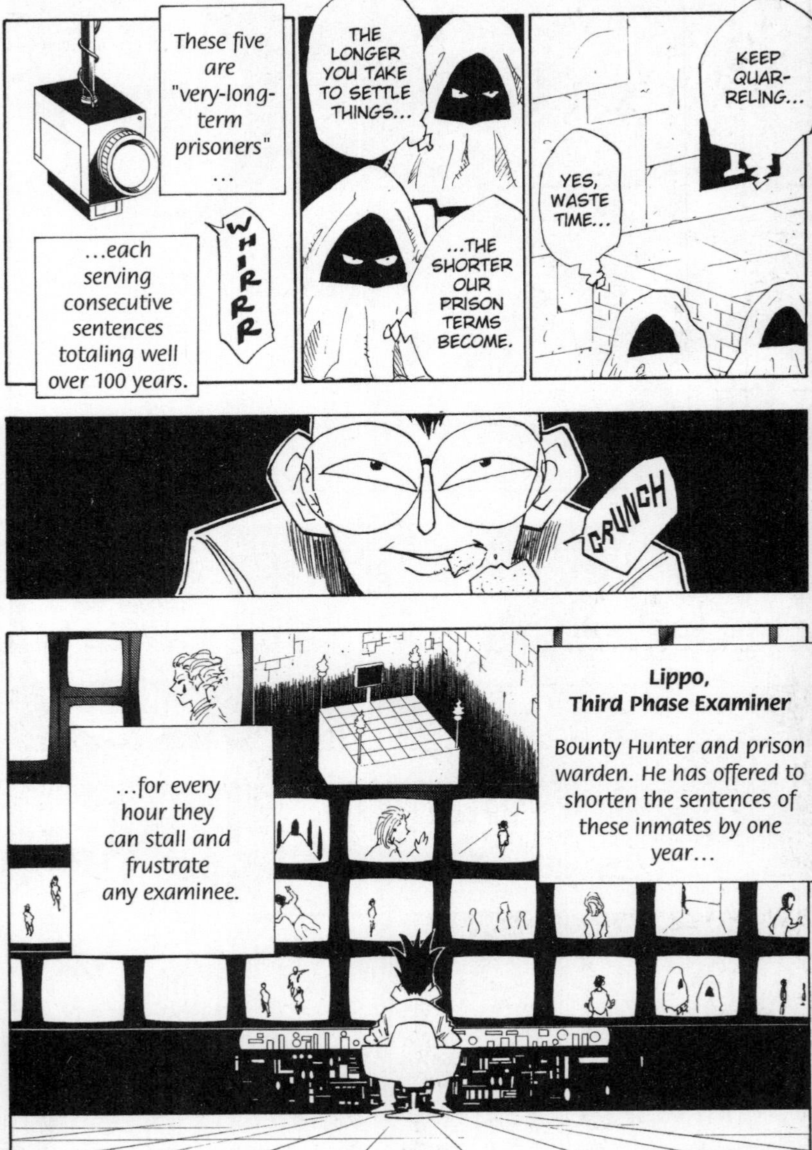

KEEP QUARRELING...
YES, WASTE TIME...
THE LONGER YOU TAKE TO SETTLE THINGS...
...THE SHORTER OUR PRISON TERMS BECOME.
These five are "very-long-term prisoners"...
WHIRRR
...each serving consecutive sentences totaling well over 100 years.
CRUNCH
Lippo, Third Phase Examiner
Bounty Hunter and prison warden. He has offered to shorten the sentences of these inmates by one year...
...for every hour they can stall and frustrate any examinee.

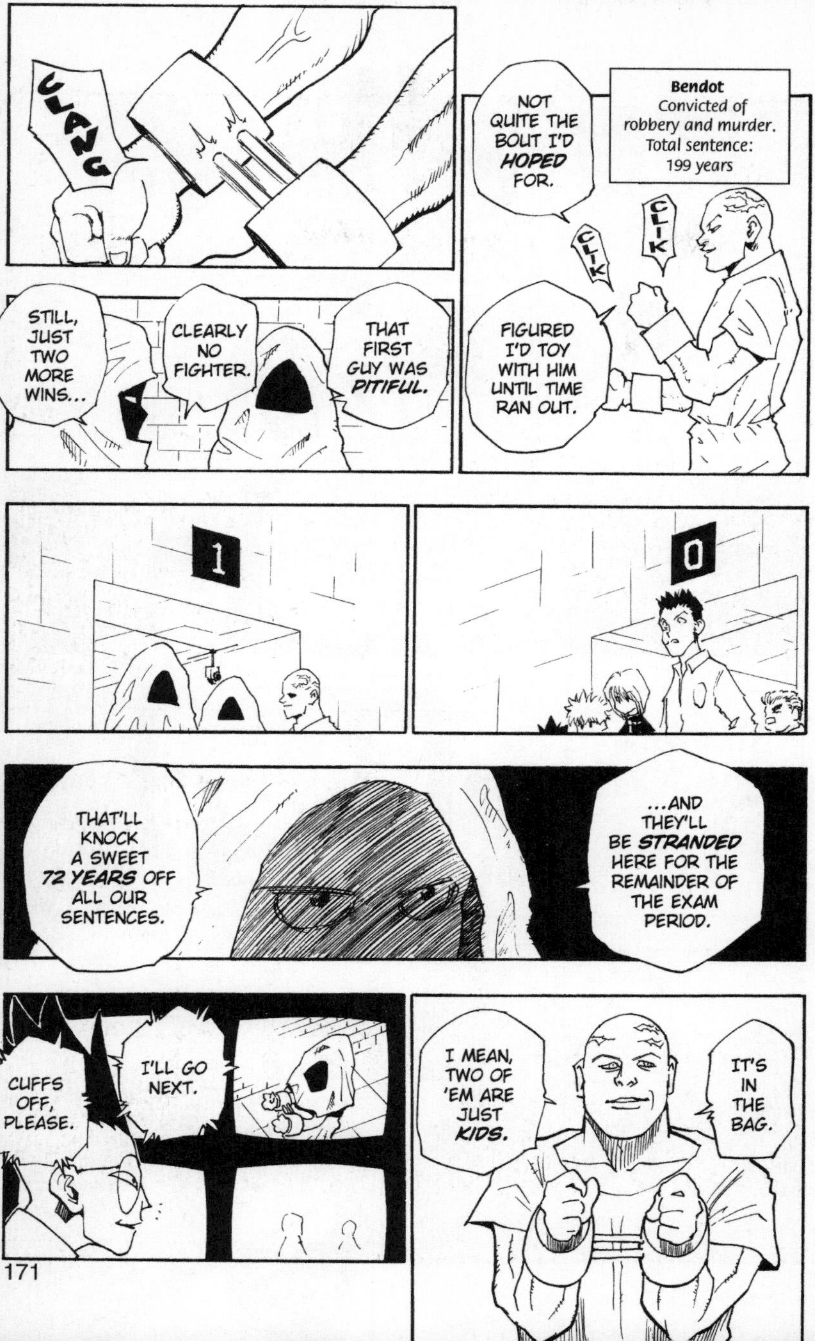
Bendot
Convicted of robbery and murder. Total sentence: 199 years
NOT QUITE THE BOUT I'D HOPED FOR.
CLIK
CLIK
FIGURED I'D TOY WITH HIM UNTIL TIME RAN OUT.
CLANG
THAT FIRST GUY WAS PITIFUL.
CLEARLY NO FIGHTER.
STILL, JUST TWO MORE WINS...
0
1
...AND THEY'LL BE STRANDED HERE FOR THE REMAINDER OF THE EXAM PERIOD.
THAT'LL KNOCK A SWEET 72 YEARS OFF ALL OUR SENTENCES.
IT'S IN THE BAG.
I MEAN, TWO OF 'EM ARE JUST KIDS.
I'LL GO NEXT.
CUFFS OFF, PLEASE.

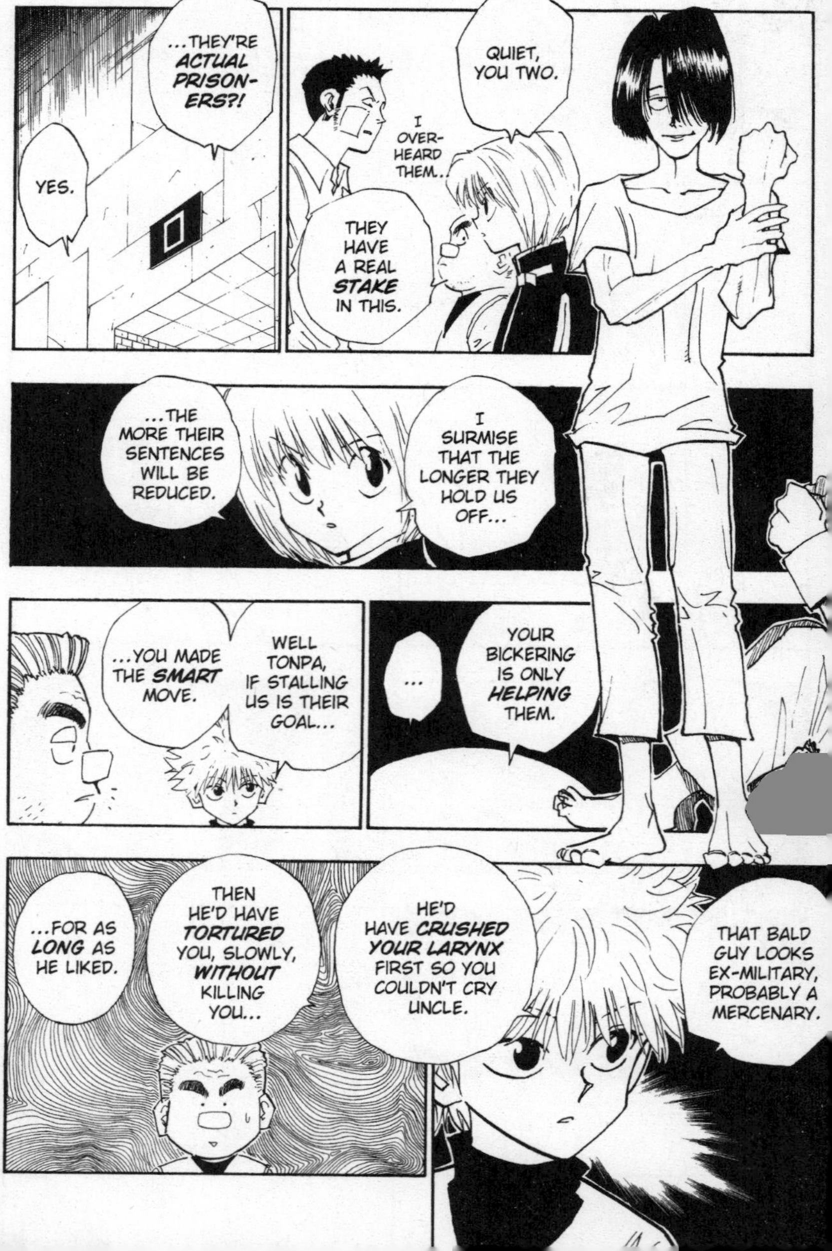
QUIET, YOU TWO.
I OVER-HEARD THEM...
THEY HAVE A REAL STAKE IN THIS.
...THEY'RE ACTUAL PRISON-ERS?!
YES.
I SURMISE THAT THE LONGER THEY HOLD US OFF...
...THE MORE THEIR SENTENCES WILL BE REDUCED.
YOUR BICKERING IS ONLY HELPING THEM.
...
WELL TONPA, IF STALLING US IS THEIR GOAL...
...YOU MADE THE SMART MOVE.
THAT BALD GUY LOOKS EX-MILITARY, PROBABLY A MERCENARY.
HE'D HAVE CRUSHED YOUR LARYNX FIRST SO YOU COULDN'T CRY UNCLE.
THEN HE'D HAVE TORTURED YOU, SLOWLY, WITHOUT KILLING YOU...
...FOR AS LONG AS HE LIKED.

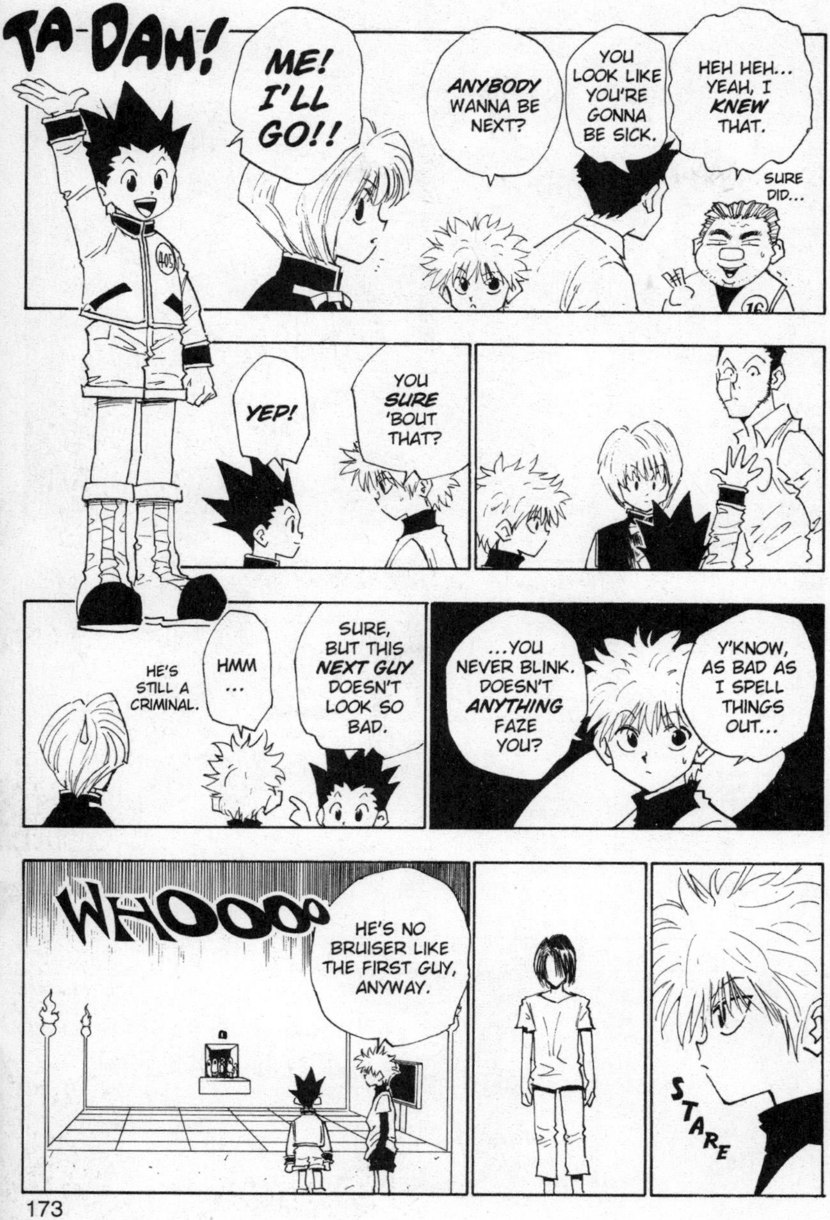
HEH HEH... YEAH, I KNEW THAT.
SURE DID...
YOU LOOK LIKE YOU'RE GONNA BE SICK.
ANYBODY WANNA BE NEXT?
ME! I'LL GO!!
TA-DAH!
YOU SURE 'BOUT THAT?
YEP!
Y'KNOW, AS BAD AS I SPELL THINGS OUT...
...YOU NEVER BLINK. DOESN'T ANYTHING FAZE YOU?
SURE, BUT THIS NEXT GUY DOESN'T LOOK SO BAD.
HMM ...
HE'S STILL A CRIMINAL.
STARE
HE'S NO BRUISER LIKE THE FIRST GUY, ANYWAY.
WHOOOO

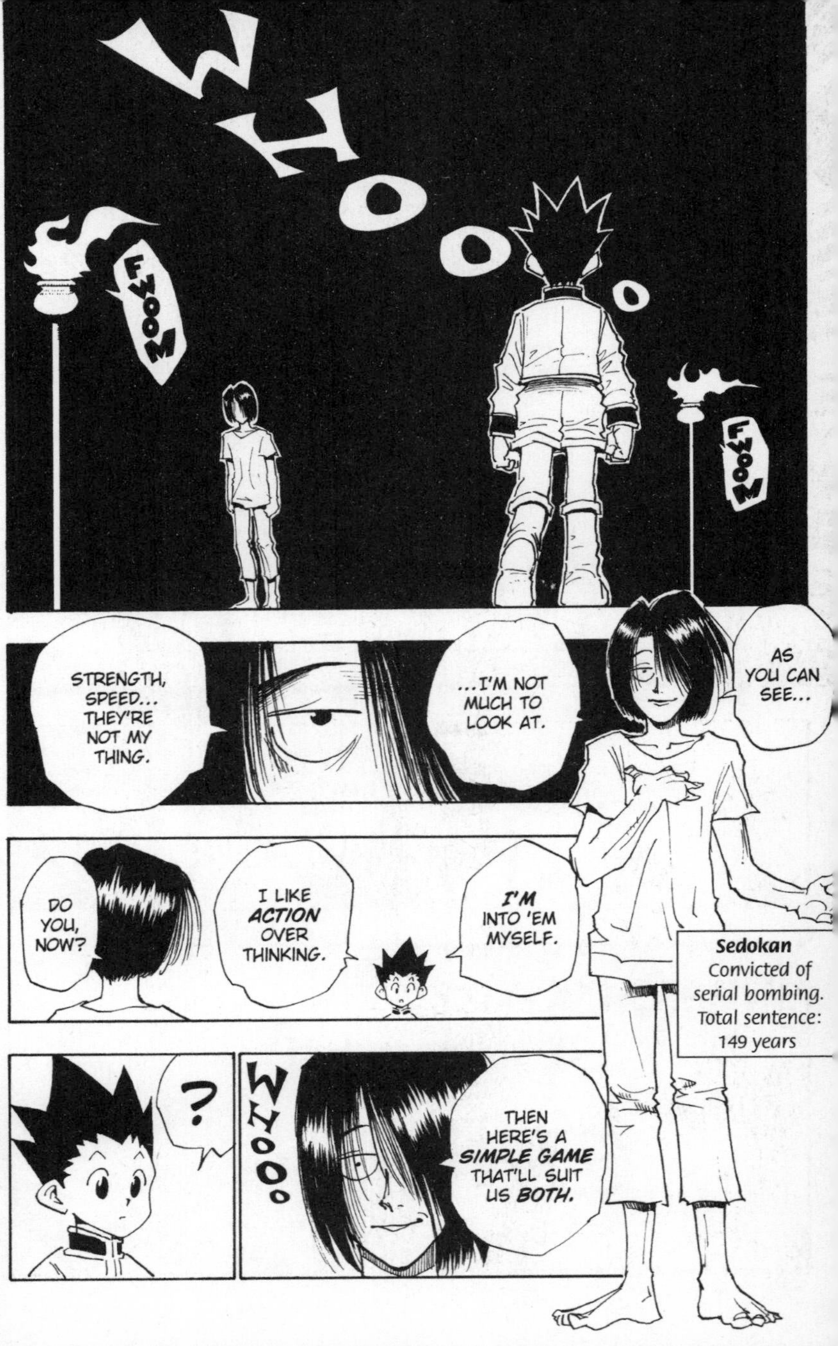
WHOOOOO
FWOOM
FWOOM
AS YOU CAN SEE...
...I'M NOT MUCH TO LOOK AT.
STRENGTH, SPEED... THEY'RE NOT MY THING.
Sedokan
Convicted of serial bombing.
Total sentence: 149 years
I'M INTO 'EM MYSELF.
I LIKE ACTION OVER THINKING.
DO YOU, NOW?
THEN HERE'S A SIMPLE GAME THAT'LL SUIT US BOTH.
WHOOOO
?

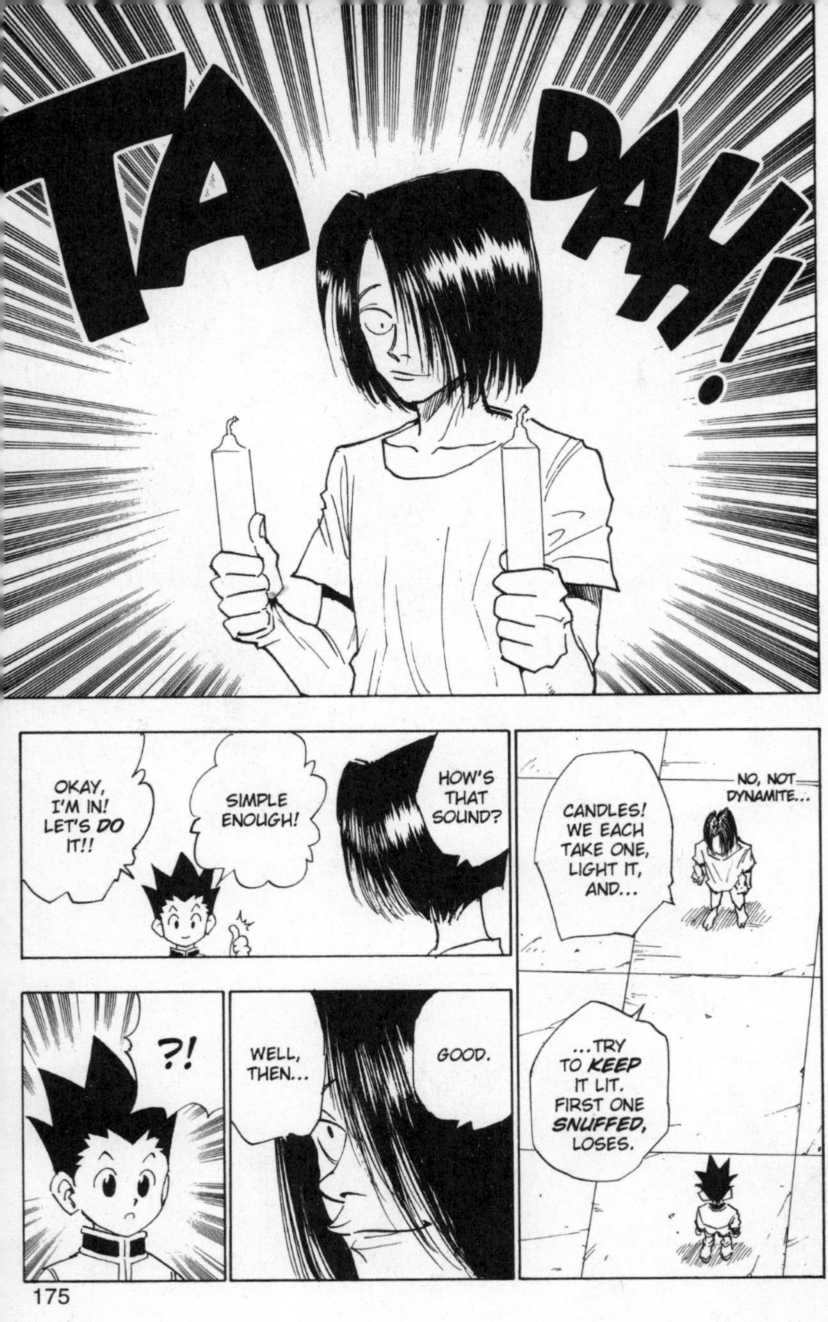
TA DAH!
NO, NOT DYNAMITE...
CANDLES! WE EACH TAKE ONE, LIGHT IT, AND...
...TRY TO KEEP IT LIT. FIRST ONE SNUFFED, LOSES.
HOW'S THAT SOUND?
SIMPLE ENOUGH!
OKAY, I'M IN! LET'S DO IT!!
GOOD.
WELL, THEN...
?!

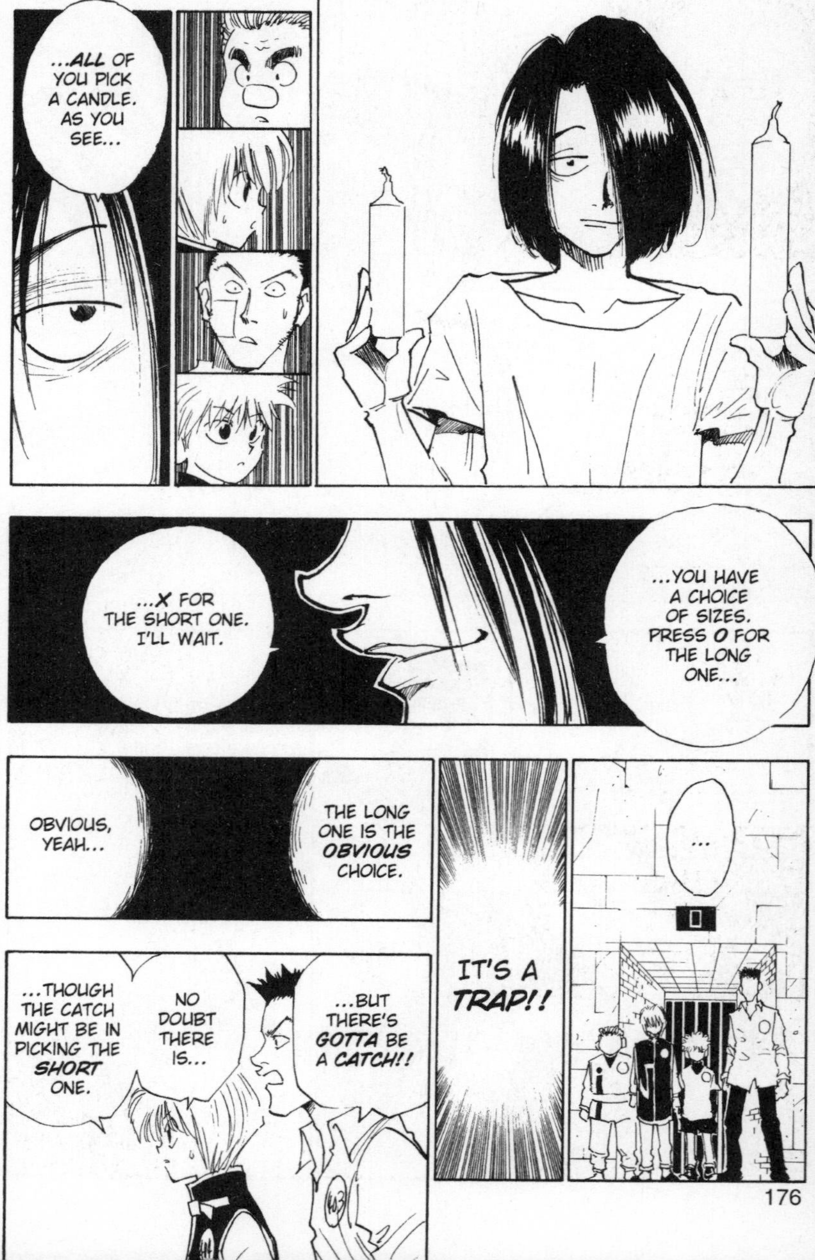
...ALL OF YOU PICK A CANDLE. AS YOU SEE...
...YOU HAVE A CHOICE OF SIZES. PRESS O FOR THE LONG ONE...
...X FOR THE SHORT ONE. I'LL WAIT.
...
IT'S A TRAP!!
THE LONG ONE IS THE OBVIOUS CHOICE.
OBVIOUS, YEAH...
...BUT THERE'S GOTTA BE A CATCH!!
NO DOUBT THERE IS...
...THOUGH THE CATCH MIGHT BE IN PICKING THE SHORT ONE.

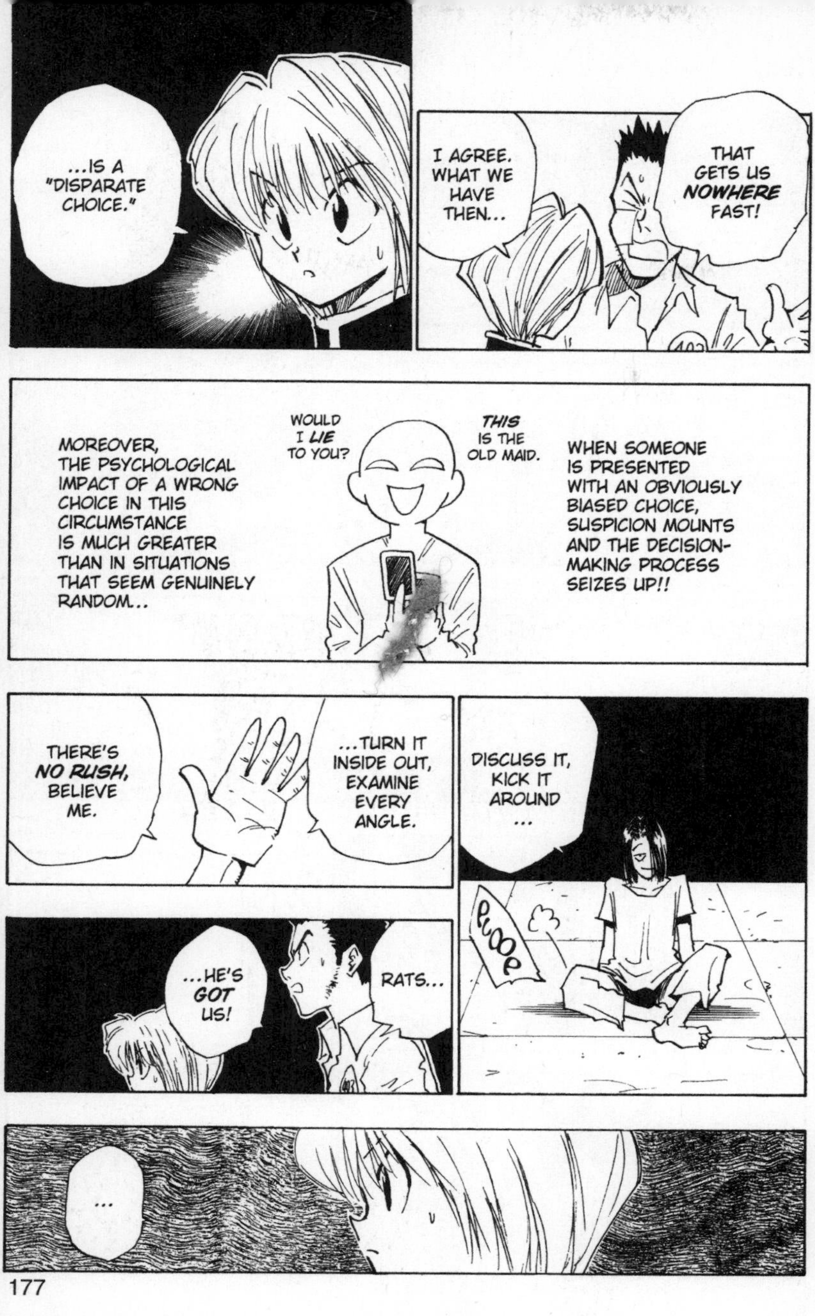
THAT GETS US ***NOWHERE*** FAST!
I AGREE. WHAT WE HAVE THEN...
...IS A "DISPARATE CHOICE."
WHEN SOMEONE IS PRESENTED WITH AN OBVIOUSLY BIASED CHOICE, SUSPICION MOUNTS AND THE DECISION-MAKING PROCESS SEIZES UP!!
THIS IS THE OLD MAID.
WOULD I ***LIE*** TO YOU?
MOREOVER, THE PSYCHOLOGICAL IMPACT OF A WRONG CHOICE IN THIS CIRCUMSTANCE IS MUCH GREATER THAN IN SITUATIONS THAT SEEM GENUINELY RANDOM...
DISCUSS IT, KICK IT AROUND ...
PLOOP
...TURN IT INSIDE OUT, EXAMINE EVERY ANGLE.
THERE'S ***NO RUSH,*** BELIEVE ME.
RATS...
...HE'S ***GOT*** US!
...

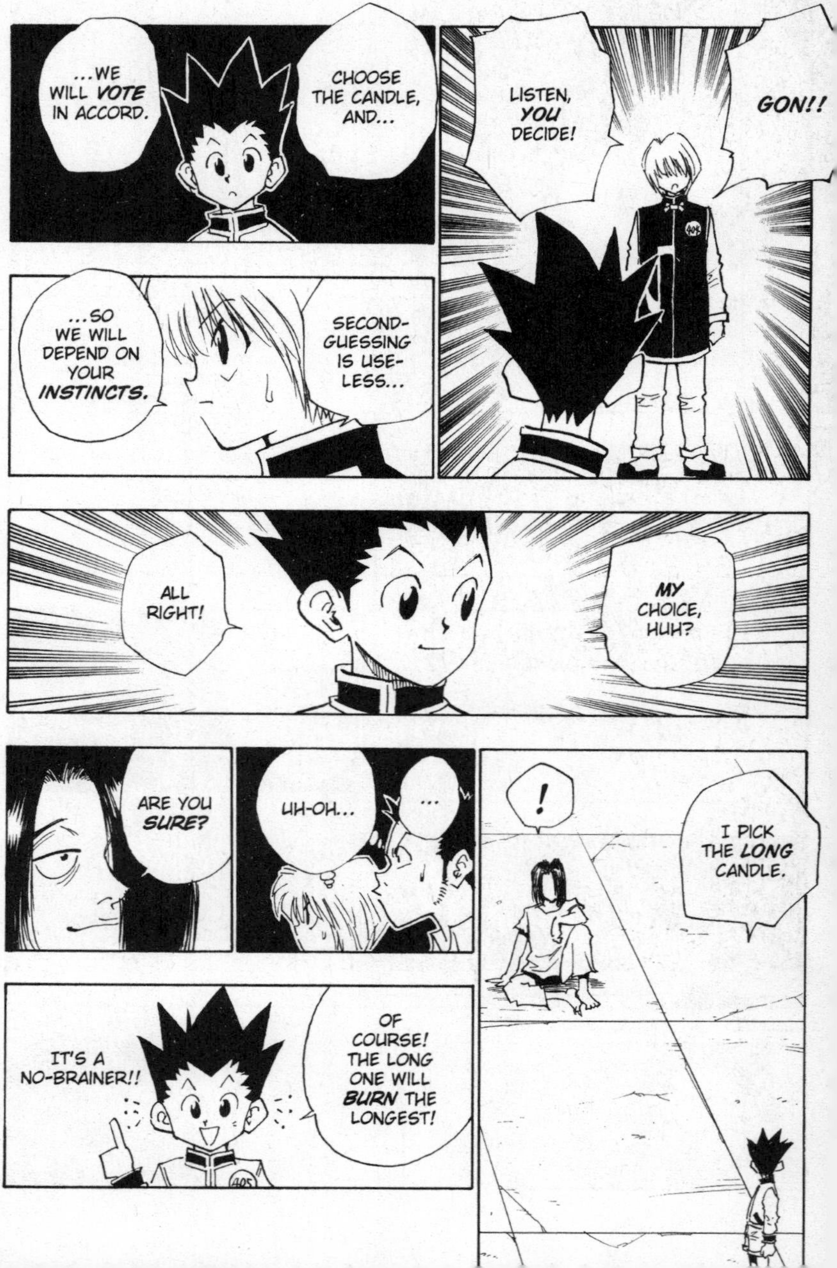
GON!!
LISTEN, YOU DECIDE!
CHOOSE THE CANDLE, AND...
...WE WILL VOTE IN ACCORD.
SECOND-GUESSING IS USELESS...
...SO WE WILL DEPEND ON YOUR INSTINCTS.
MY CHOICE, HUH?
ALL RIGHT!
!
I PICK THE LONG CANDLE.
...
UH-OH...
ARE YOU SURE?
OF COURSE! THE LONG ONE WILL BURN THE LONGEST!
IT'S A NO-BRAINER!!

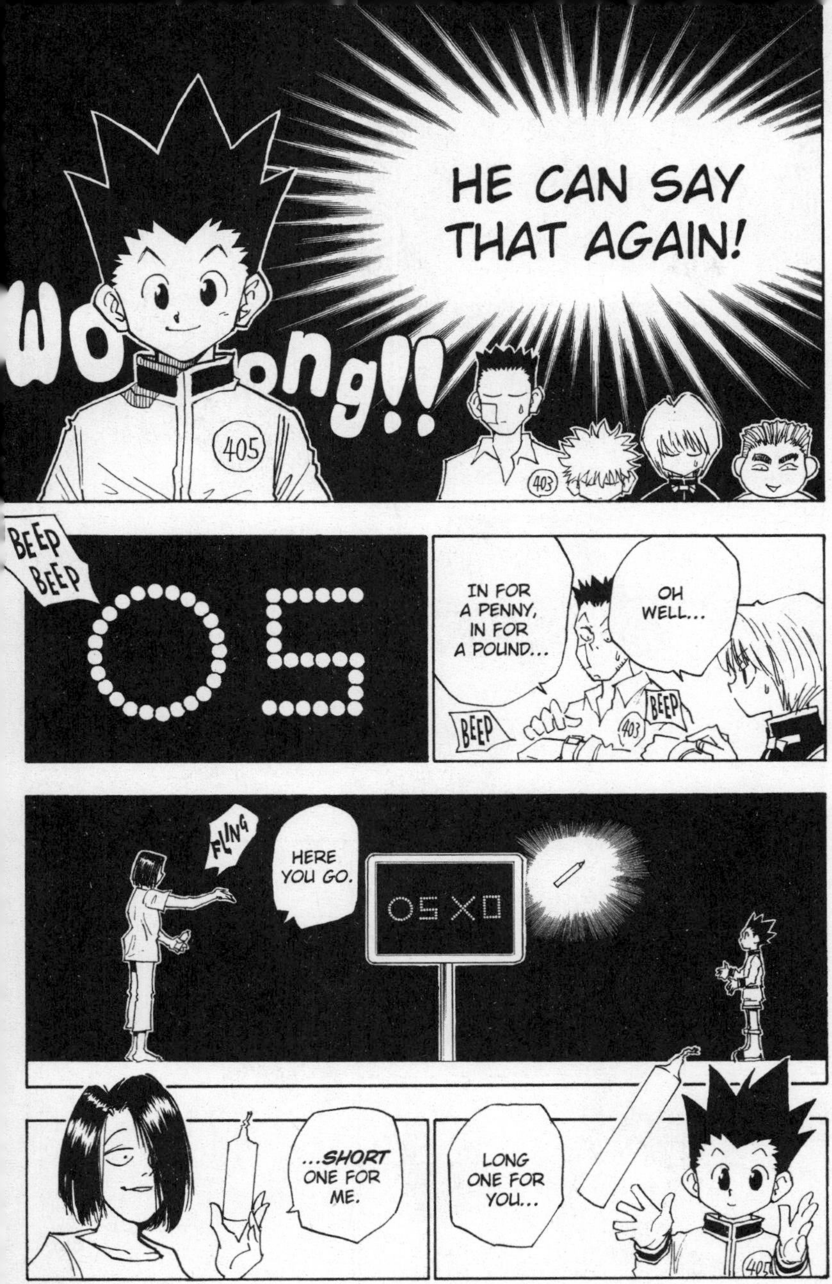

HE CAN SAY THAT AGAIN!
WOong!!
OH WELL...
IN FOR A PENNY, IN FOR A POUND...
BEEP
BEEP
BEEP BEEP
HERE YOU GO.
FLING
LONG ONE FOR YOU...
...**SHORT** ONE FOR ME.

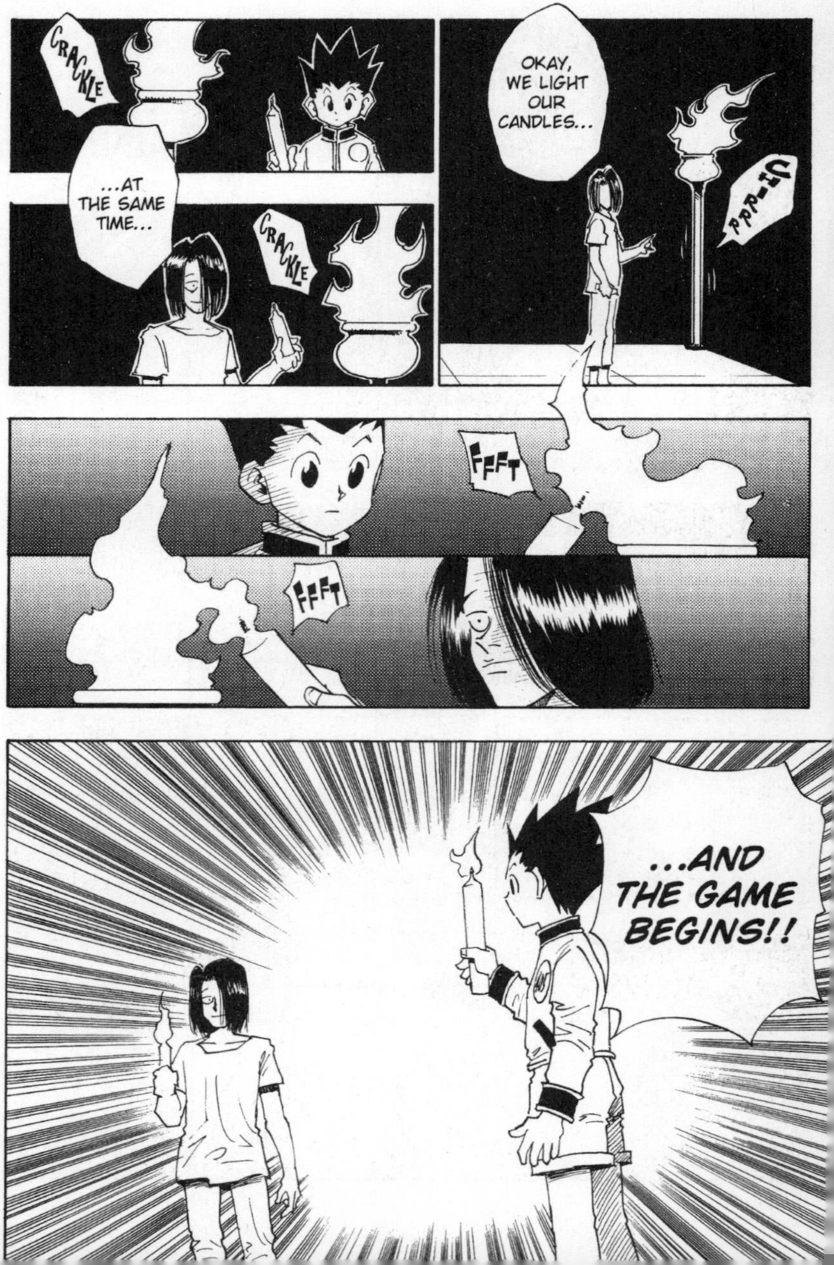
OKAY, WE LIGHT OUR CANDLES...
CHIRPP
CRACKLE
...AT THE SAME TIME...
CRACKLE
FFFT
FFFT
...AND THE GAME BEGINS!!

READ THIS WAY

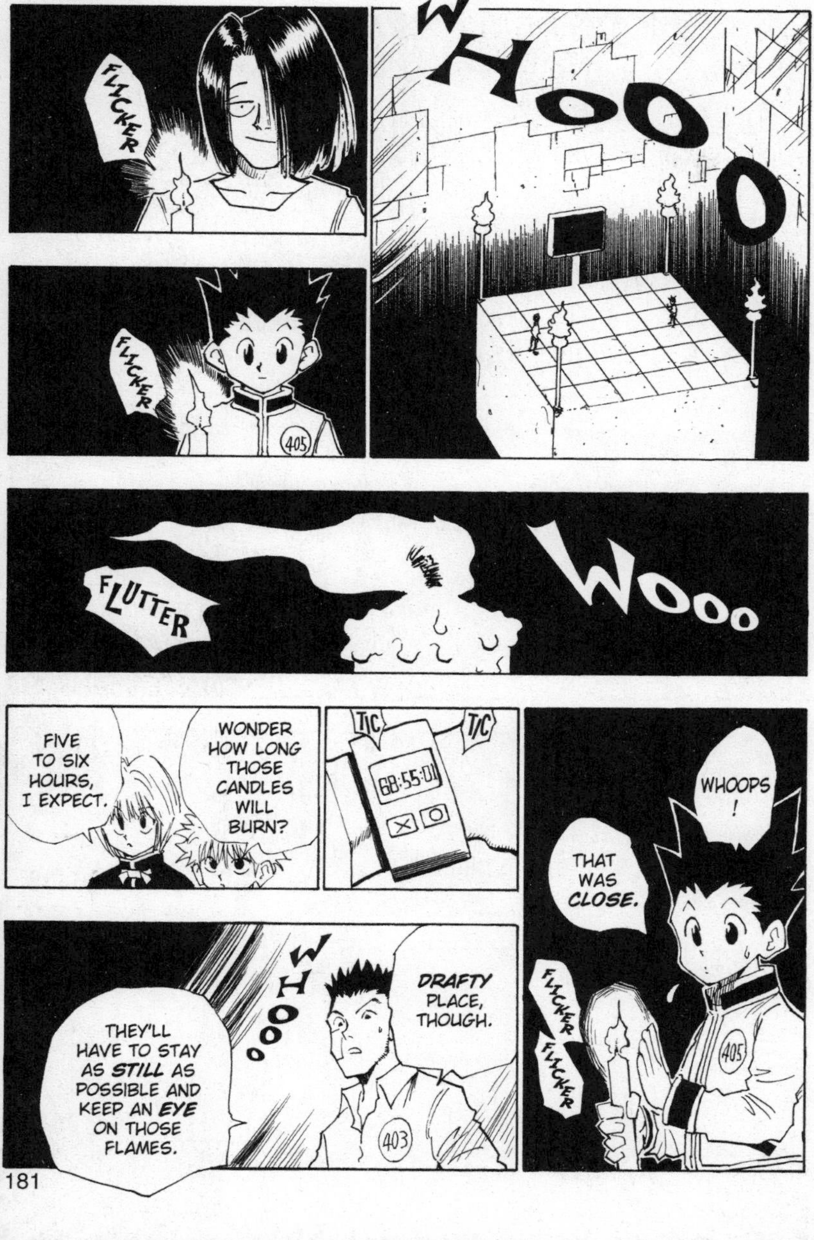

WHOOOO
FLICKER
FLICKER
WOOO
FLUTTER
WHOOPS!
THAT WAS **CLOSE.**
FLICKER FLICKER
TIC TIC
68:55:01
WONDER HOW LONG THOSE CANDLES WILL BURN?
FIVE TO SIX HOURS, I EXPECT.
DRAFTY PLACE, THOUGH.
WHOOOO
THEY'LL HAVE TO STAY AS **STILL** AS POSSIBLE AND KEEP AN **EYE** ON THOSE FLAMES.

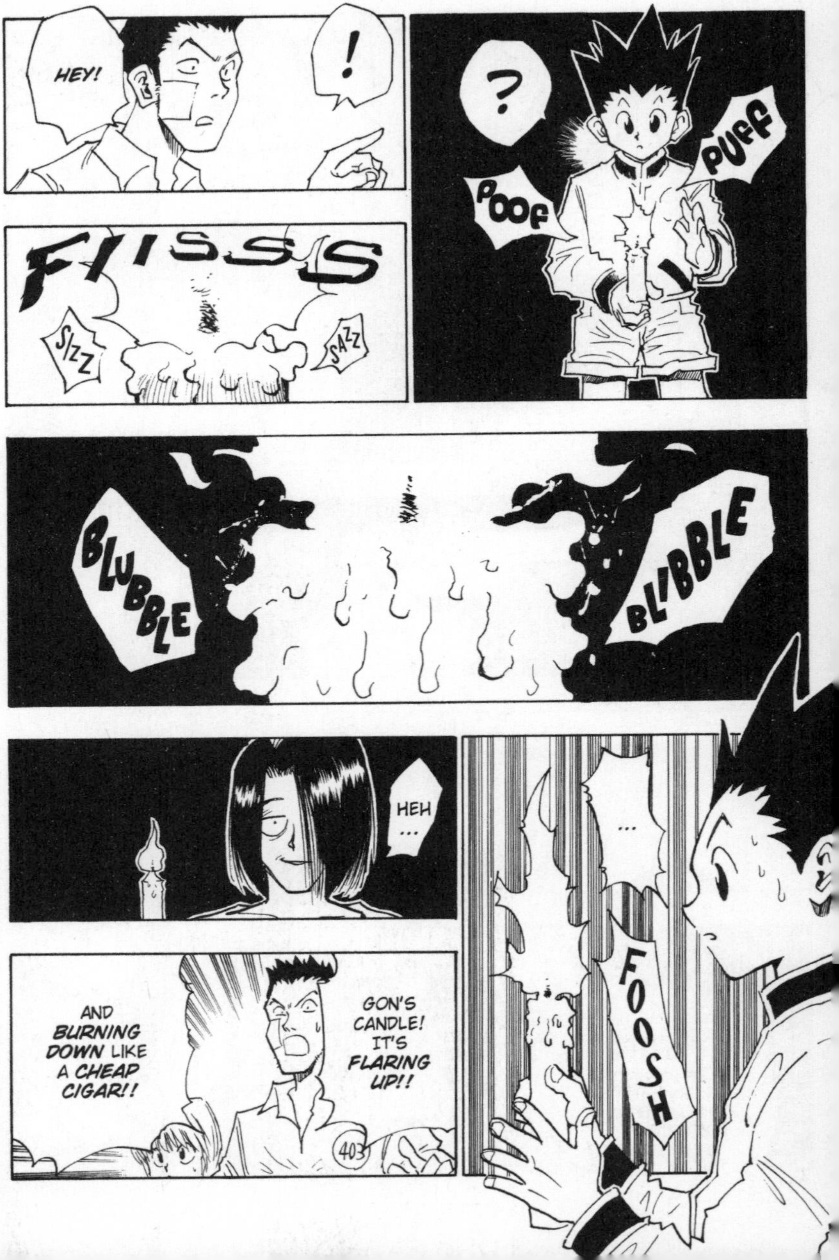
?
PUFF
POOF
!
HEY!
FISSS
SAZZ
SIZZ
BLIBBLE
BLUBBLE
...
FOOSH
HEH ...
GON'S CANDLE! IT'S FLARING UP!!
AND BURNING DOWN LIKE A CHEAP CIGAR!!

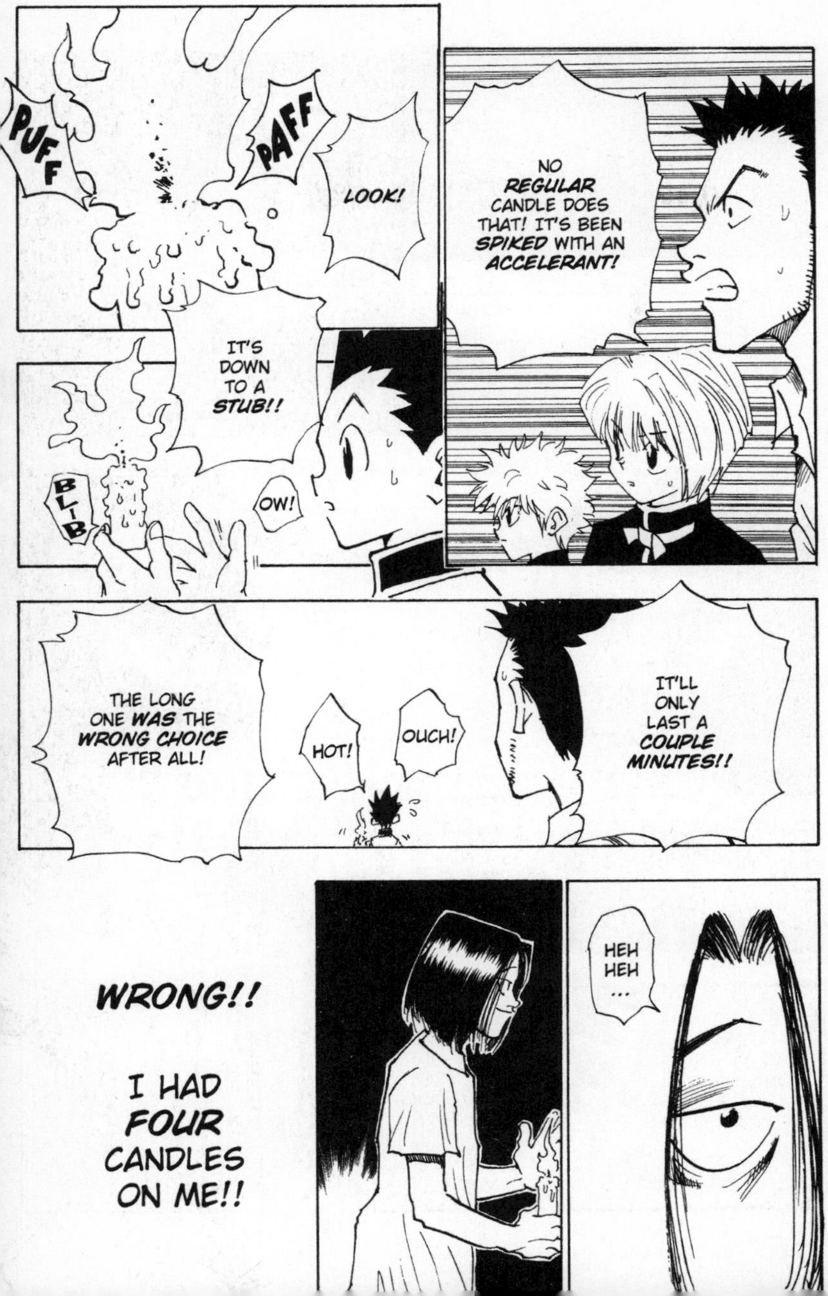
NO REGULAR CANDLE DOES THAT! IT'S BEEN SPIKED WITH AN ACCELERANT!
PUFF
PAFF
LOOK!
IT'S DOWN TO A STUB!!
OW!
BLIB
IT'LL ONLY LAST A COUPLE MINUTES!!
OUCH!
HOT!
THE LONG ONE WAS THE WRONG CHOICE AFTER ALL!
HEH HEH ...
WRONG!!
I HAD FOUR CANDLES ON ME!!

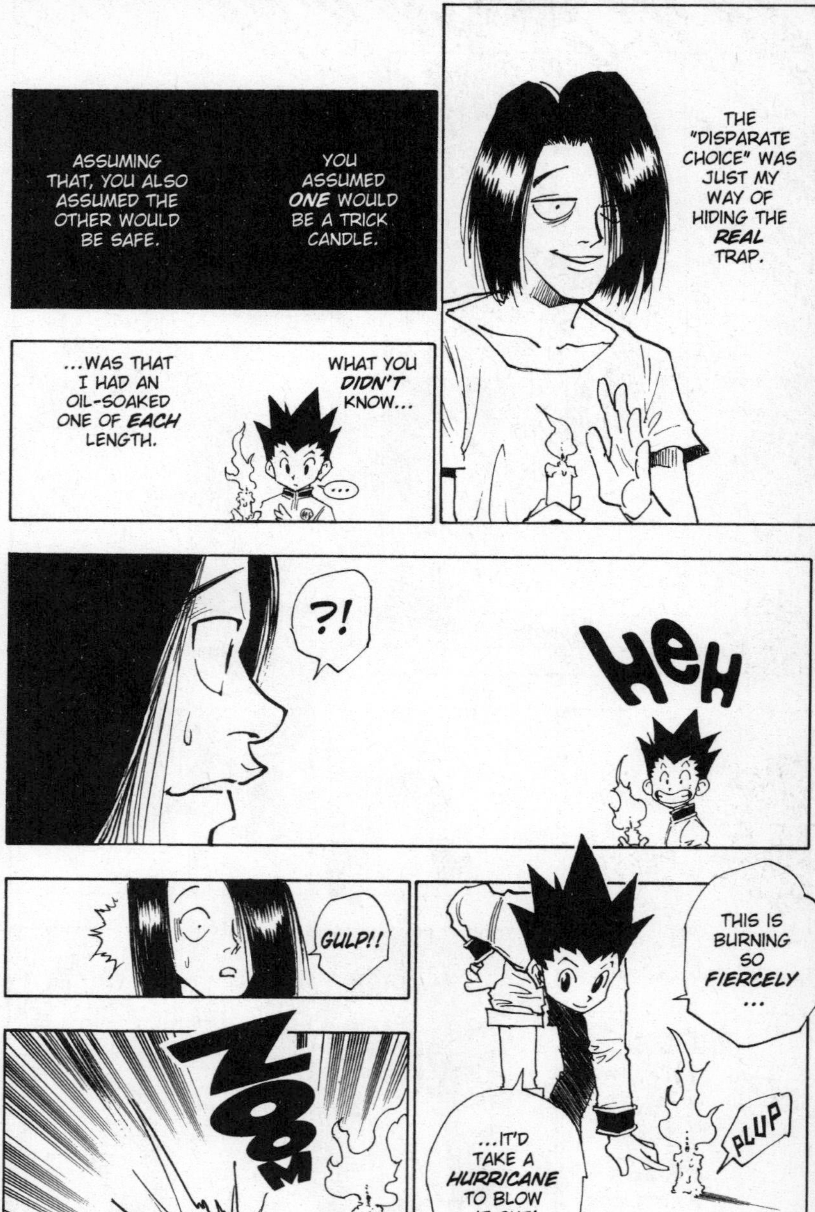
THE "DISPARATE CHOICE" WAS JUST MY WAY OF HIDING THE REAL TRAP.
YOU ASSUMED ONE WOULD BE A TRICK CANDLE.
ASSUMING THAT, YOU ALSO ASSUMED THE OTHER WOULD BE SAFE.
WHAT YOU DIDN'T KNOW...
...WAS THAT I HAD AN OIL-SOAKED ONE OF EACH LENGTH.
...
HEH
?!
THIS IS BURNING SO FIERCELY...
...IT'D TAKE A HURRICANE TO BLOW IT OUT!
PLUP
GULP!!
VOOM

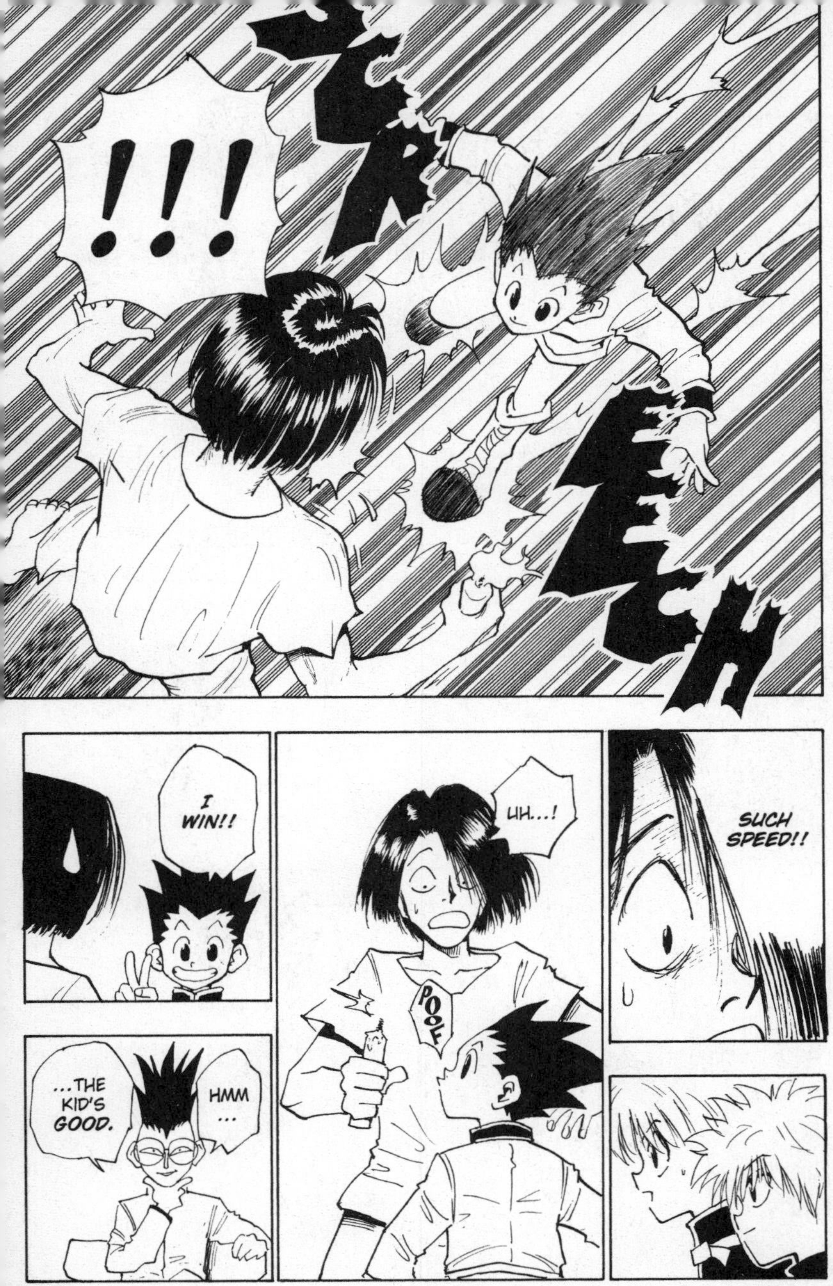
!!!
SUCH SPEED!!
UH...!
POOF
I WIN!!
HMM ...
...THE KID'S GOOD.

Coming Next Volume...

Kurapika, Leorio and Killua must battle with time and desperate criminals in order for the team to escape the tower test and pass the third round of the Hunter Exam. With so much at stake, Kurapika and Killua reveal some special abilities, while Leorio exposes his stunning lack of luck. The fourth round takes place on a deserted island, where the would-be Hunters must gain points by stalking the greatest prey—each other!

Available now!

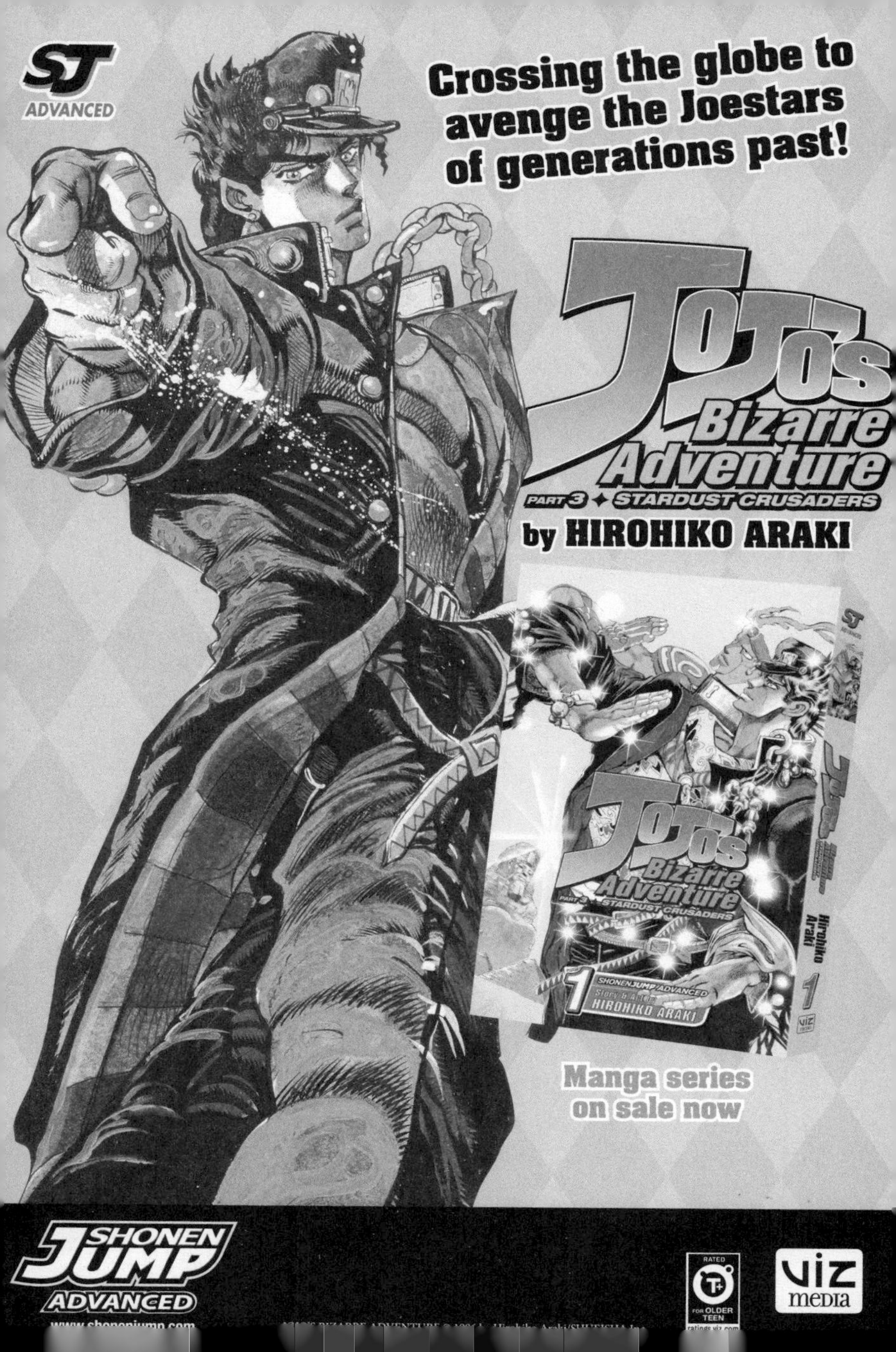

SJ ADVANCED
Crossing the globe to avenge the Joestars of generations past!
JoJo's Bizarre Adventure
PART 3 ✦ STARDUST CRUSADERS
by HIROHIKO ARAKI
JoJo's Bizarre Adventure
PART 3 STARDUST CRUSADERS
1 SHONEN JUMP ADVANCED
HIROHIKO ARAKI
Hirohiko Araki
1
Manga series on sale now
SHONEN JUMP ADVANCED
RATED T+ FOR OLDER TEEN
VIZ media

Dr. SLUMP

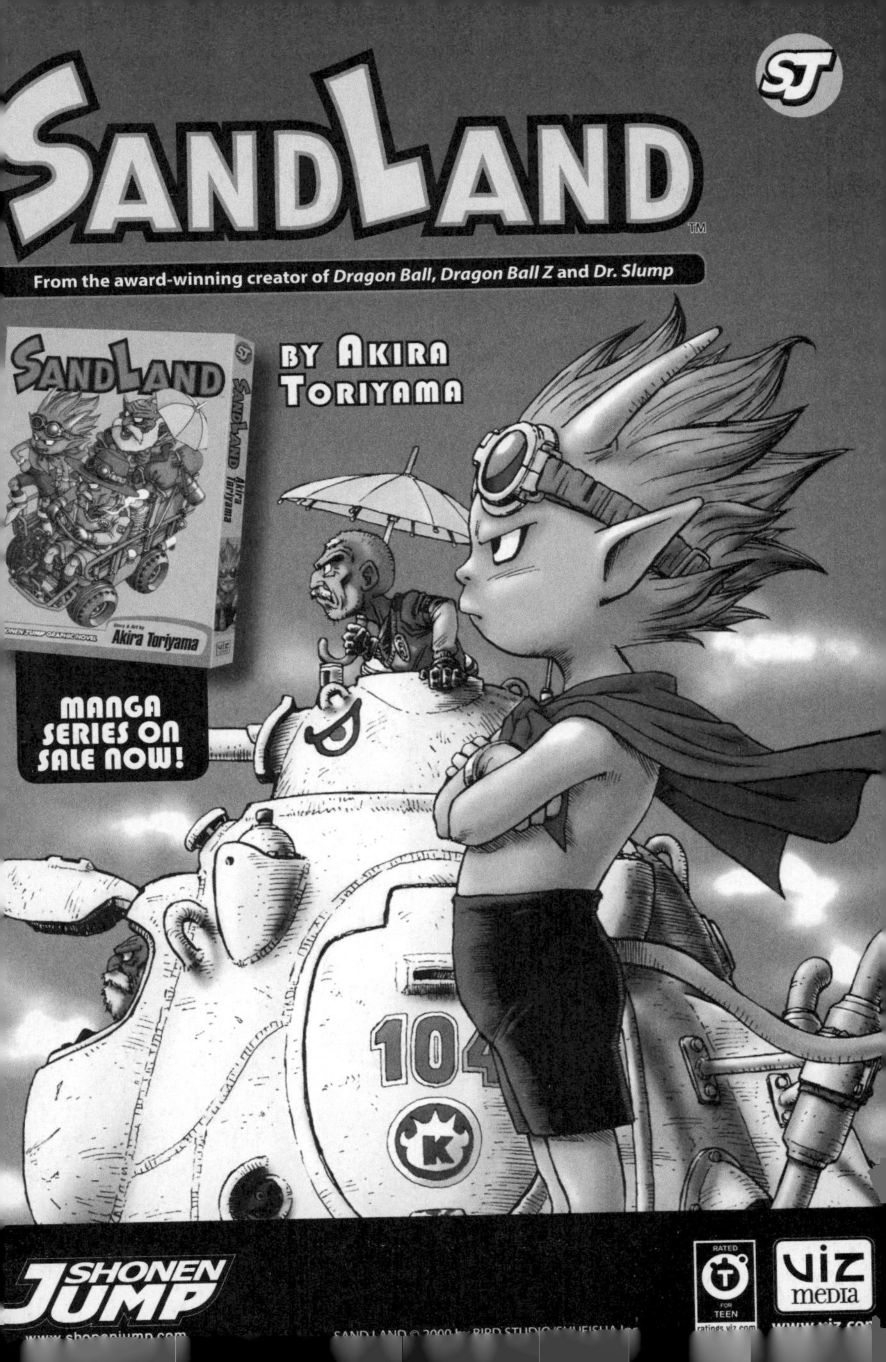
SJ
SANDLAND™
From the award-winning creator of Dragon Ball, Dragon Ball Z and Dr. Slump
BY AKIRA TORIYAMA
SANDLAND
Akira Toriyama
MANGA SERIES ON SALE NOW!
104
K
SHONEN JUMP
RATED
T
FOR TEEN
VIZ media